# Evita Burned Down
# Our Pavilion

# Evita Burned Down Our Pavilion

## A Cricket Odyssey
## Through Latin America

Timothy Abraham and James Coyne

CONSTABLE

CONSTABLE

First published in Great Britain in 2021 by Constable

1 3 5 7 9 10 8 6 4 2

Copyright © Timothy Abraham and James Coyne, 2021
Map by Liane Payne

The moral right of the authors has been asserted.

A CIP catalogue record for this book
is available from the British Library.

ISBN: 978-1-47213-252-9 (hardback)
ISBN: 978-1-47213-253-6 (trade paperback)

Typeset in Adobe Garamond Pro by Hewer Text UK Ltd, Edinburgh
Printed and bound in Great Britain by Clays Ltd, Elcograf, S.p.A.

Papers used by Constable are from well-managed forests and other responsible sources.

Constable
An imprint of
Little, Brown Book Group
Carmelite House
50 Victoria Embankment
London EC4Y 0DZ

An Hachette UK Company
www.hachette.co.uk

www.littlebrown.co.uk

For all the unsung volunteers who have selflessly given
their time to developing cricket in Latin America.

# Selected locations (historical and present-day) of cricket in Latin America

MEXICO

ATLANTIC OCEAN

Pachuca
Real del Monte
Mexico City
Orizaba
Cancún
Livingston
Belize City
La Ceiba
BELIZE
GUATEMALA
HONDURAS
NICARAGUA
Granada
Bluefields
Santiago Sacatepéquez
San Salvador
EL SALVADOR
Managua
COSTA RICA
PANAMA
Panama City
Colón
San José
Puerto Limón
Medellín
Maracaibo
Caracas
Guayana City
VENEZUELA
San Flaviano
Nieuw Nickerie
Paramaribo
Saint-Laurent-du-Maroni
Kourou
Cayenne
FRENCH GUIANA
GUYANA
SURINAME
Bogotá
COLOMBIA
Cali

Quito
ECUADOR
Guayaquil
Iquitos
Equator

Belém

PERU
Manaus
Recife
BRAZIL

Lima
Cusco
La Paz
Toquepala
BOLIVIA
Iquique
Oruro
Calama
Antofagasta
Copiapó
Jujuy
Salvador
Brasília
Poços de Caldas
Nova Lima
Barretos
São Paulo
Santos
Rio de Janeiro
Asunción
Foz do Iguaçu
Cosme
PARAGUAY
Nueva Australia
San Miguel de Tucumán
Córdoba
Concordia
Rosario
URUGUAY
Fray Bentos
Valparaíso
Santiago
Venado Tuerto
Montevideo
Buenos Aires
ARGENTINA
CHILE

PACIFIC OCEAN

Puerto Madryn

Port Stanley
FALKLAND ISLANDS
Punta Arenas

# Contents

# Foreword

I AM ASHAMED TO say that when I was researching the life of Eva Perón, having had the bonkers idea that her story would make a good musical, I did not discover that, in 1947, she had organised the burning down of the Buenos Aires Cricket Club pavilion. This was in revenge for the club's lack of enthusiasm for her Social Aid Foundation and its various chaotic welfare schemes. We did at least have a go at the foundation in the show.

Nor did I hear about this tragedy when I had the privilege of managing an MCC team on a tour of Argentina in 2006. Mike Gatting was the captain and Andy Flower a member of a top-quality squad that played five matches (a sixth was rained off) in the Buenos Aires district. This included games at the long-established grounds of Belgrano and Hurlingham, both featured in this remarkable book. It was a most enjoyable experience and it was clear that cricket at good club level has a strong foothold in Argentina, despite the rival attractions of Diego Maradona and his ilk over the decades.

So, I jumped at the chance to have an advance gander at Timothy Abraham's and James Coyne's study of cricket in all of Latin America. It is a fascinating tale, or tales.

Cricket has migrated to virtually every country of the exotic and extreme continent of South America and the simmering nations of Central America. Maybe in most places it retains only an unobtrusive presence, but the roots are often well established, and as T20 and other more instant forms of the game become more accessible on a screen near you or carried around by you, who would bet against many of these countries moving on to a more visible world cricket stage?

They already have the history, as this marvellous and original work illustrates. It achieves the almost impossible – it fills a gap in the great game's vast literary tradition.

Tim Rice
Helford, June 2020

# Introduction

'WHAT ARE YOU guys doing here? Just travelling?' our fellow backpackers would often ask us, spying strange handles peeping out of our rucksacks.

'As it happens, we are researching a book about cricket,' we would reply, a little sheepishly.

The eyes would roll. 'Cricket? In Latin America?! Expect that will be a short book . . .'

Eighteen countries (plus one overseas department of France) and four years of research later, a small part of us possibly wished some of that was true. There was enough material for three books, let alone one. The sheer scale and amount of cricket played, and its rich history, throughout a region with little obvious modern footprint in the game, was staggering even to us.

British naval, diplomatic and business interests were the driving force behind cricket's emergence across the Americas in the nineteenth century, and in most cases its decline. The sport's resolute Anglocentricity was never far from view – even outside the British Empire. There were full-page ads in English, Spanish and Portuguese-language publications from sponsors who were vital financiers of the game: a tin of Nugget White Dressing would scrub up a local cricketer's buckskin leather boots or pads; for sustenance, Bovril sandwiches 'will see you through to close of play'; 'No Pic-Nic is Complete Without Reformer Tongues: easy to open, quick to serve, delightfully appetising'. Behind every brand is a story of British influence in a mainly Spanish-speaking world. On a personal level, it was uncanny how many times we saw references to intrepid merchants from our hometowns of Liverpool and Bedford.

W. G. Grace never visited Latin America, but photographs taken by the great George Beldam of the Doctor launching his friend Arthur Weintrand's table cricket invention were widely circulated at the end of the nineteenth century: '*El Cricket de Mesa: Juego Que Promete Popularizarse como el Ping-Pong*' ('Table Cricket: A Game that Promises to Become as Popular as ping-pong'). The feted Trinidadian historian C. L. R. James did make it, though, spending a month in Mexico City in 1939, where he tried (and failed) to extol the virtues of cricket to Leon Trotsky. The exiled Soviet revolutionary was, it appears, preoccupied with conducting his affair with Diego Rivera's wife Frida Kahlo while staying at their marital home. Within 18 months the ice axe had landed in Trotsky's skull, from an agent working on behalf of Moscow rather than Rivera.

But this book is a wider tale of immigration from the Caribbean, Australian colonists, the Indian subcontinent ... and, yes, locals from every social background, intrigued by a sport that predated association football in almost every country.

Ah, football. Vast swathes of the region, to quote Pelé, '*come, dorme e bebe futebol*' ('eats, sleeps and drinks football'). Yet cricket had a head-start on football – and on baseball – and it's not so far-fetched to envisage an alternate reality where the Azteca, Maracanã and other football cathedrals we visited are crammed with Latin Americans wildly cheering sixes raining down on them. Cricket, after all, eventually broke though elitist boundaries when Parsis, Sikhs, Hindus and Muslims in India took up the game and turned it into a national obsession. At one time it was assumed that cricket in the Americas would go the same way.

Imagine, for a moment, Lionel Messi as a nuggety middle-order batsman; or Diego Maradona as a crafty leg-spinner, perhaps? Messi, in full Barcelona kit, did try his hand at batting in a TV advert for a nutrition supplement aimed at the Indian market, unfurling a bottom-handed cover drive and a slog to cow corner. Maradona, who grew up in a poor *villa miseria* of southernmost Buenos Aires, was left perplexed by the nuances of the game: 'I don't know why they throw themselves here, or jump head first there . . . And why do they greet themselves in the middle when the ball doesn't hit those three sticks? And then the crowd goes wild . . . I don't get it. But it brings out the passion in people.' While football won the battle hands down, that passion for cricket is stirring again now.

Our journey took us through myriad cultures, from Mexico City to Tierra del Fuego at the tip of South America, loosely following the route of the Pan-American Highway, and for some way retracing the tracks of Butch Cassidy and the Sundance Kid on the run. In Quito we even road-tested the effects of playing the ball exactly on the line of the Equator, so if any physicists want feedback they know where to come. We visited many of the first stopping points in the Americas during the Age of Discovery, and headed into the interior when the research called us. But we always seemed to return to the coastal towns and cities for our onward journey, which ended in Suriname and French Guiana, where backpackers and tourists rarely venture.

With the sheer amount of ground to cover we had to impose some limitations. It would have been fascinating to visit the islands of Caribbean Latin America. The reality was that time, budget and space meant we had to bypass Cuba, Haiti, the Dominican Republic and others. Someone else may feel a desire to take on that challenge.

Nor have we written specifically about Guyana (former British Guiana), Test cricket's one foothold in South America . . . at least until the tour companies decided a few years ago it was not boutiquey enough for modern tastes. Guyanese cricket has been documented as part of the West Indies, so did not really warrant further examination from us. On the flip side, while not historically part of 'Latin' America either, we felt the stories of Belize, Suriname and French Guiana were largely untold and connected to the countries around them, so merited attention. We have touched on the Falkland Islands – or Islas Malvinas if you prefer – where it's relevant to Argentina. You might be able to guess specifically when . . .

We have documented the journey and our own experiences where it feels important, so there is a travelogue running through the book. The strength, depth and variety of the stories we were telling, however, were so rich that we felt a reticence to get in the way ourselves too much.

Contrary to what some of our friends assumed, it wasn't all steak, wine and tango until dawn. We survived scorpions, violent political protests and bouts of Montezuma's Revenge, endured our fair share of dingy hostels – our personal highlight: the backpacker with a French bulldog who left it to defecate freely over the floors in Playa del Carmen, Mexico – and lost count of the number of sweaty overnight bus trips. (One of the few indisputably good British legacies to the region, the railways, has not especially flourished of late.) More than once we were asked in all seriousness if we were undercover spies for the International Cricket Council, sent to check up on a far-flung member. We weren't, just in the interests of clarity . . .

A common thread throughout our trip, however, was friendliness and openness from almost everyone we met, not least from the people who put us up in their homes, gave us lifts or ate with us. There are lessons there for those who believe the path to 'Western values' is an inherent arc of progression. Although a number of cricket's pioneers in Latin America suffered dizzying, brutal deaths – indeed, even now, 41 of the 50 cities with the worst homicide rates in the world are in the countries we covered – we should stress that we never felt in any serious danger. That's not to dismiss the grave challenges at hand across Latin America, or the protests and civil disobedience we witnessed first-hand.

We experienced the thrill of unearthing near-forgotten stories of cricket from people who strained the memory banks to recall great feats or controversies maybe 80 years old, and scoured printed newspapers, magazines and handbooks buried away in dusty archives for decades. Cricket Argentina welcomed our offer to reorganise their chaotic but impressive collection of documents and memorabilia in their offices above the Old Georgian Club in Buenos Aires – as fate would have it, less than a minute's walk to the Museo Evita and just over a mile away from where she is buried. When cricket-loving Sir Tim Rice visited Evita's grave at the Cementerio de la Recoleta, he found a well-wisher singing his own lyrics from 'Don't Cry for Me Argentina' in front of her tomb. More on Evita later . . .

Whenever we came to a border check to have our passports stamped there was a sense of foreboding that our search for historical information on cricket in the country, or city, where we were laying down our bags would prove fruitless. Inevitably, there were quite a few wild goose chases but, after scratching the surface, the deep and varied history came to the fore. Remarkably, we discovered traces of cricket in every country we visited – and the lengths that men, women and children went to play the game in a bygone, less-technological, era were quite astonishing. Sometimes the game was passed on neatly; at other times a whole new group of cricketers would have to start it up once more. The challenges have evolved for the modern custodians of cricket in the region, where the sport hangs on precariously in places. But one thing was clear in every match for which we were invited to pull on our whites (or hastily borrowed coloured kit): the passion and love people hold for cricket are a powerful base from which to reawaken the game in Latin America.

On occasions we laughed at how the quest came to occupy our thoughts. During a tourist excursion to the hilltop home of the great Chilean poet Pablo Neruda in Valparaíso, we scoured his impressive bookshelves to double-check there wasn't a yellow slab of *Wisden* nestled among his Hungarian journals and French magazines. Just in case.

We would be lying if we pretended the research didn't push the boundaries of our patience at times. Nearly a fortnight leafing through dusty newspapers in a chilly windowless basement in La Paz for something, anything, on cricket in Bolivia was time consuming, frustrating and arduous. Then, for a brief moment, exhilarating. That feeling will perhaps strike a chord with anyone who loves this glorious game – and deeply wishes it fully to spread its wings to all peoples of the world.

Timothy Abraham and James Coyne

I

# Mexico

## *After you, Claude*

A FEW DECADES AFTER he had first cast curious eyes on them, Ricardo Ludlow suddenly realised what the peculiar stakes in his late grandmother's vegetable patch were intended for. Ludlow had been studying some historical photographs of the Cornish community in Mexico at an archive in his home city of Pachuca. He was immediately drawn to a picture of men dressed in white out in a meadow. At first, he thought they might be morris dancers, or a maypole celebration, but when he examined the photo in greater detail he realised they were playing a game. 'Then I saw something and my mind raced back to my *abuela*'s garden when I was a young boy,' Ricardo says. 'I remember they were distinct and carefully crafted pieces of wood, unlike the rest of the sticks she used to grow flowers and vegetables around.' Ludlow's grandmother, it turned out, had in her possession the original cricket stumps from the old Pachuca Athletic Club, dating back more than a century.

'I guess she inherited them,' Ricardo tells us in flawless English as he reclines on a leather chair inside his pristine office, where he works as an economist. 'And she was just being resourceful putting them to use in the garden to grow runner beans.' We had come to meet Ricardo, a slim, bespectacled Mexican of part-Cornish descent in his early fifties, on the outskirts of Pachuca – some 60 miles north of Mexico City – to hear about one of his pioneering ancestors, Christopher Ludlow, whose main interests were mining, Methodism and cricket.

The first significant band of Cornish miners had arrived in Mexico in 1825, half a century before the Ludlow family. They had embarked on a fabled journey from Falmouth to Real del Monte – officially called Mineral del Monte since Mexican independence in 1810, but still usually referred to by its old name – where they had come to revive the silver mines. Denied entry into Spanish-administered ports they landed on a beach in Mocambo, famous for its rum. Sixty Cornishmen schlepped across mosquito-infested swamps, jungles and mountain peaks to the Sierra Madre Oriental. They had slung cricket bats in their bundles alongside their pickaxes and lanterns, and lugged 1500 tonnes of mining machinery over 250 miles using ropes and mules – building roads as they went – during a gruelling 14 months immortalised as 'The Great Trek'.

Ravaged by disease, 30 of the Cornishmen and 100 of their Mexican helpers would perish by the time they reached Real del Monte in May 1826. What greeted the survivors was a place with the 'air of a village sacked by a horde of Cossacks. The roofs are falling in, the walls crumbling down, and, in short the whole village converted into a mass of ruins'.

Nearly two centuries later Real del Monte – twinned with Redruth in Cornwall – is a pretty Mexican mountain town. We stroll the quaint cobbled streets with beautiful old Spanish colonial houses splashed in striking pastel greens, yellows and pinks. Nestled among them are unmistakably Cornish-style cottages of sloping double-pitched roofs and chimneys. In the heart of town is the eye-catching Iglesia de Nuestra Señora del Rosario, which has two distinctive towers: one in the Spanish style; the other a deliberate nod to the West Country.

The monuments and museums in Real del Monte are an ode to the Cornish miners. It was in the shadows of the silver mines that stumps were pitched by the first Cornish workers in search of light relief from the cavernous underground. The number of cricketers swelled as new technology from the Industrial Revolution turned the mines in the Hidalgo region into profitable enterprises. Players representing Real del Monte, including Mr C. Rosevear of Camborne, a 'very creditable round-arm bowler', jostled with two clubs established in Pachuca, with reports and scorecards from these matches even published in the *Cornishman* and *Royal Cornish Gazette* back home.

One of Pachuca's early clubs – Velasco CC – featured five Cornishmen with the surname Rabling. The veteran of the side was William Rabling, a mine agent who was held hostage in 1863 by Mexican bandits. He published *Captured by Brigands* – a colourful yarn about a month in the hands of a group of menacing *bandidos* 'all as dirty as if they never washed their face or their rags' brandishing pistols, muskets and knives. Rabling accompanied the ragtag bunch as they plundered towns and farms on horseback, and witnessed armed skirmishes with French Algerian troops. A sleep-deprived Rabling was facing death by firing squad until the Cornish community had a whip-round to pay off his ransom.

The stalwart of Pachuca CC was Francis Rule, an ever-present for four decades, his life a rags-to-riches tale. He had never left Cornwall until sailing for Mexico aged 17 in 1854, arriving without a word of Spanish or a penny to his name

(Mexican pesos would not be minted for another ten years). Rule took a low-paid job as a guard on trains taking minerals to Mexico City, and diligently saved his wages. He acquired a mule to visit abandoned mines, which he believed could be revitalised using pumping techniques. Investors were sceptical, but Rule's youthful enthusiasm persuaded them to inject the capital. He soon struck a good vein and was suddenly a miner in demand. The work was not without pitfalls and Rule survived several scrapes: he was once struck by a large rock, which smashed his teeth to pieces. Instead of complex and expensive dental surgery he had them all removed.

Rule rose to foreman of the Real del Monte mine. His judicious investments, and discovery of the lucrative vein at Santa Gertrudis, helped him accumulate a vast fortune. He was dubbed *Rey de la Plata* – the Silver King – and owned eight *haciendas* in Hidalgo and the state of Queretaro (one set aside for cricket, naturally), a house in Mexico City, and a private railway carriage to travel between the capital and Pachuca. He adopted the Spanish variant Francisco, and fathered 14 children, with 6 of his sons turning out for Pachuca's cricket team.

Rule left his mark on the city, as we discover on our return to Pachuca from Real del Monte. The Silver King bequeathed a number of public works, including the iconic Reloj Monumental in the central square. Designed in a Spanish baroque style, the clocktower was finished in 1910 to commemorate Mexico's centenary and has the same workings as Big Ben. It has become the city's symbol and remains the badge of Pachuca's professional football team. They were managed for a while by Mexico-born Cornishman Alfred C. Crowle, who took charge of the country's national side in 1935.

Christopher Ludlow, Ricardo's ancestor, arrived in Pachuca in 1875 to install one of the biggest pumping machines Mexico's mines had seen, later acquiring several concessions and establishing himself as Don Cristóbal. A pious man, he was instrumental in the building of a Methodist church in Pachuca where he preached to the congregation in both Spanish and English. He once said a prayer with his eyes closed as gunshots were heard on the streets outside – on opening them he discovered all but one of his flock had nervously sneaked out.

Hedley Ludlow and his brother Sydney inherited their father Christopher's passion for cricket. Hedley was an occasional player, but Christopher's second son Sydney was an integral part of Pachuca Athletic Club – formed in 1895 when Pachuca, Velasco and Real del Monte, with Rule as president, joined forces to provide a sterner test for Mexico's other cities. A humble preacher, Sydney skippered PAC for several years, always carrying his bible and a picture of Queen Victoria with him. He learned Otomi, the language of the area's indigenous people whom he befriended, in addition to topping Pachuca's batting averages.

Matches played by the Rablings, Rules and Ludlows were extravagant social affairs. Pachuca's cricket fraternity were synonymous with the most lavish hospitality and, in the manner of home, Cornish pasties were a staple at the tea break. Alcohol was consumed by the barrel-load and Pachuca's players were partial to a post-match session, especially if they scored rare victories over teams from Mexico City. 'To say the city is in high glee over the result is the mildest way of expressing things here tonight,' read a bulletin in the *Mexican Herald* after a win over Reforma Athletic Club in 1903. 'Champagne is flowing like water emptied from the Maravillas Shaft by the powerful Cornish pump and we are too gay to send details of the match, which will reach you in sober figures tomorrow.' Alcohol delayed Pachuca's arrival for a match in Puebla two years earlier, albeit without a drop of it being consumed, when a train carrying bottles of the famous *pulque* – made from the fermented sap of the maguey agave plant – blocked the line between the cities.

Sydney Ludlow was among the many Cornish to return to England when the Mexican Revolution broke out in 1910, but his brother Hedley remained, and could count a renowned scientist, a film producer and a flamboyant 1960s bohemian revolutionary among his descendants. Yet the affable Ricardo, fifth generation Cornish-Mexican, has a claim to fame truer to his heritage. The world's first pasty museum was opened in Real del Monte, and Ricardo took it a step further when he founded Pachuca's International Cornish Pasty Festival – persuading Prince Charles and the Duchess of Cornwall to be the guests of honour in 2009.

Cricket may have died out in Mexico's 'Little Cornwall', but the humble pasty has endured and there is a shop on every corner in Real del Monte and Pachuca – many with Union Jack bunting or the Cornish flag of St Piran hanging in the window. A short walk from Pachuca's Methodist church, our stomachs rumble as the familiar smell of oven-baked pastry carries us down the road to La Mina del Paste (The Pasty Mine). The small shop's walls are covered in black and white photographs evoking Pachuca's history and a sign outside boasts *una delicia de la gastronomia Inglesa para Mexico*.

There are a mouth-watering selection of golden pasties on offer, all handmade with the familiar crimped crusts. Distinct from *empanadas*, widespread throughout Latin America, we discover that Mexican *pastes* come in a mind-boggling variety of savoury and sweet flavours: everything from sweetened rice and pineapple to *tinga* (shredded beef marinated in tomatoes and chipotle) to spicy jalapeños and guacamole. 'Everybody in Pachuca loves Cornish pasties,' adds Ludlow, as he takes a bite of the conventional beef mince, potato, swede and onion version. 'A few years ago at the festival we baked one which was twelve feet in size. The world's longest Cornish pasty was made in Mexico!'

*　　*　　*

Hanging in the stately splendour of the Musée Royal de l'Armée et d'Histoire Militaire in Brussels is the oldest surviving photograph of sport in Mexico. Dated 1865, it shows a break in play at a cricket match, and was taken by Frenchman François Aubert. Just behind the stumps is Emperor Maximilian I – Mexico's second, and final, monarch. He is wearing white trousers, in shirtsleeves and clutching a hat in his right hand. The photograph captures a rare day of respite for Maximilian during a turbulent period in Mexico's history. The Vienna-born Habsburg prince had been installed in an attempt to legitimise French rule following the Second Franco-Mexican War, with the support of Napoleon III and conservative Mexican monarchists hostile to the liberal presidency of Benito Juárez.

Maximilian, who arrived in Mexico City the previous year, brought with him a conscience for the welfare of the people; appalled by Mexico's poverty and destitution he implemented measures of social change. He even extended an olive branch to the deposed Juárez, offering him the position of prime minister if he swore allegiance to the crown. Juárez declined, and in October 1865 Maximilian changed tack, issuing the Black Decree to capture and execute 11,000 of Juárez's supporters.

Tensions heightened and, with the threat of assassination, Maximilian turned to cricket for escapism. His interest had been roused on the occasions he looked down to the lush green fields that surrounded his lofty home at Chapultepec Castle. The grand neoclassical royal residence serves as the National Museum of History today, and offers to us the most spectacular panorama of seemingly endless Mexico City. It was built by the Spanish viceroy on a hill that had been a haven for the Aztec rulers, and from this vantage point Maximilian sighted the British practising their favourite sport on the pastures below.

William Bullock, an English travel writer, ventured to Mexico City around the time Maximilian donned his whites, and painted a colourful picture of a game he encountered on the outskirts of the capital one Sunday:

> While croquet goes on at Tacubaya, the neighbouring village of Nápoles is the headquarters of cricket. The district which it traverses consists of meadows as hard as iron, surrounded by hedges of cactus and maguey, or meadows soft as a sponge, surrounded by ditches. I had heard cricket was played in the country, but supposed it would turn out to be the cricket of that degenerate sort which one finds occasionally played by English residents in different parts of Europe. So that when I got to the ground, and found an excellent pavilion, a scoring box, visitors' tent, the field marked with flags, with the well-known letters MCC (Mexico not Marylebone, Cricket Club) marked upon them, and some eighteen or twenty players in flannels and cricket shoes, I was a little astonished.

The most surprising part of the performance was that the best player on the ground was a Mexican, whose bowling and batting did infinite credit to the training which he received at Bruce Castle School. Among the English players were several gentlemen close upon 60 years of age, who all expressed to me their conviction that they owe much of their health and energy which they still possess having stuck through thick and thin to their Sunday cricket. They assured me they had never allowed political events to interfere with their game which they had pursued unconcernedly, more than once, in view of the fighting going on in the hills around them. Being fully alive to the fact that cricket is nothing without beer, there is always a liberal supply on the ground, of a very excellent quality, supplied by the firm of Blackmore – a name revered, beyond all others, by Englishmen in Mexico.

Maximilian might have brought a touch of regal glamour to cricket, but he was swimming against the tide when it came to preserving the monarchy. Napoleon reduced his forces in Mexico under US pressure and the threat of Otto von Bismarck's Prussian expansionism. Juárez's position strengthened after the American Civil War, with support from presidents Abraham Lincoln and Andrew Johnson. Maximilian's wife, Carlota, travelled to Europe to appeal for help, but it fell on deaf ears.

Napoleon urged Maximilian to leave Mexico, but with 8000 loyalists he fought on. In May 1867, he was captured by Juárez's men and, despite pleas from prominent liberals Victor Hugo and Giuseppe Garibaldi, was shot by firing squad. Aubert had been there to snap Maximilian on the cricket field, and was present at the Emperor's death. He was permitted only to sketch the execution, but took chilling pictures of his bloodstained shirt pierced with bullet holes and Maximilian in his coffin.

The *Brucian* school newspaper, found in the old school building that is now Bruce Castle Museum in Tottenham, London, identifies Emilio Trigueros as the Mexican player of whom Bullock spoke. The school was founded by Rowland Hill, of Penny Black stamp and postal system fame, and active between 1827 and 1891. It was especially popular with the children of diplomats from Latin America, and so their school cricket XIs featured surnames such as Lopez, Rodríguez and Orellana.

Trigueros was the son of Mexico's finance minister and from a well-known sporting dynasty. Emilio attended Bruce Castle for seven years and opened the bowling for the First XI. Back on home soil Emilio and his brother Juan introduced Mexicans to cricket, which led to one particularly memorable dismissal: 'Jesus bowled Heaven 1'. The Trigueros brothers also coaxed indigenous workers employed by the family to make up the numbers – conspicuously recorded as 'Indian I' and 'Indian II' on scorecards.

The elderly players Bullock encountered had been involved in Mexico's first matches. Among those to arrive in the 1820s, after the Mexican War of Independence, were merchants Daniel and Lewis Price. The brothers retired back to Britain 30 years later, and a pamphlet from the Mexican Union Cricket Club was found in their personal archives. It contained proof that cricket was first played in Mexico's capital as far back as 1827 – not, as was widely assumed, solely at this time by the Cornish miners in the Sierra Madre Oriental.

Mexico City's early cricketers were obliged to adhere to the club's strict matchday attire: 'The dress or uniform . . . shall be a flannel jacket, a straw hat, and white pantaloons, and any member appearing on the ground in a match, or playing in any other dress, will be subject to a fine of two dollars.' There were penalties for tardiness – matches started at 8 a.m. The losing side covered the subsequent drinks bill. Alterations to MCC's Laws of Cricket were made to cope with the heat and the altitude, and were largely in favour of batsmen. One concerned the length of a Mexican 'over', which was 12 balls rather than MCC's 4 at the time. Law 34 also stated: 'If any fieldsman stops the ball with his hat the ball shall be considered dead with five runs added to the score.' The club's rules around betting were strict – payable only if the match reached a result.

Merchants and diplomats made up the bulk of the players. Charles Tadeau O'Gorman was the British consul-general in Mexico City who, at 42, had married a 14-year-old Mexican girl. George Ackermann, son of London designer and publisher Rudolph Ackermann, also took to the field. In the formative years Latin names were absent but listed among the membership in 1837 was R. González. A season later, J. M. Chávez and J. Durán joined him as the first Mexicans to play cricket. German miners even turned out, but the most interesting club member was Joel Roberts Poinsett. He was the first-ever US minister to Mexico and regarded as rabidly anti-British. The red Christmas flower – the poinsettia – would be named in his honour when he introduced it to the US from Mexico.

Mexico's cricketers were, as Bullock observed, stoic in the face of death, wars and revolutions, which would later inspire the spaghetti westerns of Sergio Leone and Sergio Corbucci. The Mexican–American War between 1846 and 1848 was no different. Even smelling the Brown Bess muskets of Mexican troops wafting into range, or hearing the whistle of bullets from US soldiers discharging Colt Walker revolvers, did not stop play. War even provided fresh opposition. An XI formed for the Gentlemen of the American Army accepted a challenge of a match at Nápoles in December 1847.

In April that year, Mexico's first baseball match was also supposedly played by the US Army, in the state of Veracruz, thanks to the ingenuity of Lieutenant Sergeant Abner Doubleday. Mexican general Antonio López de Santa Anna, who led the notorious attack on the Alamo, was ambushed while he ate lunch in his carriage. Santa Anna had lost his leg in 1838 after it was blown off by cannon fire – the limb was given a funeral and buried with full military honours. Seven years later, he had taken off his wooden replacement to enjoy a roast chicken dinner only to be ambushed. Santa Anna escaped on horseback, although in the rush to get away he left behind US$18,000 in gold and his wooden leg. The gold was turned in, but Doubleday kept the prosthetic limb. The story goes he later gathered enough men together in the plaza of Xalapa, where they played a game using the peg leg as a baseball bat. The wooden leg is now held in a glass case at Illinois State History Museum, despite calls from the Mexican government, and a petition to the White House, for its repatriation.

\*     \*     \*

The last resting place of Claude Butlin lies neglected.

A short walk from Mexico City's Tacuba Metro stop, tucked away on an unremarkable street with grey walls stained by graffiti, is the Cementerio Británico. The skyline opposite is dominated by a water tower brandishing the faded logo of Tornel – Latin America's largest tyre producer. It's a gloomy overcast day and there are no other visitors. We tentatively creep through brooding cast iron gates flanked by imposing grey brick columns. The surrounding fences have been daubed in racing green, now flaking and peeling. Passing the eerie lines of headstones, etched with British surnames, we step into a modern glass building with fluorescent strip lights where the cemetery's sharp-suited manager looks puzzled at the mention of Butlin. He has never heard of Mexico's greatest all-round sportsman, and is none the wiser as to where he lies now.

Eventually we find the headstone, nestled in front of a small hedgerow away from the main path. The bed of Butlin's grave is overgrown with weeds, while ivy climbs the headstone to the fractured remnants of where a cross used to sit. The inscription reads: 'Claude Marsh Butlin 1877–1940'. No epitaph. No fanfare. No clue to a remarkable sporting life. His accolades make him Mexico's equivalent of the renowned sporting polymath C. B. Fry. Yet Butlin has been consigned to a mere footnote.

In the salubrious surroundings of the exclusive Reforma Athletic Club there are subtle reminders of Butlin dotted around, provided you know where to look. Henry Filsinger, the club's former president, furrows his brow when the subject of the grave is broached after spicy lunchtime tacos. 'The management of the Cementerio Británico have been in contact,' he reports with a gravelly American accent before nervously lighting a cigarette. 'In the world's largest metropolitan city there is not much room to bury the dead. CMB's grave needs to be freed up.' Butlin, it seems, has no living relatives in Mexico, and the club has no power of attorney over what happens to his grave.

\* \* \*

Claude Butlin was born five years after C. B. Fry in Jaffna, British Ceylon, on 17 April 1877. His early years were spent in India where his father Alfred worked as a civil engineer. The Butlins returned to London in the late 1880s and lived in modest terrace houses in St John's Villas, Archway, and then Letterstone Road, Fulham. Young Claude was sent to board at St George's College in Weybridge, Surrey, a Josephite school, which more recently produced Adam and Ben Hollioake. Butlin is not listed among their most celebrated alumni.

At the age of 13, along with his father, mother Helen and sister Patricia, Claude moved to Mexico City. Originally built by the Aztecs on an island in a natural lake, the oldest capital city in the Americas was at this time home to just 500,000 inhabitants – a far cry from the sprawling smoggy metropolis we land in today, where 21 million battle congested roads, packed buses and a grubby overstretched underground system just to make it from A to B.

Butlin's father Alfred brought the family to Mexico having secured work on the construction of the Tehuantepec Interoceanic Railroad, one of the grander unrealised industrialisation projects of Mexico's Anglo-sympathetic president Porfirio Díaz. Not long after the Butlins arrived, however, the railroad contract changed hands and Alfred was out of work, fell on hard times and plunged into depression. Bitter and heated family arguments ensued.

Matters came to a head in May 1892, during an angry kitchen confrontation at the family home in Cuauhtémoc, the historic heart of Mexico City. Alfred seized a large carving knife and stabbed his wife four times – twice in the left arm, then once in her side and again in the pit of the stomach. The teenage Claude wounded his hand in the melee as he rushed to his mother's aid. Alfred, covered in his wife's blood, then pushed the knife into his own chest. He died of his wounds, but his wife survived.

Two months after the tragedy, 15-year-old Claude turned up on the cricket field. He gave a glimpse of the prowess that would see him dominate Mexico's sporting scene like no one else. He was picked to play for Read & Campbell's, a cricket team of railway engineers. The fixture was against Zumpango Cricket Club, based to the north of Mexico City and drawn from employees of the British construction firm Pearson & Son. Headed up by British industrialist Weetman Pearson, a friend of Díaz's, they were digging a tunnel to protect Mexico's capital from flooding.

What was going through the teenage Butlin's mind as he marked his run-up following the events of eight weeks earlier is unknown. Pent-up frustration and aggression, a raging fire in his belly? Whatever it was, Butlin's first 16 overs in Mexican cricket brought him six for 28, five clean bowled. It was a performance likened to Fred Spofforth, Australia's legendary fast bowler, and Butlin was christened the 'Demon Boy Bowler'.

*       *       *

Reforma AC's archivist unlocks a cupboard and gingerly hands us a faded silver trophy with the appearance of an oversized sugar bowl. It has two metal handles like door knockers and a number of shields – the largest of which, in the centre, is engraved 'Cricket Challenge Cup'. Between 1896 and 1909 this was the most prestigious prize on Mexico's sporting landscape, and Butlin would leave an indelible impression on it.

Reforma AC was established in March 1894 with Butlin, aged 17, the youngest founder member. Green spaces in the parks around Chapultepec had long been home to the capital's cricket. The ground, with the rolling hills leading to pine-clad mountains beyond, was lovingly sown with English grass seed when Reforma moved in. Contested by Mexico City, Pachuca and Puebla, the inaugural Cricket Challenge Cup caused such excitement that a downtown jewellery shop routinely put the trophy on display in its window.

Butlin matured from a precocious talent into the republic's leading cricketer. He grew into a man of slightly above-average height and build for the era, with a well-proportioned physique. Speed, agility and reactions were his qualities rather than super-human strength. He cut a dashing figure: slick black hair, moustache curled up at the ends and a serious demeanour.

A devastating spell of nine for 4 in May 1900 against Mexico Cricket Club were Butlin's best figures with the ball. Among his victims was Luis Amor, an affluent sugar plantation owner from the nearby state of Morelos, and the most influential Mexican national involved in cricket during the era. Amor's cricket love affair began at Stonyhurst College in Lancashire alongside siblings Alejandro, Victor and Pablo. Two of the Amor brothers were good enough to represent the school's First XI.

Luis Amor passionately devoted himself to the game. In 1896 he was instrumental in reviving Mexico CC, whose rivalry with Reforma endures to this day. He endlessly sourced equipment, filled countless administrative roles and cajoled Mexican colleagues to don whites. Inspired by I Zingari, the famous nomadic jazz-hat cricket club established in England by Old Harrovians in 1845, he founded Mexican Wanderers. Of the rest of the 'Amor Fab Four', Alejandro was a stylish batsman and the most talented cricketer in the family while Pablo seemed to possess the tactical acumen. Victor, it seems, was their Ringo Starr.

The pinnacle for the Amor brothers was in 1902 when Mexico CC foiled Butlin et al. to beat Reforma in a winner-takes-all league decider. The victory owed much to Pablo's astute captaincy and skill with the bat. But the joy, according to an old sage quoted in the *Mexican Herald*, was savoured most by Luis. 'The happiest man in this city tonight is Louis [*sic*] Amor and he really deserves the pleasure the victory has given him,' the newspaper said. 'No man in this country has worked harder for the game than Louis. The Mexico club is to him perhaps the dearest thing on earth. I am sure he wakes in the morning, thinking of the club's welfare, and he works for its welfare at every hour of the day, and his sweetest dreams are of its success.'

Mexicans, though, were not always afforded the same respect as the Amors by suspicious Brits. A waiter at Mexico CC was arrested after a wallet went missing from the pavilion during a net session. It was never recovered, but the alleged offender was thrown in prison regardless.

Monterrey – nestled close to the Texan border – was a hub of cricket during the Porfirian era, led by a British influx, but the sheer size of Mexico meant Butlin and his team-mates never ventured that far. Monterrey's cricketers instead struck up relations with counterparts in Porfirio Díaz City (now Piedras Negras) and Saltillo in the desert state of Coahuila. Scottish-born David McKellar had relocated to Coahuila from New Zealand in June 1892 when he bought a farm near Sierra Hermosa de Santa Rosa. McKellar became president of Santa Rosa Athletic Club – nicknamed *Los Rancheros* – and organised a match against railway employees from Porfirio Díaz City. A grandstand was built on his ranch to accommodate spectators, a supply of ice kept the beer cold and McKellar's wife and daughter served fresh local melon. After a 65-run victory for Santa Rosa, McKellar hosted a banquet and everyone left in high spirits.

Trouble was brewing for McKellar in the day job, though. A few weeks later he was fencing a section of land, to the scorn of other Mexican ranchers who wanted their cattle to roam freely. Heated exchanges followed and one day, when McKellar was riding back home, he was shot dead by a gunman hired by a rival Mexican rancher. He was far from the only one. The original ground at Nápoles on the outskirts of Mexico City was in a British-run *estancia*, but cricket would cease there after the death of co-owner Henry Beale. He was murdered on the ranch when 40 *banditos* attacked it during the Franco-Mexican War.

Not all Brits were on the right side of the law, anyway. Bristolian lawyer A. W. Laurie had skippered Mexico CC for one season during the Amor era. Laurie, a classy batsman, came to Mexico City via New York in 1900 and, calling himself 'Professor Alfred Laurie', became renowned on the cricket circuit for liking the sound of his own voice. Laurie's cogitations at one Puebla–Pachuca match, where he had turned up as a spectator, were particularly pompous. He strolled into the players' tent at the lunch break, then gave a lengthy monologue on the finer points of the lbw law to both teams, umpires and anyone else within earshot. There was more to Laurie than met the eye. He was masquerading under a pseudonym and had a shady past involving debts from speculation on South African mining stocks. An extradition order was issued by Britain, and Laurie scarpered never to be seen, or heard of, in Mexico again.

A few years later an 'A. G. Lawrie' turned up in Chile, where he was reported to have made 300 not out in an afternoon match at Valparaíso, before disappearing from their scene too.

Butlin, typically, continued to lead the way with bat and ball. His best knock came against Puebla in February 1901 when he struck 175 not out – a Mexican record at the time. Butlin 'handled the willow in masterly style', enthused a report of the innings. 'He drove and cut the deliveries of Puebla's best trundlers to the on, and off sides, and behind the wickets.' Puebla tried ten different bowlers but Butlin could not be moved. He then took seven for 13 in a crushing Reforma victory by an innings and 232 runs.

Puebla & District Cricket Club was established in 1899 by British textile workers. They were supplemented with players from the cities of Oaxaca – now a popular spot with tourists who come to bathe in the natural springs at Hierve el Agua, where the mineral-rich waters produce spectacular rock formations resembling waterfalls – and Veracruz on the Gulf of Mexico. Puebla encouraged a number of Mexican nationals – the surnames of Portillo, del Campo and Villavaso all appeared on scorecards, and José de Velasco was one of their best bowlers. The club played in the middle of the Puebla Velodrome, though not without tribulation. A mole infestation and damage from a French fete twice left the *cancha* unplayable. The *coup de grâce*, however, came during Mexican Independence Day celebrations when the locals 'took it into their heads to hold a cavalry charge over it'. A club outing to Orrín's Circus – featuring Londoner Ricardo Bell, the republic's leading clown – afterwards at least lightened the mood.

Before the Challenge Cup took off, Puebla used to organise friendlies with the British employed in the mill towns of

Orizaba and Rio Blanco. Orizaba counted upon a clutch of cricketing Scotsmen who played at the Santa Gertrudis Jute Mill, before the Mexico Railway Company inaugurated a new ground next to Orizaba station in 1901. In a large valley, with the green pastures of the Sierra Madre Oriental beyond, it was heralded as the most picturesque cricket ground in Mexico. An artistic pavilion was added a year later, although the club strangely used coconut matting despite the local abundance of jute.

The jute mill's Scottish cricket contingent included Duncan Macomish, a leading footballer in the early Mexican league and a regular for Orizaba in both sports. His team-mate Percy Clifford was instrumental in the construction of a pretty nine-hole golf course at the jute mill, which still exists to this day. Clifford went on to manage Club América, Mexico's biggest football team, to back-to-back league titles between 1926 and 1928; his son, Percy Jr, later designed over 40 of Mexico's golf courses. Orizaba's idyllic ground, we find out not long after arriving in the city, disappeared when the Cuauhtémoc Moctezuma Brewery, named after two Aztec rulers and now a subsidiary of Heineken, expanded its plant and built on the land.

Mexico's cricketers were compared in the press to the most famous cricketers of the era. Orizaba's wicketkeeper C. M. Hodges, for example, was dubbed the 'Mexican Blackham' after the innovative Australian gloveman Jack Blackham. Butlin, though, was the stellar name of the Mexican league. He claimed eight for 28 and eight for 5 against Orizaba in successive seasons. No comparisons were needed during his peak: he was a star in his own right. He was the reason Reforma won the Challenge Cup seven times between 1900 and 1909.

Butlin was not a flashy batsman – neither extravagant nor especially stylish with his strokeplay. Observers referred to him as graceful, but effective. Comparable in approach to Jacques Kallis, perhaps, his innings were frequently described as clinical and chanceless. It was his ability to score all around the wicket which elevated him above his peers.

Such a methodical approach ensured Butlin churned out some impressive numbers. In 89 completed innings he made 3082 runs at an average of 34.60, which put him head and shoulders above any other batsman in Mexico. This was in an era of uncovered, often underprepared, pitches, which were sticky one week and lethal the next. Bumped heads and broken bones were part of the game, yet Butlin thrived.

With ball in hand Butlin was devastating: he combined accuracy and variety with lethal pace. In his twenties he bowled long spells, clocked up countless maidens, and with a smooth, well-honed action fired it down much quicker than anyone else in Mexico. Butlin was regarded as simply unplayable by most in the republic. It brought him 463 wickets and he was a fearsome and intimidating prospect. At his peak he would even show largesse and decline to bowl in the second innings, so as not to dishearten opponents and make a game of it.

'Much of what Claude Butlin did on the cricket field has been lost, destroyed or not properly recorded in the first place,' says Craig White, not the ex-England all-rounder but secretary and historian of the Asociación de Cricket de Mexico. 'He probably took well in excess of five hundred wickets and scored between four thousand and five thousand runs, and that's a conservative estimate.'

Butlin was a colossus of Mexican cricket but the fact he never played at a high standard makes it difficult to judge his place in the global pantheon. The *Mexican Herald* claimed two of Butlin's contemporaries had county cricket experience: J. C. Parr reputedly turned out for Essex; while A. J. Simpson had rubbed shoulders with the Grace family in Gloucestershire. Butlin had the measure of both with bat and ball. Yet it was his achievements in a multitude of sports that added to his mystique. Butlin was more than just a cricketer.

\*     \*     \*

*¡Viva Villa! ¡Viva Zapata! ¡Viva la revolución!* At the Palacio Nacional in Mexico City on 6 December 1914 Pancho Villa and Emiliano Zapata took turns to sit in the presidential chair. The two iconic revolutionary leaders watched from the palace balcony as thousands of soldiers from the peasant armies of División del Norte and Ejército Libertador del Sur filed past. In dirtied white clothes, sandals and with unshaven faces they discharged their Winchester rifles into the air in celebration on a joyous victory parade. Three miles away, in the shadow of Chapultepec Castle, the members of Reforma left in Mexico were shifting uncomfortably inside the club's red-brick pavilion. 'Villa is a brigand, bandit, murderer, outlaw – absolutely a criminal,' the *Mexican Herald* proclaimed in the wake of the execution of William Benton, a British rancher, by Villa's cohorts.

In 1900, Díaz, an admirer of Butlin's sporting aptitude and a friend of Reforma, had rung the bell on a gala celebrating 90 years of a free Mexico. The highlights were a bicycle race and a cricket match. Porfirian modernisation and industrialisation, however, were not to everyone's taste. Oppressed farmers and peasants, angry at exploitation, took up arms and after two stints as president spanning 35 years the white-moustached Díaz was bumped into exile in Paris.

The elected replacement was Francisco Madero, a key figure in igniting the Mexican Revolution but lacking in experience. Britain's minister to Mexico at this time was the eccentric, bird-fancying Sir Francis Stronge, a member of Reforma and a well-known cricketer. But he paid more attention to his pet parrots than diplomacy during *La Decena Trágica* – ten tragic days – in 1913.

Stronge ceded influence to US ambassador Henry Wilson, which laid the path for a bloody military coup led by General Victoriano Huerta and Madero's assassination. 'Poor old Stronge came in for the most violent criticisms by the British colony,' wrote Sir Thomas Hohler, another member of the British diplomatic corps, who would gain fame as 'Mr H' when he intercepted the Zimmermann telegram proposing an alliance between Germany and Mexico during the First World War. 'He must have been a quaint spectacle in the midst of the firing, walking about with his head through the middle of a white poncho and his vile parrot perched on his shoulder dropping excrement and nibbling his ear.'

Huerta was himself ousted by revolutionaries, and with fighting now on their doorsteps many of those from Britain and the Dominions, on the advice of Stronge's successor Sir Lionel Carden, fled Mexico. Butlin held the fort in the family home, but in April 1914 packed the rest of the clan on to a steamer from Veracruz bound for New Orleans.

Dressed in their sombreros and crossbelts studded with bullets, the peasant soldiers occupied Mexico City's streets, but cricket managed to cling on. Just. 'Even though the deadly tap-tapping of machine guns and the ruddy rattle of rifles could be heard echoing,' said the *Herald*, 'the flower and beauty of the British colony remaining turned out in force to take part in a mixed cricket match.'

Mexico's cricketing stalwarts including C. J. Blackmore and H. G. Neumagen were supplemented by women in a fixture bridging the gender divide: 'There was some sensational slogging of the leather. The top notchers being Miss Honey, Miss Nock and Mrs Griffiths. The ladies played the regular official game but the *hombres* were handicapped by having to bat left-handed with a baseball bat, and likewise bowl, catch etc in the same manner.' The *Herald*, somewhat optimistically, signed off on 'rumours Pancho Villa will patronise [support] cricket'.

By this time Butlin had already grown weary of cricket's decline and took a back seat as clubs folded and player numbers dwindled. He relinquished his position as secretary of the Mexican League in 1907, and 1909 was his final full season. He now devoted more time to another love – tennis.

Butlin's feats with a racket in hand were staggering. With the exception of 1907 and 1908 he won the singles at the Mexico Championship every year from the first tournament in 1897 through to 1927, plus numerous doubles titles. In 1924, at the age of 47, he won Mexico's first ever Davis Cup point. Three years later he won the country's first doubles point, against Japan, when the 'crack old Mexican racquet star' became the oldest participant in the Davis Cup at 50 years and 105 days – a record that would stand until 1985.

In 1903, Butlin was given his sternest test: three encounters against George Hillyard, one of the leading British players of the time, who would become secretary of the All England Club and spearhead the move to their current site in SW19. Butlin was a 'court coverer of marvellous ability' mused the press in the build-up, but he narrowly lost two five-set doubles matches to Hillyard at Reforma. It was honours even in the singles encounter, though. The Mexico champion lost the first set 6–2 but won a thrilling second 8–6 against Hillyard, who would later win Olympic doubles gold for Great Britain. Hillyard was not too shabby a cricketer either. A fast bowler, he played for Middlesex, Leicestershire and the Gentlemen of England, and toured North America with Lord Hawke. Unfortunately, he never locked horns with Butlin on the cricket field.

Indeed, Butlin's cricket opportunities outside Mexico were scarce. Tentative plans were made for a Mexico XI to tour the US and Canada in 1900. This would have pitted Butlin against the great Philadelphian swerver John Barton King – the greatest US cricketer was in his mid-twenties and in 1908 would top the English first-class bowling averages. The *Two Republics* even went as far as to name a touring party, proposing green, white and red striped blazers in the colours of Mexico's flag. Sadly, the tour never materialised.

A relatively late starter, and reluctant convert at 26, Butlin also became the star striker of the early Mexican football league. He won the title six times between 1905 and 1912, lifting the trophy three times as captain. Butlin craftily outwitted defenders and was known for a 'deadly shot'. He was top scorer in the 1905–6 and 1910–11 seasons, and again in 1913–14 before he hung up his boots aged 36. Of the original amateur football league, the teams from Pachuca, Puebla and Orizaba, which began life as cricket clubs, still exist as top-flight professional teams.

Butlin likewise caught the eye on the rugby field, the baseball diamond and the cycling velodrome. Like C. B. Fry he was effortless with a golf club in hand, and between 1897 and 1910 won ten unofficial national golf championships. He would win the official event five times during the 1920s with the last in 1927 when, aged 50, he beat a 100-strong field.

At Reforma's annual athletics day, Butlin would routinely sweep the board and would be handicapped to ensure other entrants turned up. He could run the half-mile in two minutes flat, held the record for throwing the cricket ball, and even took the sack race seriously. Fry equalled the long jump world record with a leap of 23 feet 5 inches in 1892, and Butlin could also jump; his hop of 20 feet 4 inches not too far behind. Butlin held Mexico's high jump record for a number of years with a leap of 5 feet 4 inches and the pole vault record at 8 feet 2 inches. Fry's party trick, to leap from a stationary position on the floor backwards on to a mantelpiece would, you imagine, not have been beyond the agile Butlin.

Butlin rarely trained, but unlike many of his peers never smoked and, ahead of his time, was very careful with diet and nutrition. He would always be in the XI of the Teetotallers for their cricket fixture with the Partial Abstainers. 'Speaking for myself, I wouldn't be happy, and I doubt if I would be as healthy, if I did not play games,' Butlin said in a rare interview before a Davis Cup tie. 'I do not believe it necessary for the average man to give up athletics when he approaches middle age if he takes proper care of himself.'

Genes from active parents and experiences from childhood gave Butlin his tireless physique. His father hunted big game – elephants and tigers – and Butlin accompanied him on excursions through the dense Ceylonese jungle. 'I got quite a lot of exercise climbing because I was too young to carry a gun,' Butlin explained. 'When the game was sighted my role was to shinny up a tree and stay there until the shooting was over.'

He was a revelation in duels on the Fronton courts, where he became a champion in the Basque sport of *pelota*. He regularly beat professionals from the Basque Country and was the poster boy chosen to advertise tournaments in Mexico. 'If Mexico had been blessed with streams fit to row upon, or had the city been placed where there was good rowing water, then Butlin would certainly have added rowing to his accomplishments,' the *Herald* gushed.

Butlin's diary was so full that he had little time for matters of the heart, but in 1900 he married Mabel Wilson Morris in her home city of Topeka, Kansas. Mabel looked after their three children while Claude worked and played. He was employed initially in the auditing department of the Interoceanic Railway, then as the manager of a lumber company before finishing up as an insurance agent. Mabel would hold afternoon teas at the family house in the Popotla district of Mexico City, play bridge and visit family in the US, leaving Claude to his sporting pursuits. The couple enjoyed roller-skating together.

In 1922, they survived a light aircraft crash in which Claude broke his jaw and Mabel her shoulder, though fortunately there were no long-term complications. Butlin and his wife performed many acts of generosity for good causes, raising money for teachers, hospitals, earthquake victims as well as the hungry and homeless in what was becoming a sprawling city.

As he aged, Butlin grew more distinguished. He was tanned, relaxed, with the moustache a little more clipped and thinning hair neatly parted at the centre. His physique remained svelte and he smiled more. In cricket's re-emergence after the Mexican Revolution, Butlin, in his fifties, would briefly rekindle the old magic.

The veteran played four final cricket matches for Reforma in 1925, with and against men half his age. He scored 53 and took four wickets against the Aguila Light & Power company and then made 111 against Mexico Wanderers. A five-wicket haul followed in his third game, against the Wanderers, before two wickets and 32 in a swansong appearance versus Aguila Light & Power.

Among the photographs of Butlin we unearth in the archives at Reforma there's one that really stands out. He is smartly turned out in a tie and tweed three-piece suit. A tennis racket is resting gently between his hands. Gleaming to his left are the staggering 500 trophies, cups and medals he won. A smile of contentment hints at retirement after a remarkable sporting life. Butlin's achievements did belatedly reach Britain, with a six-paragraph wire story hailing him 'Claudio the Conqueror'. In 1938, the old boys' section of the *Georgian*, produced by Butlin's former school, announced he had been crowned Mexico's bowls champion at 61. It was to be one of his final sporting accolades. Two years later, Butlin died.

*　　*　　*

Reforma tried to lure Yorkshire's finest to Mexico in 1897. A letter was sent to the omnipotent Lord Hawke proposing his private side of amateurs sign off their landmark West Indies tour with a trip to Mexico City. The letter either never reached Hawke or it was snubbed, but one of the White Rose's favourite sons did eventually make it.

To the surprise of Mexico City's players, Fred Trueman was among the British Airways Eccentrics XI that pitched up for a game at Reforma in the 1970s. The legendary fast bowler had recently retired from first-class cricket, but Lincoln Clarke, who opened the batting for Mexico, tells us he still had plenty of zip: 'Fred dropped a shorter ball which I tried to hook. It came on a lot faster than I thought it would and went straight over the slips for four. He glared at me and growled, "What kind of bloody shot is that!" So, I replied, "Well, you look at the book, it's four runs!"'

Reforma's current ground in the district of San Juan Totoltepec claims to be the second-highest turf wicket in the world, at 7200 feet (a ground in Chail, India, is a shade over 8000). Reforma moved there in 1961, leaving a site across from the Hospital de la Defensa. Scotsman Walter Irvine, the club president at the time, instigated the switch after snooty members complained about the Mexican government using club facilities for injured soldiers to rest and recover.

Reforma is the only cricket ground in the whole of Mexico City, or 'DF' (Distrito Federal) as most of our team-mates insist on calling it when we arrive ready to play for Mexico City Cricket Club in a Sunday lunchtime encounter. Where once the wicket took pride of place, it is now sandwiched between two football pitches and Reforma's footballers are slowly traipsing off the playing area during the toss. A couple of Mexican employees from Reforma give it a hasty roll. The teams are almost entirely expats from Commonwealth countries but there is one Mexican in our ranks, Rodrigo Martínez, an ex-baseball pro. 'I really like Chris Gayle because he smashes the ball miles,' he grins, as his powerful arms essay an aggressive shadow-pull shot. 'I went to a T20 game on holiday in Australia and was hooked, so found some cricket back here in Mexico.'

As we strap on the pads and wait for our turn to bat, watching the opposition's steady medium-pacers find an extra yard of

pace at altitude, we imagine a cranky Trueman bounding in
with his trademark run-up, inspired to his old sharpness in the
thin air. Clarke is quick to point out that the locals fared a little
better when the BA Eccentrics returned a few years later with
former England opener John Edrich. 'He made all the runs as
we lost the first game,' Clarke recalls. 'However, a brilliant
catch got rid of him in the second match and we bowled them
out for 181.' Clarke, originally from the island of St Vincent
and a long-term stalwart of the Mexico City CC, re-founded in
1962, then made an unbeaten 119 to secure victory for the
home side and the praise of Edrich. 'After the match John gave
me a bat,' Clarke adds proudly in his Vincentian lilt. 'He told
me if I ever moved to England, he'd get me a contract to play
one-day cricket.' Reforma, Mexico City, plus newer clubs
Aguilas and Aztecs, now battle it out to be the capital's top side,
with the Lincoln Clarke Trophy awarded to the winners.

The England football team used Reforma as their base for
the 1970 World Cup. To alleviate the boredom during their
acclimatisation to altitude, Alf Ramsey let his players face
Mexico's cricketers in a couple of matches. It would be unthinkable for today's multimillion-pound footballers to risk injury
by playing cricket against a group of enthusiastic amateurs on
the eve of a major tournament. Yet Ramsey's side, holders of
the Jules Rimet Trophy, willingly obliged.

England divided themselves up into teams made up of northern and southern football clubs for two matches against Mexico
City. The northerners claimed a 61-run win thanks to Keith
Newton's 85 and 38 from Terry Cooper. The southerners – plus
Franny Lee of Manchester City, who had joined the squad late
– romped to a nine-wicket win. England captain Bobby Moore,
a week before the infamous Bogotá Bracelet incident, impressed

with his off-spin but Lee, despite four hours' sleep, was the star performer with the ball – which is no surprise given that he had played Lancashire League cricket. He also made a half-century, while Geoff Hurst and Martin Peters thrilled the crowd with a rain of sixes. Moore and Peters had turned out for Essex's youth teams, but it was their West Ham team-mate Hurst who was the most accomplished cricketer.

Hurst, ironically, would not have played cricket against Mexico City had his county career panned out differently. A youthful Hurst played a County Championship match for Essex against Lancashire in May 1962 in a side captained by Trevor Bailey and featuring Jim Laker. Up until July 1964, Hurst, a batsman who also kept wicket, felt he had a better chance of cracking it as a professional cricketer at Essex than as a footballer for West Ham until a twist of fate.

Hammers boss Ron Greenwood switched him from midfield to attack in pre-season. It was hailed as the managerial master-stroke that ignited Hurst's football career, although cricket had unwittingly played a part in his positional change. Because he had been playing cricket for Essex, Hurst was shorn of football match-fitness so Greenwood lightened the load by moving him up front, where he flourished. Four years later, Hurst scored *that* hat-trick in the 1966 World Cup final.

Mexico City toured Jamaica in 1973, playing against St James at Jarrett Park in Montego Bay with future Test umpire Steve Bucknor in their ranks, before England's footballers visited again in 1985. This time the cricket-loving Bobby Robson was manager, and wanted his side to get some altitude experience at the Azteca 2000 tournament, featuring Mexico and West Germany, ahead of the World Cup back here a year later.

Wearing an impromptu mix of bucket hats, Aviator shades, polo and dress shirts plus tight-fitting Umbro shorts adorned with the Three Lions, England's footballers faced Mexico's cricketers once more. The hosts were bowled out for 93, with Terry Butcher, in a pair of Stan Smiths, the pick of the attack with three for 23 from 6.5 overs. Glenn Hoddle, mid-1980s mane flowing during his delivery stride, claimed two for 27, but it was square-jawed Mark Hateley (two for 19) who left the biggest impression. 'I was surprised because they were all good cricketers,' recalls Clarke, who played for Mexico City that day. 'But I remember Hateley in particular. He was a very good fast bowler, with a nice rhythm, who could generate decent pace.'

England striker (and wicketkeeper) Gary Lineker, gold chain dangling around his neck, hit an unbeaten 45 in the reply of 95 for two with winger John Barnes (24 not out) second top-scorer. Goalkeeper Chris Woods (20) and defender Viv Anderson, for a duck, were the two wickets to fall – both to Mexico City's Mark Lawrence, who finished with two for 36. England's footballers romped to an eight-wicket victory to maintain a winning streak unlikely to be broken any time soon. 'Lineker had done well with the gloves, letting just one bye through,' adds Clarke. 'He was also an accomplished batsman and hit quite a few boundaries.'

Lineker retired from international football after the 1992 European Championship, when he was substituted in the decisive final group game against hosts Sweden, which England lost 2–1. A month later he turned out at Lord's for MCC against Germany, hoping for better luck alongside New Zealand captain Ken Rutherford, England's first black cricketer Roland Butcher, and Christopher Brown – son of Peru-born ex-England captain Freddie. But G. W. Lineker could only manage a single before he was caught at cover, and quipped to his team-mates after he walked back through the Long Room: 'I always get one against the Germans.'

* * *

'One listener is trying to introduce cricket to Mexico,' Tony Cozier informed listeners to *Test Match Special* after reading a note passed to him by fellow commentator Jonathan Agnew. 'But he's finding it hard as it is very mountainous and there are no flat areas at all. That's from a Mr Juan Carr.' Cozier was the victim of Agnew's practical joke, prompting stifled guffawing from *TMS* colleagues, yet there have been recent, and more serious, attempts to introduce the game across Mexico – including in the mountains.

The distinctive mitre-shaped rock formations of Cerro de las Mitras afford a backdrop as spectacular as Table Mountain in Cape Town for the cricketers in the north-eastern city of Monterrey, where the game has flickered back to life after a century. Monterrey compete in the national championships along with Mexico City and Guadalajara, which is synonymous with two of Mexico's most famous exports: mariachi music and tequila. Guadalajara's cricketers have even named one of their league teams Tequileros in tribute to the drink made from the ubiquitous spiky blue agave, which originates from a nearby town of the same name.

Plenty of tequila is downed in Cancún, the purpose-built party capital of Mexico and go-to destination for US college students in search of a boozy spring break. While the teeny-boppers and twentysomethings staying in the same hostel as us plan to nurse their hangovers sunbathing on the beach after a late night in crowded bars and nightclubs, we quietly pack our whites, tiptoe out of the dorm, and make our way out of town headed for a morning cricket match.

The reason for the early start soon becomes apparent – even at breakfast time the temperature and sweltering humidity of Cancún leave our cricket shirts drenched and our throats dry. 'It's too hot from midday, and in the late afternoon the mozzies will eat you alive,' advises Phillip Barkhuizen, a bull-like South African in his fifties who is organiser-in-chief of cricket in Cancún.

The Maya for Cancún – *Kaan Kun* – translates as 'nest of snakes'. Appropriate, given the perils cricketers face at their ground in the Instituto Americano Leonardo Da Vinci, where the boundary *is* the jungle. 'In there are snakes of all different colours, panthers, pumas and animals you wouldn't see in the zoo,' Barkhuizen tells us as he straps on every piece of protective kit imaginable before striding out to bat, better protected than a conquistador. 'You can even get a crocodile straying from the lagoon.' When a player spears a scorpion to death with a stump centimetres away from us as we change into our whites, we don't doubt him. 'There is a four-step rule here,' adds Barkhuizen, the unlikeliest of IT consultants. 'If you can't see the ball within four steps you give it up for lost. Or send in someone disposable.' The club built two nets at the ground in 2013 but one lane has been reclaimed by the jungle. The unforgiving foliage means the only cut shot possible would be with a machete.

A visit from Giles Paxman, British ambassador to Mexico and elder brother of *University Challenge* host Jeremy, was the impetus for cricket's relatively recent emergence in Cancún. With baseball more popular than football in the Yucatán region, Mexicans were engaged too: Alexis Juárez Sosa swapped codes with some success. Cancún's players were not the first to play in the region, though. In 1892 the short-lived Champion Club briefly played cricket in Merida, a beautiful city built on top of the Chicxulub crater formed when the large asteroid believed to have wiped out the dinosaurs struck the Earth.

Accompanied by the beats of Puerto Rican singer Luis Fonsi and Daddy Yankee's recently released chart-topper 'Despacito' – ubiquitous, with other reggaeton hits, on our bus trips the length of Latin America – we head east of Cancún to Chichén Itzá. The spectacular Mayan city was built around AD 600 and attracts 1.2 million tourists a year. It has at least one thing in common with county cricket grounds: it has staged an Elton John concert.

Chichén Itzá's Mesoamerican bat-and-ball arena is well preserved. The open-air court has steeped walls, around 30 feet, either side of a playing area measuring 225 feet x 545 feet and built with acoustics in mind. A whisper can be heard from one end of the ballcourt to the other, leading us to ponder whether the Mayans were into sledging. The walls and pillars encircling it feature a variety of curious engravings.

Our tour guide tells us of a Mayan game that would see players attempt to strike a rubber ball – larger and slightly heavier than the 6 oz cricket ball – through vertical stone hoops with a bat. Players wore protective equipment and clothing. Some carvings depict them in capes and masks; others in skirts. In general, players wore a loincloth and protective hip guards. Depending on the rules among a particular tribe or area they may also have worn a chest protector, kneepads and arm guards.

Maya viewed the game as a battle between the underworld and their earthly adversaries. Further north, Aztecs saw it as the sun against the forces of night. Games were used as a means to defuse local conflicts and disputes, although defeat sometimes meant death. Chichén Itzá has a particularly gory carving of a losing player being decapitated. Those who mastered the sport could even make a living out of it.

Hernán Cortes led the expedition that brought down the Aztec Empire in the sixteenth century and the Spanish Catholics viewed these games as heretical so sought to suppress them. Mexico City's cricketers feel differently today, adopting a red cricketing Aztec man wearing just a traditional headdress and cricket gear as their association logo for many years. Traditional Aztec ballgames survived in areas such as in north-western Sinaloa, where the influence of the Spanish conquest was not as strongly felt.

The Sinaloa people claim their Aztec version of *ulama* is one of the oldest continuously played sports in the world. *Ulama de mazo* and *ulama de palo*, which uses a two-handed wooden paddle bat weighing 15 pounds, are the most comparable to cricket. Points are scored in various ways, such as when the opposing team hits the ball out of pre-defined boundaries. Games are played to eight points, but if drawn the score returns to zero and the game starts afresh. Successive draws can lead to lengthy games and there is a record of one that lasted eight days. The Timeless Test between South Africa and England at Durban in March 1939 was played just a day longer.

\*     \*     \*

At 10 p.m. on 6 May 1940, Claude Butlin died at the Sanatorio Cowdray in Mexico City. The cause of his death was Addison's anaemia, a blood disorder caused by a lack of vitamin B12. He was 63. There were no lengthy newspaper obituaries hailing his greatness, and details of his funeral held at the Cementerio Británico are scarce. No streets, plazas or buildings in Mexico are named after him. Outside of the walls of Reforma AC his name is barely known.

Reforma believed Butlin had no living descendants. His wife Mabel would live another 20 years; his son, Claude Jr, married twice but had no children. His remains were now the property of the graveyard owners and they were to be unceremoniously disposed of unless a relative could be found. We began a quest in the hope of finding a living descendant.

Butlin had two daughters – Dorothy and Cecily – but no details existed beyond their names. We discovered, however, a marriage certificate for Butlin's eldest daughter, Dorothy, in the archives. In January 1928, she had married a Byron Chauncey Mohler, and they had children. Slowly but surely Butlin's family tree was pieced together.

A year after we first met, an email from ex-Reforma president Henry Filsinger landed in our inboxes. 'The search is over!' Filsinger wrote. 'On Tuesday I will go to the Cementerio Británico. This will be to witness the exhumation and cremation of Claude Butlin's remains. I will be given an urn with his ashes. His descendants gave me power of attorney for the paperwork. A relative of the family will, I hope, pick up the urn. If they don't, he will be next to the ashes of the cats. My wife does not like the idea.'

Mrs Filsinger did not have to put up with Butlin's remains on their mantelpiece for long. Lorraine Shartouny, Butlin's great-granddaughter, travelled down to Mexico City from Atlanta, Georgia, for a short ceremony at Reforma. On the cricket field, in front of the club's striking triangular pavilion, she was present with officials from Reforma and the Asociación de Cricket de Mexico as Butlin's ashes were scattered before the day's league fixtures. The last earthly remains of the greatest sportsman to grace Mexico were back on the fields of play. It was a low-key send-off, and you sense he would not have wanted it any other way. 'I do not give myself any particular credit for anything I have done,' Butlin once said. 'Every game I have ever played has just seemed to come so natural to me.'

## 2

# Belize

### *Stained by blood*

T HE WAIT ON Gilbert 'Bertie' Ellis's porch is long, uncomfortably so. Belize's oldest living cricketer is 99 years old. He has survived two of the world's most devastating hurricanes, witnessed British colonialism and his country's independence, and much more besides. We need not have worried: he was just rummaging around for his front-door key. When his smile beams down at us from his doorway, it's as if 25 years have been shaved off. It turns out Bertie is squeezing us in between lunch and a game of dominoes at a friend's house.

So what's the secret to such a long and healthy life? 'That's easy,' he says. 'No weed, no hard drinking, and lots of sport. I didn't do a lot of stupid things in my younger days. You can't play sport if you're drunk. And this weed and cocaine . . . that tends to ruin your body, in my opinion.' His vitality has nothing to do with fathering 19 children? Bertie chuckles quietly. 'That helps too. What can I say? In my day, when you played sport and dressed smart, the ladies liked it. Belize was a small place back when I played cricket, perhaps eighty thousand people. Almost every Belizean boy or girl played either sport or music. If you didn't, your parents were soon on to you.'

Although he hasn't played anything more strenuous than dominoes for decades, Bertie has retained a core physical strength, no serious ailments, and appears in possession of his faculties. His single-storey house, given to him in the 1950s by the Santiago Castillo wholesalers as reward for years of employment, is modest but immaculately neat, with no pensioner's clutter. We'd read in the local press that he was still driving a taxi at the age of 95, but assumed in the intervening four years that he had been required to hand in his licence. 'No way, man. That's my car outside!' he says, pointing out of the window to a rusting maroon Toyota. 'The licensing authority can't take it away from me unless the doctor says so. And he told me, "Bertie, you're fine." So I got it stamped for another two years. Who wants to walk, anyway?'

Should he ever change his mind, Bertie Ellis's house is a gentle ten-minute stroll from the Newtown Barracks – a mile-long strip of land running parallel with the seafront of Belize City. This was the centre of life in British Honduras, a 13,000-square-mile colony hemmed in between Mexico and Guatemala. The Barracks earned its name as the base of the West India Regiment when garrisons were formed across the British Caribbean in the late eighteenth century. For a while it was the closest Belize had to an airport: Charles Lindbergh touched down in the *Spirit of St Louis* in 1927 on a celebratory tour of Central America after his historic Atlantic crossing.

On Saturdays and public holidays, as many as four separate cricket matches would cram into the Barracks, watched by thousands. A hit to the western side of the wicket, barely 100 yards away, and the ball would bump along the main road and into the colony's exclusive members' clubs; a swipe to the east, and fielders would be retrieving it from the sea. Even so, on sandy wickets run scoring was not especially high. It was not until the 1930s that Sunt Trumbach scored the first recorded century in British Honduras, for Wanderers against University in the colony's crunch fixture. Evan X. Hyde, a prominent left-wing publisher in Belize, evoked this period in his columns for his newspaper *Amandala*: 'From their clubs, the colonial and native upper classes watched horse races and athletic competitions on the Barracks green in front of them. Roots Creoles swam in the Caribbean Sea in front of the Barracks and played cricket games on weekends on the green against the expats and the native elite.'

In 1947, Sir Edward Hawkesworth, a sickly man wounded in the trenches of northern France, was appointed governor of British Honduras as his last posting. On arrival, he asked if he could expect to see any cricket. Bertie Ellis remembers Hawkesworth coming along to the Barracks to watch one local club, Sussex, play Rovers, a team of businessmen, clerks and civil servants. Bertie had captained Rovers before the war, but he was playing for Sussex now.

The convention was that one team would bat from 2 p.m. until 6 p.m. on the Saturday, and the other had four hours on the Sunday to make the runs. On this occasion, Rovers, one of the strongest sides in the colony, bowled Sussex out for 106. The next day, heading into the last over, the scores were level, with Percy Davis of Sussex bowling to Rovers' number 11 Lloyd Davis – his brother. Lloyd nervously saw off the first three balls of the over, before Percy bowled him with the fourth. 'The match was tied,' says Bertie, 'and the governor said he couldn't have wished to see a better game of cricket.'

\*     \*     \*

'If the world had any ends, British Honduras would certainly be one of them. It is not on the way from anywhere to anywhere else. It has no strategic value. It is all but uninhabited.' Shortly after completing *Brave New World* in 1931, Aldous Huxley embarked on a trip to Central America, which he chronicled in *Beyond the Mexique Bay*, and was somewhat befuddled by Britain's continued possession of this small, hurricane-prone chunk of land surrounded by the Spanish-speaking world.

The clubs that emerged on Newtown Barracks reflected the colonial state of mind. The first was Wanderers, run and captained by the white and pale-skinned elite. The statutes carrying the precise date of Wanderers' foundation were swept away in hurricanes, but the *British Honduras Handbook of 1887–88* listed a joining fee of BZ$3, on top of an annual subscription of BZ$6. Forty-six people took up the privilege that year. Wanderers would enlist black or mixed-race people – known locally as the Belizean Creole – to bowl at the white gentlemen in practice. Creole cricketers eventually forced themselves into the team through their excellence.

Towards the end of the century, there were signs the military class running the colony were not having it all their own way on the cricket field. In May 1885, an intra-club match between Europeans and Creoles was won easily by the darker-skinned side. Tensions simmered over on the Barracks between Wanderers and a Garrison XI. The Garrison had been bundled out for 35, even after their captain, Lt Weir, had persuaded his opposite number, C. M. Evans, to recall one of his batsmen after a stumping to which he objected. 'It only showed Weir's ignorance of the rules,' reported the *Belize Observer*. As Wanderers set about batting, Weir instigated the changing of three or four umpires, and took real exception when a black umpire by the name of Brown, after some warnings, no-balled him 20 times.

The flashpoint that ensued went to the Police Court. Although several officers were produced to defend Weir, some claiming he had not even touched Brown, most witnesses said he had grabbed him by the arm and pushed him. 'If you push me again I'll bring you up,' Brown said in response. 'I'll push you again, and kick you besides,' threatened Weir, who then called for the town provost to come on and remove Brown from the field. Brown reluctantly put his hands in his pockets and walked off. He denied 'showing fight' on the field, but admitted saying he would 'have it out' with Weir on the Barracks Road if the soldier was willing. Weir appears to have followed him a few steps, then turned on his heels and said tersely, according to Brown, 'that he wouldn't walk after a damned nigger'. Evans felt he had no option but to abandon the game with Wanderers 65 for eight and heading for a substantial first-innings lead. The majority of the witnesses seemed to be behind Brown, but the magistrate threw the case out of court, simply declaring: 'People going to the Barracks should behave themselves.'

Wanderers, the forum through which MCC Laws filtered into British Honduras, formed a disputes committee to deal with potential grievances. Sure enough, in 1895, with 20 minutes left in one game against University, Royalist were eight wickets down, needing three runs to win. 'University saw they were going to get beaten, so all the fielders ran off the field to see if the score was correct,' reported the *Belize Independent*. 'When they had delayed about twelve minutes they set their fields again, but no sooner was that done they hit down the wickets so as to loose [*sic*] the bails; of course, they could not find them. One of the fielders had them in his pocket and when it was found, time was up. This is cricket in Belize.'

By the turn of the century there were 11 clubs in Belize Town. Robert Clarke of Rovers was famed for his 'twisting' deliveries, while Arthur Wozella of University is said to have once defied the opposition for an entire innings on the treacherous Barracks wicket, taunting them by stroking the ball around with the handle of his bat. Wanderers v. University was the talk of the papers each year.

A pamphlet written at this time by a Belizean, Isaiah Thomas, *A Concise Hint and Guide to Cricket*, found its way to London and was decades later lambasted in the *Cricketer* by the fearsome Irving Rosenwater for being 'couched in ridiculous bombast . . . and were it not for the general nature of the pamphlet, might make us seriously ponder on the following words: "I cannot conceive how the majority of cricketers nowadays are so much given to prejudice, and partiality, pretence, and double-dealing, on the whole susceptible to bribery, and flattery, self-conceit, ostentation and folly." '

But there was an unmistakeable passion for the game across the social strata. When school was over for the day, Creole boys would head out to the city's open areas at the Barracks and Yarborough to set down stumps between 4 p.m. and dusk. The damage they caused leaping over the Yarborough Cemetery fence provoked the occasional grumble, and the *Colonial Guardian* called for a local policeman to be stationed there to stop older boys bullying smaller ones.

Tragedy struck one Saturday in June 1892, when two boys, Radzival Miller and Percival Gentle, collided under a high ball. Gentle went down with a blow in the stomach, and the arrival of three doctors could not save him. He died in hospital of peritonitis two days later.

The colour-conscious authorities remained, on the whole, happy for their colonial subjects to play the grand old game – though not always through the best of intentions. A reporter in the *Colonial Guardian* wrote in 1893: 'A gentleman sometime ago told one of our governors that, in the evenings, he only saw little nigger boys playing cricket in the Barracks. The governor said that was good, else they could become "robbers or worse".'

In 1896 the Polo Club began flexing its muscles and demanding Wanderers surrender some of their dominance of the Barracks. But the cricketers could not abide the horses' hooves cutting up the wicket. The Polo Club had the backing of the *Times of Central America*; the Wanderers' case was put stoutly by the *Colonial Guardian*. At a summit meeting, Governor Cornelius Moloney ruled that polo could be played only from 15 October to 15 March, and placed the prisoners of the colony in charge of repairing the turf at the end of the polo season. The colonial government restricted the setting of wickets at Yarborough no closer than 40 feet from the roadway ditch, and 'reserved the right to stop cricket if it caused an injury or the cricketers misbehaved'.

Soldiers and police, for all their sense of entitlement, played their part in spreading the game through the entire colony. It seemed to appeal most to whites and Creoles, though some mestizos (descendants of Mayans and Spanish settlers) and Garifuna (a combination of indigenous Caribs and blacks from the island of St Vincent, who settled along the east coast of Central America in the late eighteenth century) also took up the game. Corozal Constabulary beat the might of Wanderers in 1892 when one burly policeman came off with a half century.

The Fort Cairns garrison at Orange Walk held regular matches against the townsfolk on the Mexican border. There were teams down south in the sugar-mill settlement of Sittee River; the southerly city of Punta Gorda, who battled on despite relying on equipment belonging to a few rich benefactors; and Toledo, a club of US sugar planters. The Belize Estates Company, the colonial enterprise that came to own a fifth of British Honduras, slowly milking the land of its lumber, was said to have treated its workers much like slaves, though even it would permit employees to play cricket on Saturday afternoons.

The team at Stann Creek had 'a spacious and well-kept lawn' between the sea and the district commissioner's residence, though not when the local farmer let 30 oxen graze on the field. The commissioner alienated the cricketers further in 1901 when he prevented them from practising in the lead-up to a game against the workers of the Melinda Forest Reserve, on account of the ball hitting his house – even though they had been training on that spot for 12 years. That occurred after he fined a young Carib boy $20 for setting off fireworks on the cricket ground in the direction of the sea. A more enlightened commissioner in Stann Creek had no objection seven years later to welcoming Wanderers for their first match outside the capital, when they caught the *Don Felipe* down the coast. Hemans, a black man, top-scored for the plucky villagers with 38 not out.

A tradition developed of entire villages coming out to watch. One Saturday in March 1928 Monrad Metzgen, a half-Danish tax collector and one of the architects of Belizean independence, cycled the 80 miles from Belize Town to Pine Ridge, and was taken aback by the number of spectators – he counted 40 bicycles and 4 motor cars – and was inspired to launch the first cross-country bicycle race in the colony over Easter weekend.

The race began at 5 a.m. on Maundy Thursday, outside the Belize Town courthouse, with 5000 watching the start, and covered 90 miles to San Ignacio, the biggest town in the inland district of Cayo. It seemed an improbable and reckless venture: after Orange Walk there were 15 miles of bad road; from San Ignacio to Gale Creek there was no track at all, forcing the riders to battle mudslides as they carried the bikes on their backs through the tropical undergrowth. On the Saturday evening, 22 cyclists somehow summoned the energy to play a game of cricket – Cayo v. Belize Town – which the capital won by 2 runs. After the return journey on Easter Sunday, Elston Kerr crossed the line first, and the annual Easter Cross-Country Cycling Classic remains a landmark in the Belizean calendar, marking the unofficial starting gun for the cricket season.

Back in Belize Town, tropical downpours in August and September 1929 led to the postponement of that year's Challenge Cup final between Wanderers and Cambridge until April 1930, the start of the following season. The anticipation led to the biggest crowd ever to assemble on the Barracks, the boxes of the Polo Club, Newtown Club and Wanderers Club full to bursting. But Wanderers were swept aside, mustering just 51 in 33 overs.

In September 1931 a hurricane ripped through the Gulf of Honduras, flattening Belize Town and killing 2500 people. In light of the devastation, it is easy to see why the visit of Wembley CC from Jamaica five years later, to play two 'Test' matches, is still talked and written about wistfully by the generation that witnessed it. Playing for Jamaica the previous season, fast bowler Hines Johnson and off-spinner Donald Beckford had taken all ten wickets in an innings against the touring England side boasting Maurice Leyland, Patsy Hendren and Les Ames.

The left-armer Johnson was 25 and at his fearsome fastest – a far cry from the 39-year-old wheeled out in 1950 for West Indies' triumphant tour of England. The crowd on the Barracks was sent into raptures when Beckford, opening the batting, was bowled for a duck by local boy Albert Cattouse in the first match, then again by Reginald Flowers in the second. Flowers was known, on account of his slight build, as 'Baito' – Belizean slang for *vijeto* ('little old man' in Spanish) – and produced lively pace from just a 4-yard run-up, bemusing the Jamaicans. Wembley were bowled out for just 37, and their manager offered to take Baito back for a trial in Jamaica, but he preferred to stay at home.

Clifford de Lisle Inniss was a well-off, fair-skinned lawyer who had made the first double-century in schoolboy cricket in Barbados, before going on to represent the island in the West Indies first-class intercolonial tournament and against the 1929–30 MCC side. In 1933, while up at Oxford, he put on 149 for the third wicket with George Headley in a win for the West Indians over MCC at Lord's. He pursued a diplomatic career, settling in British Honduras when appointed chief justice in 1957. Inniss could occasionally be persuaded to turn out for the Belize Club. Charles Godden, in Belize with the Foreign Office, wrote that Inniss was now 'a corpulent figure always wearing a Harlequin cricket cap, and could be taken for an elderly Billy Bunter'. There was an excruciating incident in a match against Rovers, where Inniss, not yet accustomed to the earthier Belizean game, was run out as he left his crease to do some gardening. The judge walked off without complaint.

The Barracks were still being fought over, so in the 1950s a Jamaican carpenter, R. M. 'Skipper' Edwards, decided to clear some swamp land further into the city, just west of the canal, for a cricket ground. Old-timers say Edwards would go off with his wheelbarrow, under cloak of dark, in search of sand and earth to fill in the swamp. He enlisted a working party of younger middle-class Creole boys to form Unity CC. Some of his acolytes, Telford Vernon, Charles B. Hyde (Evan X. Hyde's father), Ellis Gideon and Dean Lindo, would go on to become prominent members of Belizean society. At the new ground, named Edwards Park in his honour, the first matting wicket in Belize helped the young players to hone their back-foot play. Charles B. Hyde recalled: 'By reading instruction manuals at the Jubilee Library, Telford and I taught ourselves to bat, learning to play the strokes like the great English masters, Jack Hobbs and W. G. Grace. Telford sought perfection.'

The England team were supposed to provide the answer to the grounds conundrum. At the end of their 1959–60 Test tour of the West Indies, the MCC tourists boarded a Viscount flight from Trinidad to Belize City to play a pair of matches on the Newtown Barracks. They came at the invitation of the governor, Sir Colin Thornley, and were to officially open a new ground, named the MCC Grounds, over the road from the Barracks, to be devoted entirely to cricket. Evan X. Hyde thought it nothing less than a gift from the British to try to keep the natives sweet, at a time when decolonisation movements were on the march and a Test at Trinidad on the same tour had been held up by a riot.

England captain Peter May had gone home after three Tests due to an abscess in his nether regions, and his replacement, Colin Cowdrey, flew back from Trinidad with fast bowler Fred Trueman and the English press corps. This explains why there was virtually no mention of the British Honduras leg in reports at the time. The archives at Lord's contain just a single reference – a note of 'a handsome wooden plaque presented to MCC on behalf of the people of British Honduras'. No one knows of its whereabouts. The tourists' wicketkeeper Roy Swetman recalls them lodging with British troops, and enjoying a boat trip out to Belize's glistening cays for a barbecue and a spot of fishing.

England won both matches easily, in front of 4000 Belizeans. The Belize five-cent piece which Telford Vernon and Raman Subba Row tossed up with was pocketed by MCC's stand-in captain, who spent the entire next summer at Northamptonshire using the same coin. In the second match, tour manager Walter Robins, wearing his Free Foresters cap, applied his veto to appoint himself skipper. That was, says Swetman, entirely in keeping with Robins's general behaviour as 'a complete pain in the arse'. The English shared their connecting flight back to Kingston with George Headley, then the national coach of Jamaica, who had been coaching the British Honduras team.

By all accounts Bertie Ellis's son, Gilbert 'Chico' Ellis Jr, ought to have been in the home selection. Chico would represent British Honduras in football, basketball, baseball and softball – but not cricket. When Headley arrived to host a coaching session on the Barracks, word reached him that Chico, one of just four century-makers in the history of the colony, was playing football next door. Headley called him over, asked him to face a few deliveries, and instantly declared him better than all the other young cricketers who had turned up. 'Mr Headley walked over to me and said, "I want to take your son to Jamaica to play cricket,"' says Bertie. 'But my boy didn't want to go. I don't know why; he doesn't even know why. But there's no way I could have forced him. He was 21, he had a girlfriend, and maybe he didn't want to leave her. He lives in Chicago now, and I tease him about it. Sometimes in life you can be too young to realise the opportunities you have.'

The MCC Grounds had been captured for cricket by Albert Cattouse, president of the Belize Cricket Control Board and – handily – the minister for labour and social services in the People's United Party government, which swept the board in the colony's first elections in 1954. 'The MCC Grounds was so precious that a crotchety but outstanding groundskeeper named McMahon was imported from Jamaica to landscape and care for the garden,' said Evan X. Hyde. 'He did a beautiful job . . . It was specifically intended for cricket . . . Football was very exciting throughout the 1960s, and old "Dandy Cat" [Cattouse] had to put on a mean face to insist that cricket, slowly fading in popularity, retained pride of place.'

Cattouse was obsessive enough to break off from constitutional talks with the British over independence to consult MCC's recent changes to the Laws of Cricket. He had recovered from a political storm two years earlier, when George Cadle Price, his party leader and prime minister designate, was tried for sedition for making fun of the Queen and Prince Philip, joking that the ticker-tape unfurled on their heads by a pro-Irish crowd in New York might have been toilet paper.

Belizeans were developing tastes for glitzier American offerings. Many became Dodgers fans after Jackie Robinson broke baseball's colour line in 1947, and they could follow ballgames on the US Armed Forces Radio. The pages of the *Belize Billboard* in the 1950s and 1960s had the occasional report on the exploits of the Three Ws (Frank Worrell, Everton Weekes and Clyde Walcott of West Indies) but were dominated by baseball news from the US agencies, illustrated with inventive photographs and cartoons.

Hurricane Hattie struck land at Belize City on All Hallows' Eve 1961. It left 319 dead and 10,000 homeless, and a disturbing coating of mud and debris across the entire colony. The elegant wooden houses of Belize City were no defence against such ferocity, and one reporter described the city in the aftermath as 'nothing but a huge pile of matchsticks'. The hefty repair bill for Edwards Park prompted the government to appropriate the ground, re-badge it as Rogers Stadium after a government minister, C. L. B. Rogers, and turn it over to softball.

Dean Lindo, a passionate cricketer, had worked in the department of social services under Cattouse but, being away at university in England, was powerless to do anything about it. One writer called Rogers the 'best brain in the cabinet and the chief political strategist . . . popular with the masses', but he had no love for cricket. Softball became a popular sport in Belize: the women's team were the nation's darlings when they beat the US at the Pan-American Games in 1979. A case of a nation of less than 100,000 people beating more than 100 million – surely one of the biggest sporting upsets of all time.

'The PUP leaders *killed* cricket in the city,' Lindo tells us over tea and patties at the law practice he runs in downtown Belize City. 'I never understood why, because the West Indian governments were much more anti-colonial than ours ever were, yet they backed cricket all the way.' In 1973, Lindo split off to form the centre-right United Democratic Party. He had precious little common ground with Evan X. Hyde, a Marxist Black Power advocate, but they agreed on the issue of Edwards Park. 'The true story of the park has never been told,' wrote Hyde. 'The PUP specialises in systematic obliteration of history they consider unfavourable or undesirable.'

We walk that ten minutes from Bertie Ellis's house to the Newtown Barracks – once the centre of civic life in Belize, but now a rather sterile ode to capitalism. The wooden Newtown Club was damaged by Hurricane Greta in 1978 and never repaired. When six years later the UDP – chaired by Lindo – won power for the first time, they sold off a great chunk of the Barracks green for a hotel and casino monstrosity. Next door is the Belize Telecom Ltd Park, where one of the few concessions to history is a music stage named after Lindbergh, and a model of the *Spirit of St Louis*. A couple of miles up the road is the incomplete Marion Jones Sports Complex, dedicated to the Belizean-American sprinter before her drugs ban.

The MCC Grounds just about survive, but there is no obvious trace of cricket. From the Barracks Road, the only clue to the ground's historic importance is the Ragamuffin Bleacher, peering out above the whitewashed walls. When we drop in, a half-asleep groundskeeper ticks us off for wandering about on his playing surface. Although cricket returned to this turf for a brief period in the mid-2000s, the dimensions of the field are squared off by new fencing just beyond the touchline to deter football fans from invading the pitch. In 2016, the hotel and casino owners began renting a portion of the stadium for overflow car parking. The deteriorating state of the grounds is a perennial frustration in Belize, and sports fans are not holding their breath about its future.

'I think cricket is too slow a game for these boys growing up now,' reflects Bertie Ellis. Clicking his fingers, he says: 'They want speed sports and these video games. I used to have to buy my own bat. Then you have to get the uniform: gloves, bails, pads – it's a costly sport.' Hyde believes all sport was hurt by the introduction of hard drugs from South America and satellite television from North America, right on top of each other at the start of the 1980s: 'We have lost a lot of our young boys and men to crime and violence. The seventies were golden; the eighties became eerie. And the nineties were plain crazy.' In Belize City, it became safer – but less healthy – to stay at home and watch sport on television.

*     *     *

There is still a valley in Belize where cricket means everything. Gerald Lewis, the burly and dreadlocked taxi driver who hails *us* near the bustling Swing Bridge in downtown Belize City, is surprised when we tell him we are keen to head out to the old logging villages. He admits he hasn't been out that way himself lately. Most of the American tourists around us are clambering on to water taxis heading out to Caye Caulker or the coral reefs, or minibuses bound for the spectacular inland Mayan ruins. Belize's cricket country is a world away from the tourist trail. Lewis also knows how much it rains out there 'in the rural' in November, and hurriedly fixes a new windscreen wiper to help his rickety burgundy Honda make it through the dirt tracks of the Belize River Valley.

Lewis and other locals call the Belize River 'the Old River', as so much of the country's history is bound up with it. The river winds 180 miles north-west from Belize City into the dense jungle interior, all the way to Guatemala. It was considered so impenetrable in the sixteenth century that the Spanish – though laying claim to all of Central America – never wasted time trying to colonise it. By the time British pirates washed up from Jamaica in the 1630s, the indigenous Mayans were no longer a threat – weakened by smallpox, yellow fever and other diseases. Buccaneers began sailing up the river to cut logwood, a rich and popular source of dye in textiles back home. At first they came in ones and twos, as logwood is a small tree, requiring little work to cut and load. But British incursions grew by the 1720s to the point that they began importing African slaves, via Jamaica and Bermuda, to do the heavy lifting.

There were intermittent skirmishes between Britain and Spain over Belize in the eighteenth century, culminating in the decisive Battle of St George's Caye on 10 September 1798. The Belizean Creole legend rests on the stand that a combined force of white and black Baymen took against an impending Spanish invasion from Yucatán. When the choice was put to the settlement, it is said that a majority of 14 men – 12 of them black – paddled their dories from these villages to vote in Belize Town. 'By voting to stay and defend,' reads a monument in the village of Flowers Bank, 'they bequeathed Belize to our children, ensuring it was not forever lost to Spain, Mexico or Guatemala.' The battle is represented today on the Belize flag by the presence of a white and a black Bayman, though Evan X. Hyde for one cast doubt on the supposed equality at this time of slavery. Guatemalans have never let their claim slip: maps hanging in classrooms, hotels and public offices still portray 'Belice' as their twenty-third province.

Modest estates sprang up on the riverbanks, which grew into villages. Each one seems to play its own role in the story: Bermudian Landing is named after the grass imported from Bermuda to feed the oxen that dragged the logs to the river; Burrell Boom for the chain and anchor that stopped the logs floating downstream. In 1811, Captain George Henderson of the West India Regiment wrote that slaves were participating in dory-racing and other water sports along the river. It was not long before their emancipated black and mixed-race progeny began playing cricket in the forest clearings. White colonists would ride up on horse or mule from Belize Town, setting up camp for days at a time, and making cricket part of their festivities. As racial barriers slowly relaxed, the Belizean Creole slowly infused cricket with their own flavour.

Gliksten Bennett, the Grand Old Man of cricket in the valley, says it was known colloquially as 'ball game' or 'bat and wicket', and for the first half of the twentieth century were often scratch matches. In 1950, the demand for an organised inter-village competition led Marcelo Casasola of St Paul's Bank and Percival Flowers of Crooked Tree to formalise the Belize Rural District Cricket League. By 1960 the *Belize Billboard* was reflecting on the parlous state of cricket in the capital, and how the sport 'has been kept alive for the most part in recent years by the out-district competition' – held every season until the Great Flood of 1979, which devastated crops and livestock in the valley and submerged sports fields. It took another five years for the land to recover.

Rain is back with a vengeance today, and as Gerald Lewis struggles to peer through his windscreen he agrees that a pitstop at Charlie Belgrove's winery in the village of Double Head Cabbage would be a good idea. Belgrove pushes open the door of his unmarked concrete outhouse with his walking stick to reveal a dimly lit menagerie of maroon and gold. Tables and tables of bottles, antique and modern, are stacked in no discernible order. A heap of bark, being dried away from the rain, lies on a canvas sheet in the middle of the floor. A mestizo woman and her children patrol the room out back, which holds a Western-style bar stocked with obscure tipples.

Belgrove, in his mid-seventies, came to Belize on a scouting expedition from Trinidad at the age of 19, and never left. He is not quite mad enough to try to grow grapevines in the tropics. 'It took me thirty years here, but it came to me in a dream,' he says. 'I decided I'd do just like I dreamed, and make twenty different types of wine, using all the beautiful fruits and herbs we have here in Belize. I don't drink any of them myself, though. That's bad luck.' In Double Head Cabbage – named after the distinctive twin-headed cabbage palm trees which grow here – the cashew is the bedrock of their local economy, and the apple fruit attached to the nut is fermented into a pleasant wine, not dissimilar to port. Our attempt to save up a bottle of this ruby red for consumption somewhere in Guatemala ends up shattered at the bottom of our rucksack on a bumpy bus ride.

As Lewis's taxi chugs up a slight incline, we strain our necks to catch sight of the ground at Bermudian Landing, and the shadowy figure of a groundsman huddled in the doorway of the changing hut, unable to get on to his field.

It was in Bermudian Landing in 1984 where Gliksten Bennett delivered Belize's first season-opening 'marathon' for five years, kickstarting cricket again after the floods. Many local children hone their skills playing 'bush cricket' long before they make it to school. By the age of four, Conway Young was carving bats out of the branches of coconut trees; he and his friends would make their own balls by shaking down the fruit of the coyol palm – or *supa*, as it is known in Belizean Creole. 'We'd take a bicycle inner tube and cut it into rings, then wrap it up around the nut of the *supa* until it was big enough to be the size of a cricket ball,' he tells us. 'If you batted for a long time, the ball would change direction dramatically, and it ended up looking like spin. Ever since then, spin has been my favourite kind of bowling to face, even though there are probably only four or five bowlers who can really spin the ball in Belize.' Dean Lindo puts this down to the machismo of rural Belizean men: 'Spinning is almost seen as effeminate. Our bowlers want to bowl fast and knock down the batsman's wicket all the time. They tend to forget they have ten other people out there to help them.'

Bermudian Landing is home of the Community Baboon Sanctuary, co-founded in 1983 by Conway Young's father, Fallet. Robert Horwich from the University of Wisconsin had arrived in the area to study the Guatemalan black howler monkey. The monkey, known for its distinctive screech, was being hunted to endangerment through the wider region. Horwich approached the local villagers, who expressed an overwhelming desire to protect their 'baboon'. The villages agreed to form one of the world's first voluntary preservation areas: they would encourage locals to stop hunting the monkey, leave alone the hog plums and sapodillas they fed on, and halt their slash-and-burn farming. Fallet died in 2009, and – unimpressed at the job the men were doing – a group of women, headed by his widow, Jessie, took on the running of the sanctuary, incorporating alternative livelihood projects into protection of the rainforest.

'I started doing my first tours aged seven,' says Conway, 'and I never stopped.' For several years he juggled his role as sanctuary administrator with the role of development officer for the Belize National Cricket Association (BNCA) – all based from the same hut in the baboon sanctuary. If he swivels his chair to a certain angle, Young can see the cricket ground – one of four village grounds in Belize falling within the special conservation zone for the black howler.

The jarring screech of a black howler, just as a batsman settles down to take guard, is one of the many quirks with which to contend in Belizean cricket. The individual identity of each village runs so deep that teams are identified with their own styles of play – usually a legacy of a particular coach, family member or local conditions.

Brilliant of Crooked Tree lifted a string of titles in the early 2000s. They are known for their technical rectitude and acceptance of the umpire's decision, at least relative to other Belizean teams. Old sages still talk about the time when two Crooked Tree batsmen batted through an entire innings for just 2 runs. Excellence of Double Head Cabbage prefer to swing hard and to leg. They once dismissed Bright Star of Sand Hill for 13 in the first innings of a game . . . and lost by 9 runs, possibly due to too much cashew wine. A team from Gardenia insisted on calling themselves Taliban in the years immediately after 2001, until they were forced to rename themselves on grounds of taste.

Close to entire teams can be made up of an extended family. This was of great amusement to the commentator on British Honduras Broadcasting Service radio during a cup final between Crooked Tree and the Police in the 1960s. Crooked Tree had brought along seven players called Tillett, plus an umpire and scorer by the same name. To add to the confusion, three of the Police side were also called Tillett. 'He's out, caught behind,' Brown gleefully informed his audience. 'So it's Tillett, caught Tillett, bowled Tillett, given out by umpire Tillett, and recorded in the scorebook by scorer Tillett. And the next batsman to the crease is Tillett.'

Ingrained habits that might have been ironed out by a more organised coaching structure persist in Belize. Instead of backing up when the bowler finishes his delivery stride, non-strikers often crouch with their bat or foot rooted behind the crease until a call for a run is made. Likewise, fielders stay rooted to the spot as the bowler runs in. Yet the catching and ground fielding can be spectacular on outfields that alternate between bumpy and swampy, depending on the season. Rain, when it comes, falls hard and without much warning, rendering covers futile. A common remedy is to douse the 22 yards of the soaked pitch with gasoline, and set it alight. Wet wicket or hard, if a batsman inadvertently makes contact with his own stumps, he would be marked down in the scorebook as 'murder wicket', rather than hit wicket.

As for protection from these uncovered pitches, many of the older players shun batting gloves – or 'tips', as they are known in Belize – and wear a pad on the front leg only. Helmets are a relatively new addition. James Brodie's, a wholesalers that stocked cricket equipment since the 1870s, stopped doing so when the import duties grew crippling. Now it is a case of begging and borrowing from Belizeans travelling back from the US. Cal-Bel CC are the club of the Belizean-American community in Southern California, and have been known to run on to the pitch waving Belizean flags after winning crunch matches in Woodley Park, Los Angeles.

Aggression is the norm. When a European wine merchant, Richard Price, arrived from England in the early 2000s, his cautious approach to batting met with voluble derision, especially from females in the crowd, who often make up a majority of spectators, and feel less inhibited about shouting advice – or abuse – at players or umpires. They give up their Saturday afternoons to watch the men strike towering sixes and send stumps flying out of the ground, so did not take kindly to Price, in the spirit of a classic English opening bat, diligently seeing off the new ball. One season Price finished second in the league batting averages, much to the dismay of team-mates, opposition and the crowd.

Modern Belize is a society bombarded with American influences, yet one of the few countries in the world without a single McDonald's, Burger King or KFC. To hunt and eat turtle is frowned upon these days, but some clubs still barbecue an iguana steak and serve it with rice and beans for tea. It is said to go down especially well with Belikin, the national beer, which enjoys a virtual monopoly after its late owner, Sir Barry Bowen of the Belize Estates Company, frustrated local competitors by buying up all of the country's glass bottles. Almost every aspect of life in Belize was affected by Bowen's business activities in some way, so it is no surprise that, after he died in a plane crash in 2009, his name was added as a prefix to the cricket league. Much the same applies to Lord Ashcroft, the Conservative peer, pollster and businessman raised in the colony, who owns a seafront mansion in Belize City. He loves cricket and has invested in myriad enterprises in Belize during his life. But when contacted about cricket in Belize his office replied that it was 'not something of interest at the moment'.

The disputes committee is one survivor from colonial times. Although teams will go to some length to avoid losing games to rain, it is not unusual for matches to be halted in protest at one decision or another, especially in the knockout phase. In 2014, Excellence abandoned their semi-final against Brilliant because they disagreed with the dismissal of their number nine batsman. The case was referred to the disputes committee, who ruled the game should continue from where it left off. The next

Saturday, just four Excellence players turned up in an SUV to complete the run chase (and lost).

Sometimes anger spills over. In a match on the Governor-General's ground in Belmopan – the purpose-built inland city made the capital due to its protection from hurricanes – one player responded to being given out by running back on to the field waving a gun. He was an off-duty policeman. Lindo served for several years on the disputes committee, and even all his years as an attorney-at-law were not adequate preparation. 'I quite liked it,' he said, smiling mischievously. 'I went all the way out for the umpires, let me tell you.'

Each week, the league archivist, Peter Young, contributes a heartfelt and informative round-up of the league action to *Amandala*. More often than not Young signs off with an impassioned plea to players and supporters to respect their opponents and the umpires. He threw in the towel after the 2018 Championship was blighted by abuse towards an umpire in a crucial match between Easy Does It of Lemonal and Summer Fever of Bermudian Landing, but could not resist making a quiet return to the column the following season.

In the mid-2000s, the Rural District competition was named after Harrison Parks, who had collapsed and died on the cricket field. The running of the league passed back from the BNCA – the ICC-recognised national body, led by the amiable postmaster-general Elston Wade – to the Belize District Cricket Association (BDCA) in 2007. The following season, both organisations began staging matches under the Harrison Parks banner. Rival presidents – Wade of the BNCA and Elihue Bonner of the BDCA – traded blows in the press, each claiming to be the rightful administrators of the league, and accusing the other of misusing or misappropriating ICC funds. Matters were only reconciled after Parks's widow, Vincent, stepped in to plea for the two factions to stop fighting over the competition bearing her late husband's name.

Much of this flew over the head of Conway Young, who was so besotted with cricket that he was bunking off school to score hundreds in club cricket. When, aged 16, he struck a century against Suriname on Belize's international tournament debut in 2004, Young became a poster boy of the ICC Development Programme. He was invited to train with West Indies age groups, did his coaching badges in Argentina, and persuaded Sir Hilary Beckles, the esteemed Barbadian vice-chancellor of the University of the West Indies, to guest for his team in Bermudian Landing on a visit to Belize.

Young's attempts to play club cricket in England and Australia fell foul of visa criteria. In early 2016, he applied to attend trials for the ICC Americas Combine competing in the West Indies one-day domestic competition, but was turned down due to a lack of evidence of his performances. Young once made 200 not out for his village side, but newspaper cuttings from *Amandala* and the *Belize Times* were not sufficient proof. Belizean cricket hasn't always been the best at collating its records, with many of the scorebooks lost in hurricanes.

Now in his thirties, Young channels his energy into coaching Summer Fever and the Belize national side. As a result of tightened ICC regulations – and Belize's own failure to put its players, coaches, umpires and scorers through training courses – the BNCA's annual funding from the ICC fell by two-thirds across six years. Young was for some time the only ICC-qualified coach in the entire country, somehow required to be in every village on every school sports day.

In Gliksten Bennett's Lemonal – a village of just 150 people – cricket is the only team sport for men. Some of Lemonal's best young players had to play for other villages if they could not break into the established team, Surprise. Eventually, Lawrence Banner, Denvo Banner and Michael Muslar overcame local opposition to form Easy Does It. 'Insulting remarks were thrown at them,' wrote Peter Young. 'Some fans were rough on the team, who were thought of as being friends or family. But wherever they traveled, you would see their crowd following . . . not least [coach] Muslar, who everyone could hear telling his team how to bat, and who to bowl.'

In August 2014, Easy Does It beat Brilliant in the two-day Harrison Parks final to lift their maiden league title. Shortly after leaving the victory party in Lemonal the following Saturday night, one of their players, 27-year-old Denvo Banner, was shot multiple times and dumped in a shallow grave behind a primary school. Many believe it to be revenge for the killing of a lab technician in Belize City seven years earlier; Banner had been charged with the murder, but walked free when the case broke down due to lack of evidence.

Nine months later Mykelt Anthony, opening bowler for Easy Does It and the national team, narrowly escaped with his life after being shot in broad daylight in Belize City, as he waited to collect his bicycle. He was shot three times; one of the bullets grazed his spinal cord, another lodged in his chest. Doctors were able to extract one of the bullets, but at the age of 32 he was left paralysed from the waist down, with no feeling in his legs. Anthony appeared in a wheelchair to celebrate with his team-mates when Easy Does It retained their league title. He will never play again but, desperate to contribute to cricket, he joined the BNCA committee.

Belize, starting afresh after five years in the international wilderness, selected a young team under the management of Conway Young for their return to regional competition in 2018 and their first official T20 internationals the following year. Many of the team were products of the Easy Does It and Summer Fever youth projects, and too shy to tell of the bloodshed they had experienced.

Cricket is still referred to without irony in Belize as 'the gentlemen's game' – a way for young men to come together for the honour of representing their village or their country. Aaron Muslar began playing bush cricket aged two, and 20 years later is scoring centuries and taking wickets. In Mexico City in early 2019, Belize's young team were crowned champions of Central America after shock victories over Panama and MCC, with Muslar taking three for 15 in the final.

They proudly lifted the silver-plated Central American Championship trophy in front of the Reforma Athletic Club pavilion. The team bus was jumping as it approached the border crossing at Chetumal, with the promise of a parade to the centre of Belize City from cricket's spiritual home in Bermudian Landing. Until, that is, Mexican border guards confiscated the most-prized trophy in the history of Belizean cricket.

# 3

# Guatemala, El Salvador, Honduras and Nicaragua

## *Cricket, coffee and Contras*

IN JUNE 1979, a thousand Sandinistas in brown fatigues reached the southern tip of the Vaughan family farm in the village of San Francisco, Nicaragua. One mile to the north were opposition forces loyal to Nicaragua's dictator, Anastasio Somoza, the tyrant backed up to then by the United States. The Sandinistas were launching their offensive towards Managua, and the Vaughans were caught in the middle.

This Anglo-Jewish family had cultivated coffee and poultry in the hills south of Managua since 1871, when two brothers on pack mules hacked their way through the jungle from British Honduras with 1000 guineas each to their name, a gift from their father, who had made his fortune in mahogany. They cut out a swathe of the undergrowth, built houses among the snakes and monkeys, and went for tea dressed in top hat and tails.

By 1910, their San Francisco *finca* was producing more coffee per acre than any competitor in the region. They even had a coffee-pruning technique named after them, the *poda Vaughan*, more efficient and elaborate than any methods used in Central America. The farm got by comfortably enough under the notoriously brutal Somoza regimes, which virtually owned the country. But the coming of the Sandinistas, with their proclamations of land redistribution to the masses and their avowed anti-Zionism, was a potential danger to entrepreneurs such as them.

Arturo Vaughan Jr leans back on his chair in his office in Managua, where he is now the commercial director of an agricultural management firm, and relives what was at stake. 'My father received a call from the British ambassador in Costa Rica. He said: "It's time to pull up stumps, my friend."' The Vaughans were given strict instructions to reach the US Embassy in Managua by 5 a.m. on 19 June, with no more than one bag of hand luggage each. They made the 45-minute car journey without running into any roadblocks, and were raced by convoy to an airbase at Montélimar, on the Pacific coast, then still just about under Somoza's control. The US Air Force arranged for two Hercules C-130s to evacuate the US and British communities to safety. The Vaughan family, young and old, boarded the second plane, sprinting across the airfield with 100 other people, as the sound of gunfire rattled in their ears.

The US attitude to the Nicaraguan regime had been defined by Franklin D. Roosevelt's assessment of Somoza's father: 'He may be a son of a bitch, but he's *our* son of a bitch.' That, as Arturo Vaughan reflects, had been pushed too far. 'I think we were stunned. There was a feeling that the Americans wouldn't allow a second Cuba to emerge on its doorstep. Yet the Carter administration's foreign policy switched to an emphasis on human rights, and it reached the point that the Americans were blocking Israeli ships full of weapons bound for Nicaragua. So we had to go.' Britain after the Winter of Discontent was not deemed the most attractive proposition, so the Vaughans holed up in a Miami hotel room for a few weeks, until taking up an offer on a farm in Missouri.

Through deft politics and good fortune, the San Francisco *finca* emerged from Nicaragua's revolution, though not quite unscathed. The local Sandinista commander rushed to occupy it on account of its high productivity and strategic position close to the Pan-American Highway. Arturo Vaughan told us how his father and grandfather would ride up on Sunday afternoons to the top of the hill to watch the American gangs build this section of the great road that runs the length of North and South America (with a 66-mile break in the road between Panama and Colombia for the Darién Gap). With the Sandinistas inside, Somoza instructed his forces to bomb the beautiful old wooden family farmhouse. 'But on that very day – July 17, 1979 – Somoza ran out of bullets and fled the country,' says Arturo, still incredulous at their fortune. 'Fancy that? Maybe we're blessed.'

The worst of the damage left by trigger-happy young Sandinistas were a few bullet holes in their antique chairs, which the first generation of the family had shipped over from England, and slogans ('VIVA SANDINO', in homage to the revolutionary hero Augusto C. Sandino, who had led resistance to US occupation in the 1930s) daubed on the walls. The farm was not collectivised as such, but the Vaughans would be instructed to run it by proxy, under Sandinista observation. The three brothers – Arturo, Tomás and Ricardo – would come down from Missouri on rotation, entering on their Nicaraguan passports rather than their British papers, to check up on the farm.

We retread the Vaughans' regular journey up from sweltering sea-level Managua in a crowded *colectivo*, which is a typically Nicaraguan hum of activity. Boys run through the bus selling cola in plastic bags tied to the roof; utterly fearless women, one visibly pregnant, file through time after time hollering '*platanitos, platanitos, platanitos . . . chicharrón, chicharrón, chicharrón . . .*' As the bus climbs up the hills and we bump past coffee fields, cool air mercifully buffets through the windows. We get off in San Francisco and walk up the path to the ancestral farmhouse, welcomed in by Arturo's younger brother Tomás, and settle down for *jugo de naranja* in the same chairs peppered by the Sandinistas.

Tomás recalls how Fidel Castro once sent his officials to inspect the farm's chick incubators. The Soviet-manufactured lightbulbs the Vaughans were instructed to use were so unsafe that they unwittingly generated enough warmth for the animals to survive and grow. Trade with the US was prohibited, so the Vaughans could no longer update their crumbling equipment: they had no choice but to let the chicks live on the floor, meaning the farm became inadvertently free range. A family operation that had once produced half of a country's eggs, and distributed 95 per cent of them, was slowly run into the ground.

Worse still, the Sandinistas chopped down the centuries-old forest canopy in the entire department, on the pretence of ridding the area of leaf rust. The wood was reportedly sold to Cuba in exchange for AK-47s, and the coffee has never recovered from the loss of shade. The Sandinistas handed the Vaughans a large bill for their trouble, but the astute Arturo, foreseeing the hyperinflation to come in socialist Nicaragua, urged the family to wait before paying it off. Sure enough, they did so quite easily.

*     *     *

As for the real stumps, the Vaughans had to pull them up too. Although the Vaughans knew nothing of it, cricket had been popular on the rain-drenched Mosquito Coast, around the Caribbean port of Bluefields and the offshore Corn Islands, since the days of the Miskito Kingdom. The Miskito, a mixed-race people descended from a combination of indigenous hunters, African-Caribbean labourers and British merchants, had first formed an alliance with British traders from the Providence Island Company in 1638, and their 'kingdom' – a loosely governed 225-mile stretch of Nicaragua and southern Honduras – became an on-off Crown protectorate. So Anglicised were the Miskito that they would sail up the coast to crown their kings – christened Oldman or George – at St John's Anglican Cathedral in Belize Town. Even in the late nineteenth century, the peoples of the Mosquito Coast still spoke English, danced Highland reels and pinned Union Jacks on their walls. Naturally they played cricket too, among themselves and against British and American timber and banana merchants working out of Bluefields.

For a port established by pirates, it was a prudish environment: the by-laws of the three cricket clubs, Caledonia, Peace and Invincible, prohibited 'indecent language and quarrelling or contention of any kind'. Caledonia, the longest-running club, had 17 members, with practice every Friday, and shared their pavilion with the Bluefields Amateur Dramatic Society. Attempts to spread the game to the locals had patchy results. One British merchant was particularly impatient, as he reported to a colleague back in England:

I have instituted your favourite old game, cricket, among the natives. But they are such a lazy race that half an hour of it at a spin completely does them up. I, however, wrote home to our directors, and they immediately kindly sent the officers out a complete outfit. We call ourselves the Anglo-Nicarauguan [*sic*] team, and I have no doubt you would manage to put us out in half an hour, provided you escaped from your innings alive, as the native bowling is very uncertain.

Not every merchant in Bluefields fell for cricket. Albert Adlesberg was a German-American who traded Nicaraguan lumber in New Orleans in the late nineteenth century, and was active in the Bluefields am-dram. He grew tired of watching what he considered an excessively slow English pastime. Worse still, he claimed the local Nicaraguans were equally bored of it. In 1888, Adlesberg came down from New Orleans with baseball bats, balls and mitts, and introduced what he considered the 'more dynamic' American sport. When in 1892 the Gentlemen of Caledonia issued their traditional Boxing Day challenge match to Peace, there was no response: the opposition were all playing baseball.

The following year, the Nicaraguan Liberal Party, determined once and for all to rid the Atlantic coast of British influence, invaded Bluefields, stuffed a Union Jack into a cannon, and blew it into a thousand pieces. The British beat an embarrassing retreat to Jamaica, and Adlesberg had the space to form two fresh baseball clubs, White Rose and Southern. US influences grew, and baseball – introduced at the same time to Managua and Granada by Nicaraguan students returning from the States – quickly became the national sport.

Yet isolated pockets of cricket remained dotted along the Mosquito Coast. The entry of the United Fruit Company – the vast New Orleans corporation that walked virtually hand in hand with US foreign policy – into already shabbily run Spanish-speaking countries led the American writer-in-exile O. Henry to coin the term 'banana republic'. Fruit pickers from the British West Indies played cricket on fields next to their huts along the Northern Railroad from Guatemala City to Puerto Barrios, the country's purpose-built banana port. F. S. Ashley-Cooper, the frail but fastidious editor of *Cricket* magazine, was none too impressed at one scorecard he combed from a plantation newspaper in 1909. 'Cricket cannot be in a very flourishing condition in Guatemala,' he tutted from leafy Surrey, 'if one may judge from the manner in which the scores are reported.' Cayuga West's total did not add up; three stumpings in Cayuga East's innings (two by T. O'Connor; one by F. Douglas) were not attributed to the bowler; and there were no bowling figures listed at all.

That same year, a team from the English-speaking enclave of Livingston, Guatemala, had planned to tour British Honduras, but the trip fell through when their company changed hands and the funding for the boat was withdrawn. Invincible CC, from the port of La Ceiba in the Republic of Honduras, did make it to British Honduras in the 1920s, but were beaten by local side Cambridge CC and promptly sailed straight home. The result was gleefully pinned up in shops across Belize Town minutes after the finish. The Limón Pathfinders of Costa Rica were set to tour to Bluefields and the Corn Islands in 1939 before news of war in Poland made it impractical.

Bluefields has historically always been cut off from the rump of Nicaragua. Until the completion of a highway in May 2019, a rickety trip by panga boat through the jungle was the only way of reaching Bluefields from the middle of the country. Nicaragua's long-serving ex-Sandinista president, Daniel Ortega, has promised to stimulate the east coast by realising the construction of the long-promised canal from the Atlantic coast through to Lake Nicaragua. (It was this journey that a young Horatio Nelson attempted in 1780 in one of many inglorious British expeditions to capture the fabled Spanish gold from the beautiful lakeside city of Granada.) But Ortega's project hit the buffers when Hong Kong investors saw their worth plummet in a Chinese stock market wobble. And so Bluefields has become a sad, impoverished outpost of the drug trade that flows north through Central America, many of its people indirectly owing their livelihoods to the kingpins. Others comb the shore in the hope of finding discarded bundles of cocaine and suitcases of dollars.

\* \* \*

Arturo Vaughan Sr, bored of farm life, lied about his age and volunteered for the RAF during the Second World War, flying Lancaster bombers in the Far East. On his return he was looking to indulge more sedate pleasures. Over a game of golf with Tony Skinner, a former Barbados batsman now high up in British American Tobacco (BAT), they formed a cricket club to challenge other teams in Central America. There was always *some* interest in the country: in 1948, Gerald Pedder, who was working in Nicaragua, earned headlines when he travelled 5000 miles home for a crucial club match in Ditchling, Sussex – only to be bowled for a duck.

Skinner sorted out a large sports field at the back of BAT's office near the airport, running down towards Lake Managua.

Ian Ross, who played for the club in the late 1970s, remembers a dog once being pressed into action, so short were they on numbers. Most games took place in oppressive heat, although the wickets did not always reflect the prevailing conditions. 'The pitches reached a greenness unseen in the rest of Central America, thanks to the use of tobacco dust as a fertiliser,' Ross wrote in none other than the *Helsinki Cricketer*, a magazine published in Finland drawing on unlikely tales from around the world. 'Before each match a roadmender would be "encouraged" to divert his road roller over the pitch to generate sufficient bounce out of the normally soggy Bermudian grass.' There is no suggestion that Bianca Jagger (née Pérez-Mora Macías) ever dropped by to watch her home-town team, though she was dragged along to Tests at Lord's and The Oval during her seven-year marriage to Mick, the Rolling Stones frontman.

Each Vaughan boy made the annual journey – initially by boat, later by plane – to Eagle House prep school, Berkshire, followed by Wellington College, which more recently produced the three Curran brothers. Even today, Eagle House present the Smith–Vaughan Trophy for prowess at cricket – a legacy of a departing headmaster whose first head boy had been Arturo Vaughan Sr, and his last Ricardo 'Dickie' Vaughan. One opponent recalled Arturo as a wicketkeeper keen to 'indulge in Australian-type sledging'. Arturo Jr and Tomás did not share their father's love for cricket, and were content to keep score. But Dickie, the youngest, was a superb cricketer who captained the Wellington First XI and took the new ball for the English Public Schools XI. He was selected to tour Hong Kong with England age groups, but was unable to go due to summer commitments on the farm in Nicaragua.

When Dickie returned permanently to Nicaragua in his early twenties, 6 feet 4 inches and fearsomely quick, he proved far too good for the rest of Central America. In the first game played by the Costa Rican Cavaliers of San José in 1975, two balls, one bat and five stumps were all broken – only partly a result of having been kept unused in storage for so long. Dickie was responsible for dismissing the Cavaliers for 11 and 7 in consecutive matches. The Cavaliers secretary, Bill Caines, gently informed Arturo Sr that the fixture would survive only if he could persuade his son to slow down.

Dickie was the reason Managua were crowned champions of the Central American Cricket League – contested between the clubs in Guatemala, El Salvador, Nicaragua and Costa Rica – seven times in a row up to 1976–7. Managua had to pull out in January 1979, when cross-border travel to Nicaragua simply became too risky, in light of the Sandinistas' tendency to take hostages, especially Anglos with business interests. It was the last cricket in Nicaragua for a quarter of a century, and the BAT ground was overrun by squatters.

*     *     *

The most picturesque cricket ground in Central America could be found on the slopes of a volcano. Roberto Cristales, the mop-haired head of projects at El Salvador's Walter A. Soundy Foundation, drives us up there one morning from their offices in Santa Tecla, the pretty satellite town next to brooding San Salvador. As we pull through the big iron gates of the San Antonio El Quequeisque coffee *finca*, we catch a glimpse of the *quequeisque* itself – a plant known as the elephant's ear in English, for the shape of its leaves. There are tropical flowers all around, and the air is sweet with the smell of roasted coffee beans.

We climb on dirt tracks up the foothills of the volcano, to 3000 feet above sea level, bumping our way past grinning coffee pickers on their way down for lunch, hanging out of an old army truck. After ten minutes there is a clearing above the jungle, and the unmistakeably flat profile of a sports ground. Cristales, now in his fifties, used to kick a football about here in his youth, and the eight-a-side goals dug into the ground for the *campesinos* are still intact. But for many years cricket held pride of place at El Quequeisque. It was among the most spectacular vistas in world cricket: batsmen would jog out from the pavilion in front of the labourers' quarters into the mountain air, glancing through the canopy to the city and Pacific Ocean in the distance. Waiting batsmen would help themselves to the abundant cacao fruit growing around the boundary.

Walter Soundy's parents had moved out from England in the late nineteenth century to open the El Quequeisque plantation. They made their fortune when the worldwide price of coffee went through the roof during Prohibition in the US, and they became one of the 14 coffee families holding El Salvador's shaky economy in their hands. Yet Soundy was not one to hoard his money. During the dark days of the Battle of Britain, he contributed a Spitfire to the RAF – with 'El Quequeisque' stencilled on the fuselage – and even chose to leave the relative calm of Central America to join up for the chaos in Europe, being taken a prisoner of war.

Soundy was a great patron of sport: members of El Quequeisque's football team, made up of the plantation *campesinos*, became household names in El Salvador for winning the national league for five consecutive seasons. Photographs of the football team in their 1930s and 1940s heyday hang in a modest museum next to the old cricket pavilion, alongside Soundy's old furniture and personal trinkets.

A painting survives of cricket played at El Quequeisque in 1917 – the year the volcano last blew its top. Soundy formed and financed the Fincona Cricket Club, whose early opposition came from British Honduras or Royal Navy ships passing through Puerto de la Libertad on the Salvadorian coast. When Guatemala CC made their first overland trip to El Salvador in March 1953 it was tracked by regular updates from the British Embassy in San Salvador, and resulted in a suitably tense finale. Fincona were dismissed in their second innings for just 39, leaving Guatemala 73 to win. The visitors were a dozen runs short with four wickets in hand, but suffered late heartbreak as a hat-trick allowed Fincona to claim a one-run showstopper.

Charles Godden, serving with the Foreign Office in British Honduras in the 1960s, journeyed to El Quequeisque on Remembrance Weekend 1963 with the Belize Club. This was an annual home-and-away two-day fixture dating back to 1948, with the Soundy Cup at stake, marked by a shared club tie that imagined a volcano spewing out a cricket ball. Godden's team flew from Belize City via San Pedro Sula in the Republic of Honduras, in an old Dakota that had seen wartime service. They arrived to find a 'manicured outfield, smart pavilion, big scoreboard, sightscreens and a perfect wicket'. Fincona called on a couple of former Minor Counties cricketers and Dutch employees of Shell, who thrashed the Belize Club, their techniques admittedly loosened by cocktail parties on consecutive nights at the British Embassy, by an innings. On the return visit Fincona's players gleefully snapped up the British clothes and cigarettes they could not come by in San Salvador. Cricket even played on through El Salvador's Soccer War with Honduras over a fortnight in 1969.

The steep slope down the volcano at El Quequeisque and the short straight boundary behind both ends of the wicket meant top edges frequently flew for six, and anything missed by the slips or the infield was a certain four; balls lost in the coffee trees or down the slopes were a constant problem. Dickie Vaughan can be seen in one photograph bounding in with a perfect Lillee-esque side-on action, against the backdrop of a jacaranda tree and the coffee pickers' houses. Jerome Mostyn, a tobacco executive working in El Salvador, recalls lounging in the shade of the jacaranda before plucking up the courage to walk out to face Dickie's vicious pace. Once a year in the 1970s, Managua, Fincona, the Cavaliers and Guatemala would select their best players for a combined Central America XI to take on the might of Mexico City CC. Carlos Avila, who picked up cricket while at Oxford, was one of the locals who proudly took his place in what was effectively the first El Salvador national cricket team.

Soundy died in 1975, a few months after his wife, Consuela. They had no children, and he bequeathed the entire plantation to the workers and an educational trust for San Salvador's poor. In doing so, his plantation skirted around the bloodshed and upheaval of civil war. As in Nicaragua, there was a large-scale British exodus in 1979, which gathered pace after Archbishop Óscar Romero was assassinated by right-wing militia in March 1980 as he held mass.

The Vaughans returned permanently to Nicaragua only in the 1990s, after the Sandinistas' surprise defeat at the ballot box by Violeta Chamorro, the first female elected head of state in all the Americas. Dickie, the first to come back, built a new, modern house, overlooking the ancestral farm. The cricket equipment had been safely stowed away in a cabin, so the fervent young Sandinistas probably never swung the willow while they took pot shots at the family furniture.

In 2002, Arturo Sr dusted off his old bat and entered the ground at Managua for one last time before BAT plastered warehouses all over it. Before he died, he donated all the gear to a new posse of Nicaraguan cricketers, who took on Costa Rica at a polo ground in the picture-postcard, cobblestoned colonial city of Granada. While in Granada we watch as tourists roll past the ground on horse and cart, the wagons splashed in the garish colours of whichever mobile phone company holds the sponsorship – right now, it's the scarlet red of Claro and Movistar purple and green. But Dickie Vaughan, the greatest cricketer in Nicaragua's history, did not live to see cricket's return. In 1999, distraught by marital problems, he had taken his own life.

*    *    *

San Salvador's reputation as one of the most dangerous cities on earth seems a little overblown. But there are frequent reminders, such as the armed guards whose Aviator shades pan on to us as we enter the British school, the Academica Británica Cuscatleca in Santa Tecla, a few miles down the volcano from the old ground.

In December 2005, a gimlet-eyed, tousle-haired Zimbabwean geography teacher at the school, Andrew Murgatroyd, took whoever would follow him out on to the football field facing the Pan-American Highway, and pitched some stumps into some hastily shaven grass. At the time, none of Murgatroyd's motley crew knew they were rekindling El Salvador's cricketing heritage. But Philip Mostyn, son of Jerome, was working for Dell in San Salvador. He got wind of the experiment, and together, Murgatroyd and Mostyn did what the pre-civil war cricketers had not managed to do: inject El Salvador's cricket with a bunch of Salvadorians.

By season three of the experiment, Murgatroyd was heading up the El Salvador Cricket Federation, and had constructed a makeshift net at the school. It is still there, pinned down by old Coca-Cola cooler boxes. In this tatty single net Murgatroyd produced the first generation of Salvadorian schoolboy cricketers. He enlisted the three Arbizu brothers, who knew the game from their childhood in Australia (a possible hotbed of cricketing knowledge for El Salvador, for as many as 10,000 Salvadorians emigrated to Australia in the 1980s); Lucas di Mauro, who bowls nagging medium pace honed from spells at university in Leeds and Edinburgh; Guillermo Estrada, all bulging pistons and wild left-arm pace; and Miguel Villalta, a marathon runner who never runs out of puff between the wickets. In 2013 Villalta became the first Salvadorian to score a century – and that after finishing a half-marathon in the morning. El Salvador play in the cool of the evening, thanks to lights beaming from the school building, and the luminescence of the *Panamericana*.

Murgatroyd achieved so much in 15 years but, through no fault of his own, El Salvador cricket missed the boat. By the time he had got his act together, the ICC had retrenched from their open-arms globalisation policy of the 1990s and early 2000s, and membership now required multiple grounds and multiple clubs. 'To be honest, we've given up with the ICC,' he admits. 'We'll keep doing what we do, and bringing on

Salvadorian cricketers, but it's impossible to think we can suddenly access more grounds and have eight teams in such a small country.' The federation is entirely self-funded, and beholden to the connection with the school. Were that link in the chain to break, like so many others in Latin America, there is no guarantee cricket would survive. But Murgatroyd has given this unwieldy sport the best chance it will ever have.

# 4

# Costa Rica and Panama

## *Birth of the Black Bradman*

E VERY SUNDAY AFTERNOON, an elderly black man with
spindly legs would climb out of his armchair in Paraíso, a
once-segregated dredging village on the east bank of the Panama
Canal, and wander down the steps to watch his local cricket
team. He was known to them only as Jackman, and he wasn't
the politest of spectators. 'Man, bowl the ball straight!' he
would holler. 'Throw me the ball, I'll knock him over!' His
frankness got under the skin of some of the more sensitive souls
on the team. But, until his legs gave way, it was he who watered
and rolled the wicket in the week before a game.

The more perceptive of Paraíso's cricketers understood
Jackman was the umbilical cord that linked their sport to
another era. The roller he used was the same brought over in
1954, when the black community of La Boca moved en masse,
just past the Pedro Miguel Locks, to Paraíso – the spot where
Captain Henry Morgan is said to have first set eyes on Panama
City during his bloodthirsty seventeenth-century raids on the
Spanish Main.

When we visit Paraíso's cricket ground on a sunny Sunday
afternoon, the same roller is leaning up against the corrugated

indoor sports complex. It has lain stationary for some years: the young men of Paraíso – whose grandfathers were cricketers – are out in the field playing baseball.

Running alongside the highway and the canal, elevated above the ground, is the track of the Panama Railroad, all the way from Panama City on the Pacific coast to Colón on the Atlantic. Like most of Latin America, Panama has abandoned the collective nobility of rail travel for the individual convenience of diesel SUVs. A passenger service still traverses the narrowest stretch of Central America on this route once a day, but mostly for tourists, and the train no longer stops at Paraíso. We ourselves are touring the canal in an air-conditioned imposing black Mercedes 4 x 4, with Saleh Bhana, the kindly peacemaker of contemporary Panamanian cricket, behind the wheel.

We glance south over the sports ground, and a vast cruise ship moves slowly through the canal. J. D. Arosemena, governor of Colón and president of Panama in the late 1930s, declared that the canal was 'built with French brains, American money and West Indian blood'. Jackman's ancestors were the 'silvermen' behind this man-made wonder, as were the parents of George Headley, the great West Indies batsman who C. L. R. James was moved to call 'the first Caribbean folk hero'. Jackman and Headley even knew each other as boys. We knock on the door of Jackman's house, hoping for a window into that world, but the next-door neighbour tells us he has died. We are two years too late.

*　　*　　*

Today Panama City is the gleaming, modern financial hub of Central America – even if the provenance of some of its money is questionable. The city at the other end of the canal, Colón, is a sobering place to walk around. Entire buildings have been condemned; sewage runs through alleyways; unemployment, delinquency and drug addiction have been endemic for decades. The city hospital has liquid streaming along the floors and rooms full of files just dumped in them. Plenty of cruise ships are passing through the port; not many passengers are advised to get off. Film crews even started using Colón as a double for Haiti, the most deprived country in the Americas.

The New Hotel Washington, Colón's grand palace overlooking the Caribbean Sea, was put up in 1913 after the US president William Howard Taft complained of nowhere decent to stay. It is now an Arab-run casino, its seafront vista neglected and overgrown. Most of its patrons are there to visit the bustling and utterly functional Colón Free Trade Zone, the oldest of its kind in the world. The money changing hands inside seems to be doing very little for the ordinary people of Colón.

Then again, the ordinary people of Colón have never had it easy. In 1905, the New York *Independent* journalist Poultney Bigelow landed to report on the US construction of the canal, a project that had proved beyond the French. After witnessing half-naked boys playing in mounds of rubbish left to rot in the interminable rain, he wrote: 'Through my pestiferous excursion up and down this filthy city, I could not find a single man or woman who had not suffered from fever of some kind.'

US engineers and politicians had convinced themselves that black West Indians, whose ancestors had toiled in the cane fields of the Antilles, could cope with the harsh tropical climate in a way whites could not. It does seem true that a mild bout of yellow fever in childhood seemingly protected many West Indians for life, whereas infection tended to prove deadly to other workers. But they were equally as susceptible to malaria. The snakes and tarantulas in the swamps dredged by West Indians were like nothing they had seen on their island homes.

'I shall never forget the trainloads of dead men being carried away, as if they were so much lumber,' said Alfred Dottin, a Bajan worker, about his construction years. 'There were mosquitoes, I say this without fear of exaggerating, by the thousands attacking one man. There were days that we could only work a few hours because of the high fever racking our bodies.'

Sugar workers in Barbados were so badly paid that between 1904 and 1914, the ten years of US canal construction, a third of adult Barbadian men sailed to Panama. One was William 'Tommie' Burton, who had opened the bowling for West Indies on their first two tours of England. Burton had already left highly colour-conscious Barbados for British Guiana to get a game. On the 1906 tour, he questioned why the task of lugging the team gear and cleaning the players' boots always fell to the darker-skinned players. When he had the temerity to bowl a bouncer, he was packed off home, where British Guiana refused to pick him. He was forced to emigrate to Panama in search of a job. In 1907 Burton became a sanitary inspector in the belated drive to rid the workers' huts of mosquitoes. He returned to Barbados only for the last days of his life, so he could die where he was born.

De Coursey Headley, 20, also from Barbados, began work on the canal in March 1908. Shortly after arriving he met Irene Roberts, a Jamaican woman of the same age. There is not so much as a plaque in Colón to George Alphonso Headley, but the world's first great black batsman first saw light on 30 May 1909 in the pier district of Cristóbal.

Headley was born into a formalised second-class citizenship. During the days of French construction, black workers could be placed on the gold payment roll and employed perhaps as division engineers, foremen, clerks or teachers. But in the year of Headley's birth, Taft effectively ordered that all black workers in the Panama Canal Zone be moved on to the silver roll. Aside from better pay, gold workers were entitled to sick and home leave, better housing and more subsidised entertainment. Black people had to use separate toilets and shops. It was segregation and Jim Crow Law in all but name.

The Headleys moved around temporary quarters, depending on where De Coursey was working in the Zone: permanent accommodation was not made available to silver-roll workers until as late as 1913. Many West Indian families lodged in flats in the terminal cities, the rents ratcheted up by unscrupulous landlords. The American writer Harry Franck, working as a plainclothes policeman, told of 'windowless, 6x8 rooms, always a dirty calico curtain dividing the 3ft parlour in front of the 5ft bedroom behind, a black baby squirming naked in a basket of rags'.

De Coursey worked a few months in the Quartermaster Department in Paraíso, before signing up as a powder helper for 32 cents an hour. This was among the most hazardous work on the canal, carrying 50-pound boxes of dynamite and handling the charges, in stifling heat and humidity when the slightest drop of rain or sweat could set off an explosion. The Culebra Cut involved 300 steam drills cutting through an entire mountain range for nine miles so the canal could join up with the sprawling artificial Gatún Lake. Accidents and fatalities were commonplace.

In 1911 De Coursey had transferred to the Panama Railroad, diverting the route of the line, when he suffered serious injury.

'We had an explosion there which knocked me unconscious,' he wrote in 1946 when applying for his belated pension from the US government. 'When I found myself I was in Ancon Hospital. I almost lost my right arm.' As a silver-roll worker he would not have been entitled to any sick leave, and when discharged from hospital he simply resumed the same job.

The canal was completed on 15 August 1914, at an official cost of 5069 lives, though the real toll must have been much higher. In 1917 De Coursey moved on to Cuba to work on another US project, the Guantanamo Bay naval centre, while Irene stayed behind with the children.

The cherubic George Headley, dressed in a chorister's gown, would file into Christ Church by the Sea, Colón, every Sunday. The family were regular churchgoers at the oldest Episcopal church in Central America, built in 1864 to serve the railroad. Young Headley became known for poking his head around doors and curtains in the church, only to be apprehended by the vicar each time. 'Ah, yes, George Headley,' says Robert Lovat, the kindly flaxen-haired junior warden, as he unlocks the church door for us. 'When I started here, some of the older congregation remembered him as a boy.' Their children and grandchildren have long since spoken Spanish at home and in public, but the book trolleys in Christ Church by the Sea are still stacked with English versions of the King James Bible and Thomas Cranmer's *Book of Common Prayer*. There are black Panamanians alive today who were named after George Headley.

Schooling for the children of the 'silver people' was rudimentary. Irene made the call to send George 'home' to Kingston for a 'British' education when he was ten. It was a rough boat journey, and his stomach was settled on the last day only by a flagon of fish tea made by his mother. Irene, who doted on her first-born son, left George with her sister-in-law and sailed on to Cuba to join De Coursey.

Bradman had a cricket bat in his hands from a very young age; Headley was a significantly older, and self-taught, cricketer. When he arrived in Jamaica, he spoke much better Spanish than English – occasionally he would find himself muttering '*vamos*' under his breath, or humming a Spanish song. Contrary to generally pessimistic accounts of race relations in the Zone, Headley had mixed with Panamanian children in the streets and on the baseball diamond, and became so accomplished at baseball that all the boys in the area wanted him on their side. He told C. L. R. James that his exceptional eye stemmed from having to watch the ball right out of the pitcher's hand; those free-flowing horizontal bat shots that would confound Test bowlers were a legacy of his upbringing in baseball. When he took up cricket at Calabar Elementary School in Kingston, his throwing arm was superior to other youngsters, and he thought nothing of keeping wicket bare-handed, having learned to catch the baseball with soft hands in Panama. While watching a ballgame in Colón, the eight-year-old Headley leapt in front of a gallery of spectators to catch a home run that was about to take someone's head off.

*       *       *

Almost as much blood was spilled in Costa Rica trying to build a railway from San José to the Caribbean coast. The track had to pass through unforgiving jungles and swamps, and by the time the rail gangs had made it 25 miles east of San José, 4000 men had perished.

Among the dead were three brothers of Minor C. Keith, the American in charge of the project. Keith reportedly never took a day off work, even when laid low by fever; he survived when a bridge collapsed into a torrent; and plunged headlong into a river in an attempt to save a monk on horseback. He too subscribed to the view that black West Indians had a unique capacity to withstand the tropics, although scores of them were soon among the dead. There's a saying in Costa Rica that a dead black man can be found under every tie of the railway.

Keith's luck changed one day in 1873, when he spotted wild bananas rotting in the fields along the lines. It dawned on him that he could funnel this cargo up to New Orleans and into the southern states, as well as use it as a cheap source of food for his workers. Financial setbacks forced Keith into a merger with the Boston Fruit Company in 1899, and the result was the United Fruit Company. He rode triumphantly into Limón 19 years after he set out and, in 1900, the first steam train ran from San José to Puerto Limón. Three months had been shaved off the freezing journey around Cape Horn.

At its peak in the late 1920s United Fruit owned a chunk of Central America equal to Yorkshire and Lancashire combined, and was declaring bumper profits. It was, depending on your worldview, either a shining example of the American entrepreneurial spirit or *el pulpo* ('the octopus') – a ruthless capitalist machine exploiting every corner of Latin America, eagerly supported by US politicians. United Fruit's antics in Colombia were the inspiration for the 'banana massacre' fictionalised by Gabriel García Márquez in *One Hundred Years of Solitude*. The 1954 CIA-organised coup of Guatemala came after the democratically elected Jacobo Árbenz tried to end some of United Fruit's worst exploitation.

By 1927 an informal colour bar prevented the 10,000 or so British West Indians in Costa Rica from being employed west of the Central Highlands, the lush protected rainforests on which the country has built its reputation. Limón Province's isolation led to the black, English-speaking, predominantly Protestant population of the Atlantic coast having very little to do with Costa Rica as most would know it. Fruit workers lived in drab makeshift accommodation, with Jamaicans, Trinidadians, Barbadians and Martiniquais housed separately. Many of the white American foremen carried guns, especially on payday, and drunken brawls became part of the monthly routine.

In 1910 hundreds of Jamaican fruit workers stormed a boat carrying strikebreaking rivals from St Kitts. Ricardo Jiménez Oreamuno, the president of Costa Rica, washed his hands of it. 'The West Indians are responsible for whatever bloodshed there has been,' he announced. 'The government is not responsible for the disagreement between the United Fruit Company and the West Indians.'

Marcus Garvey joined thousands of Jamaicans seeking work, spending part of 1910 and 1911 lodging in Puerto Limón with his uncle while working as a timekeeper for United Fruit. He started a newspaper critical of the company, but when an editorial questioned the motives of the fire brigade during a blaze, Garvey was run out of Limón by the town's elite, and left for Colón, where he fell ill and returned to Kingston. He would have to wait until the Great War for his Universal Negro Improvement Association and African Communities League (UNIA-ACL) to find support along the Atlantic coast of Central America. Liberty Hall, the glorious aquamarine wooden former headquarters of Garvey's UNIA Black Star Line shipping company in Limón, was the epicentre of the struggle for black rights. It was a sickening irony when the building burned to the ground in April 2016.

In a monolithic existence, a Sunday, Monday or public holiday was when West Indians could be found at their happiest. At plantation settlements dotted along three railway lines, they hacked away at the undergrowth, flattened the land, mixed the whitewash and set down stumps. Play would begin around 10 a.m., and for lunch and tea women and girls would prepare huge pots of rice and beans, sticky buns, ginger beer and *agua dulce*. In season, fishermen would catch green or hawksbill turtles – now critically endangered – for steak or soups. 'You could still get some . . . if you want it,' one barman whispered to us in a bar on the main strip of Puerto Viejo, an old fishing village that attracts tourists to the biggest surf in Costa Rica.

Some of these villages raised women's teams, although many girls would instead play skitlolly, a rural Jamaican game similar to ten-pin bowling; for that reason, Costa Rican women cricketers tended to bowl underarm well into the last century. For the big celebrations such as Emancipation Day or the king's birthday, special excursion trains would be laid on from Puerto Limón, sometimes carrying dance bands. The visiting side would stay overnight, dancing to calypsos, mambas or meringues, and more besides, before catching the train home next morning.

Shocking though some of United Fruit's labour practices clearly were, they did work with the British Consulate and UNIA to fund leisure for the West Indian workforce. The company ran churches, private schools and hospitals, usually superior to the state alternatives, and twigged that cricket allowed the West Indians to let off steam, which might otherwise have been directed their way. By 1922, clubs in Limón were sparring for the Frank Sheehy Cup, named after a senior United Fruit executive.

Costa Rican cricket became wrapped up in a complex web of class, race and inter-island rivalry. Charles Brown, a wealthy man, muddied his whites during a game in Limón. When he walked off the pitch a few days later a woman in the crowd hollered 'Dirty Brown!' He snapped back that she had the 'vulgarity of a whore'. Another man stepped in, and Brown stabbed him to death.

The first matches in Limón pitted Jamaicans against other Caribbean islanders. The Revd A. N. McDonald was a demon bowler for Waterloo CC of La Junia. Samuel C. Nation, editor of the *Limón Times* and a pillar of the moderate black leadership hostile to Garveyism, was a top-order batsman who used his editorials to harrumph about bad sportsmanship and sloppy protocol. In the 1912–13 season alone, his paper ticked off Estrada for not sending a telegram to explain why they could not fulfil their fixture at St Mark's; criticised the Matina captain for refusing to carry on after a disputed boundary; and sniffed at Siquirres for requesting their supporters be allowed in to watch. 'We hope the UF Coy Mandadors will tackle the Lindo Mandadors,' challenged the *Limón Times* in February 1913, at a time when Cecil Lindo, a renowned Jamaican plantation owner, was refusing to hand over lands to United Fruit. A team even emerged bearing the name Jiménez CC – a curious inspiration in light of the president's declared indifference to the West Indian cause.

It wasn't just a black man's game. Juan Gobán, a highland mestizo born in 1904, moved to Limón and became a superb cricketer, baseball player and footballer, featuring in the first Costa Rican national football team. He died prematurely of cancer aged just 26, and the sports stadium in Puerto Limón is named after him.

The first cricket game on the isolated Talamanca coast, running from Puerto Limón down to the Panamanian border, was played in 1909 between Cahuita and the Bluff. Old Harbour, the English name for Puerto Viejo, formed their team, Bee Hive, at a honey farm next to the old health dispensary. These were the days before any rail or road link to Puerto Limón, meaning visitors trekked to Old Harbour on horseback through the jungle or sailed a boat down the coast. The American historian Charles B. Kepner labelled these fishing communities 'transplanted Jamaican villages in which cherished folkways prevail and old mores still hold sway'. He was talking of *obeah* – the spiritual healing that dated back to the days of plantation slavery – and bush medicine.

The sturdiest boat in Cahuita was the 50-foot-long *Whisper*, which carried everything the settlement needed from Limón, including cricket equipment transported all the way from Jamaica. Selles Johnson, born at Cahuita Point in 1894, remembered being the only player in the settlement to own a full set of whites. 'The money we take in from the dance, we use that to fix the ground and to buy the gears,' he recalled in *What Happen*, Paula Palmer's folk history of the Talamanca coast, which she recorded verbatim in their patois. 'Then if a player becomes sick, we able to help.'

Spanish-speakers from San José were billeted to teach in these villages, but most went down with malaria or yellow fever inside the first few weeks and, apprehensive about the local bush medicine, dashed home at the earliest opportunity. 'Once we had a German came here,' one man related to Palmer. Noticing an umpire, clad in white, during a cricket game, the German asked: 'What the hell those is? Are they parson?'

In 1932 the first wireless radio appeared in Cahuita. Townsfolk would gather in Sylvester Plummer's house to listen to commentaries of big horse races and Test matches, broadcast through an English-language radio service in Limón. Plummer's house would have been full to bursting in July 1933, when George Headley wowed Old Trafford with 169 not out, leading West Indies to a landmark draw against England.

One warm evening we seek out the old Bee Hive ground on the outskirts of Puerto Viejo. The night takes its own course as we relax in a typically Caribbean wooden open-air bar nearby; with Augustus Pablo and Dennis Brown blasting out to a mixed crowd, many apparently openly enjoying marijuana and cocaine, the sea lapping against the beach, it's hard to tell where authentic Afro-Costa Rican life ends and global backpacker hipsterdom begins.

\*     \*     \*

It is strange that Headley did not play cricket in Panama as a boy, as the game had been enjoyed there since the days of the Panama Railroad. When the Americans turned the marshy crop of Manzanillo Island into the northern railroad terminus they named it Aspinwall, after their boss; the Spanish-speakers called it Colón, after Columbus, the man who discovered the Americas for Europeans.

The Aspinwall Regular Cricket Club, an Anglo-American initiative, made its debut on US Independence Day 1869, with Team Blue, led by Captain Gardiner, scoring 126 to the 114 made by Team Red, skippered by Captain Scott.

In 1887, local cricketers announced – in separate English, Spanish and French notices – the organisation of a match at

Plaza Chiriquí, 'to the *small* danger of passengers-by, and houses in the vicinity'. In most cases, the clubs were Anglophile set-ups: Kensington, Belgravia, Newcastle. Maduro e Hijos, the agents for Spalding kit suppliers, were advertising 'leg-guards, batting-gloves, wicket-keeping-gloves, all-cane cricket bats' at the turn of the century.

In 1890, the Panama Athletic Club formed a cricket division, patronised by Panamanian gentlemen Gaspar and Rafael Arosemena and Julio Arias, who made his runs against Isthmian 'in a first-class style', according to the *Panama Star & Herald*. The battle between baseball and cricket, settled in the US during their civil war, was still raging on the isthmus. In April 1891, Panama AC's baseball and cricket sections met in a game of cricket on the Cocoa Grove grounds – positioned, handily for some, next to a popular brothel – each wielding the bats from their favourite sport.

We make a pilgrimage to Colón's main ground at Monkey Hill, now known as Mount Hope or Monte Esperanza. A cemetery was dug into the hillside to bury those who fell building the railroad and later the canal. As the wind whips through the palm trees, to the backdrop of inmates screaming in a prison next door, it is a haunting memorial to the 'silver people' who paid with their involvement on the French and American projects. The old Monkey Hill cricket ground has been turned into the Estádio de Softbol y Béisbol Infantil Jaime Veléz.

On 25 December 1905, Pacific CC caught the train to Colón to play their annual Christmas cricket match at Monkey Hill. Colón was the nightlife capital of Panama, and strictly segregated. 'As is usual during the wet season in the Sister City, the rain managed to undo all the other arrangements,' lamented the *Star & Herald*. 'The players walked about a quarter of a mile through the woods from the station, but the ground was very wet.' Eighteen runs into the first innings there was a tropical downpour, and all the players and spectators traipsed back to the station, muddied, for the 4 p.m. return train home, just in time for their Christmas dinner, 'abandoning their intention to do up Colón on Christmas night'.

Five years later, the first MCC-organised tour of the Caribbean took place. This was the first time top-class cricket brushed up against Central America. MCC captain A. W. F. Somerset was an amateur of the classic sort – great-grandson of the Duke of Beaufort, useful in the scrum for Richmond and a heavyweight boxer of some repute, combined with first-class outings for Sussex. The English press were decidedly sniffy about the calibre of the touring party, despite the presence of county players George Brown, Jack Hearne, Sydney Smith and Cecil Burton.

Leaving Trinidad, their ship called at Colón before turning north-east to the final leg of the tour in Jamaica. At Colón, a special committee of the International Club went on board and challenged MCC to take on the cream of Panama. The match is completely absent from the established record books, but the *Limón Times* reported that the International Club of Colón beat Somerset's XI by 140 runs to 94. J. W. Gill led the way with 53, then ran through MCC with four for 10.

As early as 1882 the governor of Jamaica was complaining that his subjects were being left to die on the streets of Colón. The West Indians learned to fend for themselves with their own mutual societies and clubs. In 1896, the black West Indian clubs Perseverance CC and Surprise CC were staging fixtures against Anglo-American teams at Monkey Hill and Cocoa Grove. Twelve years later, H. L. Kilburn took a white team from Colón to play a fully Bajan side at Gorgona, and won by just one run. By 1909, the year of Headley's birth, there were 300 active players in the Isthmian Cricket Club League. Panamanian cricket was at its zenith as the domestic champions played off against Jamaican club champions Lucas; the winners of that, trumpeted the *Star & Herald* with some grandiloquence, had a right to claim the arguable title of 'Champions of the Isthmus of Panama and of the West Indies and Central and South America'.

At the same time, anguished letters were appearing in the press from the British community. 'What has become of the Panama Cricket Club?' asked one. Perhaps if the British had shown more inclination to forge links with their colonial subjects, then something might have endured. On Remembrance Day 1926, Sydney A. Young, writing in the West Indian section he had fought for in the *Panama American*, complained 'the conservative Britisher accepts the current standard . . . of social separation among whites and black . . . and displays no interest in nor attempts any connection with the large and multi-complexioned British West Indians'. This he thought at odds with the climate in the British West Indies, where 'there is mutual respect and mutual regard'. If anything, race relations seem to have worsened after the canal's completion in 1914; to some, no doubt, the West Indians had outlived their usefulness.

When Young was told by his editor that he would never be paid as much as a white man, he marched out of the *Panama American* and founded the *Panama Tribune* with George Westerman. The local cricket action was faithfully reported each week by the tireless Westerman, whose cricket columns appeared under the nom de plume 'Center Stump'. Born in

Colón to Barbadian and St Lucian parents in 1910, Westerman was an impeccably dapper, bow-tied man about town: journalist, historian, diplomat, politician and Panamanian national tennis champion. His list of complaints was legion, and usually connected to standards of behaviour, which – in line with cricket writers down the decades – he believed to be in perpetual decline. He took a dim view of the legendary rowdiness of West Indian crowds: 'Spectators enjoy the privilege of free admission here and yet few appreciate it. On the contrary the majority abuse the opportunity.'

In 1929, the Atlantic–Pacific play-off between Wanderers and East End at La Boca was, Westerman declared, 'another exhibition of poor sportsmanship, necessitating a change of four different umpires'. Not that he had much time for the men in white coats either: Panamanian umpires appear to have pre-empted MCC's 1935 change to the lbw Law, which meant that a batsman could no longer pad the ball away outside off stump without playing a shot. 'The practice of padding the ball [away] is little known and less practised here,' wrote Westerman, 'and those who have attempted it have paid the penalty as a result of the inefficiency of umpiring.' In one game at the end of the season, an umpire called time on a draw when two balls were still left to bowl in a tight finish, causing uproar.

These were low-scoring encounters, with 100 in the first innings usually enough to win. The grounds were owned and controlled by the US-run Canal Zone, so assiduous preparation of a 22-yard featherbed was presumably not top priority. Far from being rolled and watered during the week, most pitches were prepared with just a few hours' notice. Westerman did, however, single out for praise one groundsman, Matthews, for the way he consistently produced good pitches on the difficult Guinea grass at the Clovelly–Ancon Oval. He called out the club in print for not honouring Matthews's backbreaking work: 'THAT'S NOT THE WAY.' Westerman fought for the rights of black Panamanians for the rest of his life.

In early 1927, Pelham Warner's MCC team sailed through the canal on its way back from South America. As the ship passed through the Gatún Locks approaching Colón, the passengers spotted a match barely 300 yards away, between two teams of black players. When the West Indians noticed the bacon-and-egg MCC flag fluttering from the *Orita*, they paused, waved their caps and cheered raucously. Warner spent the next day recuperating in the salt baths of the Washington Hotel christened by President Taft – who, had he been a cricketer, would surely have been the barrel-like Warwick Armstrong.

In the *Cricketer*, Warner wrote: 'In the evening we were going on board at Colón when we found a deputation from the West End club waiting on the wharf. We had a long and enthusiastic talk on cricket.' The other British players were surprised there were seven clubs around Panama City and nine on the Atlantic end of the canal. Warner, born in Trinidad and raised in Barbados, claimed kinship with these West Indian cricketers, stemming from his childhood days when Killebree, a black boy hired by his parents, would bowl to him. Previous generations of Warners had grown wealthy from the slave labour on their Trinidadian plantation before the abolition of slavery in 1833, though Plum himself had done much to encourage the first West Indies and island teams to pick the best black cricketers. 'Meeting these men brought back memories,' wrote Warner, 'of my boyhood days when I used to bat in my nightshirt to a black bowler on a marble gallery.' Warner did not, however, seemingly give much thought to engaging these black men on the field.

\*     \*     \*

George Headley sailed back into this world in early 1930, when England were visiting for their first full Test series in the Caribbean. He had been considering a move to New York – where his parents had settled and taken US citizenship – to study dentistry, but a delay in his immigration forms being posted allowed him to make his first-class debut for Jamaica against Lord Tennyson's XI in early 1928.

On Test debut at Bridgetown, he was booed to the crease by home fans angry that a young Jamaican had taken the place of a Bajan. Headley soon wowed them and the English with his lightness of feet and front-foot cut shots in a near-faultless 176 in the second innings, containing just one, hard hit, return chance. For the third Test at Bourda, Georgetown, he was forced to share a bed with Learie Constantine, such was the substandard accommodation for black players, yet would be proclaimed an 'immortal' – one of six men to hit centuries in each innings of a Test – inspiring West Indies to their landmark maiden Test win. There was a gap of five weeks until the finale, for the teams to make the long boat journey from British Guiana to Headley's Jamaica. These being the days of chauvinistic home selections in West Indies cricket, just two players – Headley and the Trinidadian opener Clifford Roach – kept their places from the third Test to the fourth; in came seven Jamaicans. Roach, Headley and the England party took the Elder & Fyffes banana boat SS *Ariguani*, calling at Colón and Puerto Limón.

In Headley, the Jamaican prime minister Michael Manley would write, West Indians had found 'black excellence personified in a white world and a white sport'. At Cristóbal pier, yards from where he was born, Headley was greeted by representatives of the West Indian Colony of Panama, led by its president Cyril Lawrence, who waxed lyrical about his achievements. 'Although domiciled in a foreign land, we are keenly interested in everything that attends to the material and social advancement of our homelands,' he said. 'When the news was flashed to us that you had made the magnificent score of 176 . . . the jubilation of every West Indian was indescribable.' Community activist Linda Smart Chubb presented Headley with a belt and gold buckle made locally. The *Star & Herald* sang: 'George Headley, famed cricketer. Onward to victory and achieve your goals, righting the wrongs.'

Headley always kept the sharp dress sense of a Latin gentleman, with his taste in fedoras, pristine suits and fetching cravats and socks. At Puerto Limón, his wardrobe was boosted by a pair of Costa Rican gold cufflinks presented to him by the Limón Friendly & Literary Association, plus a sterling silver cup by the United Fruit Company; Headley had worked for a subsidiary of United Fruit back in Jamaica, and it was under the profession of 'fruit selector' rather than 'cricketer' that he first entered New York to visit his parents. While Headley was being endlessly garlanded, the England players went off to Portette beach for a picnic and a dip.

When the ship finally reached Kingston, West Indies and England played a timeless Test to decide the series. England amassed an almost unthinkable 849 in two and a half days. Headley's monumental 223 in the fourth innings – ended when he was stumped on the seventh day's play, and tenth in all – was the last meaningful act before England had to catch the boat home, so the match was drawn. Headley had struck up a long correspondence with Sydney Young's *Panama Tribune*. He wrote in after his Sabina Park innings: 'I was rather lucky to fulfill your desire by making the double century at the last moment.'

It was not the last they would see of him. That October, the West Indian party for Australia and New Zealand assembled in Colón before making the long journey together across the Pacific. A match against an Isthmian XI at Mount Hope was abandoned after a few overs due to wet weather, even though kerosene was poured on the wicket and set alight in an attempt to dry it.

The Australians would meet with success on their faster pitches by bowling at Headley's midriff, until he altered to a more front-on stance, leaving Clarrie Grimmett to conclude he was the best leg-side player to whom he ever bowled. On his euphoric return journey, the RMS *Mataroa* was greeted at Colón by members of the Atlantic Council, troops of boy scouts, and a delirious thousand-strong procession at 11th and Front Street. A further 3000 crammed into the thoroughfares and the Ideal Auditorium, as the West Indian population of Panama downed tools to set eyes on their hero.

The four Jamaicans in the party agreed to delay the last leg of their journey home to guest for an All-Jamaica XI against the Atlantic-Pacific All-Stars at Mount Hope. Headley, as the best of the quartet – not to mention the only one black and working-class – was the real draw. Headley's great frustration was that he never bowled more in Test cricket, so he lapped up the chance to unfurl his leg-cutters, taking two for 17. To the crowd's audible dismay, though, he was caught behind for 10. Headley presented one of his best bats to a Panamanian called Joseph, who made the home side's highest score of 43. Headley, eager for more practice, took himself off to Gatún, where he enlisted young locals to bowl at him in the middle.

The English writer Owen Rutter witnessed him in action in Puerto Limón in early 1933, when Jamaica's best players were on their way back from Test trials in Trinidad. They were challenged on a scorched-earth pitch, with the *Ariguani* stewards making up the numbers. 'An immense crowd of negroes lined the square,' wrote Rutter. 'Two or three times in every over he would scatter the crowd with a clean, low drive that reached the encircling road. Every time Headley sent a ball crashing on to one of the corrugated iron roofs they sent up a delighted roar.' Bradman famously honed his rotary technique by hitting a golf ball against a wall at his home in Bowral; Headley's mastery on wet wickets, superior even to Bradman's, surely owed something to these sawdust-and-kerosene experiences in Central America.

Headley and Rutter spoke at length on the banana boat back to Kingston. Headley managed to keep his calm when some white passengers insisted on extending the segregation of Panama and the wider US to the ship's swimming pool. The irony was not lost on Rutter. 'Here was a man whom the British public would be cheering in a few weeks' time; whom the cricket savants of the British press would be honouring in columns of expert appreciation. Yet because his hide was black we couldn't bathe in the same swimming pool.' Rutter made a point of jumping in alongside his companion. Headley had already made his point when entering Australia, which then employed a whites-only immigration policy. When asked to fill in his nationality, he wrote not Jamaican, not British, not Panamanian, not American – but 'African'.

\*     \*     \*

Thomas Spencer was among the first generation of Jamaican immigrants who brought cricket to Costa Rica. We talk and sip lemonade with his son Daniel, now well into his nineties, on the balcony of his modest, elegant green and yellow wooden house in the village of Estrada, with the train line from Siquirres to Puerto Limón running in front of us. There was once a passenger train every hour, he says, but now you were lucky if you saw two a day, and they are all carrying fruit freight. Daniel pauses from his reminiscences to wave at the fruit workers cycling past on their way home.

In Daniel's playing days, Estrada were one of 37 cricket clubs in the outlying towns and villages, together with nine in Puerto Limón itself. Across the railway line, beyond the undergrowth, is where Estrada played, on an open clearing long marked down for a housing development that has never materialised. Estrada's fixtures were always on Mondays, and mostly against their local rivals on the line, with special trips down the Talamanca coast or to Bocas del Toro, the United Fruit town built on stilts just over the border in Panama. The strongest team of his time were Pacuarito, who had in their side Nathaniel Samuels, the grandfather of Joel Campbell, the Costa Rican footballer who spent time at Arsenal.

Daniel's daughter digs out his old cricket stash, including a battered burgundy-coloured ball, which he grips as if to deliver an off-cutter. He has not played since 1975, when the village team packed up, but his eyes glisten, as if he were 25 again. 'I bowled seam, but when I want to twist the ball, I twist,' he says, doubtless a successful formula on such damp tropical wickets. He confesses, though, to nursing headaches caused by *cacique*, a homemade Costa Rican *guaro* liquor, in the post-match libations.

In 1937, the Pathfinders of Limón despatched 72 cricketers, boxers and baseball players for an ambitious tour of Jamaica. Cleveland Clarke, the tour manager and secretary of the Costa Rica Cricket Board of Control, formed six years earlier, declared it 'the biggest excursion of its kind attempted in Costa Rica by the working classes'. The Pathfinders cricket team came back smarting from eight defeats and just one draw. The baseball game against the Ortega Stars was lost, as were all three bouts by the boxers. Clarke blamed underprepared Costa Rican wickets for their technical deficiencies on better pitches. He also managed to upset his hosts by airing his views in Kingston's *Daily Gleaner* about the relative merits of Costa Rican and Jamaican life. 'One thing our trip revealed is that the condition of the working classes in Costa Rica are not as bad as those existing in Jamaica as we were previously led to think. Your capital is much larger and commercialised. But for scenic beauty I think San José has it over Kingston.'

The Pathfinders pitted their wits against Headley, after the touring captain Stanley Dixon issued a request for the Jamaican hero to appear in order to bring in the crowds. Young Sylvester Cunningham was to drop Headley off the bowling of his brother Winston in front of thousands of spectators – a mistake that would haunt Sylvester for the rest of his life.

The Pathfinders returned to Jamaica the next two years, even taking a full orchestra with them in 1938. The Excelsior left-arm spinner Simeon Maxwell was the star of that tour, taking 48 wickets at an average of 11, including five-fors against West India Cold Storage, Puros, Wolmer's School and the Unknowns. 'Longfield', the *Gleaner*'s cricket correspondent, reckoned Maxwell as good as any left-arm bowler in Jamaica. However, 'Longfield' did not hold back in criticising Dixon's bowling changes and field placings; the wicketkeeper and slips apparently stood too far back, even after opposition team-mates and local journalists had politely pointed this out to the captain.

The Hylton Affair of 1939 laid bare how much cricket meant. Leslie Hylton, a towering but troubled fast bowler, had been among the Jamaican triallists who stopped over in Limón in 1933. Six years later, he was omitted from West Indies' tour of England. There were six Trinidadians in the party, against just four Jamaicans, and 'Longfield' was apoplectic. He labelled it 'Trinidad's West Indian team for England', and argued that Jamaica should withdraw its quartet in protest. A group of well-wishers in Jamaica launched a fundraising effort to raise the £400 needed for Hylton's boat fare, board and lodging.

The blowback reached Limón and Colón, where sales of the *Gleaner* went through the roof as the diaspora sought daily updates. 'The whole affair actually caused broken friendships and in some cases fisticuffs between the Jamaican section and those of Trinidad and Barbados,' reported Clarke. Eventually the West Indies board climbed down and added Hylton for the opening Test at Lord's. But he had run-ins with his team-mates, including Headley. There would be no happy ending: in 1954 Hylton shot his wife dead after he discovered she was cheating on him. His defence that it was an instinctive act was undermined by the fact that he fired seven bullets into her, which suggested he had reloaded the gun. He was hung for the crime, and remains the one Test cricketer to have been executed for murder.

It became more difficult to play in Costa Rica after the authorities commandeered the Limón Oval – where Marcus Garvey had spoken to thousands in 1921, and Headley wowed just as many with his bat in 1933 – for use by the Red Cross.

When we drop by it has become the Tony Facio Hospital. The Pathfinders were able to play just once at home between their second and third tours of Jamaica. 'As a result the players have turned attention to baseball and football,' lamented Clarke. 'Cricket is almost at a standstill.' In 1938, Cyril Lawrence of Colón was expressing his regret that cricket in Panama was 'on the downgrade . . . quite different to when George Headley made a passing visit'. The Second World War hastened this decline, as bats and balls – which used to come in from England by ship through Jamaica – became harder to access.

By 1952 the Panamanian league still had 171 cricketers at the Atlantic end, including the clubs of Fenwick, Midland and Rainbow City, who all played at Mount Hope. On the Pacific side, 98 players represented Clovelly, Ancon, Red Tank, Spartan and Gamboa, playing at La Boca and the Clovelly–Ancon Oval. 'When the La Boca XI play at Mount Hope, they are met with to-do at the station, to be escorted to the playing field,' reported the *Panama Canal Review*. 'The local umpire also often adds an "elephant hunter" hat to his traditional white duck "duster". After the match, dinner is laid out at the home of a home-town team member. Then a party follows to make anyone forget the most wicked battle at the wickets.' Cricket's last gasp as the number-one sport for black Panamanians is touchingly captured in photographs collated by Aston Parchment, a teacher in La Boca, of schoolchildren in cricket training, and adult teams of fit, muscular black men lining up proudly in traditional caps, belts and whites.

It was only with the civil rights movement of the 1960s that segregation on the Panama Canal Zone was phased out. In March 1965, Benarro Thompson, an electrical engineer from Trinidad, accepted a job on the canal. He brought his eldest son, Micky, joined later by the younger two, Jimmy and Ronnie. Micky, looking sharp in a loose-fitting shirt when we meet him at a game in Panama City, tells us with a cocksure grin: 'We joined the Paraíso team, and lo and behold they suddenly started winning again.' In 1969–70 Benarro arranged for a Trinidadian side to tour, bringing with them future Test spinners Raphick Jumadeen and Inshan Ali, and the seamer Pascall Roberts, who had just returned from West Indies' tour of the UK, where they were famously bowled out for 25 by Ireland at Sion Mills. 'One day, Ronnie was struck right in the mouth,' recalls Micky, regaling the story with characteristic Trini cool. 'We took him to a private clinic, where they did some work on him. We spent about $750. I said, "Well, let's take you home." He said, "No, take me back to the ground." He went back, put on his pads, finished the game, and hit the winning runs.'

Prince Charles did not quite meet with the same success. In 1974, the 25-year-old Prince of Wales had just seen Camilla Shand marry his polo partner Andrew Parker Bowles, and instead embarked on a military career in which he served as a ship's communications officer on HMS *Jupiter*. The ship called at Acapulco before passing through the Panama Canal en route to Bermuda. Charles's arrival prompted the British Embassy in Panama to arrange a cricket game at Paraíso, in which the Prince of Wales' XI would take on a local combination. The Panamanians racked up around 250 for four before declaring, and swiftly dismissed the Prince's XI. 'I think the British couldn't take the heat, it was so hot,' says Micky Thompson. 'His Highness was a lovely man, but he wasn't much of a cricketer.'

Charles's father, Prince Philip, always had more pretensions with bat and ball, having captained the Gordonstoun First XI.

He was in his second term as MCC president when in March 1975 his Royal Yacht XI took on the Cavaliers of San José at the Republic Tobacco sports ground at Zapote, since turned into a condo. The 63-year-old Duke of Edinburgh was obliged to carry out ceremonial obligations while the Cavaliers chased down 85 for the loss of five wickets.

Cricket was flickering back into life in both Panama and Costa Rica by the 1980s. Work by the British embassies, assisted by Ken Armitage, a Cheshire businessman residing in San José, resulted in a Costa Rica v. Panama match at Zapote in 1986. Thanks to contacts in Manuel Noriega's government, Indian nationals on the Panama side were waved on to a flight to San José, without the requisite papers. When the plane landed, the team were taken through a back door, avoiding immigration or customs. Thompson remembers them not being entirely prepared for the formalities of a black-tie dinner at the ambassador's residence. 'Someone in the British Embassy came to me and said, "Michael, there's lots of diplomats here, and some of your boys are not properly attired." Some of our players were wearing BATA sneakers made in Czechoslovakia. I asked, "What shall we do?" We sent out one of the guys to buy a load full of smarter shoes, all the same size. The guys with smaller feet had to stuff newspapers in the end of them.'

They pulled on their trainers at the unlikely start time of 7 a.m. next morning to avoid the worst of the tropical heat. Ronnie Thompson and Kendrick Thomas – serving with the US Air Force in Panama – racked up 250 for the first wicket before Maurice Macphail, one of the San José team, shattered his collarbone as he hit the ground holding on to a catch. After the Panamanians completed an innings victory, they were presented with trophies by their sports minister Rigoberto

Paredes, one of Noriega's closest allies, and met Oscar Arias, the president of Costa Rica.

The event acted as an unofficial summit for the two countries – peace-loving Costa Rica had abolished its own army in 1948 – and Armitage was obviously using the occasion as a publicity stunt. 'Something just looked wrong about him,' says Richard Illingworth, the doyen of Costa Rican cricket. 'I remember him wearing some pretty dodgy cufflinks.' Eventually the source of Armitage's wealth slipped out and he was arrested and sent down on fraud charges for swindling $10 million out of an orange grove investment. Noriega's own deadlier activities finally caught up with him: he was toppled in 1990, after the US invasion of Panama, in which several Chinooks landed on McGrath Field, the old cricket pitch in Gamboa. Noriega was incarcerated for the last six years of his life in Gamboa prison.

Costa Rica's top scorer that day in 1986 was Lancelot Binns. A lifetime of sun and tropical fruits had been kind to him, so much so that the British diplomat Tim Willasey-Wilsey – who penned an evocative article on Costa Rican cricket for the *Cricketer* a few years later – was taken aback to learn that Binns and his contemporaries Standford Barton and Sylvester Cunningham were well into their seventies. Barton was even one of the Limón Pathfinders who ventured to Jamaica way back in 1937. Now he was serving as president of the Limón branch of the Jamaican Burial Scheme Society, helping to organise the Limón Carnival, which had on its roster the one guaranteed cricket fixture in the country each year, preserved as a cultural relic.

Binns, though, was the would-be superstar of Costa Rican cricket. He was born in 1916 into a relatively wealthy family in Siquirres and, like Headley, sent to Kingston at the age of ten to complete his studies. There he benefited from better coaching and facilities, developing his square drive and leg-spin. In 1936, he was selected for Jamaica Schoolboys to play against a touring Yorkshire team containing eight past or future Test cricketers. Binns made 30 at the start of the match, seeing off Bill Bowes with the new ball, before falling in both innings to Ken Smales. After graduating from the Jamaica School of Agriculture, he was hired by United Fruit in Kingston, and played for their cricket team in 1939 alongside his uncle Michael and cousin Allie, who would go on to keep wicket for West Indies. In one match, against the British Garrison, Lance took eight for 18 – including a hat-trick – and followed it with a century. A future in first-class cricket beckoned.

Then, on the outbreak of war, Binns decided to make his fortune in coconut farming and livestock in Costa Rica, and became the first *regidor* (a kind of alderman) of West Indian origin in Siquirres. Binns's commitment to cricket endured well into old age, and he would drive around the Atlantic coast collecting players on matchday morning in his pick-up truck. He was still taking wickets in eightieth-birthday celebration matches for himself in 1996 and Barton in 1998, playing his last game when he was 84.

Illingworth – not the Worcestershire and England spinner turned Test umpire, but an MCC member, stoic opening batsman, long-serving president of the Costa Rica Cricket Association, and a US doubles champion in croquet – bonded with Binns over a shared love of growing coconuts. 'I was very fond of old Lance,' says Illingworth as we lunch on ceviche at his home in San José. 'For reasons we could never quite work out, he always wanted to play for San José rather than Limón, even though he was from that side of the country. It's possible that he saw himself as slightly better than the rest of them.' Binns owned much of Siquirres by the time he died in 2005 and, according to Illingworth, he attempted to leave his last 100-acre farm to his nephew, Donald, with 5 acres set aside for a cricket ground. But the move was blocked by his lawyer, who persuaded him to sell it off for housing.

Such setbacks would dispirit most ordinary folk, but Illingworth is the kind of civic enthusiast who believes in doing things properly. It's as well that he lives in Costa Rica, the neatest and most organised country in Latin America, because it's hard to imagine him putting up with more precarious places. Illingworth finds himself repeatedly drawn back to the crumbling grandeur of the rain-drenched Atlantic coast – a life apart from the yoga-retreat, eco-tourist rainforests that define modern Costa Rica. He has plunged much of his later life into travelling the length of Limón Province, across the old West Indian towns and villages, trying to rekindle the memory of cricket.

He was handed a gift in 2016, when West Indies shocked Australia to win the Women's World Twenty20. That year, 23 female PE teachers, all members of the Asociación de Cricket Femenino Costa Rica, affiliated to the national federation Fedecric, signed up for coaching clinics run by Ann Browne-John, a former West Indies player, with the backing of Limón MP Trudy Poyser. They entered schools armed with a YouTube clip of Hayley Matthews and Stafanie Taylor belting it around Eden Gardens. It was something of a two-fingered rebuke to the former West Indies board president Dave Cameron, who blamed the influence of female PE teachers for the decline of cricket in his native Jamaica.

Fedecric has set up Escuelas de Cricket in more than 100 schools across Puerto Limón, Siquirres, San Miguel de Heredia,

Cocles and Bri Bri, of which 45 are competing regularly in the Standford Barton Cup. In the village of Bri Bri, home to an indigenous tribe of the same name who speak their own language, cricket is making footprints in an entirely new demographic. There are week-long cricket *colonias* in the tropical setting of EARTH University in Guacimo, where bananas are cultivated sustainably and a disused railway line runs through the campus – an instant history lesson about the industries and the people who brought cricket to Costa Rica in the first place. Undergraduates at EARTH, drawn from all over the world, are obliged to enrol in a club in their first year, and some are choosing cricket.

Before we leave Costa Rica, Illingworth puts us on to his old friend Armando Foster, the man on the ground in Puerto Limón – though as a Seventh-Day Adventist we are advised not to contact him on a Saturday. We meet him and his twenty-something son, Roderick, at their home. Armando says he doesn't see cricket as a black sport in Limón any longer; more a means of lifting up a depressed region that needs a new purpose.

Ultimately it will be down to Roderick's generation if *Limonense* cricket is ever to undergo a true renaissance. He is cautious but thoughtful about the task ahead. 'I feel aware that, back in the time, they used to play cricket and it was something strong,' he says in considered and pristine English. 'My great-grandfather played cricket here. But the characteristics and the way of thinking when we were playing cricket have vanished from Limón. You can see some kids knocking the cricket, but others appreciate what it can teach them. Those who've played cricket, you see a lot of change in that person.'

\*    \*    \*

Cricket is hurtling on in Panama at an unprecedented pace, on the wings of the most passionate diaspora in the game. A generation ago, Panama's Indian cricketers may have been wearing humble Czech sneakers, but today they are big players in the most successful economy in Central America.

On one stifling Sunday we are invited to make guest appearances for Saleh Bhana's Revolución CC. Every Sunday the arid Parque Felipe E. Motta, in Panama City's sterile but powerful business district of Costa del Este, is transformed into a slice of India. Four matches take place side by side on earth wickets completely devoid of grass, endlessly rolled and cracking in the sun, which pounds off the glass on the skyscrapers surrounding the park; many of the banks and financial institutions housed inside were implicated in the 2016 Panama Papers financial scandal. Under the merciful shade of a jacaranda tree, Hindu wives and daughters chat away with a picnic; Muslim players gather under another with their young sons. On the top pitch, Dhaiz v. Dada produces a standard of cricket as good as anything in many Associate nations.

The first immigrants from the Indian subcontinent began making their way to Panama in the 1920s. When Albert Einstein made a covert visit to Panama's United Fruit banana plantations a few years later, he insisted on having his picture taken with Indian clerks in Colón. One Gujarati Muslim, Mahmood Bhana, arrived from the small village of Manekpor in 1927, and rose from a humble street seller to owner of a thriving household store in Panama City, Bazar Bhana, which specialises in offering luxury trinkets from the East.

It was rare for these early Indian migrants to play in the West Indian-dominated leagues. But the opening up of the Colón Free Trade Zone after the Second World War led to more

Hindu and Muslim traders and wholesalers making their way to Panama. They formed an Indian Society, which began looking for cricket fixtures.

The presence of Indians in Panamanian cricket grew until they outnumbered West Indians, and gradually took over the running of the league. By the time the Thompson brothers were retiring from cricket in the late 1990s, they were the only West Indian players in an otherwise Indian Muslim team. Where their Trio side would once have celebrated with rum, calypso and rotis, we relax after our intense outing for Revolución by downing invigorating cashew nut and fig milkshakes in the underground car park next to the family offices. Bhana has even squeezed a makeshift net into one of the parking spaces.

From 1988 to 2002, Panama's Hindu and Muslim teams were happy to compete in separate tournaments – a communal split more prevalent in cricketing nations than the authorities would like to admit. The ICC awarded Affiliate membership to Panama in 2002, but made it clear that unless all communities competed together they could just as quickly remove it. Clubs in Panama still exist along communal lines, but at least compete in the same league. Both communities need each other to continue receiving ICC funds, so the Panama Cricket Association – currently headed by a Muslim, Ismail Patel, and with Bhana a calm and moderating influence on the committee – holds the uneasy truce, and there is little open sign of discord during our visit. When united, Panama are the strongest team in Central America, and crowds for domestic finals have numbered 9000.

Over at another ground, Panama Pacifico – site of the former US Howard Air Force Base – the backdrop is truly eerie. Rusting 1980s cars emblazoned with UN World Food Programme stickers sit half-demolished between an aircraft hangar and two cricket pitches – like *Repo Man* transplanted to the tropics. Planes and helicopters take off all around us; cadets march on their weekend drills behind the bowler's arm. Out on the field an under-15 tournament features 44 players across four teams . . . all but one of Indian origin. Cricket remains half-forgotten by black Panamanians and half-understood by the rest of the country.

Panama's cricketing history came full circle in 2015, when Pacifico hosted the Central American Cricket Championship, with MCC invited guests for their maiden appearance in an international tournament. Neither MCC's players nor officials had any inkling that A. W. F. Somerset's XI had played that landmark game in Colón more than a century ago, even less that the Panama side had won.

This 2015 MCC team of hardened Minor Counties and ECB Premier League club players breezed through every game up to the final – where they met Panama. The technical rectitude and tactical nous of seasoned English cricketers was set against the Panamanians' brazen hitting and unorthodox bowling. Panama kept hitting out, even when wickets tumbled, and – helped by a controversial no-ball call off the last delivery – they scampered to their target. Thousands of Panamanian Asians invaded the pitch in exaltation. On two occasions, a century apart, Panama had beaten the best Lord's could send.

# 5

# Colombia and Venezuela

*Hostages to fortune*

O N A HAZY early English summer's day in 1977 Phillip
Witcomb slung his Duncan Fearnley bat into a brown
leather cricket bag then hopped on a coach waiting to take him
and the rest of his Lucton School team-mates to an away match.
As the busload of schoolboys, in dark blue blazers, wound its
way through the sleepy Herefordshire countryside for the
fixture, against nearby rivals Malvern College, it was tailed by a
sleek black Mercedes with tinted windows.

After the toss, Witcomb fastened the metal buckles on his
pads, merrily clapped his wicketkeeping gloves together and
did a few stretches before striding out to take up his position
behind the stumps. Out of the corner of his eye he saw, as
usual, a burly man with bushy sideburns wearing a tight-fitting
black suit and Wayfarers. The man took a seat on a wooden
bench next to Malvern's listed pavilion.

Witcomb's father, Patrick, had been a top MI6 secret agent
and during his Colombian childhood this had been a familiar
sight for the young teenager. Bodyguards, often with guns,
were part of everyday life. It was nothing out of the ordinary.
At least, that was what Witcomb always thought. It was only in

1989, at the age of 24, that he discovered the real reason for those years of armed protection. Phillip was adopted, and actually born Roberto Sendoya Escobar. His biological father was Pablo Escobar. *That* Pablo Escobar.

In 1965, the future Colombian drug lord, narco-terrorist and richest criminal in history, aged 16, fathered a son from a non-consensual encounter with a 14-year-old named Maria Luisa Sendoya. During one particular secret-service mission Patrick, who was involved with tracking drug money, had taken part in a shootout and in the aftermath discovered a baby boy. The infant, only a few months old, was named Roberto.

Patrick and his wife Joan adopted the boy and with the Colombian authorities discreetly changed his name to Phillip Charles Robert Witcomb. Maria, who died young, had managed to keep the child a secret from the future leader of the notorious Medellín Cartel, who would later be worth an estimated US$30 billion. Inevitably, though, Colombian tongues wagged, and years later Escobar discovered the existence of his eldest son. He wanted him back – Escobar's first-born was, theoretically, the heir to a cocaine empire.

It became too dangerous for Phillip in Bogotá, especially as his father was one of the men tasked with helping to bring Escobar down. The threat of kidnapping was a daily reality so young Phillip – oblivious to the true reason – was packed off to boarding school in England: first to an Oxfordshire prep and then to Lucton School in Leominster. And Lucton meant cricket.

'Pablo Escobar's son became a crafty wicketkeeper!' Witcomb tells us at his remote *finca* on the Spanish island of Mallorca. 'I wasn't the best batsman in the world. I was regularly number eleven and it was usually six, miss, six, miss and out, but I was a sly fox behind the stumps.' Witcomb has a stocky prop forward's frame, a tanned complexion and a boisterous laugh. He sports a thick moustache and his resemblance to Escobar is striking, but he is itching to reminisce about his glovework first. 'My favourite trick was using a piece of thread and matchstick under the bails, which I'd pull, and then we'd all celebrate a player being bowled,' he says before roaring with laughter again. 'I was always looking to use sneaky little cheats to get batsmen out in school games – it must have been my Colombian genes. Usually a doddery schoolmaster was umpiring so often I'd get away with it. I used to love sledging too. Of course, nobody would have known they were being sledged by the offspring of Don Pablo.' Phillip would even receive visiting dignitaries at Lucton: '"Witcomb, get your suit on," the teachers would shout, and limousines flying the Colombian flag would arrive and I would be taken out for lunch and the likes.'

His grandfather Sir John Renton Aird, an extra equerry to the Queen and son of John Aird who built Egypt's Aswan Dam across the Nile, was an MCC member who turned out for I Zingari. 'He gave me the Duncan Fearnley bat I used in school matches,' Witcomb adds, reclining on a wicker chair on his veranda. 'Sir John got it signed by a load of players at Lord's but I just wanted to try to smash sixes.' The Airds fostered Witcomb's early love of cricket. 'I'd stay with them in Swiss Cottage for three weeks every year as a little boy. My grandmother would plonk me in front of the cricket on the telly with my Meccano set,' he recalls. 'She adored cricket but would potter about in the kitchen while it was on. I'd have to run down the corridor at the end of every over with an update. It was a nightmare when Geoff Boycott or Chris Tavaré were batting.'

It was in Bogotá that Witcomb, bodyguards *in situ*, watched his first live cricket. His father preferred to play golf with MI6 chums, but the Witcombs socialised with other Commonwealth families at the Bogota Sports Club (BSC; as elsewhere, the British gave their club an English name and didn't lend themselves to the accent on Bogotá). 'The British bigwigs from the banks and oil companies would turn up,' Witcomb remembers of a time when he would be called 'Don Felipe' by Colombia's president Misael Pastrana and bounced on his knee. 'Back then, I wasn't interested in cricket – just playing marbles and swapping football stickers. I remember tearing around annoying all these old Empire types. They would say, "What! What! Who is this little oik misbehaving and disturbing the cricket?!" But I'd be the only person with security guards carrying guns so nobody dared to say anything. I was a bit of a spoilt brat, really.'

\*     \*     \*

'Don Pablo, in this house you will be very comfortable,' Akbar Bilgrami told Pablo Escobar before showing him around a $4000-a-month mansion in Panama City. 'The location is perfect for your purposes since it is at the end of a cul-de-sac.' Escobar grinned and then replied: 'I thank you for your attention, Don Bilgrami. I promise you we will collaborate much more with new deposits.' In 1984, Escobar had fled to Panama to lie low in the wake of the murder of a Colombian minister who had tried to take cocaine traffickers to task.

Bilgrami, the slick director of the Latin American division of the Pakistan-owned Bank of Credit and Commercial International (BCCI), always liked to be accommodating to one of his most lucrative clients. The property, in the Altos del Golf district, had been used by Bilgrami's predecessor and had a huge terrace for wild parties. There was a jacuzzi in the master bedroom. It would be the operations hub of Escobar's cocaine-smuggling business for the next three years. The $10,000 bills for telephone, fax and telexes would eclipse the monthly rent.

The office found on the third floor at the headquarters of Banco de Crédito y Comercio de Colombia (BCCC) – a subsidiary of BCCI – in downtown Bogotá was less ostentatious. On the front desk a receptionist would paint her nails while three employees made trips to other floors carrying unmarked bundles of paperwork. There were no fax machines, no teleprinters and the office was inconspicuously furnished.

Officials from Colombian banking authorities, with their sensible suits, briefcases and diligence, arrived at BCCC on a routine visit in 1987. Except they took wrong turn and visited the wrong office, on the wrong floor. What the regulators discovered on the third floor was a phantom bank operated by BCCC. It was neither registered nor licensed to operate in Colombia. The clandestine operation was being used to launder millions of dollars through the Bahamas, washing cash for Escobar and the Medellín Cartel.

BCCI had expanded rapidly to become a serious player in the global banking industry with assets of $4 billion by 1980. BCCC employed Colombians at management level but the company's movers and shakers were all from Pakistan and BCCI. 'We used to have an "All England" versus BCCI match,' former Bogota Sports Club president Anthony Letts tells us over a cup of coffee. 'These were particularly lean years for cricket in Colombia so BCCI, with a number of Pakistani cricketers, usually won those matches. Their presence, however, was short lived. Although that had little to do with cricket . . .'

In addition to the violent Colombian drug lords José Gonzalo Rodríguez Gacha and Escobar, BCCI counted dictators Saddam Hussein and Manuel Noriega – a one-time golf partner of Witcomb's father – among its clientele. The institution was nicknamed 'Bank of Crooks and Criminals International'. The initialism's clash with Indian cricket's governing body is an unfortunate coincidence.

Aziz Rehman, a former driver for BCCI, remembered delivering sacks of dollar bills, sometimes too heavy to carry, illegally into the US. When they were unable to wash it, the cartel hid piles of cash in farmers' fields, rundown warehouses, in the walls of houses, mattresses, and spent $2500 a month alone on rubber bands to hold the wads of cash together. 'Pablo was earning so much that each year we would write off ten per cent of the money because the rats would eat it in storage or it would be damaged by water or lost,' his brother Roberto Escobar, the cartel's chief accountant, claimed.

BCCI's unscrupulous modus operandi could last only so long and an undercover US customs operation, with special agent Robert Mazur as the linchpin, would blow the lid off the whole grubby business. Mazur created the alias Bob Musella, a bogus financial high-flyer, and ingratiated himself with BCCI's Pakistani top brass, who were hell-bent on furthering their own careers by managing the shadowy banking needs of the Medellín Cartel. 'They were all very passionate about cricket,' Mazur explains to us. 'I can even recall an occasion in Miami when they hosted the Jamaican cricket team at a bank event.'

Mazur developed friendships with BCCI's cricketing bankers, who in turn had forged close relationships to cartel leaders. Bilgrami, with a polished charm and flawless English, was the darling of the drug lords. 'Bilgrami in particular was an avid cricket enthusiast,' remembers Mazur, who still lives behind a hidden identity decades later to protect him from violent reprisals. Bilgrami would receive invitations to spend weekends at Escobar's Hacienda Nápoles, east of Medellín, where he kept a zoo of exotic animals not native to Colombia. Escobar's menagerie included lions, kangaroos, elephants, giraffes and, most famously, hippos.

Bilgrami had served as the personal banker of Zayed bin Sultan Al Nahyan, BCCI's biggest shareholder and the man after whom the 20,000-capacity cricket stadium in Abu Dhabi would be named. 'Amjad Awan was another interested in the game,' Mazur adds. 'He handled the most sensitive clients including Manuel Noriega and Pakistan president Muhammad Zia-ul-Haq.'

Patrick Witcomb played a role in the BCCI investigation, but it was chief infiltrator Mazur who collated enough evidence to bring the corrupt bankers down. An ingenious plot was hatched to gather them all in Tampa, Florida, in October 1988 for the fictitious marriage of Mazur's alias to his fiancée, another undercover agent. The sting took place the night before when guests were whisked from the airport by limousines to a special 'bachelor party' but actually into the hands of the authorities in front of NBC News.

Colombian drug cartels laundered close to a billion dollars through BCCI and six of the bank's employees served jail time. BCCI was forced to close in July 1991. BCCC, the only subsidiary of BCCI in Latin America that did not shut its doors, was sold and renamed Banco Andino. It severed all ties with BCCI, and removed its Pakistani administrators. The cricket team disbanded not long after.

*     *     *

Even after morning rush hour our journey to Bogota Sports Club, sat in the back of a battered yellow taxi, takes an age. Colombia's capital is the most congested city in Latin America and diesel fumes belch out from exhausts as we crawl at snail's pace to the outskirts of the city. When we finally arrive at the place where Witcomb spent his childhood weekends, and BCCI's corrupt bankers wielded the willow, it is practically deserted.

The club's matting wicket has been ripped up, leaving a stretch of bare concrete in a grass field. Inside the main building our footsteps echo down the BSC's long empty corridors. Sporting trophies gather dust on the shelves, while Colombia's first snooker table has a thick maroon cover undisturbed in months. A large portrait of the Duke and Duchess of Cambridge in their wedding attire hangs next to a wood-panelled bar.

Hidden away, next to the toilets, are framed, fading reminders of BSC's cricket past. 'The majority of those pictured in the team photos from that golden era have gone – either died or moved away,' explains ex-BSC president Anthony Letts, a translator and former banker from his office in an uptown part of Bogotá later that day. 'The city has plenty of people from all around the world living here. But enthusiasm to be part of this type of club, even among the British, has withered.'

Bogota Cricket Club – which spawned BSC – was founded in 1955 and originally played on the fairway at San Andres

Golf Club, where Witcomb's MI6 father was a member. 'Cows and kikuyu grass are problems. The nature of the pitch seems to give dominance to the fast bowlers,' read one of club's annual reports from the era. Facing the quick bowling of John Weymes was described as a 'terrifying experience' and the highest batting average in the 1958–9 season was a modest 12.6. Weymes, a Foreign Office official who later became British consul in Guatemala and ambassador to Honduras, took 48 wickets at 4.04 the same season. Bogota CC made trips down to the southern tropical city of Santiago de Cali after matches were struck up with the office of Shell.

Ross Salmon, who later became the Test match statistician for BBC television, managed a ranch in Colombia at this time until he broke 14 bones in a jungle air crash. After recovering Salmon headed home where he became a children's TV star, as the Jungle Cowboy, riding into school playgrounds around Britain wearing a Stetson hat. In 1975 Salmon claimed to have discovered a lost city of the Incas in the Bolivian Amazon, bringing back axes, statues and 2000 feet of film on the indigenous marvel – all this some years before the Indiana Jones movies.

British residents in Bogotá were less fussed with such outlandish endeavours – they just wanted a club where they could spend their leisure time. Potential members were canvassed over a name, with 'The Spotted Dog' among those rejected in favour of Bogota Sports Club. In 1961 Bogota CC disbanded and amalgamated with the sports club, bringing with them '$3,730.50 plus 10 bottles of Black and White whisky'. The new club initially rented a wooden Spanish-style colonial house but it had structural problems and, during a card game, the floor collapsed.

Eventually BSC found a permanent home, which boasted a cricket pitch with a sizeable outfield, sightscreens and a scoring hut. Maintenance of the cricket facilities fell to members, although this was fraught with comical danger. Brian Chart once fell into a large barrel of whitewash while painting one of the sightscreens. The club suffered its first burglary at the end of the 1960s with bottled spirits and cash pilfered. BSC's care-taker asked for a shotgun to protect the cricket ground – a request the annual report notes was 'gracefully (and mercifully) turned down' by the club president.

Over the border in Venezuela, cricket also set down roots. A cadre of cricketing Scotsmen had, with 'their Sassenach breth-ren', set up Caracas CC in 1947 with matches against a team made up of West Indians. Oil companies with head offices in the Venezuelan capital then put up the cash for a ground and the cricketers founded the Caracas Sports Club in June 1951. A site was chosen in El Peñón, away from the city with views of the El Ávila mountain range, and heavy-duty machinery sliced away half a hillside to create a cricket ground. To this day, a hooked six rebounds off a chiselled, quarried face.

Caracas Sports Club's membership mushroomed from 30 to 300 throughout the 1960s but the British still insisted on certain things. 'In all my time there, Venezuelans never got to understand how to make a pot of tea,' says Ian Keys, one crick-eter from the era. 'Players brought sandwiches and cakes but it was left to one of the Venezuelans employed by CSC to make the tea. He always had to be told to put the heater on for the water, how many tea bags to put in and so on.'

Cricket relations were struck up between Colombia and Venezuela as Commonwealth populations in the two countries looked for rivalry, camaraderie or just a weekend jolly. Their fortunes would ebb and flow, mirroring the political and social situation in their respective countries. When the New Zealand Ambassadors XI turned up in Caracas in March 1970, they caught oil-rich Venezuela at its peak as South America's wealthiest country. The visiting Kiwis lapped up all the trappings of a city with some of the region's glitziest nightlife and swankiest restaurants thronging with the rich and beautiful.

CSC were easily brushed aside by the tourists in the first match, so former West Indies and Barbados batsman Norman Marshall hatched a plan the night before the second game. Marshall liberally plied his visitors with Cacique – a brand of dark Venezuelan rum – at a raucous party at his house and when CSC declared on 219 for eight against woozy opponents the following day it looked to have worked. But Barry Hadlee, brother of Richard, had a stronger constitution than most and compiled a beautiful 120 not out to see the tourists home. 'It was a very true wicket of rubberised compound plus a very hard fast outfield made batting easy,' Brian Adams of the Ambassadors scribbled in his tour diary. Caracas Sports Club's pitch even allowed close-fought matches to continue in tropical downpours according to Keys: 'Watching the incredulous expressions on some of the Venezuelan spectators' faces normally made the soaking worth it.'

Marshall, brother of Hampshire's daredevil batsman Roy Marshall, had been working in Caracas as an executive for sewing-machine company Singer, a position that later took him to Lima. But Robert Jones, a Barbadian financier and long-time resident in Caracas, remembered him as a cricketer who was never anything but full-blooded even when playing with humble clubbies. 'CSC were the first team to play at Windward Cricket Club's new ground up in Saint Philip,'

Jones tells us of one particular occasion where Marshall showed his competitive streak. 'Peter Short, then the president of the West Indies board, came in and guested for us and opened the batting with Norman. Even though he had finished professionally, Norman still took his cricket really seriously and was determined to be the first person to score a century at this new ground. Only for his good friend Peter to run him out without facing a ball! I don't think Norman ever forgave him.'

Caracas's proximity to the Caribbean afforded such links with Trinidad and Barbados, and CSC played at the Queen's Park Oval and Kensington Oval Test grounds. While Venezuela's economy boomed there was always an ex-West Indies Test cricketer around to sprinkle some stardust. Tony Skinner had played first-class cricket in the same Barbados side as the Three Ws, and turned out for CSC into his sixties. Denis Atkinson, who played 22 Tests for West Indies and helped nurture the young Garfield Sobers, hit the biggest six ever seen at CSC according to Jones: 'It came off Norman Marshall's son, Ray, up the hill and landed in the water tanks.'

CSC also ventured to the neighbouring Dutch Caribbean islands of Curaçao and Aruba. 'Curaçao was basically an oil refinery and oil terminal,' says Keys. 'It had four languages – Spanish, Dutch, English and Papiamento, a mixture of all of the others. We played on a matting wicket and there was not a blade of grass on the whole field as it rarely rained on the island. The outfield was dusty and quick.'

Life in Colombia, meanwhile, grew more dangerous as the 1970s became the 1980s. During a turbulent period, conflict raged between the government, organised crime, Marxist guerrillas and other paramilitary groups. 'Bogotá had been cleaned up for the Pope's visit,' observed Brian Adams, 'although there was a plane on the tarmac in the process of being hijacked to Cuba when we arrived . . .' The Ambassadors needed future Test players John Morrison and Andrew Roberts to bail them out against Bogota Sports Club as the hosts fell agonisingly short in pursuit of 95.

Venezuelan and Colombian nationals periodically joined in. Gustavo Gonzalez was perhaps the most accomplished, winning BSC's bowling award in 1974. Trips made between Caracas and Bogotá occasionally aroused the suspicion of officious border guards. BSC members returning by land one year had their precious cricket balls confiscated as 'suspicious objects', before overzealous officials sliced them open to look for drugs, in front of the heartbroken travelling cricketers.

One sun-bleached photograph at BSC from 1979 shows the team that took on the D. H. Robins XI, a side of leading under-25 English county players on a South American tour. Bogota's cricketers gave the visiting county tyros a fright. Norman Bracht took five for 74 as BSC bowled out the professionals for 184 – the only time on tour they were dismissed – but fell short in the chase. Bracht, a Canadian-Colombian, grew up in the city of Pasto, south-west of Bogotá, and with a slender and athletic 6 foot 2 inch frame was a dashing all-round sportsman.

Witcomb was high on Colombia's lists of kidnap targets because of his Escobar connection, but was never successfully captured. (His claimed ties to the drug kingpin were, however, later disputed by Escobar's recognised eldest son, Juan Pablo Escobar Henao.) Others were not so lucky. In July 1997 Bracht, who worked with precious metals, was seized by members of the Marxist terrorist organisation Ejército de Liberación Nacional (ELN) in El Bagre some 300 miles north of Bogotá. By coincidence, it was not the first time he had encountered his captors. Bracht had helped the heavily pregnant wife of one the guerrillas a few months earlier when his truck was flagged down in the Antioquia jungle.

The ELN, citing environmental damage along with their class struggle, demanded the titles of the gold mine from the company for which Bracht worked. In the wait for them to be handed over Bracht spent two months trudging around remote jungle areas of Colombia with his captors. He was eventually released unharmed by the ELN commander, who remembered his good turn, although he had to make his own way back to civilisation. When Bracht was reunited with his family at Bogotá Airport after three months, they recognised him only by his shoes.

Bracht's ordeal was far from an isolated incident, and three years later two British travellers were held hostage by suspected Fuerzas Armadas Revolucionarias de Colombia (FARC) rebels in the Darién Gap bordering Panama. Tom Hart Dyke, the horticulturist cousin of comedian Miranda Hart, was captured in 2000 while searching for rare orchids along with companion Paul Winder, a merchant banker. The health of the pair suffered in the jungle as they witnessed violence and feared for their lives. Eventually, though, they formed a rapport with their insouciant captors and taught them how to play cricket using equipment fashioned from the jungle. Hart Dyke and Winder were released after nine months. 'Every one of them had the usual ubiquitous AK-47,' Winder said of the FARC guerrillas. 'They also had trouble with lbw.' FARC disarmed itself in June 2017 after signing a peace deal and re-formed as a political party, but around 2000 dissidents remain active.

Bracht was blighted by gout but championed cricket in Colombia until he died of a heart attack in a Medellín restaurant in 2011. Sharing the new ball with Bracht against the

D. H. Robins XI in 1979 was a guest from Caracas Sports Club and a former West Indies Test cricketer. Tony White was a fair-skinned tenacious Barbadian who toured England in 1963, without playing a Test, as back-up for Lance Gibbs. White switched between medium pace and off-spin and was a diligent middle-order batsman who top-scored with 57 not out against Australia at Kingston on his Test debut in 1965 under the captaincy of Sobers. 'White flew up to BSC from Caracas and still bowled tidy little off-cutters,' recalled Henry Blofeld, joint manager on the Robins tour.

Even in his early forties White's pedigree was beyond South America's amateur cricketers. When CSC toured Peru in April 1980 he made an elegant 114 in a two-day match against Lima Cricket & Football Club. 'It was his judgement of a single, ability to rotate the strike and running between the wickets which stood out,' remembers Michael Palmer, whose father Norman worked for Shell and was a founding member of CSC. 'All of his shots were stroked, beautifully and effortlessly, along the ground.'

Caracas's former players believe White's talent was never quite realised in the West Indies. He was alleged to have fallen out with selectors during his playing days and turned down a post in the leagues in Lancashire. 'He should have played more than two Tests,' says ex-CSC cricketer Colin Wedge, who gave White a job with his IT company for a time. 'He was a superb cricketer and one of the greatest fielders in the world at one time. But he had a habit of getting into rows on the field. He had a habit of having a row with everybody in life, really.'

*　　*　　*

A Colombian with the blood of an Irish Catholic liberator running through his veins was the original cricket pioneer in Bogotá. Daniel O'Leary was the son of a Cork butter merchant but sought swashbuckling adventures in the wars of South American independence. O'Leary had not fought in the Napoleonic Wars, but was nonetheless appointed aide-de-camp to Simón Bolívar, became a bona fide hero of Venezuelan independence, married the daughter of a high-ranking general, and was awarded the prestigious Order of the Liberator.

Bolívar died of tuberculosis in 1830, though arsenic poisoning was later suspected. Gabriel García Márquez imagined his final days in *The General in His Labyrinth* as a gaunt, coughing and bedridden man. During this sickly end Bolívar instructed O'Leary to burn his myriad writings, letters and speeches. O'Leary's love and devotion for *El Libertador* extended to naming his first-born Simón Bolívar O'Leary, but he ignored Bolívar's deathbed request and devoted much of the rest of his life to organising and chronicling the papers alongside 32 volumes of his own memoirs. The Corkman – who corresponded with 'The Emancipator' Daniel O'Connell back in Ireland – later settled on a *hacienda* in Bogotá.

O'Leary's grandson was sent to St Edmund's College in Ware, England's oldest Catholic school, and returned to Colombia with a passion for cricket. Julio Portocarrero O'Leary coached, taught the Laws of the game and sourced equipment. Naturalist Carlos Michelsen bequeathed land for Colombia's first cricket ground south of Bogotá. His father Karl, a Danish Jew, had been sent by relatives in the Rothschild family to further their banking empire. Old Etonian Carlos Ordóñez became Bogota Cricket Club's captain on its foundation in 1897.

Portocarrero O'Leary and Ordóñez looked to the Bogotá liberal elite, including students from the Colegio de Rueda, for their cricketers. Among them was Dr Carlos Esguerra, who later persuaded fellow physicians to allow space for a small cricket ground at the Marly sanatorium he opened in Chapinero, north of Bogotá. Ordóñez would only occupy the crease for a couple of years. He became an officer in the government's army during Colombia's Thousand Days' War and died of a fever on the Río Magdalena.

After the civil war, foreigners joined the fray with matches now social occasions at La Magdalena jockey club, compared to Longchamp by Bogotá's press. They included William Boshell, a suave Colombia-born British secret-service agent, who took time out from espionage assignments to open the batting. A write-up from *Bogotá Ilustrado* in April 1907 was particularly effusive in its praise of cricket, claiming it would equip young men with the virtues to become *filipichines* – the best turned-out gents in Bogotá.

Shortly after his death, Daniel O'Leary's remains were moved from Bogotá to the National Pantheon in Caracas, near to those of his beloved Bolívar. Venezuela's favourite son even appears to have dabbled with cricket. The teenage Bolívar was sent from Caracas to undertake military studies in Spain between 1800 and 1802. *The Delirium of the Liberator* cited a conversation at the Palace of Aranjuez, in Madrid, between the commander of the guard and Manuel Godoy, eventual prime minister of Spain. Godoy enquired after Bolívar's whereabouts only to be told he was 'playing cricket with Prince Fernando [of Asturias]'. The author went on to write 'the product of the match, Simón knocked down the cap of who in years later would be King of Spain'.

Cricket surfaced in Bolívar's home city 60 years after his death. Influential Venezuelan merchant Marcos Santana was the early benefactor of the Caracas Cricket Club. 'After a hard struggle there is a club together of thirty members – more than half are Venezuelans,' the *Venezuelan Herald* reported in March 1894. 'The Englishmen in the country have been trying for some time to infuse interest in true sport into the Venezuelan mind.'

The club's first match was a 14-a-side affair between teams named after Santana and Mr E. Woodard. Santana made a useful 13, outscoring three family members, who managed a combined total of two runs across both innings. However, Albert Cherry, who was behind the city's first electric tram network, gave Santana's side the win with 12 wickets and 35 runs. 'We had the best people in Caracas as onlookers and they all seemed interested; we greatly hope to make cricket a national game here,' the *Herald* optimistically added.

Whenever Caracas's players assembled at the club's ground, next to the Petare railway station, they were accosted by the flotsam and jetsam of society. One legless beggar was a well-known figure at railway stations. He claimed to have lost his legs after being crushed by a monstrous serpent, which coiled around him and prepared to make a meal of him before friends had come to his aid.

The soothing wiles of play at Caracas CC gave sporadic comfort to the incumbents of Petare's Hospital de Lázaros, an infirmary whose intake was afflicted by leprosy. 'A plaza covers almost the entire frontage, and the rows of white pillars look quite pretty for a stranger approaching from the cricket grounds,' wrote a *New York Herald* correspondent in 1896 after a chilling visit.

It is a long white building of probably 200 feet. A cow tied to a tree before the main entrance was tugging at her rope and the place looked not unlike a well-kept farmhouse. On one side of a passageway sat two patients. They were both mulattos and the only outward evidence of the infirmity was both wore great green goggles. On the steps facing them sat men with the most hideous faces I have ever seen. An odd fellow in the centre had enormous ulcers on both his cheeks; others were swollen and discoloured.

Petare today is an uncompromising working-class neighbourhood, and one of South America's toughest slums. Half a million people occupy every nook and cranny in 15.4 square miles of houses built on top of each other in an area that used to be a bastion of support for the Bolívarian socialism of Hugo Chávez. Incredibly, cricket returned to Petare a couple of years ago when it was chosen by the United Nations for an International Day of Sport for Development and Peace. The cricket ground has long gone, but in a baseball diamond in the shadows of the barrios, lined by carts selling *arepas*, children were introduced to the game, affording a few hours' respite from life's daily struggle.

*   *   *

Old-timers sitting out on wooden verandas in Cabimas, on the banks of Lake Maracaibo, can still just about recall the spots where they used to gather during their leisure time at weekends. The majority are originally from Trinidad which, seven miles off the Venezuelan coast, had long been a trading partner as well as a haven for smugglers and sanctuary for political exiles escaping mainland South America. These mainly black Trinidadians came in their thousands in search of work and a means to better their lives. What brought them was oil.

Lake Maracaibo sprawls over a vast 5100 square miles. It is home to an atmospheric phenomenon known as Catatumbo lightning, caused by unsettled weather systems, which brings on average 260 storm days per year, and more electrical storms than anywhere else in the world. But what defines the Maracaibo Basin is the large reserves of crude oil.

The first foreign oil companies were welcomed to Maracaibo with open arms by the Venezuelan government, though that was not to everyone's taste. In 1918 Venezuelan novelist José Rafael Pocaterra compared the oil prospectors to the Spanish conquest: 'One day some "Spaniards" mounted a dark apparatus on three legs, a grotesque stork with crystal eyes. They drew something (on a piece of paper) and opened their way through the forest. Other new "Spaniards" would open roads . . . would drill the earth from the top of fantastic towers, producing the fetid fluid . . . the liquid gold converted into petroleum.'

The trickle of oil became a torrent. Immigrants from all over the world descended on the port of Maracaibo and the lake's new source of wealth. There seemed again to be a suspicious preference for African-Caribbean workers. One internal memo from an oil company said: 'The British negroe is thrifty, home-loving and industrious and has an excellent temperament, with few of the Latin characteristics such as excitability, irresponsibility.'

But the arrival of so many workers from Trinidad put the frighteners up Venezuela's elite. In 1936 the Maracaibo newspaper *Panorama* ran an anonymous story under the headline '*El Peligro Negro*' – 'The Black Threat'. A Trinidadian vendor named Joseph Cook was shot three times by a police officer in Caracas after an argument following the heinous crime of selling ice and sweets outside a permitted area.

Royal Dutch Shell, Standard Oil and Gulf Oil became the big players in Lake Maracaibo and the oil camps were communities within themselves. The inauguration of the Caribbean Club at the Cabimas camp in 1928 brought a crowd of 500 and the Caresser's Home Sweet Home calypso played until 4 a.m. the next morning. Early workers from the Caribbean brought cricket equipment for informal knockabouts, and by the 1930s it became more organised. Cricket leagues in the oilfield danced to a complex mix of inter-camp and inter-company rivalries. The West Indian oil worker returning home with his 'splattered khaki clothes, aluminium hardhat, boots and shiny metal lunch pail' would clean himself up and pull on his spotless pressed whites.

English-language match reports were carried in the *Maracaibo Herald* and then the *Maracaibo Times*, the latter owned and edited by Phillip Citroen and his brother. Citroen's name cropped up in a recent declassified CIA report from Maracaibo, as he produced what he claimed was a post-war photograph of himself and Adolf Hitler. Hitler, Citroen claimed in the mid-1950s, was living among Nazi sympathisers in the Colombian town of Tunja who saluted and addressed him as '*Der Führer*'. Investigating CIA officer George Warbis noted the 'negatives of the photograph were too poor to make copies from', and dismissed Citroen's claims as 'apparent fantasy'.

In 1941 the local press hailed the Campo Rojo team of Lagunillas – a town built on wooden stilts – as they beat all-comers from Zulia to be crowned 'champions of Lake Maracaibo' with medals and a trophy provided by Creole

Petroleum. Later that year, the sports pages of the national newspapers were dominated by another bat-and-ball sport, which had jostled with cricket for space on the multi-purpose sports grounds of the oil camps.

A substantial US influence in the country's oil industry had put baseball in the mind of Venezuelans, but a shock win over home favourites Cuba in the final of the World Amateur Baseball Series in Havana cemented it firmly into the nation's hearts. The victory sent Venezuela into a baseball frenzy: schools, businesses and offices closed as a third of the country's population crowded the 21-mile stretch of road from La Guaria to Caracas to welcome the players home as conquering heroes. A Venezuelan professional baseball league followed in 1945 and, in a rarity for South America, football firmly plays second fiddle in the country.

The flow of British West Indians to the oilfields declined after the war, but those who remained and hoped for a game of cricket would have been lucky to make it past the security gate. While bread-and-butter workers lived in the oil camps, the senior company workers enjoyed a privileged existence in expensive houses where the wants of their families were met. In the private homes, a whole sub-industry for maids, cleaners, cooks and drivers was created. The preference for English speakers ensured West Indians, especially women, filled the positions. Richard Schroder, whose Dutch father worked for Shell, gave a more benevolent appraisal of this life in the late 1950s as racial barriers began to come down. 'We had a woman from Trinidad and later her daughter arrived. They were never treated as slaves or servants but we considered them maids,' he tells us. 'They had their own quarters in the house. My parents helped pay for their younger children's schooling in Trinidad.'

Segregation along racial lines was still commonplace in the 1950s. The white wooden door of a lavatory in the office of a major oil producer in Maracaibo used to have a note pinned on it: 'Toilet only for Americans'. Even when the US civil rights movement began to change attitudes an old-school elitism still prevailed. 'Lubrication oil sales have dropped five percent,' said a famous cable telegraphed to Shell's commercial London office. 'Send two more cricket Blues.'

The lavish expat hangout in Maracaibo was the Bella Vista Club, and it was here the upper crust pulled on their whites and public school caps, ate cream teas and pined for home on Sundays. One member was Michael Pocock, who would subsequently become the chairman of Shell in 1977. Pocock's son Nick learned his early cricket at the club, and would become the only first-class cricketer born in Venezuela, going on to captain Hampshire in the first half of the 1980s. 'My father was right at the top of Shell,' says Nick. 'He played in Maracaibo where my mother used to complain about making the sandwiches, before we moved to Caracas.'

Representatives from the Pocock and Schroder families would make the journey to neighbouring Colombia, where Maracaibo Shell would face Bogotá's cricketers. The first 'international' match in February 1958 was one of the first live sporting events outside of football televised, in black and white, by Colombia's state broadcaster.

The winds of change were blowing through Venezuela's oil industry, especially at Shell. Dutchman John Hugo Loudon rose from working on the rigs and derricks of Lake Maracaibo to Shell's managing director in 1952. He subsequently made a key change to company policy, encouraging more nationals to be hired in regional bases, which reduced the number of cricketing Shell expats across the globe. He was a distant cousin of Alex Loudon, once of Kent and Warwickshire, who played a solitary ODI for England in 2006.

Of greater impact on cricket was nationalisation. In 1970 Venezuela's oil industry had reached an all-time high of 3.8 million barrels per day, contributing to a GDP not far behind the US. Four years later the industry became a state monopoly, and a long and steady decline followed. Political interference saw skilled foreign workers dismissed, and a failure to invest in technology. Corruption became rife. Oil production in Venezuela today has fallen to under 900,000 barrels a day – closer to 1950s levels – with environmental issues swept under the carpet. The effect of government over-reliance on a misman-aged industry has left the country in turmoil.

Trinidadians who came to the oilfields in Lake Maracaibo were neither the first significant groups from the Caribbean to settle in Venezuela, nor the first cricketers from the region. More than 3000 West Indian labourers had worked on cacao plantations between Carúpano, Yaguaraparo and Güiria in the previous century. One of the companies who imported cacao from Venezuela was Bristol-based Fry's, later to become synonymous with Turkish delight. The Fry's company cricket team began life at Pembroke Road, Clifton, in 1872 and despite being 5000 miles away played under the banner of Caracas Cricket Club, in homage to a new cocoa drink the company was making at this time.

Venezuela's first matches were played in more remote areas. El Callao had been a gold-mining centre since 1853, but the rush arrived two decades later with British engineers and geolo-gists. The mines became the world's leading producer of gold, with the back-breaking labour reserved for West Indians. From the 1870s workers and owners would put status aside for cricket in towns such as El Callao and El Dorado, named after the mythical gold city.

El Callao was an almost entirely English-speaking town but firmly on Venezuelan soil as defined by the Schomburgk Line, the hotly disputed border with British Guiana drawn up by a German-born British explorer in 1841. Many West Indians settled in the region, and by the time Henri Charrière – Papillon – permanently walked free from El Dorado prison in 1945, cricket was still played in the area. North from El Callao, up the Río Caroní from the Guri Dam, Guyanese immigrants in San Felix and Puerto Ordaz – the two towns that make up Venezuela's Guayana City – still play the odd game. Venezuelan–Guyanese relations continue to flare up over oil-exploration rights in disputed maritime areas. The Caribbean flavour in the region is warmly celebrated at *carnaval*, though, when the sound of Calypso de El Callao – a unique fusion of West Indian and Venezuelan music with steel drums – fills the night air.

*       *       *

In a makeshift wooden hut near where the Pomeroon River meets the Atlantic on Guyana's coast, a group of indigenous Arawak were at breaking point. They watched their brothers and sisters slain in the bloody Rupununi uprising of 1968 – three years after the country's independence from British colonial rule. They endured political marginalisation in the 1970s and were festooned in economic deprivation. Arawak elders debated long into the night, and eventually declared: enough was enough. Guyana was their beloved home, but toleration of ethnic and cultural persecution could continue no longer. It was time to start afresh. Away from the brutality of the regime of Guyanese president Forbes Burnham, which had brought the Arawak and other indigenous groups two sorrowful decades of pain and anguish.

So 17 families, many from the villages of Wakapoa and Santa Rosa, packed up their belongings and left Guyana for the jungle. They walked on foot, the Arawak elders guiding the group along traditional routes used by their ancestors. The Arawak's hand-crafted machetes cut a path through the bush, as they evaded deadly snakes, and did not stop until they found sanctuary. Men, women and children crossed into neighbouring Venezuela away from the eyes of the Guyana Defence Force and border guards – many of the Arawak never owned a passport anyway. This small Arawak group mourned their past, shed a tear for Guyana, and started to rebuild their lives.

Daniel Gomez, now in his late fifties but with a shock of long black curly hair and a flat torso, was among those who made the journey as a young man in 1986. 'Many of us chose Venezuela, because they were our neighbour and also knowing that indigenous people are treated as the equal of any man,' he says. Even though Burnham's policies were African-centric, the Arawak harboured no resentment towards their black Guyanese cricket heroes; they had celebrated Clive Lloyd, Colin Croft and Roy Fredericks like any West Indian – although they especially idolised Basil Butcher, who had been the first person of part-indigenous descent, via his mother, to represent West Indies.

The Arawak had been the first people to greet Christopher Columbus when he arrived in the New World. Nobody can quite recall when watching and playing cricket became stitched into their lives. Peeking through the gaps in the walls to watch

Test matches at boisterous Bourda, Georgetown, where the Arawak sold fruit on Regent Street and North Road, piqued the interest of some. As if stuck in a time warp, Gomez regularly namechecks the Shell Shield when discussing his West Indian cricket idols – the oil company sponsored the West Indies' domestic first-class competition from 1966 to 1986.

Crossing the border into a remote part of Venezuela ought to have spelled the end of cricket for Gomez and the Arawak. After they were issued with Venezuelan citizenship the focus, naturally, was on establishing life on land given to them by the government in what is now known as San Flaviano in KM 46. But, improbably, some of the elders had felt compelled, against a backdrop of political and cultural oppression, to pack some cricket kit and haul it across the jungle. 'We kept the English language alive by talking and listening to English music,' explains Gomez, who originally answers to the Portuguese 'Gomes' back in Guyana. 'But most of all we brought cricket. When we came, the whole Arawak community cleared a cricket oval in the jungle.'

Once the initial bats and balls broke the Arawak had no way to obtain fresh supplies. So they used whatever they could to keep the game alive. 'We made cricket bats out of corkwood trees, pads out of cardboard boxes and played with baseballs,' Gomez enthusiastically adds in his soothing Guyanese accent. 'Spectators used coconut leaves with painted numbers on them to post the score.' Word spread, and in its 1980s heyday San Flaviano's ground staged tournaments with visiting teams, largely from the displaced Guyanese diaspora in Venezuela. 'Our cricket brought people from as far south as the Gran Sabana Plateau,' Gomez says. 'Huge crowds came to see us play. Once an English tourist came to us. He was so impressed that he sent a complete set of cricket gear a month later. Then we *really* played cricket.'

A faded photograph gives a snapshot into this period: two captains with their backs to the camera captured moments after the toss. One is wearing full whites, and both are examining an immaculate pitch and lush outfield. Gomez tells us the Arawak mastered how to prepare a 'true' deck in the jungle: they dug the earth down 6 inches, filled it with straw and then packed red clay on top. It was rolled by Toyota pick-up trucks then finished with a light roller. 'The tournaments were held in a carnival atmosphere,' beams Gomez. 'The players were treated like royalty. Guyana is a nation of six races, so we had a whole range of different food and drink. Nobody would want to leave.'

Two Australian brothers – Kendon and Ben Glass – were cycling through Venezuela in 2003 and were flagged down by Gomez as they passed San Flaviano, when he spotted a Kookaburra bat poking out of a rucksack. Although the jungle had reclaimed most of the cricket ground and the last pieces of kit had perished sometime in the previous decade, the Glass brothers were itching for a hit. Gomez dug an old cricket ball out of a trophy cabinet housing the community's cricket memorabilia, and the trio gathered the town's children out on to the green sward for an impromptu match. 'Cricket is still in our blood,' Gomez says with a smile. 'There's a man here who is eighty-six years old and when he hears of cricket his face lights up. You want to get something out of him? Just start talking cricket.'

Gomez still dreams of one day clearing the cricket field for matches once again. 'Some of our cricket players emigrated to the US, some went back to Guyana and some went to other

A contender for the oldest cricket photograph in Latin America – a match underway at the City of Mexico Cricket Club, 1865, with Chapultepec Castle in the background. *(Roger Mann Collection)*

Vienna-born Emperor Maximilian I, Mexico's last monarch and a cricketer, pictured near the stumps clutching a straw boater. He was shot by firing squad in 1867. *(Musée Royal de l'Armée in Brussels/François Aubert)*

Mexico's greatest-ever all-round sportsman Claude Butlin, pictured with some of the 500-plus trophies. His name is barely known in the country today. *(Reforma Athletic Club/Claudia Cervantes)*

Mexico City's Mark Lawrence, wearing a headband, sighs after John Barnes belts him down the ground for four at Reforma Athletic Club in 1985. Gary Lineker, at the non-striker's end, would top-score and keep wicket in a comfortable victory for England's footballers.
(Bob Thomas, Rex/Shutterstock)

The striking pavilion is the perfect place to watch play at Reforma, where Fred Trueman bowled with a bit more zip at high altitude on the world's second-highest turf wicket.
(Ben Chaplin)

(above) James Coyne fends off a delivery from fellow author Timothy Abraham in Cancún. A statue of NFL running back Walter Payton nestled inside a mock-Roman archway provides the curious backdrop at the Instituto Americano Leonardo da Vinci. (Timothy Abraham/James Coyne)

(left) A modern Claude Butlin? Mexico's Anjuli Ladrón has represented her country at cricket, football, NFL and footgolf. She's also a handy boxer, rugby player and javelin thrower. (Cricket Mexico/Magdalena De Gante)

Bertie Ellis at his home in Belize City. A fine cricketer in his day, and just as good a storyteller at a healthy 99 not out.
*(Timothy Abraham/James Coyne)*

For many years Belizean batsmen played without gloves, wearing perhaps only one pad and it was customary for non-strikers to crouch with their bat or foot rooted behind the crease until a call for a run.
*(Elston Wade)*

Belize's Mykelt Anthony takes a Panama wicket in an ICC World Cricket League match at Hurlingham, Buenos Aires, 2014. The following year Anthony sustained spinal injuries in a shooting which left him unable to play the sport he loves. *(ICC Americas)*

From left to right, brothers Marvin, Kevin and Geovanny Jolón Yucute in Guatemala. The trio turned to cricket and God as they escaped the gangs of Santiago Sacatepéquez. *(Timothy Abraham/James Coyne)*

Miguel Villalta pictured at the Volcano Cup in El Salvador with Costa Rica's players in a huddle behind. Marathon runner Miguel became the first Salvadorian to score a century in 2013, after winning a race earlier in the day. *(Timothy Abraham/James Coyne)*

Tomás Vaughan at the family finca in the hills south of Managua. The farm was in the eye of the storm when the Sandinistas ousted the Somoza dictatorship in Nicaragua in 1979. *(Timothy Abraham/James Coyne)*

George Headley's early days in Panama helped shape him as the first great West Indies batsman. He always kept his snappy Latin dress sense. *(National Library of Australia)*

Colón, Panama, in 1913, when George Headley was living there as an infant. *(Ullstein Bild/Getty Images)*

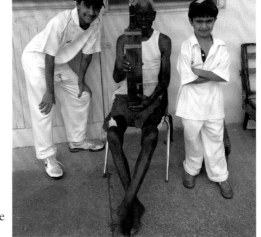

'Jackman', the irascible groundsman at Paraíso, a six-hit away from the Panama Canal, with two young cricketers. He was a childhood friend of George Headley, but sadly passed away before we could meet him. *(Saleh Bhana)*

The Parque Felipe E. Motta in the otherwise sterile business district of Costa del Este, Panama City transforms into a slice of India every Sunday. *(Timothy Abraham/James Coyne)*

Phillip Witcomb, born Roberto Sendoya Escobar and the son of notorious Colombian drug lord Pablo Escobar, sitting first on the left with his teammates for Lucton School U15s in 1977. *(Phillip Witcomb Private Collection)*

Mechanic Tony Williams, with protégé Kevin David, carving cricket bats and stumps at his workshop in Santiago de Cali, Colombia. *(Timothy Abraham/James Coyne)*

Cricket was played in the simmering heat all over the Atacama Desert by miners in the 19th century and again on a concrete wicket at Toquepala, Peru in the 1970s. *(Walter Rodriguez)*

Cricket Peru's development officer Samantha Hickman runs some wide-eyed Peruvian youngsters through a few batting drills at the Colegio Johannes Gutenberg on the outskirts of Lima. *(Cricket Peru)*

Indigenous Ecuadorian children prove that ponchos are no barrier to strokeplay after being introduced to cricket at the Foundation Sumak Kawsay Yachay in Salasaca. *(Foundation Sumak Kawsay Yachay)*

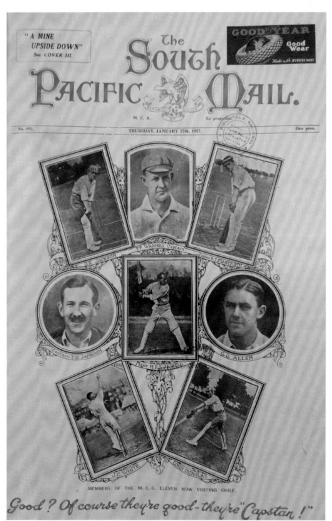

Chile's *South Pacific Mail* heralds the arrival of the star English players in Plum Warner's 1926–7 MCC side for the match at Viña del Mar. *(South Pacific Mail)*

The breathtaking vista of the snow-capped Andes provides a stunning backdrop for cricket in Santiago, Chile during the Junior South American Championship. *(Mike Meade/Cricket Chile)*

places,' he tells us wistfully. 'Maybe with the younger generation . . . there is space in the village, still. I will never lose hope.'
San Flaviano just needs equipment which, given Venezuela's
recent plight, has been beyond their means. For the time being,
a tinny radio tuned into the BBC World Service, listening out
for crackly updates from international matches around the
globe, is his only link to the global cricket world.

*    *    *

Colombian diners at Restaurante el Kioskón de Rozo, 12
miles north-east of Cali, used to flinch whenever they heard a
loud thwack. Englishman David Muirhead had revived
cricket in Cali and, short of a place to practise, persuaded his
partner to let him build nets in the garden of her restaurant.
It meant patrons had to look up from their bowls of *sancocho
de gallina* to keep an eye out for flying objects. The food on
offer was so good it was a minor inconvenience for bemused
customers as cricketers sheepishly interrupted family get-
togethers and romantic soirées to retrieve their battered net
balls. We miss out on the chance of a net, though, as our visit
one Sunday coincides with a monthly gathering of Cali's
British community, so all the cricketers are too busy wolfing
down fish and chips and mushy peas while guzzling imported
cider.

The Cali v. Bogotá rivalry resumed in 2002, after a 21-year
hiatus, when the sides played for the Ernie Field Cup, named
after one of Colombia's star cricketers from the 1970s. Cali
play at Colegio Colombo Británico and, like the bulk of
modern cricketers in South America, are likely to be English
teachers, translators or hostel owners. Among Cali's cricketers

is Mancunian Dave Procter, who founded La Leyenda del Dorado, a mountain stage race in a country obsessed with road cycling. Ike Isaksen, another Brit, carved his own niche in the Caleño community with a range of homemade chutneys and marmalades.

Cali, the tropical home of salsa dancing, has produced most of Colombia's home-grown cricketers and almost all of them have come to it via Tony Williams. He tells us the most important items he takes with him to cricket training on the school-yard over the road from his garage every Saturday morning are not bats and balls. 'I took one thousand pesos-worth of sand-wiches and five hundred pesos-worth of drinks to my first session,' he says. 'They all disappeared within a few minutes. I soon realised what I was dealing with.'

Williams is a black Guyanese, and when he left school, he ignored the friends who told him to head to England, instead crossing south into Brazil, where he worked for three years as a mechanic, before washing up in Colombia. We meet in the organised chaos of his workshop in Cali, which he established 35 years ago.

Far from the stereotype of Escobar's drug-ridden playground, tourist-friendly Colombia is now among the safest and most prosperous countries in Latin America. But dissident groups will continue to gain support while there is such a divide between rich and poor.

'In Colombia, they talk a lot about peace,' says Williams, a softly spoken man of Christian conviction. 'Peace is not some-thing that falls from the sky. The real change must come from the younger ones.' He points out of his window up the hill. 'We're not far from the Cauca River here. By the dam of the river, there are illegal houses made from bamboo and plastic.

There's lots of prostitution, crime and drugs there. The good people up there are the ones who really need help. In my classes we keep them off the road, and give them a distraction, something positive to do.' Williams believes a couple of teenage girls have been saved from drugs and prostitution by coming along to these cricket sessions.

He encourages boys such as musclebound Kevin David, the most promising of his Cali Juniors, to come by and use his workshop to carve their own bats. They are painted in a dazzling range of colours, and out of some old car parts Williams has constructed durable spring-loaded metal stumps for practice. 'At first I had cast-off bats from the Cali club, which quickly got worn out. So I made the first from a plank of wood under my bed. That was just to show the kids how to play. Back home in Guyana we used to do the same thing.'

It can be hard to win over families on the breadline, who tend to see cricket as a foreign frippery. 'One of the boys didn't come last week because he was punished for not doing some chores at the house. He has a broken bat, which he had painted and tied over his bedhead as a treasure. For a mother, it's just an old piece of wood, and she wanted to throw it away. For him, it's his first bat.'

Williams chose cricket for the instances it throws up where the participants have to make a reconciliation – with the opponent, the umpire's decision or themselves. 'There are some tricky moments in cricket. Like when you know someone is lbw, and you ask the batsman, "Well, was it?" He can say, "Yes it was." That makes my skin stand on end. He could just say "No," but he admits, "Yes, I'm out." Sometimes I provoke the kids: they know it's the wrong decision, but then they respect the wrong decision. I'm not looking for the best batsman or bowler. I'm looking for the complete person.'

\*      \*      \*

There is a smattering of Colombian cricketers in the capital, among them Jairo Andres Venegas. He is Colombia's first cider producer, keeps wicket, and tells us over a sparkling glass of his Golden Lion brew that he is so fascinated with the game he is writing his PhD on it. But Bogotá's cricketers have been forced to switch play to the Los Pinos Polo Club in Mosquera, on the outskirts of the capital, after Bogota Sports Club fell into financial strife and ratcheted up the ground fees.

The presence of 1000 British Petroleum staff in Colombia during the 1990s turned out to be a brief false dawn for BSC. BP's presence was highly controversial amid local human rights abuses, alleged payments to the Colombian army, and environmental issues with the Ocensa pipeline. BP sold the remainder of its Colombian assets in 2010 to pay for the Deepwater Horizon oil spill, leaving Amerisur, headed by former England & Wales Cricket Board chairman Giles Clarke, as the UK's largest oil producer in Colombia. If anyone from the Colombia Cricket Board was contemplating sending Clarke an email for sponsorship it may be best left in the drafts folder. Oil and cricket, it seems, are a volatile mix. Ever since BP packed up their Colombian operations, BSC was living on borrowed time, and the clubhouse was sold in 2018 to a nearby hospital as a social club for its staff.

Over the border, Caracas Sports Club limps on. Venezuela did make a fleeting appearance at the South American Championship in 2000, but barely scraped a side together. In their match against hosts Argentina, three local schoolboys aged 10, 12 and 14 made up the numbers. At that time, it was still safe enough for touring sides to visit Caracas. Former West Indies opener Faoud Bacchus, then in his mid-forties and enjoying a second international career as USA captain, struck twin centuries for the Miami Masters at CSC. The last Caracas v. Bogotá match was in 2002, to celebrate CSC's fiftieth anniversary.

Venezuela has since plunged into a humanitarian crisis following hyperinflation that has left its currency next to worthless. Shelves are empty and refrigerators bare while queues to obtain essentials such as toilet paper can be several hours long. The politics of Chávez's successor Nicolás Maduro, president since 2013, has taken Venezuela and its citizens to the brink. Starvation and desperation have fuelled a dizzying homicide rate. Four million Venezuelans have emigrated since 1999 – a staggering 13 per cent of the population.

Almost all of CSC's cricket-playing members beat a hasty retreat. The equipment they left behind has been raided and sometimes put to barbaric use. A cricket bat was used by prison officers to beat up political prisoners critical of Maduro at the Uribana Penitentiary Center. The guards had inked a harrowing inscription on the blade: 'Defence of human rights'. CSC members cling on to the hope the situation will improve. 'The irony is that when we used to go to Colombia *they* had bars on the windows. Venezuela was paradise!' says Colin Wedge. 'It has all turned around. I think there's a point when governments give up on the population and just worry about themselves.'

It is a great irony that nowhere is doing better in Colombia than Medellín, Escobar's city. Medellín Cricket Club, founded in 2014 by Jake Macmillan, compete in the Colombian

National Championship alongside Bogotá and Cali. Macmillan shows us where their informal games started at the back of the city's modern art museum in downtown Parque Lineal Ciudad del Rio, to the curiosity of grungy skateboarders and bohemian marijuana smokers.

That encapsulates the journey cricket has made since it was played under a veneer of formality at Medellín's exclusive Club Campestre in the 1920s and 1930s. Escobar and his Medellín Cartel cronies were never granted membership of Campestre, as Colombia's upper classes took a sneering attitude to their tawdry flashiness. Just down the road from the club we gaze up at the Monaco building, a brutalist eight-storey concrete criminal fortress which Escobar put up in the 1980s. Escobar's bunker had been empty since he was killed in 1993, a day after his forty-fourth birthday, by Search Bloc, a Colombian task force, as he attempted to flee across the rooftops.

The Netflix series *Narcos* sprinkled glamour on the Escobar years, and many of our fellow backpackers gleefully sign up for tours of Pablo's hotspots in Medellín. But most Colombians we speak to want to move on from a turbulent period and the association with cocaine. In the grip of the Medellín Cartel the number of homicides surged to 7723 in 1991 as the city became the murder capital of the world. By 2017 this figure was down to 577. The Medellín we experience is a thriving, vibrant and welcoming city, with seemingly the most integrated – and cleanest – transport system in all of South America.

Two years after our visit, in early 2019, a crowd in the thousands gathered on the old cricket ground at Club Campestre to watch as the Monaco building was blown up in a government ceremony. 'It is not about deleting the past, it is not about deleting history,' declared Medellín's mayor Federico Gutiérrez, after Escobar's home went up in a cloud of smoke. 'It is to return and tell the story from the right side, the victims' side, not the perpetrators'.'

It is a sentiment Phillip Witcomb, who now works as an artist, shares concerning his biological father, even in spite of the ongoing obsession with Escobar. 'I am not proud of my father's achievements,' he adds sombrely. 'Pablo Escobar was a mass murderer, had sex with children and caused misery for the world. Nobody would be proud of that. I was relieved when he died, it was a weight off my shoulders.'

# 6

# Peru

## *From Lima to Lord's*

HARRY HILDEBRAND WAS pacing down the aisles of his local branch of Santa Isabel supermarket one Sunday morning with a tad more urgency than normal. Those who know him will tell you that Harry, a tall, congenial guitar-playing Australian teacher in his fifties with a near-permanent grin, sometimes leaves things until the last minute. On this occasion he had enlisted the help of locally born Julian Walter to find a trophy for that afternoon's Peru v. Brazil international at Lima Cricket & Football Club (LC&FC). Eventually they spotted it. Gleaming under the shop's lights, big enough to represent the magnitude of the occasion, without being garish and overly flashy. It was to be called the Copa Amistad – Friendship Cup – and would be the coveted prize on offer every time the men from Brazil and Peru met on the cricket field.

The tradition began in 2011 and when Peru took the honours, by two runs, at the 2019 South American Championship (SAC), their national team proudly held it aloft then posed for pictures. The 'cup' Hildebrand and Walter bought eight years ago was, in fact, a small Thermos flask. 'I guess cricket trophies have always been a little unconventional,' says Hildebrand, Cricket Peru's president, in his husky Aussie twang as we munch on *dulce de leche*-flavoured *alfajores*, a kind of biscuit. 'Try explaining to anyone here unfamiliar with the Ashes about playing for a tiny urn.' The losers of the contest take away a plastic spork, attached inside the lid of the flask. 'The only regret with the Amistad Cup is it is not suitable for engraving,' Walter adds. 'It proved so popular that when Peru and Brazil played at under-seventeen level a few years later the teenagers wanted a trophy of their own – we got them a cocktail shaker.'

The Amistad Cup, in many ways, embodies the joyous spirit of improvisation required to help cricket thrive in Latin America. At the 2019 SAC in Peru, we watch as black bin bags are hastily taped to white sightscreens by LC&FC's befuddled Peruvian staff when ICC umpires kick up a fuss during the opening women's match between Argentina and Peru. Thankfully, the beautiful communal singing by Brazil's women's team each time they take a wicket continues without interference.

One thing Cricket Peru did not have to worry about when planning the SAC was the rain gauge. Lima is the world's third-largest desert city, and cricketers at LC&FC uniquely claim to have never lost a ball to rain in the club's 162-year history. When we play a morning match, a couple of weeks after the Championship, however, the fog and mist rolling in off the Pacific, fused with the city smog, make it difficult to peer through the murk to see if a fielder at long-on has cleanly pouched a catch.

The South American Championship was started in 1995 to encourage greater interaction between nations in the region. It expanded to include youth and women's competitions. Argentina have dominated the men's tournament on the pitch.

But the events, played predominantly by enthusiastic amateurs, are more remembered for what happens off it. A Peruvian player bragged to a flight attendant on a plane to one SAC about being an international cricketer – he ended up marrying her. In true rock 'n' roll style, a Chilean batsman once threw a television set out of his hotel window. Mexico's men celebrated the title with a trophy parade on a bouncy castle squeezed on to the back of a cattle truck.

Unsuspecting reporters from the region can have the wool pulled over their eyes. When a Peruvian journalist asked for the names of three cricketers he had just interviewed, he thought nothing of their deadpan responses: Wally Hammond, Geoffrey Boycott and Vivian Richards duly appeared in national newspaper print the following day.

Of course, it's not always bonhomie and goodwill to all men (and women). Colombia's preparations for the 2019 Championship were disrupted when an ex-player, possibly with a grudge to bear over money, allegedly spun a yarn to the Peruvian Embassy in Bogotá about some old team-mates. The aggrieved made claims that three of Colombia's players were in the country illegally, and the trio were promptly denied entry into Peru for the tournament.

*　　*　　*

With just the one permanent ground in all Peru, at LC&FC, the men's tournament on our visit is held at the Cortijo Polo Club, which means a tortuous two-hour bus ride through the smog, incessant beeping horns and chaos of Lima at rush hour. When we belatedly arrive at Cortijo, our eyes are drawn immediately to empty wooden watchtowers on top of sandhills encircling the playing area. For many years these boxes were manned by guards to protect the club from armed members of the *Sendero Luminoso* (Shining Path) movement – an extreme Maoist group seeking to overthrow Peru's government through guerrilla warfare.

Throughout the 1980s they carried out assassinations on political figures, detonated bombs and sabotaged power stations, causing blackouts. *Sendero Luminoso* received a measure of support from *campesinos* in the countryside and impoverished areas in Lima until their leader Abimael Guzmán, who used the nom de guerre Chairman Gonzalo, was captured in 1992.

The Shining Path once had pockets of followers in the district of San Juan de Lurigancho – a Lima slum of one million where some of the region's poorest people try to eke out a living. We head out there with Cricket Peru's Steve Hallett, who advises us to 'wear your daggiest clothes, bring only a handful of Peruvian *soles* to pay for the bus there and back – and nothing else'. On an artificial football pitch Hallett, a stout fair-haired Aussie country boy wearing a red Peru jersey and with sun cream smeared across his pink face, leads a small group of eager Peruvian youngsters through a few basic cricket drills for an hour. 'Some of those kids have nothing, absolutely nothing,' Hallett tells us we pack up and look up to the rows of tiny makeshift houses that stretch as far as the eye can see on the dusty sandhills above. 'The broader aim of this project is to find and develop Peruvian cricket talent, but just giving some kids a few hours of respite can feel just as important.'

At the other end of the spectrum, we visit the plush Cambridge and Markham colleges, two of Peru's most prestigious private schools, where cricket is part of the curriculum. Hildebrand is deputy headmaster at Markham College – dubbed the Eton of the Andes – and both have produced a steady stream of Peruvian cricketers for the national team, with Joaquín Salazar and Diego de la Puente among recent alumni to progress to senior level. Legendary Peruvian wicketkeeper Jorge Pancorvo, a former Markham pupil now in his sixties, is still pulling on the gauntlets for LC&FC in league matches, decades after he played at school.

The men's national team of Peru are nicknamed *Los Llamas*. The llama was an extremely valuable animal to the Incas, providing food, clothing, dung to fertilise crops and beasts of burden to traverse the Andes. Yet it is their smaller cousin, the alpaca, which produces much of the beautifully woven, brightly coloured textiles associated with Peru. Alpacas are half the size, but produce much more fleece, and their fur is softer, lighter, more lustrous and thermal than coarser llama. The women's team of Peru are *Las Vicuñas* – a relative of the llama, and actually the national animal – and count the granddaughter of controversial ex-president Alberto Fujimori, a Peruvian of Japanese descent currently in prison for embezzlement, among their number.

Peruvian cricket hosts its domestic league entirely at LC&FC's ground in Magdalena del Mar – a few hundred yards up the road from the Victor Larco Herrera psychiatric hospital. In keeping with football in Latin America, it has an *apertura* and *clausura* splitting the season into opening and closing sections. Lima's cricketers are fortunate they do not have to wander too far to quench a post-match thirst. The club is home to a wonderful English-style pub named the Cricketers, where the décor is British racing green.

We head to 'El Pub' after an afternoon league game between Eidgenossen, a collection of teachers who derived their team name from the German word *Eidgenossenschaft* (confederation), and the Kiteflyers, the cricket wing of a British football team active in Lima since the 1980s. Peruvian cuisine – infused with a variety of Inca, European, Asian and West African influences – is famed as some of the best in Latin America, but the Cricketers is the place for old-fashioned British fish and chips. The drink of choice for Peru's cricketing fraternity is not beer, but pisco sour. We're plied with tumblers of the moreish cocktail, containing pisco brandy, egg white, syrup and lime juice, which we hazily learn is a source of fierce dispute between Peruvians and Chileans. There can be no doubting the nationality of the man who pioneered Peru's most famous and popular soft drink in 1935, though. Englishman Joseph Lindley made a green-coloured carbonated beverage, with a bubble-gum taste, and called it Inca Kola. In Peru it comfortably outsells its more well-known US cousin.

*　　*　　*

Pelham Warner suggested Rio de Janeiro, the Transandine Railway and the Panama Canal as worthy of being added to the wonders of the world after MCC's 1926–7 tour of South America. 'To which I would add a fourth,' declared the Grand Old Man of English cricket. 'The guano birds of the Peruvian coast. No guardsman, no Sandhurst cadet, was ever more adept at a drill. There must have been 50,000 manoeuvring.'

Peruvian pelicans, boobies and Guanay cormorants were spied through binoculars in the 1840s but not quite with the same ornithological curiosity as Warner. British prospectors instead eyed two things: poo and pound signs. Of all the industries that brought imperialist speculators to Latin America in search of their fortune, guano – bird droppings – was surely the most malodorous.

The profits were not to be sniffed at, though. The excrement of birds became valuable as a fertiliser for plants and crops due to high levels of nitrogen, phosphate and potassium. On Peru's Chincha Islands alone there were piles of guano 150 feet high. Chinese immigrants were recruited to harvest it, and for around four decades Peru supplied much of the world's fertiliser.

Callao, the port of Lima, became a key staging post for the export of guano. The boom ushered in an era of peace, prosperity and stability under President Ramón Castilla – liberator, slavery abolitionist and the man who signed treaties with Antony Gibbs & Sons, the British company that had commercialised guano in Europe. It made William Gibbs one of the richest men in Britain. A Victorian music-hall ditty – 'William Gibbs made his dibs, selling the turds of foreign birds' – was a small price to pay for the vast wealth he accumulated. A member of the Gibbs family was among the cricketers in the first recorded Callao v. Lima fixture played in September 1860.

Tranquil grassed areas on the Pampa del Mar Bravo, on the outskirts of Callao, had staged cricket matches involving British sailors since the 1830s. A notice in *El Comercio* in 1854, however, announced a proposal 'to form a cricket club in Callao', with the owner of the Bellavista racecourse enclosing the field to 'provide a superior cricket ground in the centre'. Nowadays Callao is a dirty, wheezing port dominated by cranes and cargo ships, and a naval base where Guzmán of the Shining

Path is incarcerated. The cricket fields have long since been paved over for housing metal containers.

Lima Cricket Club grew out of the city's Salon de Comercio and was established in 1859 – becoming South America's longest continuous club in both cricket and football. Norman Evans, who came to work for Gibbs during the guano boom, was among its founders. Their first ground at Santa Sofía was 'a moderately green but not moderately level' bowl located just down the hill from a particularly beautiful hacienda and surrounded by *Brugmansia* flowers, better known as angel's trumpets. The plant is potentially poisonous and one of the side effects of ingesting it is hallucination, which may go some way to explaining a bizarre incident involving Sir Charles Mansfield. Britain's minister to Peru was attacked while returning from a cricket match 'by a furious cow, which gored him'. Mansfield was left 'seriously injured in the body, throat and head', but survived.

Estrella, Independencia and 28 de Julio were entirely Peruvian clubs in Lima and Callao. Others, such as Unión Cricket, converted to football. Their ground in Santa Beatriz eventually became the national football stadium still on the same site today. Club Bolognesi – named in honour of Peruvian military hero Francisco Bolognesi – were one of the few all-Peruvian cricket sides still active at the time Warner's MCC tourists docked in Callao on the *Orita* in February 1927. The oldest team in Peru's capital, known as Lima Cricket & Football Club since 1900, ensured, however, the fixture was staunchly an all-Commonwealth affair.

Not that it made a jot of difference to the outcome. Gubby Allen took 12 for 22 as MCC dismissed the hosts for 28 and 56, and won by an innings and 89 in front of Peru's president, Augusto B. Leguía. It left Warner's side a little more time for sightseeing in Lima. 'We saw something of the "City of the Kings", and paid a visit to the cathedral, built by the mighty conquistador, Francisco Pizarro, whose bones are to be seen within a glass-covered coffin. He was great, but in a cruel age he was a cruel man. Their cruelty was one of the causes of the eventual downfall of the Spanish Empire in South America.'

Pizarro had crushed the Inca Empire in 1532, executing the last emperor Atahualpa a year later. The Spanish conquest destroyed much of the Inca culture, while many of the indigenous people who survived the bloodshed died after contracting European diseases. The obsessive search for El Dorado consumed the conquistadors and one of them, Lope de Aguirre, nicknamed *El Loco*, seized power of a bloodthirsty expedition up the Marañón and Amazon in 1560, famously depicted by Klaus Kinski in Werner Herzog's *Aguirre, the Wrath of God*.

In 1909 HMS *Pelorus* sailed rather more sedately 2000 miles up the Amazon to Iquitos, where it took cricket to one of the remotest parts of Peru during the Rubber Boom. No warship had ever been so far up the Amazon, and its arrival brought the port to a standstill. During its seven-day stay the crew of the *Pelorus* attended dinners, parties, dances and found a patch of grass for the obligatory cricket match. Unlike Kinski's half-Irish immigrant in Herzog's *Fitzcarraldo*, the ship's captain did not try to pull the *Pelorus* over a hillside.

Cricket appeared in other isolated pockets of Peru. A team popped up in Arequipa, in the highlands. 'The English residents started a cricket club,' wrote Captain Prescot Stephens in 1886. 'But it had to be given up, as the exertion to make the runs was found to be too great. Arequipa is 9,300 feet above the level of the sea and the rarefied state of the atmosphere causes some persons to feel a difficulty in breathing.' Matting would occasionally be put down in the Lobitos oilfields of the north, with an annual match played between 1900 and 1950 by teams based in Talara and Negritos whenever there were enough British staff present. The area is now a surf hangout. Another club emerged on the blazing glare of the desert flats near the Toquepala copper mine in the 1970s, and in the nearby free-trade zone of Tacna a few decades later.

The superior quality of Peruvian Pima cotton – grown along the northern coastal valleys all year round – brought cricketers from northern England's cotton towns in the 1960s when the Fabrica de Tejidos la Unión Lima textile mill set up shop. LC&FC were boosted by an influx of former Lancashire League players right up until the early 1980s. These included the hot-headed Bryan Conroy, whose fiery encounters with ex-West Indies batsman Norman Marshall sometimes ended in fisticuffs. 'All of Lima would come out if they were facing each other – it even spilled over into social events sometimes,' says Peter Relton, whose father Bernard played for LC&FC against Warner's MCC.

A six-a-side tournament in Cusco is the closest cricket has come to Machu Picchu, the iconic Inca citadel, which remains a must-see for every touring team. Warner's party made the trip not long after US archaeologist Hiram Bingham III rediscovered the lost city in 1911. Unlike today's Gore-Tex-clad hikers, MCC came decked out in formal dress shirts, ties, jackets and shiny brogues. Most tourists now fly to the city of Cusco, standing at 11,200 feet and home to the nearest major airport, though the flight from Lima was a little hairy for the New Zealand Ambassadors in 1970. 'It's never a good sign when the air hostesses are crouching in the back of the plane and the doors are flapping open,' remembers John Morrison. 'I think the pilot had been drinking heavily for twenty-five years.' At least they made it to Machu Picchu, unlike Oxfordshire team Stanton Harcourt CC. The village cricketers were left holed up in a Lima hotel for two weeks by the Covid-19 outbreak in March 2020 as the Peruvian army kept people off the city's streets.

*    *    *

Inside the cosy bar of the Cricketers, among the memorabilia, we find a joint team photo of LC&FC and MCC before their match in February 1927. The players are intermingled, bedecked in striped blazers and sporting a range of impressive headgear. Warner is sat in the middle of the front row in his MCC touring blazer, legs akimbo, hands resting on the outside of his knees. Sat immediately to his right, a little uncomfortably given Warner's manspreading, is Roger Brown. He is wearing possibly the least jazzy jacket on show, with a cap pushed back slightly further, exposing all his forehead. He appears impatient at the formality of the occasion.

Brown was a battle-hardened league cricketer, rubbing shoulders with the likes of dual international Harry Makepeace back in England. He was the most accomplished all-rounder in the Lima side and their captain against MCC. He relished the visit of so many high-class players – even though he was the wrong side of 40 himself. Brown's seam bowling claimed five for 50 from 24 overs – all his victims frontline batsmen.

Brown was the son of a Liverpudlian painter, and had a modest upbringing. He moved to Lima with his two brothers to make their fortune in mining. While his younger siblings made a quick buck, a change in labour regulations meant Roger's investment turned out to be less lucrative. He stayed in Lima, and drew upon experience from his time as a shipping clerk in Liverpool to land a job with the import–export house Duncan Fox.

In 1909, Roger married an Anglo-Peruvian, Inéz Milne, and on 16 December 1910 their first son, Frederick Richard Brown, was born in Lima. Freddie would become the second Test captain born in the mainland Americas (a few months after George Headley) and one of England's more charismatic, colourful and combative skippers. With his trademark silk neckerchief, sunhat and jovial disposition, Australian cricketer-turned-journalist Jack Fingleton noted Freddie 'lacked only a wisp of straw in his mouth to make him look like the original Farmer Brown'. To others, especially professional players, he was considered the archetypal amateur: pompous and arrogant (although, perhaps with a nod to his father's humble back-ground, he did encourage greater interaction between Gentlemen and Players). When he later became a cricket administrator, manager and selector, he frequently clashed with colleagues. Fred Trueman, in particular, held little affection for him and labelled Freddie 'a snob, bad-mannered, ignorant and a bigot'.

As a young boy Freddie had a cherubic face, showing no hint of the divisive figure he would become, although, at the family home in the Miraflores district of Lima, he irked his father with one particular trait. He'd eat his dinner with the fork in his left hand. He would draw with the pencil in his left. When he chucked a ball around on the boundary at LC&FC while watching his father play, he would do so with his left. 'Nature ordained I should use my left hand for doing everything,' Freddie said. 'From scribbling on walls to batting, bowling and throwing.' Among Incas, lefties were thought to possess special spiritual abilities – but Roger had grown up in Toxteth, and forced Freddie to become a right-hander.

So when an eight-year-old Freddie was packed off to boarding school at St Peter's School in Viña del Mar, Chile, in 1919 there was no switching back. Cricket master G. P. S. Crofts, a middle-order batsman for Valparaiso Cricket Club, was tasked with keeping a close eye on the youngster in the classroom and on the cricket field.

By May the following year, young Freddie's natural coordination meant he was able successfully to make the adjustment to the right. 'F. Brown had a large hand in winning the match,' reads the only report of a game of cricket he played in South America as a boy. 'It was a hard-hit innings of 29 which came at a critical moment.' It was a presage of what was to come. Brown's big hands gave him the dexterity with the ball in hand to mix up his variations of seam, leg-breaks and googlies. His swashbuckling style with the bat would continue into his first-class career. He was not the only one of Roger Brown's children to enjoy a cricket career. Freddie's younger sister Aline, also born in Lima, would represent Middlesex and England Women.

Freddie Brown's last cricket in Chile came not long after his tenth birthday in an end-of-season Parents v. Pupils match. The scorecard has not survived, but a post-match photo has. Freddie is sat on the front row, bolt upright, wearing pads and gloves. A circumspect Roger is back left with a white-brimmed sunhat pulled down close to his eyes.

With a few hours to kill before our overnight bus to southern Peru we venture to the Miraflores district of Lima where

Roger Brown and his family lived, stumbling across a statue of Paddington Bear on the seafront. A Union Jack has been added to Paddington's signature blue coat and he is doffing his hat with one hand, and holding a briefcase in the other, with the vast expanse of the Pacific Ocean behind. A few decades before Paddington – by coincidence adopted by the Brown family in Michael Bond's story – young Freddie made his way to England from Lima. After emerging from 'Darkest Peru', even the task of leading the weakest England side on an Ashes tour in 1950–1 must not have felt so daunting.

# 7

# Ecuador and Bolivia

## *Cricket with altitude*

'BOLIVIA DOESN'T EXIST!' Queen Victoria asseverated when informed by an aide it would be impossible for Her Majesty's Navy to launch an attack on the country's capital La Paz. The difficulty was that it stood 11,975 feet above sea level and 300 miles from the coast. The monarch drew a thick black cross over the country on her map of South America instead. Her reaction followed an incident that has entered Bolivian folklore.

A British diplomat reputedly refused a glass of *chicha* offered by Bolivia's president, Mariano Melgarejo. A traditional welcome offering to guests, *chicha* is made with corn chewed by humans then spat into water to ferment. The repercussions inflicted by the black-bearded eccentric Melgarejo were bizarre. The British official was instead forced to drink a gigantic bowl of cocoa, stripped naked, then tied to a donkey. He was paraded three times around La Paz's main plaza before being packed back to Blighty. Victoria wanted war, but settled for a suspension of diplomatic relations.

In 1888, Anglo-Bolivian tensions eased sufficiently to allow cricket. The Sporting Club of La Paz, founded by the British community, played at the city's horse-racing track. Bolivian writer and politician José Aguirre de Achá wrote of the venue 'standing out in the vegetable fields with cheerful plantations located on the road leading to it'. We navigate our way around La Paz's impressive Mi Teleférico cable-car network, with stomach-churning views of the tortuously inclined capital city, and spot the site of the old cricket ground from above. It has been Bolivia's national football stadium since 1931 and now looks as if it has been plonked in the middle of the urban jungle.

Hampshire cricketer-turned-traveller Godfrey Vigne found little evidence of the game elsewhere in Bolivia when the British first started playing in La Paz. 'In the absence of cricket people amuse themselves with regular pitched battles, fought across a large ravine, with slings and stones, one parish against another,' he wrote. 'A severe contusion is often inflicted. I watched them once, and two people were struck – one very severely, in the face.'

Cricket had disappeared from Bolivia by the time Butch Cassidy and the Sundance Kid were killed in the southern canton of San Vicente in 1908, though not for long. Newspapers excitedly announced the 'first cricket match in the sporting history of La Paz' in 1918, unaware of the previous century's matches. The fixture was between the XIs of the Town and the Railway after a pitch was found on the fairway of a golf course – now the site of La Paz's El Alto International Airport. Three years later La Paz and Oruro, once a key station in the railway network but nowadays a stopping point for tourists heading south to Bolivia's breath-taking salt flats in the Uyuni, both had active clubs. The telephone directory for La Paz contains the surnames of three regulars – Thompson, Garrett and Connal – but their descendants were oblivious to our requests for information on the pursuits of their ancestors.

In an unusual place we spot the biggest cultural imprint apparently left by the British. As we clamber up the steep streets of the Witches' Market in La Paz's old town, where Yatiri witch-doctors sell llama foetuses, dried frogs and potions used in traditional Bolivian rituals, there is a curious familiarity about the headwear donned by the indigenous Aymara women customers. Along with big skirts, blouses and jackets in a dazzling range of colours, many are sporting bowler hats. Called a *bombín* in Spanish, the bowler – donned by Brits since the mid-nineteenth century – was introduced in the 1920s, reputedly more by accident than design. Two brothers from Manchester are said to have manufactured a line of bowlers to sell to British railway workers. On arrival in Bolivia the hats were too small for most men. The enterprising duo, lumbered with a pile of unsellable stock, concocted a story: they told indigenous Bolivian women the hats were all the rage with women in Europe. The trend caught on and the bowler is an integral part of the style for those who identify as *cholitas* to this day.

*     *     *

Ask anyone from High Altitude Cricket Club (HACC) in La Paz and they will agree – the need to bowl 'a heavy ball' has a different meaning here. Cricket in the highest capital city in the world brings challenges not faced by most players. The air is so thin that when a batsman connects the ball *really* stays hit. The result is balls frequently lost beyond the confines of their postage-stamp ground. Supplies are dwindling and a permanent solution is needed. 'We need somebody to design a special cricket ball to play at altitude,' explains Vimal Menon of

HACC. 'Preferably a ball that is heavier to cope with the thin air, but still feels, looks and plays like a normal cricket ball. Maybe NASA's scientists and Dukes could get together to help us?'

The lack of oxygen, at just a shade under 12,000 feet, means bowlers and batsmen, particularly newcomers such as us, are left gasping for air after sending down a couple of deliveries or taking a quick single. One solution used by visiting players to combat altitude sickness is chewing coca leaves. The leaf is the organic compound of cocaine, although for Bolivians it is sacred for its medicinal properties. In 2013, Bolivia won the right to consume the leaf in their country after a UN concession. Ex-Bolivian president Evo Morales, himself a former coca grower, advanced the cause when he chomped on the leaf at a UN drug convention.

In 2012 HACC rescued some kit gathering dust at the British Embassy. Edgar Claure, who represented Bolivia in judo at the 1984 Los Angeles Olympics, was listed as the country's ICC contact at this time. But in 2016, having allegedly embezzled millions of dollars from sporting bodies, he disappeared, and hastily slipped off the ICC's contacts list. Bolivia's cricketers had wisely kept him at arm's length. Some of HACC's kit was used by British staff at Compañia Boliviana de Electridad in the 1960s at a time when Che Guevara was plotting a revolution in the country. Guevara was executed in October 1967 on the orders of Bolivian president René Barrientos, amid alleged CIA involvement. His killing was carried out by Mario Terán, a young Bolivian army sergeant, and British journalist Richard Gott was among the witnesses called to identify Guevara's corpse. Terán still lives in Bolivia under a different name.

High Altitude CC's current crop is a hotchpotch of expats. Alistair Matthew, a Kiwi, moved to the country in the 1990s and became the first person to run bicycle tours for tourists on Bolivia's infamous Yungas 'death road' – a 35-mile stretch between La Paz and Coroico. Built by Paraguayan prisoners during the 1930s Chaco War, the road barely stretches more than 10 feet wide, and has no guardrails despite terrifying 1000-foot drops. Fog, waterfalls, landslides and drunk drivers have added to the number of casualties. It routinely used to claim the lives of between 200 and 300 people a year, with the worst crash in July 1983 when a bus veered off the road and plunged down a ravine, killing 100 passengers. 'As strange as it sounds, I'm more of a cyclist than a cricketer,' Matthew tells us, as we nervously clunk the gears on rented mountain bikes and prepare to ride the perilous route ourselves. 'So I'm more worried about getting injured on the cricket field than the death road.'

The American Calvert School, located in a swish area of La Paz, has been Bolivian cricket's home since the 1960s. The distinctive rock formation of the Muela del Diablo – Devil's Molar – overlooks the ground and is a reminder to Matthew to protect his teeth by swapping his bicycle helmet for a cricket lid. Another player, Englishman Thomas Lynch, runs Nemo's Bar in Copacabana, on the shores of Lake Titicaca – which requires a 12-hour round trip by bus for matches. There is a sprinkling of Bolivians including teenager César Caro, a former junior national dressage champion who now prefers spin bowling to show jumping. Bolivia can lay claim to at least one fully fledged international cricketer: flame-haired ex-Ireland women's wicketkeeper Valmai Gee was born to missionary parents in Cochabamba.

Aussie backpacker Rusty Young knew nothing of cricket's presence when he rocked up in Bolivia's capital in 2000. During his stay, Young befriended convicted drug trafficker Thomas McFadden, a British-Tanzanian who showed tourists around La Paz's notorious San Pedro Prison while incarcerated. Young bribed guards to let him stay inside for three months to document McFadden's story. 'My father was a first-grade cricketer in Sydney and I played in my teens,' Young tells us. 'I would have loved a game while I was in La Paz.'

Young's bestselling book *Marching Powder* captured the curious way of life in San Pedro, which was a society within itself. Inmates earned their keep to purchase their own prison cells, while children lived and went to school within the walls. During McFadden's time inside, the jail housed a cocaine factory, and backpackers spent weekends partying with the cons. The environment appears far removed from the world of cricket. Yet not entirely. 'San Pedro didn't have internet,' Young adds. 'The only way to get the latest Test score was to hope Thomas was showing a cricket fan around.'

We discover from surly prison guards outside its walls that San Pedro is now off-limits to tourists. Backpackers in search of a high these days seek out Route 36, christened the world's first cocaine bar. Curiosity gets the better of us one evening and, egged on by some new friends, we jump into a taxi with them, explaining our plan to the driver in broken Spanish. The bar moves every month, its whereabouts spread by word of mouth, so we're a little apprehensive as we whizz through dark and deserted streets into a sketchy part of town. The taxi driver winds down the window at a convenience store with bars on it and brazenly shouts: '¿Dónde está la barra de cocaína ahora?' After some pointing and gesticulating, we arrive at what looks like a basement shop and are greeted by two burly doormen in black bomber jackets. We clamber down some steps into a dimly lit bar lounge with an illuminated dancefloor to find a polished operation: English-speaking waiting staff, a fully stocked bar, and a menu offering plenty of Charlie. Given the British gap-year students and Aussie travellers filling the venue, it could be a useful recruitment base for the local cricket club.

A more pressing concern for La Paz's cricketers is a new ground. Their agreement with the school recently ended. A site at an even higher altitude near the spectacular Valle de la Luna – lent its name following a visit in late 1969 by Neil Armstrong, who remarked on its similarity to the lunar landscape – has been found. The prospect of even thinner air does have some upsides for the club's evergreen pacemen. 'I'm in my forties and the altitude makes me feel like I'm bowling the same pace as in my twenties,' adds Menon. 'Maybe I'll feel like a teenager again at the new ground.'

\*      \*      \*

It was a fascination with the effects of high altitude that lured English mountaineer Edward Whymper to Ecuador at the end of 1879. Having been the first person to ascend the Matterhorn, Whymper turned his focus to Chimborazo. At 20,549 feet, and located on the bulge of the Equator, its summit is the farthest point on the Earth's surface from its centre. In other words, it is technically the highest place on the planet. On arrival in the Pacific port of Guayaquil, Whymper enlisted the services of H. Perring, a Spanish-speaking British ex-courier. Perring had the distinction of playing in the first cricket match in the history of Ecuador, which took place in Guayaquil six years earlier.

Whymper was an avid amateur cricketer. His diaries recorded his ups and downs on the field, his role in founding the North Lambeth Cricket Club and visits to The Oval. The mountaineer's account of his time in Ecuador does not relay whether he talked cricket with Perring, but he did have a curious fascination with him. 'Perring was a man of enfeebled constitution. He could not walk a quarter of a mile on a flat road without desiring to sit down,' Whymper wrote. Perring's more eccentric behaviour during the rest of their Ecuadorian adventure was reluctantly tolerated by Whymper. He would mysteriously disappear for hours and had a taste for booze. On one occasion, under the influence, he fell from his mule into a fast-flowing stream, which completely drenched him from top to toe.

Yet when the group made the first-recorded ascent of Chimborazo on 4 January 1880, Perring did not suffer altitude sickness. The rest of the party of experienced mountaineers, meanwhile, were blighted by dizziness, nausea and headaches. It left Whymper bewildered that 'a rather debilitated man, distinctly less robust than ourselves' was barely affected. We both suffer severe thirstiness, and a few cramps, a few hours after arriving in Quito but after drinking lots of water, and slurping down *encebollado* – a popular Ecuadorian fish soup, ideal for hangovers – the effects of what the locals call *soroche* slowly dissipate.

The inaugural 1873 cricket fixture in which Perring played was highly unusual compared to elsewhere in South America at the time. The teams were not made up by expatriates, but Ecuadorians. It was officially billed as 'La Inglaterra v. Guayaquil', although the English team was itself bolstered by a number of Ecuadorians. Alongside the British consul Henry Cartwright, his brother Alfred and Perring et al. were a Dr

Miguel Castro – who founded the Cruz Roja Ecuatoriana – and the England-educated Don Enrique Seminario.

The Guayaquileños all had surnames from well-known families. Some were relatives of those wrapped up with Ecuador's very existence as an independent nation. Carlos Aguirre, who top-scored in Guayaquil's second innings with 20, was a descendant of General Vicente Aguirre, a trusted aide of both Marshal Antonio José de Sucre and Simón Bolívar in establishing Gran Colombia. Opening the batting for Guayaquil in the 1873 fixture – won by La Inglaterra by 4 runs – was Pedro Pablo García Moreno, brother of then Ecuadorian president Gabriel García Moreno. Despite his elder sibling's lofty status he was not lobbed any gentle half-volleys, and bagged a pair.

President Moreno did much to enhance the social and economic climate of Ecuador, including the initiation of a railway network. British engineer Marcus Kelly oversaw a line extension in 1885 including bridges designed by Gustav Eiffel, three years before the construction of his iconic Paris tower; the Frenchman was also behind La Paz's central railway station, painted in a natty yellow and – inevitably – now converted into the bus terminal. The railways were close to the heart of Eloy Alfaro during his presidency a decade later. He instigated an ambitious railroad to connect the mountainous capital Quito with Guayaquil.

Around 4000 workers from the Caribbean, predominantly Jamaican, were recruited to build it, and played impromptu games of cricket and football en route. The most infamous section was *Nariz del diablo* – the devil's nose – which supposedly earned its name because of the number of people who died in its construction. Another popular explanation was the Jamaicans who built it practised witchcraft and were only able to finish the stretch of track after they made a pact with the devil. Some of those who built the railway remained in Ecuador, and the country's most famous footballer (Alberto Spencer) and musician (Julio Jaramillo) are both of Jamaican descent.

The Guayaquil Sports Club was founded in April 1899 by brothers Juan Alfredo and Roberto Wright. They were the grandchildren of Thomas Wright, an Irishman from Drogheda who joined the independence wars and became the founding father of the Ecuadorian navy. The club's cricketers imported clothing from New York, and President Alfaro even enlisted local police officers to undertake the task of removing the weeds from a ground at Plaza del Corazón de Jesús to ensure a superior outfield. Alfaro's Guayaquil–Quito railway project, meanwhile, was finished in 1908, and shortened the arduous journey to two days.

The legacy of Alfaro's father, however, lives on in cricket in an altogether more recognisable way, as any visitor to a match, especially on a warm day at Lord's, will testify. Manuel Alfaro arrived in Ecuador from Spain in the 1830s and settled in Montecristi where he began to export stylish handmade straw hats crafted in the mountain town. Alfaro eventually made Panama the base for his business, and it was here the reputation of the headwear grew and the iconic Panama hat was born.

International drug trafficker Pieter Tritton used the hat's association with cricket as a cover story when curious family members quizzed him on his regular trips overseas. 'They wanted to know why I was going to South America,' he said. 'I told them I was going to Ecuador to buy a container-load of Panama hats to sell at cricket matches.' In reality Tritton – or 'Posh Pete' in the criminal underworld – had smuggled cocaine with a street value of £3.5 million into the UK. He was caught and served time inside two of Ecuador's most notorious prisons where he witnessed gang-related executions, gunfights and riots.

\* \* \*

Outside official cricket associations, away from swish country clubs, crisply ironed flannels and the chink of post-match glasses of Pimm's, there is another form of the game. It takes place in the dimly lit car parks of Argentina's capital Buenos Aires at night, in the blazing glare of the Chilean desert flats near the Antofagasta copper mines at the crack of dawn, and jostles for space in public parks across the region on weekend afternoons. The participants are South Asian and games involve a tennis ball, sometimes wrapped in electrical tape, which negates the need for pads, gloves and other inaccessible equipment.

Ecuador boasted arguably the most competitive and lucrative tapeball league in the region. Dominated by Quito's Pakistani community, the league had a dozen clubs sporting names such as Quito Lions and Boom Boom Quito. Colourful kits, extravagant trophies and oversized cheques for the man-of-the-match award, worth more than the monthly salary of the average Quiteño, encapsulated the excesses of the league bankrolled by Pakistani businessmen. 'The Muslim community needed cricket to keep the boys out of trouble,' Sonny Mohammad, one of the league's former players, tells us over cups of sweet *manzanilla* herbal tea and *humitas* at a café in Quito's Plaza Foch. 'Otherwise they would be tempted by drinking, dancing and womanising.' The highlight of the season was a three-day tournament to celebrate the festival of Eid al-Fitr, marking the end of Ramadan.

Fiercely competitive matches took place inside a running track in bustling Parque Carolina, close to the site of the original racetrack where cricket was played in 1903, now a short walk from the city's main mosque. Playing inside a public city-centre park has its pitfalls – stray dogs, drone enthusiasts, homeless people and dance troupes have all stopped play. Shirtless macho bodybuilders, a large picture of Pope John Paul II to commemorate his visit to Ecuador in 1985, and the entrancing cloudy peaks of two active volcanoes – Pichincha and Cotopaxi – provide the backdrop to breathless games at 9350 feet. During anti-government protests towards the end of 2019 an army helicopter landed on the dusty cricket strip one Saturday afternoon, although a military curfew meant that day's match had already been cancelled.

The star player in Quito was all-rounder Aamer Raza. He played in the same Multan Under-19 side as Pakistan Test left-arm seamer Rahat Ali and ODI batsman Sohaib Maqsood in the mid-2000s. A raw 15-year-old by the name of Mohammad Amir was in the same two-day inter-district championship. Raza was part of the Quito XI which made the ten-hour bus trip to take on cricketers in the sweltering bustling port of Guayaquil. It's a journey we later repeat to join in with tapeball games played on a baseball diamond with views of the hulking great ships on the Río Guayas holding containers packed with bananas, cut flowers and shrimp – three of Ecuador's biggest exports.

In 2012, however, a shadow was cast over Ecuador's Pakistani community and its cricketers. A total of 66 foreigners were detained in the country after an undercover sting. Six were on an Interpol list and deported to the US. The most high-profile was Eritrean Yaee Dawit Tadesse, who used the alias Jack Flora.

He had links with al-Qaeda and was reported to be a cousin of Osama bin Laden. It was, though, the arrest of Pakistan nationals Irfan-ul-Haq, Qasim Ali and Zahid Yousaf, all well known in Quito tapeball, which shook Ecuadorian cricket. The trio pleaded guilty to conspiring to smuggle a member of the Taliban into the US and were imprisoned for links to terrorist activities. Pakistanis in Ecuador have kept a low profile since and the tapeball league wound down.

A fresh group of cricketers has filled the void in Quito. They include Dutch-Liverpudlian Paul Hagendyk, who previously spent his free time judging national spelling competitions. Volunteers working at the Katitawa School in the indigenous Andean village of Salasaca have also introduced cricket to Quechua children using homemade bats and tennis balls. Katitawa's uniform of white shirts and trousers kept up the best traditions, and a poncho does not impede strokeplay. Quito's players hope to welcome touring teams in the future. They can expect to sample the traditional Ecuadorian delicacy of *cuy* – part of the guinea-pig family – served during tea breaks.

Quito cricketers sympathetic to the cause of Julian Assange, exiled in the Ecuadorian Embassy in London until April 2019, and since then incarcerated in Belmarsh Prison and reportedly ill, even wrote to him offering honorary membership of the club. Born in Townsville, Queensland – the home of left-arm quick bowler Mitchell Johnson – he boasted in *Julian Assange: The Unauthorised Autobiography* of his family cricketing pedigree: 'My paternal great-grandfather, James Greer Kelly, had four sons who were brilliant sportsmen, well known for their prowess at cricket.' The founder of Wikileaks has, though, yet to respond.

# 8

# Chile

## *Stumping Pinochet's grandson*

' To Colonel John Thomas North,' W. G. Grace wrote,
'a thorough all-round sportsman, and the first subscriber
to my national testimonial fund, I dedicate this book.' The
doctor had a soft spot for the colonel – North, after all, had
swelled his bank balance considerably, and Grace was known
for loving money almost as much as he loved runs and wickets.
So, on publication of *The History of a Hundred Centuries* in
1895, Grace showed his gratitude to the stout, ruddy-faced
Yorkshireman.

He was plain old John North, born in Holbeck near Leeds in
1842, when he arrived in Chile in his mid-twenties to work on
a contract for Messrs Fowler & Co. after a spell at their Steam
Plough Works in Hunslet. Fowler's had sent North south to
work on machinery in Chile's lucrative copper-mining region.
Two years after the job finished, aged 29, he decided to remain
in South America. North gained employment in the port city
of Iquique – at this point Peruvian territory – at the Santa Rita
*oficina* where he got his first taste of the nitrate business and
opportunities out in the *salitreras*. Sodium nitrate – a powdery
crystallised substance sometimes referred to as Chile saltpetre

or white gold – had become an important ingredient in the production of fertilisers, explosives, food preservatives, glass and pottery. It was North's first foray into an industry that would make him, for a time, one of the richest men in the world and universally known as 'The Nitrate King'.

From the mid-nineteenth century there was an appetite for nitrate all over the globe, and North positioned himself to meet the demand. The War of the Pacific plunged Chile headlong into a conflict with Peru and Bolivia, and they fixed their territorial ambitions on key ports and nitrate-rich areas in the Atacama Desert in the far north. Iquique, where North had based himself, had been a major hub during the formative years of the saltpetre boom in the early 1860s, and there was a sufficient number of British workers to sustain cricket.

War between 1879 and 1884 was generally seen as a minor inconvenience for the cricketers. When Iquique travelled up the Tarapacá coast for a fixture with Pisagua, and a naval bombardment began, one cricketer lamented as he saw smoke rising from his office in the town: 'There goes my best bat!' Players from both sides then retreated to a hillside, still in their whites, to watch the Battle of Pisagua. En route to Iquique, we stop off at Pisagua to visit its haunting old graveyard, with wooden crosses spread over a desolate desert hilltop, which dramatically plunges into the ocean.

North was passionate about cricket, but preoccupied with plotting how to make his fortune. During the fighting, he purchased vast numbers of bonds in the Peruvian nitrate industry. Depreciation in the value of the Peruvian certificates meant North bought them at a knockdown rate – in some instances for 90 per cent below their original value. When the victorious Chileans annexed Iquique and its surrounding areas they transferred nitrate ownership to the bondholders. North was sitting on a fortune, and a monopoly in the Tarapacá region. Seventy-four lines of Pablo Neruda's poem *Canto General* vilified North as an unscrupulous exploiter of a desperate situation.

British workers filled positions in the vast network of mines and railways – many under the umbrella of North's companies. Cricket spread throughout northern Chile during the nitrate boom, with clubs established in Antofagasta, Tocopilla and Taltal, the ports exporting the saltpetre. Not all players were directly employed in the nitrate industry. Travelling magician 'Professor' Anderson appeared one Saturday night in July 1895 at the Teatro de la Calle San Martín in Antofagasta. A week later he exchanged his wand for a willow and top-scored with 20 for the Antofagasta Cricket Club.

We encounter the remnants of the British legacy after spying a bright red telephone box inside the grounds of the museum of the Ferrocarril de Antofagasta a Bolivia (FCAB). The museum's elderly curator, wearing a bright blue FCAB cap, grins as he pulls out a weathered bat and a battered stump, with dirt still on the spike from its last match many moons ago.

Cricket was played in the hundreds of *oficinas salitreras* where many of the mine superintendents, engineers and foremen were based. Bellavista, Irene and Victoria all had teams, while Francis Watson gave an insight into matches at Lagunas. 'We played in the winter months as in the summer it was too hot,' he wrote. 'It was difficult for us to keep up the enthusiasm, because our field was on a vacant lot on railroad grounds and covered with sand and soot. There was no grass or anything remotely similar. Rubble from the mine was used to level the ground.'

The emergence of new clubs afforded fresh opposition for teams around Chile's copper and silver mines, which predated the nitrate rush. The Caldera–Copiapó railroad was Chile's first train line and connected the port with the mine in 1851, when cricket hostilities hinted at familiarity breeding contempt. 'As is often the case, the spirit of rivalry prevails among the members of both clubs,' read a report in the *South Pacific Mail* after one feisty encounter. 'Only to the extent of keeping them in working order and until a return match is played at Copiapó Club, their Caldera friends will not rest.' Elsewhere in the region of Copiapó, the Descubridora miners in Chañarcillo used to play a match between those who worked underground and those on the surface. The world's media descended on the area in 2010 when 33 miners were rescued after being trapped 2300 feet underground for 69 days.

South of Santiago, coal miners founded clubs in Coronel and Lota. Teams also sprang up in Concepción, where one club was named Pedro de Valdivia after the Spanish conquistador who founded the city. Precious little has survived in Chile from a time when cricket blossomed in its mining regions, beyond a handbook containing the regulations of Calama Cricket & Football Club, and some photographs.

There is, however, a rare fragile letter we find at the C. C. Morris Library in Philadelphia, written by the secretary of Caldera Cricket Club and dated 21 October 1876. It is on special headed notepaper with a depiction of the desert scene before a match. The players are relaxing under a giant tent; some hold bats, others rifles. There is a flag with yellow and black bands, and the letters CCC along with a Merchant Navy Red Duster and the Chilean standard. The letter conveyed a heartfelt thanks from secretary John Peack addressed to former

Caldera captain George O'Brien, an Irish engineer. Peack expressed gratitude for O'Brien's 'service in the formation and keeping of the club', and his departure would 'cause them the loss of a good-natured and efficient captain'. A bat was enclosed in the letter as a token of the club's appreciation and signed off by Peack with a 'three cheers for CCC'.

The most prestigious games in the mining regions, especially in Iquique, were the Town v. Pampa clashes. Those working out in the nitrate fields would assemble their best XI, including Gamble North, brother of the *Rey del Salitre*, and head down to take on the ports. The Town were frequently too strong for their opponents, although vast lunches of tripe and onions, sausages and mash or steak and kidney pudding softened the blow.

One of John North's closest personal associates in Chile was Maurice Jewell, the British consul in Iquique. All three of his sons would play first-class cricket. Two of them – Maurice and Arthur – were born in Iquique and would go on to represent Worcestershire, playing the bulk of their cricket between the wars. Maurice Jr would have three stints as Pears captain and also skipper the Gentlemen of Worcestershire on their 1937 tour to Nazi Germany. His swarthy complexion led to him being nicknamed *el chileno* in the family.

We stroll down Iquique's Calle Baquedano, with its wooden Georgian buildings, before making a beeline for the city's charming canary-yellow railway station, behind which cricket was played. Here fielders once had to contend with peculiar religious rituals taking place within the boundary. William Russell, a nineteenth-century traveller, observed it first-hand:

The cricket ground is an asphalted quadrangle. Not many yards distant from long-stop's whereabouts, and within range of a good drive, you may observe a mound of earth. There are generally two or three, sometimes more, women in black, kneeling devoutly before the mound. The story I heard was some years ago the body of man was found on the beach and carried to this spot and buried. Lo and behold! The leg of the dead man presently popped up out of the grave! It was put under ground once more. But up it came as before. Repeated instruments could not keep the uneasy limb in place. So, the people concluded the man was a saint. For myself I thought it very touching to see these poor worshippers kneeling and praying before their shrine, caring little for the shouts of 'Run! Run! Throw it up! Well caught!' and alike from the cricket clubhouse.

North became an honorary colonel in 1895, by which time he was attempting to ingratiate himself into London high society. He bought Avery Hill, a swanky mansion in Eltham with its own private cricket ground. That year he stood as a Conservative candidate in Leeds West. During his election campaign he instructed supporters to round up as many dogs as they could find, dip them in blue fabric colour and send them out on to the streets. North lost by just 96 votes to the Liberal candidate, William Gladstone's son Herbert. On 5 May 1896, half an hour after he had eaten some oysters, North died, aged 54. His vast wealth had dwindled. The saltpetre boom was already over and by the 1930s synthetic nitrates forced many mines to close, leaving abandoned works dotted across the Atacama Desert.

One of the best-preserved *oficinas salitreras* is the Humberstone and Santa Laura Saltpetre works. We catch a bus from Iquique's promenade, watching the surfers grow smaller until they are tiny specks in the ocean as the bus winds its way up into the imposing desert hills that overlook the city. The landscape shifts dramatically as concrete buildings are replaced by parched sand and all trace of greenery disappears. It's a weekday mid-afternoon and we are the only visitors to the works, founded in 1872 by an Englishman, James Humberstone.

Not all of the saltpetre works became ghost towns like this; others took on more sinister guises. The works at Chacabuco were later used as a concentration camp by the callous regime of General Augusto Pinochet, and remain surrounded by unexploded mines. At its peak Humberstone had 3500 employees but nobody has worked there since the 1960s, leaving the works to decay in the sands of the Atacama.

Everything in the town is rusted, giving it a post-apocalyptic feel. We walk past a copper-coloured bandstand, and hear our footsteps make a metallic echo as we clamber down into an empty, corroded metal swimming pool. The wind whistles and we are both relieved the eerie silence is momentarily broken by the rattling of corrugated roofs and gates squeaking on hinges. Some of the workers' houses still have bedframes and kettles left on hobs. There are occasional reminders of the British presence stamped on the machinery: 'Rufford of Stourbridge' from the West Midlands, and 'Ashton & Co of Buckley' in Flintshire.

On an old map of the town we find the *cancha* where cricket was played in Humberstone. The brooding spectre of the rusty chimney and the exposed pipes, cogs and wheels of the Santa Laura saltpetre works loom menacingly over the old ground. The entirely sand 'field' is now scattered with rocks, old wood, decaying scraps of metal and other detritus. In the distance are the withered branches of dead trees. The sun starts to set, casting haunting shadows across the sepia-filtered landscape. On the horizon we see clouds of dust forming, and with a sandstorm on the way beat a hasty retreat back to Iquique. With Russell's ghoulish tale and the horror of Pinochet's concentration camps fresh in our minds, Humberstone does not feel like the kind of place you want to be hanging around at night.

*      *      *

The bombastic Sea Wolf was humbled and disgraced: sentenced to 12 months in prison, fined and put in the stocks. He was dismissed by the Royal Navy, stripped of various titles, expelled from Parliament and given a ceremonial kicking on the steps of Westminster Abbey for good measure. Lord Thomas Cochrane was a charismatic, bold and enterprising British admiral, but his reputation was in tatters. Convicted of defrauding the Stock Exchange, after a hoax which claimed Napoleon Bonaparte had been captured and murdered by Cossacks, he left Britain under a cloud despite protestations of innocence that have divided historians since.

He sailed for Chile and arrived in the port of Valparaíso in November 1818, and into the country's War of Independence. On arrival Cochrane was appointed vice-admiral of Chile and commander-in-chief of the country's navy. Over the next few years Cochrane would score audacious and spectacular victories at sea, reorganise the Chilean navy, and be scorned and loved in equal measure by subordinates and superiors.

Cochrane's naval flair, self-confidence and larger-than-life personality were the inspiration for the swashbuckling fictional adventures of Jack Aubrey and Horatio Hornblower.

He would become an integral part of the social scene during his four years in Valparaíso; relishing his status as the 10th Earl of Dundonald, he would dress up for banquets in full Highland regalia.

Cochrane also 'occasionally participated in solemn cricket matches', according to Chilean historian Alamiro de Avila Martel, although he had no great ability as a player so found himself standing as an umpire. General William Miller recounted in his memoirs Chile's first recorded cricket match in 1818, not long after Cochrane had arrived in Valparaíso:

> A succession of diversions rendered Valparaíso more than usually gay. Captain Shirreff and the officers of HMS *Andromache*, who had made themselves popular with all parties, contributed largely to vary the general stock of amusement. A match at cricket between the officers of the *Andromache* and those of HMS *Blossom* led to the establishment of a club, the members of which met twice a week and dined under canvass. The play-ground was a level on a hill, jutting into the Pacific, so that passengers in ships entering the bay of Valparaíso witnessed, from the deck, sports not to be looked for round Cape Horn.

Cochrane's time among Valparaíso's cricketers came to end in 1823, later joining Brazil's bid to win independence. His departure from Chile was bittersweet – he felt short-changed for his efforts. The city would continue to raise an XI to play visiting ships, with some 200 a year docking in the port by 1830.

Unlike Colonel North, Neruda revered Cochrane for his part in Chile's liberation. We make the short walk from Neruda's house, taking time to admire portraits of Cochrane hanging in his study, to see what became of the old *cancha* in Cerro Alegre, Quebrada, where cricket was first played by British naval officers.

The club had a quaint pavilion, surrounded by red geranium bushes, and was looked after by a caretaker called José, who had three English bull terriers and two revolvers at his disposal to protect the property from robbers. It was here in 1860 that Valparaiso Cricket Club (VCC) was founded. Lyndhurst Ogden worked as a clerk in the port between 1869 and 1873 and recalled a peculiar occurrence while batting at VCC. 'I made a hit to leg into a bunch of natives who were sitting on their ponchos and looking on with astonishment at their first cricket match,' he wrote. 'One suddenly jumped up, clapped his poncho on the ball and bolted, notwithstanding the shrieks of long leg, and was never seen again.' The scorer initially scribbled a four next to Ogden's name in the scorebook but, he noted, it was 'deemed a lost ball' so the 'umpire decided six runs!'

Cerro Alegre has the same striking views over the Pacific, above the hustle and bustle of the port below. The area is now a built-up bohemian spot popular with tourists for its colourful houses, trendy cafés and fashionable shops on higgledy-piggledy streets.

VCC would play Santiago, Concepción and, for a short period from 1882, the Aconcagua Cricket & Football Club. The breathtaking Aconcagua region was where the family of Maximiano Errázuriz, a famous Chilean winemaker, would at one point own the biggest vineyard in the world. His son, Maximiano Jr, would later open the batting for Santiago.

The celebration of Chile's independence in the Fiestas Patrias – colloquially known as the *Dieciocho* – on 18 September traditionally marked the start of the cricket season with four days' holiday. It would run until May after which, Ogden noted, 'the rains set in and we were able to hunt the Chilean fox, a larger kind than the English'. VCC annual subscriptions covered the cost of the club's four donkeys, which became indispensable. The quartet ferried barrels of water to prepare the pitch, and hauled lunches and drinks up on matchdays, ascending some 1200 feet up a corkscrew road from the port round a steep hill to the ground.

Their burden, though, was a light one compared to that on the backs of mules carrying cricketers across the Andes in November 1893. Under the auspices of Buenos Aires v. Valparaíso, a group of Argentines made the ambitious excursion for a maiden fixture with their Chilean counterparts. They took the train to Mendoza, at the foot of the Andes, before a three-and-a-half-day trek through the spectacular mountain range and down to Santiago, as there was not yet any Transandine Railway. The travelling party of 24 – 12 players, 10 supporters, of which 6 were women, an umpire and a reporter from the *Times of Argentina* – hired a mule each for the journey. 'The party's attire and travelling implements was the subject of much hilarity and jokes,' reported *La Nación* on their departure. 'The extravagant headgear, the goggles to protect the eyes from dust, the baggage, truly Noah's Arks, in which toothbrushes were dancing among flannel trousers, books and cigarettes, the entire proverbial luggage of English travellers.'

From Santiago the party took the train to the coastal resort of Viña del Mar, where Valparaíso's cricketers had been based on a ground that bordered a section of the racecourse since 1881. Argentina's visit was lauded as a diplomatic opportunity for the Argentine and Chilean governments to mend fences after years of squabbling over water rights and the border lines. 'It is quite possible that in the future lasting reconciliation between Argentina and Chile will be attributed to a famous expedition by a few cricketers, accompanied in this endeavour by beautiful ladies,' *La Nación* pronounced. The interest was such that the West Coast Cable Company posted a staffer at VCC to transmit updates.

The visiting team was strong: all-rounder Paddy Rath was the fastest bowler in Argentina; John Garrod and E. R. Gifford could be relied on to churn out the runs; former Middlesex man Henry Mills was behind the stumps. Despite the efforts of Frank Quennell, who top-scored in all four of Chile's innings and topped the averages on both sides, the Argentines won the two encounters by six wickets and 55 runs. Not content with that, the visitors also scored wins over the Chileans at football, tennis and billiards.

Valparaíso's captain was an Anglo-Chilean, Alfred Jackson. Two of his sons, John and Alfred Jr, would go on to become eminent cricketers for Chile during the interwar glory years. John went to Sandhurst, survived the hell of the Somme, and went to Cambridge to read political economy. He made his first-class debut in May 1920, although against his university for Somerset, and would play another 19 first-class matches that English summer. For Somerset he frequently appeared alongside Argentina's Axbridge-born all-rounder Philip Foy, and they both made their best first-class scores against Essex at Leyton – Jackson 106 and Foy 72.

John Jackson cited financial pressures for dropping out of Cambridge, and he came back to Chile at the end of a solitary county season to work in the Slavonia nitrate *oficina* for Gibbs & Co. He would open the batting with his brother Alfred against Argentina at Belgrano, Buenos Aires, in 1925 – Alfredito making a century, although Chile would be whipped by 320 runs.

The pair would play one more high-profile match on the same side, against Pelham Warner's MCC tourists at Viña del Mar in January 1927. MCC won easily by seven wickets, although two Chilean batsmen stood out: Oliver Bonham Carter, of the well-known British family, had travelled up from Concepción and with wanton abandon hit 62 and 36; opener Edward Cutler, who played with a black patch over one eye, was understandably more circumspect in making 35 and 40. 'Cutler lost his right eye in the Great War,' wrote Warner. 'It was an inspiring sight to find a man overcoming so successfully a great disability.'

MCC's game in Chile was most notable for an over of Gubby Allen's when an earth tremor shook the ground and the bails fell off. His next ball was whacked for six. It was a homecoming for Iquique-born Maurice Jewell, who opened the batting in the second innings and was dismissed with victory in sight. Earlier in the tour he had made a similarly poignant trip to Rosario, Argentina, where his relatives had given birth to the Plaza Jewell ground. The major skipped the game to socialise, and Warner handed a game to Victor Mallet, the British chargé d'affaires in Rosario.

Alfred Jackson moved to Argentina where he became part of the cricket furniture for the next couple of decades, earning selection as the only Chile-born player in the 1932 South Americans' squad that toured Britain. When he refused to walk and was given not out by the Argentine umpire after seemingly edging behind against Sir Theodore Brinckman's XI in 1937–8, the chirpy Yorkshire wicketkeeper Arthur Wood pursed: 'Ever tried walking on water?' A year later, Alfred would play a three-day match at Viña del Mar for Argentina against a Chile side featuring his brother John. When Chile wicketkeeper Harold Senior stumped Alfred off one of John's occasional leg-breaks it was an exceptionally rare feat of dismissing a sibling in an international match.

John Jackson was instrumental in fostering a school cricket rivalry in Chile which, for those who played in it, was taken every bit as seriously as Eton v. Harrow. Jackson had been a teacher at St Peter's School in Viña del Mar but, prompted by the British community in Santiago, founded a school in Chile's capital. He used his old school, Cheltenham College, as the template for the Grange School in 1928, and inevitably while Jackson was headmaster the cricket match against St Peter's became the most important event of the year.

In one match in November 1933 St Peter's thrashed the Grange by an innings and 135 runs, largely down to the performance of four Cooper brothers – Gerald, Wilfred, Ronnie and Leslie. Jackson was so perturbed by the thrashing he promptly visited the parents of the Cooper brothers and persuaded them to move to the Grange. Jackson was famed for giving tactical briefings on excitable train journeys from Santiago to Viña del Mar.

He was a stickler for doing things properly – the detail in a pre-season letter to parents on cricket clothing bordered on the ridiculous. Yet he showed a lighter side. He encouraged stray dogs to be taken in by the school, and they were adopted as mascots for the cricket sides, appearing in team photographs. When the number of Anglo-Chileans decreased in the years after the Second World War Jackson still enthusiastically taught cricket to those completely new to the game.

One day never forgotten at the Grange School was 13 March 1958. It was the first academic day of the new term and began as normal with assembly and prayers. In the midst of that busy first day John Jackson, unusually, found time to make an inspection of the entire school. He finished by taking a look at the school's new central heating system. Not long afterwards, Jackson went back to his house nearby. On arrival he told his daughter Wendy that he was feeling tired and went upstairs. Jackson loaded a gun and used it to end his life. He was 59.

\*     \*     \*

Santiago's cricketers were long considered poor relations to Valparaíso, except when it came to the backdrop. VCC's ground, nestled in a racecourse, had charm, but the spectacular natural beauty of the Andes as seen from Chile's capital is unmatched in Latin America. During the political turmoil and suppression in Chile's not-too-distant past the quality of the cricket rarely matched the surroundings. That the game continued at all was perhaps due in part to the desire for players to lose themselves in the tranquillity.

The Prince of Wales Country Club (PWCC) was established at the foot of the Andes in 1925, with a foundation stone laid by the future Edward VIII on a tour of the country. Since 1870, a Santiago CC had folded and restarted more times than anyone could remember. But, with hospitality to match a stunning setting, PWCC quickly found its way on to the fixture lists of touring teams. Tony Lewis, on MCC's 1964–5 tour of South America, reckoned it was 'certainly among the most beautiful half-dozen grounds in the world'. It is a picture-post-card sight on our visit as snow-capped mountains glisten under light-blue skies on a cloudless sunny day. Even the club's irrigation ditch, fed by fast-flowing snowmelt straight from the mountains, holds a mysterious appeal.

PWCC originally had an almond grove next to it, and Old Grangeonian Alan Mackenzie remembers munching on them while waiting to bat. 'John Jackson even allowed us to drink watered-down gardenia cocktails in the PWCC bar when the school played there,' he tells us. 'But only if we beat St Peter's.'

There was a minor panic in 1949 when a plane malfunction led to a bomb being dropped on the club, but except for the legacy of a large hole on the outfield the damage was minimal. Among PWCC's cricketers in these post-war years was Eric J. B. Hobsbawm, a cousin of the influential communist historian Eric J. E. Hobsbawm. He was another to have attended the Grange School after many of the family headed to Chile having fled Germany during Hitler's rise to power.

Mackenzie remembers the club tactfully negotiating Chile's political turmoil. PWCC officially mourned the sudden death of Salvador Allende in 1973, who had been an honorary member in spite of his avowed Marxism . . . then promptly put the club's facilities at the disposal of the military junta who had overturned him. Although they were lean years generally, cricket continued under the Pinochet dictatorship against a milieu of fear and brutality. In the 1970s the bodies of two women with their throats slit were discovered on the golf course next to the cricket outfield at PWCC. Nobody was ever convicted. Disappearances were commonplace, but Pinochet was known for his Anglophile leanings.

The former Middlesex and England opener Peter Parfitt certainly sensed something when the D. H. Robins XI rolled into Santiago in 1979. 'At PWCC I asked whoever was our twelfth man to collect everyone's valuables,' Parfitt says. 'But the dressing-room attendant was having none of it. He insisted in broken English, "There will be no need to collect them, *señor* manager." It was when he gesticulated if anyone dare nick anything, they would have had their hands chopped off, or worse, I thought it wise not to argue.' Most British members kept their heads down during the Pinochet years, burying their heads in three-month-old copies of the *Financial Times*.

Uncorroborated stories abound in Chilean cricket of Pinochet padding up at PWCC while at the nearby military academy in Santiago in the 1930s. Certainly two of his grandchildren played youth cricket in Chile. 'The Pinochet brothers, Diego and his twin Nicolas, were both good cricketers,' remembers Joseph Williams, who coached Chile's youngsters for many years. Their cricketing talent was missed on a tour to Buenos Aires in 2006, when the family were slapped with a travel ban while under financial investigation.

At the other end of Santiago's cricketing political spectrum is La Casa Roja, a youth hostel that doubles up as a city-centre training facility. The striking mansion house, which has many of the original wooden beams and features, was originally a Catholic girls' school, but under the Pinochet regime it became a centre of strategic significance for the left-wing guerrilla resistance.

In 2001, Aussie owner Simon Shalders took over the building and converted it into a hostel. He later installed a swimming pool with blow-up palm trees, a bar serving cocktails and, naturally, a full-length cricket net. 'We didn't have any

proper practice facilities in Santiago at the time,' Shalders says.
'I had space in the yard, and thought, "Why not build a cricket
net there?"' It proved popular not only with Santiago's players,
but with cricket-loving tourists. Some of them would even be
roped in for league games. 'It upset the dress code a little bit,'
Shalders adds. 'But you would rather have eleven-a-side even if
some of them are wearing hiking boots.' International guests at
the hostel, without any prior cricket knowledge, can sometimes
have their curiosity pricked by the nets. 'I thought the owner
kept dogs in here!' laughs Belgian backpacker Raphaël Vorias,
before striking an unorthodox cover drive off one of the authors'
non-spinning leg-breaks.

There are still nets at PWCC but only boutique fixtures are
played at the club now. League matches in Santiago are played
at the equally picturesque ground in La Dehesa. The fields were
originally owned by Craighouse School, where cricket was
taught, but bought by supermarket group Cencosud to stop
Walmart building a store on the land. Among those to have
represented Chile is firefighter and wicketkeeper José Tomás
Andreu – all firefighters in Chile are volunteers – who, in
January 2017, battled some of the worst forest fires in recent
memory in the country's south. Sadly, Andreu was not on hand
when the pavilion in Santiago by coincidence itself caught fire
later that year and turned much of the cricket equipment to
ash.

Chile's biggest contribution to world cricket – if true – is the
standardisation of the six-ball over. The claim appeared in the
obituary of W. G. Sewell in the *South Pacific Mail* in July 1920.
He was the grandson of William Henry Sewell, aide-de-camp
to William Beresford at the 1806 British invasion at the Río de
la Plata, and a member of Valparaiso Cricket Club since 1880,

playing in the inaugural match against the Argentines. 'It is only a few years ago that he sent his old friend Mr A. H. Price a cutting from an English sporting paper, written by his younger brother E. H. D. Sewell,' reported the *Mail*. 'The famous England county player, on the subject of the six-ball over, claimed this was started first in Valparaíso as a saving of time. This is a fact, and it was Mr W. G. Sewell's suggestion.' E. H. D. Sewell turned out for Essex, London County and MCC before a career as a prominent journalist, author and civil servant in India, which adds credibility to the assertion. In 1889 MCC officially increased the length of an over from four balls to five, then as late as 1900 to six for all cricket other than one-day matches.

The overs dragged on longer than was comfortable for Chile in February 2006 during an ICC Americas Championship Division Three match in Suriname against the Turks & Caicos Islands. Behind the stumps for the Chileans was Guy Hooper, once lauded in a round-up by *The Times* as the best schoolboy first slip in England. Hooper's quick glovework and astute captaincy, however, were not of much use that day at Dr E. Snellenpark in Paramaribo when the radars of Chile's bowlers went haywire. 'After wide number thirty went down I didn't know whether to laugh or cry,' says Hooper, who works in the wine industry and produced a special vintage in 2018 to celebrate two centuries of cricket in Chile. 'But that was only the half of it – the wides kept coming.'

Of the seven Chile bowlers used, Tim Messner and Shalders were the only ones not to suffer from a scrambled radar with just one wide apiece. The other five would prefer to remain nameless as Chile set an unwanted record in an official ICC men's 50-over international. Chile sent down 66 wides in 46.3

overs as Turks & Caicos chased down their 289 for nine. 'Given the preference for T20 now, I think it is unlikely to ever be beaten in men's international cricket,' sighs Mike Meade, Cricket Chile's Californian stats guru, who was in their XI that day.

Chilean cricket seems a magnet for unusual firsts. Five years before the IPL, their league adopted an American-style player draft system for the 2002–3 season. It was an attempt to dilute the dominance of their domestic league's big two clubs – Las Condes and La Dehesa – with the previous season's bottom side, PWCC, given first pick. The same season Anthony Adams Jr, national parachuting champion, caused a stir when he arrived for one club match at the ground from the air. Adams descended on to the ground at fine leg, peeled off his parachuting gear, and took his place on the field exactly where he had landed.

There is a grittier underbelly to cricket in Santiago, away from the affluent schools, country clubs, neoclassical nineteenth-century architecture of the *centro histórico* and 'Sanhattan' – the portmanteau used to describe the financial district. Miguel Ángel Hernández, a Christian missionary in his mid-forties with a goatee, caught the cricket bug while in southern India shooting a documentary. While there he bought up all the cricket books and newspaper reports he could lay his hands on. On his third trip to India he brought home a bat and pledged to join a Chilean club. But he found the English-flavoured game in Chile too formal for his liking.

Hernández headed into Santiago's poorest *barrios*, including Villa Francia. It is a district notorious for when two brothers were slain during the 'years of the disappeared' under Pinochet. Every year on the anniversary of their death there is a 'Fighting

Day', which usually ends with someone killed. In one school, Colegio Echaurren, girls and boys would scrap in the playground. But Hernández took cricket into the school, and soon 90 out of 300 were playing the game. 'Cricket helped shape their values,' he tells us over *pastel de choclo* in the cafeteria of a noisy bus station. 'Especially in the way boys should be respectful to girls.'

One of the teachers bluntly told Hernández 'the kids were bad', and he should not involve them in Chilean youth teams. When the Villa Francia kids arrived for their first match at the fee-paying Grange School, Hernández was asked to remove the soap from the toilets over fears the kids would steal it. Hernández found a ground for them in Estación Central, and soon they were playing 50 games of cricket a year. When he took the national under-15 side to Argentina they were beaten easily, but he encouraged a pride in playing for Chile, insisting on the anthem being sung before the game.

Pedro, one of the youngest players, had a gun put to his head in his own home. His parents simply packed him off on a bus to the far south of Chile to live with relatives; he was lost to cricket forever. Another boy, Javier, was killed by a drunk driver. His friends asked for a cricket bat to be placed next to his grave. 'At that point,' explains Hernández, 'I really did think that maybe God led me to cricket for a purpose.'

Hernández had given it his all by the time he moved north to work at a Christian ranch near Iquique. He even tried to organise a game against a team from Tacna, the southern city in Peru, but the only suitable pitch was on an army base. When he wrote to the Chilean army for permission to use the ground, he was investigated by military intelligence, and decided to back off. Cricket is still coached to Chile's youngsters by

Edward Seisun, an Australian with Chilean heritage who worked as a leading chef alongside Jamie Oliver. And with Hernández appointed as Cricket Chile's president in 2020 there is fresh hope of inculcating the game in the *barrios*.

*    *    *

The legendary *Tangata manu* – birdman – competition of Easter Island is well known to all its inhabitants. Contestants had to collect the first sooty tern egg of the season from the islet of Motu Nui, swim back to Easter Island and climb the sea cliff of Rano Kau to the clifftop village of Orongo. Competitors were frequently eaten by sharks, died from falls or slain by rivals, but the winner would enjoy a lavish life for a year. In addition to growing his nails and wearing a headdress of human hair, the birdman would spend time eating and sleeping without any other responsibilities. So, when Patricio Caamaño pitched up on Easter Island and invited some of the indigenous Rapu Nui to give cricket a whirl, the sport did not seem quite so bizarre as might be imagined.

Caamaño, a Chile national team player, was visiting for an environmental study and brought his bat and ball along to the remote Chilean possession 2000 miles from the mainland. The Moai headstones, carved by the Rapu Nui people, provided one of the more surreal backdrops to the ad hoc games played during Caamaño's stay. However, he ensured the island's novice cricketers were careful not to venture too close to the monolithic statues in case a stray six might hit one during their knockabout games. Around this time a Finnish tourist, Marko Kulju, broke the earlobe off one Moai for a souvenir and was threatened by Easter Island's mayor with having his own ear chopped off, before being landed with a US$17,000 fine.

Caamaño is a bit of a maverick. His unorthodox promotion of the game sometimes rankles with Chile's governing body. Nevertheless, for the past decade he has kept the sport going in Viña del Mar and Valparaíso through beach cricket. The form of the game best suited to Latin America's coastal resorts has never really caught on, perhaps due to the rigid focus placed on hard-ball cricket by the ICC. Caamaño managed to make a beach cricket tournament one of the chosen showcase sports at the Viña del Mar International Song Festival – the oldest and largest of its kind in Latin America. 'Beach cricket is one of the best ways to introduce the game here,' he says. 'It's fast and fun. Everybody gets to bat and bowl. Fielding is also more enjoyable.' After joining in a last-ball thriller on the *playa* on a Saturday morning – temporarily halted after a huge breaker almost swept away ball, stumps and players – we can see the appeal.

In the afternoon, Caamaño drives us to the Viña del Mar racecourse for a peek at the ground where Valparaiso CC had begun playing in 1881, to visit its classical Victorian pavilion. The Valparaiso Sporting Club was a hive of activity as last-minute preparations were made for Chile's most prestigious horse race *El Derby*, taking place the following day.

VCC has existed as a cricket club in name only since the 1960s, with hockey the only sport played under their banner since then. Everyone we had spoken to did not know what kind of state VCC's beautiful old clubhouse would be in. Since cricket was no longer played there, they had not visited it in a couple of decades. A few of the old guard said it contained a treasure trove of historic photographs, club handbooks and mementos from the golden era. Inside the cricket pavilion there was also a notice that drew attention to the occasion when a jockey, ahead of the field and a furlong and a half from home, was knocked off his horse by a ball hooked out of the ground through deep square leg.

When Caamaño pulls up in the car park, however, our hearts sink. The old cricket ground is now covered with floodlit 3G football pitches and called the Centro Deportivo Marcelo Salas. A dispute between the hockey club and the racecourse over ownership of the land ended in a legal victory for the latter, and VCC were promptly booted out.

The racecourse turned the old cricket ground over to Salas, the legendary headbanded former Chile striker, who bank-rolled the construction of a state-of-the-art football centre. When we turn the corner, the situation is worse than we had feared. The old wooden pavilion is gone – bulldozed by a demolition company sometime in 2007 with no apparent consideration for its historical significance. 'It had no lights, no running water and was not fit for use,' deadpans Juan Silva Fuentes, a childhood friend of Salas who oversees the centre.

Where the pavilion once stood there is a modern café, which has shirts from Salas's various club and international games hanging on the walls. And the prized artefacts inside the pavilion? Fuentes shrugs his shoulders, oblivious of the heritage within. 'It was completely empty when it was demolished,' he says. 'I guess it must have been thrown out.' More than 125 years of cricket history in Chile had been destroyed forever with a few swings of a wrecking ball.

\*     \*     \*

Miguel Cáceres cocks the rifle, lifts it to his shoulder and takes aim. A direct hit. The pigeon's body makes a dull thud as it nosedives into the wooden floor. He walks over and calmly breaks the bird's neck. Four more decapitated *palomas*, blood slowly oozing from their carcasses, are lined up on the dusty floorboards nearby. 'We are preparing to put a full-scale replica of a blue whale skeleton here,' Miguel says, wiping his hands on his jeans before shaking ours. 'But these pigeons keep shitting everywhere, which is making life a real pain for us.'

We are inside the bowels of the dilapidated Río Seco Meat Works outside Punta Arenas, at the freezing southern extent of Chile – the world's longest country. It seems even further away than the 2500 miles from the Nitrate King's world up in the Atacama Desert. This *frigorífico* opened in 1905, and at its peak slaughtered 300,000 sheep and lambs during the season. It was the furthest, and possibly most remote, point in the Americas that the tentacles of the Vestey meat conglomerate would touch.

Production ceased in 1964 and nowadays the plant is a shadow of its former glory. The current owners are Japanese and use it to store seaweed. Miguel leaned on his father, who is the site's general manager, for some space to indulge an artistic passion – reconstruction of the skeletons of animals from their bones. The result is an unofficial natural history museum-cum-art project, supported by donations from interested benefactors and visitors.

In a side door to the main exhibition room, Miguel grins as he picks up a walrus skull in the museum workshop. The bones of dolphins, eagles and various mammals are all neatly organised and labelled. It's a typically cool day but we sup from large bottles of Patagonia's Cerveza Austral while exploring the rest of the derelict Río Seco plant with Sebastián Vargas, our unofficial guide in Punta Arenas, who we met at the British School, and is possibly Chile's coolest teacher. The corrugated facades of the warehouses are rusting, but inside the giant refrigeration units the wooden interior remains in remarkably good condition. 'Over there is where, I guess, the cricket pitch once was,' Sebastián says, before taking another large gulp and pointing through an empty window frame to a large field next door.

In 1910 Tom Jones left behind English summers watching Surrey to become the first clerk of the Río Seco *frigorífico*. He turned up without a word of Spanish and having never ridden a horse – hardly ideal preparation for life in the cold, southern-most extent of Patagonia. 'There was no question of learning to ride; one just mounted and hoped the animal would go in the direction one wanted,' he wrote in his memoirs. When he first arrived, Punta Arenas seemed almost like a British colony. English was spoken as much as Spanish, and when Spanish was spoken it was with a beautiful singing lilt. The majority of shepherds came from Berkshire; some were Scottish and Irish. Labourers were paid and sheep purchased in sterling. Jones herded together the sheep-dip agents, farmers, wool exporters and others from the mercantile industry to form the British Athletic Club (BAC).

On a return trip to England, Jones made a beeline for Jack Hobbs's sports shop on Fleet Street and invested in some equip-ment to take back to Punta Arenas. 'Mr Hobbs very kindly autographed two of the bats,' Jones remembered. 'It was not the custom I was told, but as the gear was to inaugurate the game in Patagonia, with his usual generosity, he agreed to my suggestion.' Matting was put down in a horse paddock at the

Río Seco works, where Jones had become manager, or in the middle of the Punta Arenas hippodrome.

The biting Antarctic wind that whipped through Punta Arenas ensured multiple layers were needed and bails rarely used. Everyone wanted to run in and bowl with the gale blowing behind them. Some players would simply go AWOL after the lunch break, unable to tolerate the chill. Those who stayed kept their sense of humour. 'I remember bowling out Alf Parfitt,' Jones recalled of one Freezer v. Town match. 'He remarked to me on his way back: "It wasn't a good ball, Tom. The sweat got in my eyes!"'

When Punta Arenas held its annual stock show, the Camp v. Town match would be the highlight of the season. The Camp, with younger men fresh out of school, Jones remembered, 'proved too strong for the has-beens and never-wassers playing for the Town'. We find the ground in Punta Arenas still exists, though it is a somewhat tired-looking stretch of land inside a neglected horse racetrack. The British connection endured in later years when Pinochet, in a clandestine arrangement with Margaret Thatcher, permitted the RAF to covertly use an airbase in Punta Arenas during the Falklands War.

BAC laid claim to the world's most southerly cricket club, edging out the British Club of Río Gallegos, who played on a sheep farm at Chimen Aike some 160 miles north-east in Argentina. Cricket was played, however, even further south – south of the Beagle Channel and the Straits of Magellan, at the very tip of the Americas, in the Chilean portion of the imposing Tierra del Fuego archipelago.

The indigenous Yaghan were said to number around 3000 when Europeans began colonising the 'Fireland' in the early nineteenth century. The Yaghan were incredibly resourceful given the freezing climate, living naked with only guanaco skins draped around them, covering themselves in whale blubber and resting in a squatting position around fires. The women swam among the chunks of ice in the impossibly cold forty-eighth parallel hunting for shellfish. Over time their bodies developed a higher metabolism to retain heat.

In January 1830 some Yaghan stole a whaleboat belonging to the HMS *Beagle*, captained by Captain Robert FitzRoy. After a fruitless month-long search for it, FitzRoy captured four young indigenous Yaghan in a canoe, seemingly as revenge, though they were not from the same group of Yaghan. The 14-year-old Orundellico was nicknamed Jemmy Button by the sailors by dint of the mother-of-pearl button thrown back down at the other Yaghan as a nominal payment. He and the other surviving two Yaghan were taken back to England with a view to 'civilising' them in Victorian mores.

They were enlisted in an evangelical infant school in Walthamstow, where Orundellico was taught English, maths, Victorian deportment . . . and cricket. When FitzRoy embarked on his famous second voyage of the *Beagle* a year later, with Charles Darwin in tow, they returned the Yaghan home. Darwin was less than impressed with the condition of the Fuegian people, who he ungenerously concluded were 'the most abject and miserable creations I anywhere beheld'. Orundellico was left behind in the expectation he would teach the other Yaghan to tend European crops, drink from tea sets and play cricket – but the items (including the bats, balls and stumps) were distributed among the Yaghan, who had little truck for possessions in a European sense. Visiting Europeans were always astounded to come across Orundellico, a Fuegian who spoke good English, even if he slipped back into traditional Yaghan life.

By the 1890s the indigenous Fuegian peoples were under existential threat. The South American Missionary Society outpost in Tekenika Bay on Hoste Island, south of the Beagle Channel, did their best to Christianise the Yaghan under the watchful eye of minister the Revd John Williams. Several times the Revd Williams engaged the Yaghan in games of cricket on the sandy bays. 'Our Christmas festivities are just over,' wrote Mrs Knowles of the mission at Christmas 1896. 'The natives met for their feast on the 24th. After dinner we rowed on to the opposite shore, and they thoroughly enjoyed playing cricket, quoits and battledore.' There remains only one surviving full-blooded Yaghan and native speaker of the language, Cristina Calderón, 91, who lives in Puerto Williams.

*     *     *

On the port side of the Río Seco plant we find the rotting wooden quay, known locally as 'Shackleton's Jetty', where boats would line up to take lamb and mutton to Europe. Ernest Shackleton arrived in Punta Arenas in July 1916 depressed, desperate and fearing defeat in his effort to save the 22 men he had left behind in the bleak frozen isolation of Elephant Island after his attempted trans-Antarctic expedition fell into trouble. They were stranded there after their boat the *Endurance* was lost to ice, and Shackleton had departed in an open lifeboat with six colleagues to try to obtain a vessel for a rescue mission. Shackleton had twice failed in attempts to save his colleagues, from the Falklands and South Georgia, by the time he washed up in Punta Arenas.

One of the men to whom Shackleton turned was Punta Arenas church minister Joseph Cater. A keen organiser of cricket, Cater had captained a Punta Arenas XI against All Patagonia the previous year, and he was an acquaintance of Shackleton from the Royal Scottish Geographical Society. Cater and another cricketer, Charles Milward, housed Shackleton and his men, then galvanised the British community to fund a rescue boat.

They raised enough money for Shackleton to charter the *Emma*, a 40-year-old oak schooner, which got within a hundred miles of Elephant Island before ice and harsh weather forced them to turn back. Among those stranded was zoologist Robert Clark, a cricketer good enough to represent Scotland. Clark tried to keep spirits up with a homebrew of methylated spirit, sugar, water and ginger, which he dubbed 'Gut Rot 1916'. After three months on the desolate island, supplies were low and the morale even worse. The men hunted penguins and seals to survive and played football on the shifting ice floes.

Eventually, the Chilean government gave permission for the *Yelcho*, a Scottish-built tug, to make the trip to Elephant Island. Despite the boat's unsuitability the rescue mission was a success. On 30 August it chugged up the Magellan Strait and Shackleton rowed out to the jetty at Río Seco, which would later be christened after him. The *frigorífico* foreman Arthur Bishop ran down the wooden pier to greet Shackleton but in his heightened excitement blurted out: 'Welcome Captain Scott!' to which Shackleton, biting his tongue before deciding against a firmer rebuke, replied: 'Captain Scott be so-and-soed! He's been dead for years!'

Shackleton forgave Bishop's faux pas for it was the people of Punta Arenas, and its cricketers, who had responded in his hour of need. The *Yelcho* made its way from Río Seco to the town's port where the men were given a riotous welcome. A few days later Shackleton gave a chronometer saved from the *Endurance* to the British Club in Punta Arenas – now held at the National Maritime Museum in Greenwich – as a token of his thanks. 'I lie always under a debt of gratitude to you all,' Shackleton said in a speech. 'Here, I have received help and encouragement. It is our second home. We shall go as missionaries for Punta Arenas.'

# 9

## Argentina and Uruguay

### *The Test nation that never was*

THE CARETAKER, ALEJANDRO Chacón, had just woken up for his daily 6 a.m. inspection when he saw smoke billowing from the pavilion. Fire was coursing through the handsome wooden structure. Chacón rushed back to the groundsman's hut to call the *bomberos*, but it was too late. In the space of a couple of hours on the Saturday morning of 26 July 1947, more than a century of a nation's sporting heritage – the clubhouse of Argentina's equivalent to MCC, containing some of its earliest scorebooks and photographs, and priceless memorabilia donated by W. G. Grace – had gone up in smoke.

'The old pavilion on the Buenos Aires Cricket Club ground was a miserable travesty of its old self,' sighed the *Buenos Aires Herald*, pillar of Argentina's English-speaking community. 'Charred uprights, piles of twisted galvanised sheets, black ruination.' One by one, cricket lovers in Buenos Aires traipsed into the offices of the country's newspapers to relay the awful news.

Buenos Aires Cricket Club (BACC) members were called to give evidence during the police investigation, and none could explain how the pavilion – which was not electrically wired, did not have anyone staying there, and had not been used for three days outside of the cricket season – could have caught fire without human agency at such a mild time of the year. There was no trace of evidence, no reports of any suspicious activity. That did not stop members writing in to the *Herald* and the *Standard* with their theories. Many, fearful of Peronist retribution, hid behind the cloak of cricket-themed pseudonyms, which populist politicians were unlikely to decipher.

For more than a century the sight of *ingleses locos*, clad in white flannels in the piercing sun, had been part of a Porteño's weekend stroll through the Bosques de Palermo. Roy Gooding, a tireless promoter of cricket in Argentina, remembered 'a lovely ground, set in the great park, ringed by high eucalyptus trees and with, over the fence, a lake running down one side of the field. It had a great atmosphere of peace.'

Privately, most in the cricket community were convinced the fire was ordered from the offices of the president's wife. That summer, Eva Perón had landed with 12 trunkfuls of clothes on her 'Rainbow Tour' of Europe. She was at the height of her glamour, lapped up by crowds, received adoringly by General Franco and Pope Pius XII.

Column inches from London to Buenos Aires were stuffed with speculation over whether the British government would grant Evita an official reception. She was after the kind of red-carpet treatment rolled out during wartime for her heroine Eleanor Roosevelt. But the Attlee government were reluctant during post-war austerity, especially so soon after Evita had been garlanded by Franco – something the Foreign Office felt 'would be misunderstood by the British public', and could lead to open agitation. Yet they could ill afford to upset a major trading partner who produced a third of the meat consumed in Britain. A carefully apolitical itinerary was drawn up containing various junkets for Evita – a day in the royal box at Wimbledon, an RAF air show, cutting the ribbon on a shipload of Argentine beef unloaded at Tilbury docks, and afternoon tea with the Duchess of Gloucester.

By the end of June, intrigue over whether she would meet King George VI and the Queen was causing Evita stress, and she was threatening to sidestep Britain altogether due to flu and general fatigue. 'I am no politician,' she declared. 'I mean only to be a messenger of goodwill from the people of Argentina to the people of Europe.' Evita sailed on from Paris to Lisbon, and into the arms of Portugal's dictator António Salazar, then back south to Buenos Aires.

Beneath the silly-season tittle-tattle there were deeper issues at play. Post boxes in Argentina were red. Argentines drove on the left until 1945. British companies still ran two-thirds of the country's rail network. Argentine meat factories, railways and utilities floated on the London Stock Exchange, their share prices listed in *The Times*. The esteemed Anglo-Argentine writer Andrew Graham-Yooll reckoned the British legacy to be greatest in commerce, education, transport and sport – 'not that they were thinking of doing Argentina a favour'.

Now president Juan Perón was calling time on this cosy arrangement, which had generally worked nicely for the British upper crust for more than a century. Perón was pledging to nationalise Argentina's crumbling and underfunded railway system, and invest money in schools, hospitals and welfare projects run by his wife, to deliver an overdue rebalancing of the economy towards the 'shirtless ones' on the streets from where he drew his support.

Evita began suggesting that companies and societies make generous donations to the Maria Eva Duarte de Perón Social Aid

Foundation. Reginald Leeper, the British ambassador in Buenos Aires – and by extension the president of the BACC – cabled the foreign secretary Ernest Bevin to report that 'most of the big businesses in Buenos Aires are now being more or less openly dunned into contributing large amounts' to her foundation. Help for the poor was no doubt overdue, but this was a private company, paying no tax: a state within the state. Evita declared: 'Keeping books on charity is capitalistic nonsense. I just use the money for the poor. I can't stop to count it.' Leeper warned Bevin: 'This woman is now the real president of Argentina.'

Evita approached the BACC to free up their ground and pavilion for one of these social-aid events, and encouraged club members to donate a month's salary. The committee declined. This spot in Palermo had been their home since 1868; it was where football, rugby and hockey had first been played in Argentina. They did not want their hallowed turf wicket ripped up by ignorant nationalists. Five days after it was announced that his wife's London trip was off, the pavilion of the first cricket club in South America lay in smouldering ruins.

All that marks the cradle of Argentine sport, at a busy inter-section leading into the city centre, is a simple stone monu-ment in a patch of turf, somewhat lost among the picnickers and open-air drinkers in the park. When we reach it the inscrip-tion is disfigured by graffiti, but we can still make it out: '*Aquí se instaló el primer campo de deporte del Buenos Aires Cricket Club: 8–XII 1864*' ('The first sports ground of the Buenos Aires Cricket Club was opened here on 8 December 1864'). A forgiv-able error, perhaps . . . the club is even older than the stone suggests, and this was not the club's first ground in the Palermo parks. But the BACC were in no position to complain. The stone was laid by hasty agreement with the heritage commission after Perón used his executive powers to 'save the ground from the bulldozer and the park architect'. The front page of the *Herald*, cowed into support for the new regime, blared: 'Argentine "Cradle of Sport" Saved by President Perón'.

Not for very long. The field was soon renamed the Plaza Benjamin A. Gould, after Argentina's landmark astronomer, and the city observatory built on it. The dome sticking out of the Planetario Galileo Galilei dominates the skyline. A bulldozer must have been used at some stage to install the flower beds and the artificial lake. Our visit coincides with an artistic exhibition celebrating world sport, featuring lots of inflatable sports balls bobbing around the Plaza Gould. There is no cricket ball among them.

With Perón and his political dynasty twice since booted out of power, Kenneth Bridger, the foremost Argentine cricket writer of his time, could afford to be a little more explicit. 'Evita Perón had the clubhouse burnt down,' he wrote, poison dripping from his pen, 'in a fit of rage at the Englishmen's obstinate refusal to give up the ground in favour of some wild welfare scheme of hers.'

\*     \*     \*

Cristóbal Nino unlocks the catches on each side and thrusts open the long wooden shutters of the committee room in the Belgrano Athletic Club. The air rushes in and reveals one of the great sights in world cricket, in its own way rivalling Lord's, Cape Town and – outside the Test world – perhaps only the Padang of Singapore.

It is February, and out on the field below Argentina are taking on the might of the Cayman Islands for the right to compete at the level their Argentine cricket forefathers once took for granted. February and March, the most enervating months in Buenos Aires, are the time of year when the rugby players of Belgrano rest their weary limbs and let the cricketers roam free on the turf.

When Belgrano AC moved here in the early twentieth century, the modest houses and bungalows of this genteel district ringed the *cancha* and there was a steel windmill to power the clubhouse. But as Buenos Aires expanded rapidly after the Second World War, 18-storey tower blocks sprang up at the Incas End of the ground, where the road behind runs down towards the Río de la Plata. These high rises should be an eyesore; instead the enclosed brutalism lends a feeling of accidental serenity.

For decades here, the chat out in the field would have been mostly polite, crisp, almost all in English, and the long, lazy day's play would have taken in lunch and tea. The crowd would applaud calmly as they fanned their faces in the shade of the grandstand. Today's players, as is now the way at all levels of Associate cricket, are dressed in slim-fit coloured kit, their caps Americanised snapbacks, the ball is white and there are 30-yard circles for the six-over powerplays in this Americas sub-regional qualifier for the T20 World Cup. Furious Spanish incantations keep *Los Guanacos* going as they try to stay on terms with the Caymans.

The grand history of Argentine cricket hangs off the walls of the handsome Edwardian clubhouse – in the framed photos of the great XIs on the top floor, to the memorial hall for the First World War where so many Belgrano members paid with their lives. As we look out right from the committee room window, the clubhouse is still flanked by clay tennis courts, the cricket pavilion and a shaded stand, which is empty but can hold hundreds; beneath us to the left is the constant hum of splashing and chatter of the club swimming pool. For the Anglo-Argentines who called this place home – literally so, for those who lodged in its bedrooms on their time down from 'the camp' – Belgrano was the centre of British influence and ideas in a place they did not call 'Argentina', always 'the Argentine', and in clipped tones pitched somewhere between the Queen's English, Argentine Spanish and a colonial lilt hinting at the British Caribbean.

The descendants of these Anglo-Argentines have almost all married into Spanish-speaking families and become solidly Argentine. Cricket is a family game in Argentina and so three or four generations of Fergusons, Forresters and Kirschbaums remain active. Some of the last straggling Anglos can be found sitting in ones or twos around the halls and bars of Belgrano AC, insisting on certain things being done properly, by which they mean the British way – or at least the perceived British way – and carrying a friendly but solemn air as they reflect on the state of Argentine cricket.

As we settle down in the bar for mid-afternoon steak and chips, we are regaled with the childhood reminiscences of Luis Ross, combed from listening to England Tests on the BBC World Service and syndicated reports in the *Buenos Aires Herald*. The man with him, the impressively robust David Parsons, was the *Herald*'s loyal correspondent on Argentine cricket for years until the paper folded in 2017. The eccentric, tweed-jacketed, Brylcreemed Ross carries a walking stick now but was a decent batsman for Argentina in his day. 'Ah yes, Peter May . . . Brian Statham, fine fast bowler . . . Mike Smith, he came out here to the Argentine . . . do you know him? Colin Cowdrey . . .'

Every day for years, an ageing lady and her friend would sit out on one of the apartment balconies for afternoon tea – a British tradition that clings on in middle-class Buenos Aires despite the regional preference for coffee or yerba *mate*, the green leaves stewed in hot water and sucked through a *bombilla*. One Sunday a batsman sent a six flying up towards the unassuming old dears, clattering the ladies' most precious china out of their hands and triggering a spat between the club and the residents. Donald Forrester, the biggest hitter in Argentine cricket, is said to have shattered more windows and sent more swimmers and tennis players scurrying to safety than anyone. Ironic then, that for a time many of Belgrano's cricketers were insurance salesmen for companies who loyally sponsored the club and the Asociación de Cricket Argentino. As more tower blocks went up, so did the number of complaints, and 50-foot-high mesh fencing has now been put in place to stop flying cricket balls.

The high rises inflict slow revenge when the mercury climbs towards 40 °C. As the sun beat mercilessly off hundreds of apartment windows, it was a pressure cooker engulfing John Morrison, the 22-year-old Wellington batsman destined for Test cricket and expected to score the bulk of the runs for the 1970 New Zealand Ambassadors. Their world tour almost began with disaster when he collapsed at the crease and had to retire ill. There were serious concerns for his life until he was revived in the clubhouse through a mysterious tonic whipped up by an alert barman.

The fair-skinned, fair-weather Kiwis were garlanded with sumptuous *asados* (barbecues) and cocktail parties, and expected to wolf down *bife de lomo y patatas fritas*, dessert and multiple gin and tonics over leisurely 90-minute lunch breaks. But in the days before air conditioning, DEET spray or secure bottled water, they were ravaged by mosquitoes bigger than they had ever seen, and their stomachs churned.

The New Zealand Ambassadors rated the 22 yards at Belgrano to be superior to their Test wickets back home. Many of the top English first-class batsmen down the years – including Bob Wyatt and Mike Smith – filled their boots at Belgrano, unfurling the full range of their strokeplay in a country that, unlike most of Latin America, has always insisted on batting on grass. 'Belgrano must be one of the fastest wickets in the world,' reflected the Somerset batsman Dennis Silk, touring with MCC in the late 1950s. The knowledge behind these legendary surfaces was all in the head of Charlie Vignoles, a taciturn man who ran cricket at Belgrano, and his pint-sized chief grounds- man Pedrito. Vignoles moved up north to Córdoba in his later years, limiting his appearances at Belgrano, but Roy Gooding could still recall him watching the action 'grim-faced . . . he generally appeared completely impassive, but this was appar- ently a cover for his extreme shyness. In his own words he was "laughing like hell inside".'

There has been a week of steady rain in Buenos Aires during our stay, and as we wander out to peer at the square between innings the 22 yards are greener and slower than the legend of Belgrano suggests. At least there is a pitch at all. Vignoles's turf almost met with a fate worse than Palermo, when Juan Perón hatched plans for a new 200-mile highway from Buenos Aires to Rosario, intended to boost the Argentine motor industry and wean the country off its reliance on rail. He apparently drew the line directly through the Belgrano ground. Not for the first time, a military junta came to Argentine cricket's rescue, booting Perón out of office before he could go further than a blueprint.

And so Belgrano remains as a place of refuge in a chaotic city. Never more so than for Gooding when his wife was conducting a long affair with the novelist V. S. Naipaul. 'For years, in one of the buildings, someone endlessly practised Chopin's Revolutionary Etude on Sunday mornings,' Gooding wrote. 'I have always imagined it was a she.'

Argentina's last pair traipse off the field, unable to overcome handy Cayman seam bowling – a proud sporting nation of 44 million beaten by a tax haven of three tiny specks south-west of Jamaica. But, as the warm evening sun flickers off the apartment windows and the Belgrano faithful spill on to the outfield with their G&Ts, one of the strangest, furthest-flung cricket cultures is not done yet.

\*　　\*　　\*

Cricket came to South America through an especially vainglorious Royal Navy officer. In August 1805, Commodore Home Riggs Popham sailed at the head of a task force of 6600 charged with capturing the Cape of Good Hope from the Dutch. At the same time, Popham was being sent intelligence reports from the other side of the Atlantic by a Scotsman named Russell. He claimed there were no more than 6000 Spanish troops stationed in the Viceroyalty of the River Plate, defending a population so discontented that an invading British force would be welcomed. Popham began to imagine the mouth of the Río de la Plata as an exit port for the Peruvian silver mines where he could make his fortune.

Popham sought no permission for his move, and decided to gamble on being rewarded for his initiative. Seventy of 250 vessels were loaded with cotton and other consumer goods, which Britons were barred from selling in Europe due to Napoleon's trade blockade, betraying the naked self-interest of the venture. On 25 June 1806, his subordinate, Brigadier-General William Beresford, landed at Quilmes, 12 miles south of Buenos Aires, with a force of 1635. They entered the town and raised their standard three days later. Barely a shot was fired. Russell was half-right: they were garlanded by the black population of Buenos Aires, the descendants of slaves imported by the Spanish, 6000 of whom held a short-lived uprising in the hope the British invaders would honour the cause being pushed by William Wilberforce. Alas, Beresford's intentions were not so philanthropic.

The viceroy made off with the town's gold to Córdoba. There he rallied, and some British soldiers were induced to switch sides for 16 pesos a month. The Spanish needed just 47 days to retake Buenos Aires, making the Beresford Expedition one of the shortest and most inglorious occupations in Crown history.

British soldiers were left scattered around, many taken prisoner under casual terms. One woman took ten officers hostage when they burst into her house pleading for water. She plied them with wine, led them to a room and locked the door, and would not let them leave until two of them had agreed to marry her daughters. 'The inconvenience of an invasion apart,' wrote Andrew Graham-Yooll, 'the arrival of these visitors was the most exciting thing to happen in the dull life of the colony in years.'

Fourteen officers were held captive in San Antonio de Areco, 70 miles north-west of Buenos Aires, and whiled away their time with various British pursuits. An entry in Major Alexander Gillespie's diary read: 'The arrears due being settled at Esquina and a repose of some days being allowed us, full pockets and vacant time revived the national diversions of horse racing and cricket, for which we always carried the materials.'

A second invasion in 1807 was even shorter lived, and a third in 1808 by the cricket-loving Arthur Wellesley, the future Duke of Wellington, was abandoned when his troops were diverted to Portugal. Popham was handed a court martial for deserting his post, though it did not stop him being knighted and garlanded by the City of London for 'opening new markets'.

Argentina declared independence in 1810, ushering in years of unrest between a despotic cowboy-general, Juan Manuel de Rosas, and a dizzying array of rival militia. Britain's George Canning was one of the first European foreign ministers to recognise Argentine independence, and by 1823 there were more than 2000 Britons resident in Buenos Aires.

As early as 1819, James Brittain, who would establish the first bank in independent Argentina, was flattening the land at his *quinta* in Barracas to play cricket. Brittain was in Team White, captained by Thomas Hogg, who faced Team Colorado, led by John Harrat, in the first game there. Cricket was the natural sport of choice for British merchants, though James McGough – or 'Leatherite', a peerless chronicler of Argentine sport – attempted to explain the lack of action in the years that followed: 'The dignity of the staid, middle-aged business man would naturally have deterred him from making a public spectacle of himself in the eyes of the people of the country, who would be liable to ridicule his athletic exertion.'

They had dropped any such reticence by 22 October 1831, when a notice in the *British Packet and Argentine News* reported the formation of the first cricket club in the country, with 25 members. 'Perhaps many of our readers are not aware that a cricket club has been formed in Buenos Ayres, and that the members thereof have lately played some excellent games in that manly exercise. Some of the players might not feel ashamed to take up a bat, even by the side of the men of Kent . . . Among the best players are some "hijos del pais" who had been educated in England.' The sporting interests of the Spanish were assumed to go little further than bullfighting, sack racing and soaped-pole competitions, but the club had a refreshing mix of British merchants and *criollo* gentlemen bearing the names Muro de Nadal, Martínez de Hoz, Ortiz Basualdo, Pereyra Iraola and Álzaga Unzué.

One letter-writer recounted his morning amble across the Retiro, the central square:

> I was suddenly and agreeably surprised by observing a very neat field-tent . . . over which floated a flag with the follow- ing inscription: 'BUENOS AYRES CRICKET CLUB'. A field was turned out which would not have disgraced our native country. The play commenced with some fine, swift and true bowling by the Messrs Nadal and Isla, both natives of Buenos Ayres . . . I cannot refrain from wishing that this Noble Game may be encouraged by many more of the natives and other gentlemen residing in this country.

An intra-club match between the Greens and the Pinks was played in the shadow of the Socorro church on St George's Day 1832. The Pinks blamed a shoddy pitch for their defeat, and insisted on the return match taking place in La Boca, the neigh- bourhood closer to their homes. For some years the Boca ground was marked by the presence of a beached schooner in one corner, which had blown off the Plata during a particularly violent storm. Boca Juniors would be formed in the district by Greek and Italian immigrants 75 years later.

Cricket clubs disappeared as quickly as they had emerged. Anglo-Porteño CC played on a field in front of the German brewery in Palermo, the district named after the patron saint of the Sicilian city; pupils at Revd John Chubb Smart's English school had access to the Whitfield family *quinta* in Flores, battling against ant infestations and swarms of locusts.

The British did their best to ruffle feathers in 1833 by seizing the Falkland Islands, on the pretence of seal-hunting rights. One of His Majesty's gunboats was placed on standby in the Plata to guard British interests. When Rosas met his comeuppance in 1852 at the Battle of Caseros, the Buenos Ayres cricketers stopped play to applaud a company of his defeated soldiers as they trooped past their ground. Tellingly, when he was sent packing into exile, the British granted him asylum and allowed him to live out his days as a tenant farmer near Southampton.

During a later siege, the ground became stranded behind the battle lines, and the cricketers needed to ask permission from General Justo José de Urquiza to head back across to fulfil their fixture. Urquiza assented, as the British ran the banks holding his money. The match took place with two opposing armies flanking either side of the ground. 'One day as we began the game our noses were assailed by an intolerable dead horse,' wrote Thomas Woodbine Hinchliff, who was sneaking in a game while exploring South America. 'The poor beast had strayed into the cricket ground to die. He had been very carefully skinned by the first finder, and then left to pollute the air. The effect was disgusting, and we could do nothing till we found a man who tied a rope to his legs and galloped away with him.'

The building of the railways by the British, fanning out of Buenos Aires into the pampas, did as much as anything to create modern Argentina. When a reformed Buenos Aires CC emerged in 1858, it was a telling alliance between British interests in the railways and the banks. Frank Parish, the British consul, was president, and Frederic Wanklyn, head of the biggest British bank in Argentina, sat on the committee. The duties that fell at Parish's door included representing the railways, the property of intestate immigrants, running the British Hospital and chairing the cricket club. The British had established their hospital to deal with the bulging queue of drunken British sailors suffering from cirrhosis of the liver.

Parish was a hard-nosed businessman prepared to use the most brazen tactics to further British interests. The British community bent to his needs, cancelling fixtures at BACC when his family endured 'a domestic calamity'. Once, when the government tried to recoup a large sum owed to them by the Central Argentine Railway, which Parish chaired, he effectively held the country to ransom: he stopped the flow of freight and demanded the debt be cancelled. He and other railwaymen knew that speculators used rail construction to build up the value of their land.

To head out to the Argentine frontier was openly to court danger. In 1857 the Bell brothers, from the Scottish borders, established their *estancia* of Adela, south of Chascomús in Buenos Aires Province, in the face of floods, dust storms, cholera and raids by the indigenous Mapuche. Since they derived no pleasure from hunting slow-moving animals, the Mapuche left the Scotsmen's sheep well alone. The oldest known cricket photograph in Argentina shows the family and entourage lined up outside Adela – 'the prettiest place about Chascomus' – with one man leaning up against a bat, as if catching breath at the non-striker's end.

Parish's ever-lucrative Great Southern Railway reached the lakeside town of Chascomús in December 1865. A team of railwaymen there soon raised a side to face Adela, who triumphed by one wicket. The following year's fixture was marred by rain and a cholera outbreak. 'There were several heavy sighs and pathetic solicitations for "Umbrellas and Mackintoshes",' grumbled the *Standard*. 'None being forth-coming, the plucky players took overcoats and ponchos to keep them dry outwardly, and a slight application of Martell's [cognac] to render the under apartment tolerably waterproof.'

On New Year's Day 1874, Adela took on the South American I Zingari, a wandering side inspired by the exclusive southern English club. The club's president was Señor Gomez, who was a justice of the peace in Belgrano and 'thoroughly conversant with our language . . . [who] understands a good deal about cricket, having played in former days'. It was some years before the real I Zingari got wind of their South American imitators, and the merest 'semi-official intimation' that they were upset was enough for the Argentine club to change their name to 'Zealots'. 'This is rather an absurd idea,' reported the *Anglo-American Review*. 'Zingari simply means "Gipsies" or "Wanderers". There are hundreds of Wanderers AC scattered all over the world.'

Some Brits who fled to Montevideo formed in 1842 the Victoria CC, the first cricket club in the Banda Oriental later known as Uruguay, which served as a demilitarised buffer state between Brazil and Argentina. They played out the back of a slaughterhouse, in the Arroyo Pantanoso, owned by the Liverpudlian businessman Samuel Lafone, and grew accus-tomed to fishing the ball out of stinking meat silos. Its location outside the city walls meant cricket was banned on safety grounds during Uruguay's interminable civil war, which dragged on until 1851.

Ten years later came the Montevideo Cricket Club. Their first ground, now the site of Uruguay's military hospital in downtown Montevideo, was then in open countryside. The club made its first bulk import of cricket equipment from Britain, and the Bank of London opened a branch in Montevideo for the first time, making all its employees automatic members of the cricket club. Montevideo lacked reliable drinking water until the government issued a water works contract to a British company – leading to a further influx of cricket-playing engineers. In 1889 the club moved to a nearby spot named La Blanqueada – 'the bleaching' or 'the whitewash' – after an old *pulperia*, though it was also a cute summation of the members' skin colour.

Buenos Aires CC and Montevideo CC each had just about enough players to survive on internal club games, most dredging up rivalries from the old country – Liberals v. Conservatives, English v. Scotch, English v. Argentinos and, by 1863, Liverpool v. Manchester, underlining the number of Lancastrian engineers involved in the Industrial Revolution in the New World.

The two clubs were all set to clash for the first time in 1864, but war between Argentina and Uruguay stymied the plan. That did not stop HMS *Bombay*, an 84-gun screw-propulsion ship, sailing blissfully through the gun smoke to fulfil fixtures in both capital cities. The match between All-Buenos Aires and the *Bombay* officers on 8 December 1864 – the Feast of the Immaculate Conception – marked the inauguration of BACC's new ground in Palermo, a secluded spot surrounded by gum and palm trees. BACC had moved around Rosas's old gardens in Palermo for a number of years, grumbling about dodgy pitches and muddy changing tents. Once Parish knew where the Buenos Aires Northern Railway was to run, he advised BACC of the wisdom in renting a plot next door. And yet the Arroyo Maldonado, the city's underwater sewage system, had a nasty habit of spilling out on to the ground – a handy fertiliser but a nasty odour.

'All town is going,' gushed the *Standard*'s two Dublin-born editors, Michael and Edward Mulhall. 'We cannot disguise our apprehension as to the result, as the Montevidean gentlemen got such a terrible beating.' Betting was two to one against the Bombay XI. The game began at 10.30 a.m., in front of a sparse crowd, until the 12.30 p.m. train stopped at Palermo, 'bringing the Anglo-Argentine fashion in hundreds . . . a most enchanting scene: magnificently dressed ladies, reclining beneath the shade of Palermo willows, carriages arriving each moment'.

All-Buenos Aires, inevitably captained by Parish, claimed a comfortable victory, dismissing the Bombay XI for 23 and 58, with BACC founder member James Darbyshire sweeping up 11 wickets. A third innings was arranged, this time edged by the Bombay XI. Bowling over the shoulder had finally been legalised the previous English summer, so the bowling was likely a heady mixture of overarm, roundarm, underarm and lobs. Parish's wife presented Mr Trollope of the Bombay XI with a white satin wreath as a parting gift.

*Bombay* was on routine target practice near Flores Island on 14 December when smoke was discovered in the hold at 3.35 p.m. Its ventilation system, efficient for the time, caused the flames to spread quickly. Uruguay and Brazil were at war, so when the Brazilian steamer *Gerente* arrived on the scene at 4 p.m., she was ordered to lower her flag and neglected to help in the rescue operation. The *Bombay* exploded at 8.30 p.m. One of the launches could not be freed when the boat was being evacuated, and 91 men drowned or burned to death out of a crew of 616. No personal effects were saved. 'A disaster of almost unprecedented magnitude,' reported the *Standard*. 'The flames assumed the appearance of a blazing tower . . . at times they seemed to move upon the waters.' The disaster was immortalised on canvas by George Cochrane Kerr, whose painting hangs in the National Maritime Museum in London.

*Bombay*'s visit proved tragic, though it set off a frenzied cricket programme. A group of women formed their own club in upmarket Belgrano in January 1865, and challenged the ladies of downtown to do the same. This, incredibly, gives Argentina a claim to the first women's cricket club anywhere in the world, more than two decades before the Nun Appleton CC was formed by eight noblewomen in Yorkshire including Lucy Baldwin, wife of future prime minister Stanley.

In February, peace broke out in the Plata, clearing the path for a long-awaited first international match between Uruguay and Argentina in any sport. It happened 24 years after the USA first played Canada at cricket, six years after H. H. Stephenson's English XI went to Australia, but nine years before the first official Test match at the Melbourne Cricket Ground. The first England v. Scotland rugby and football internationals had not yet taken place.

To the Mulhall brothers, campaigning for more Brits and Irish to settle in the Plata, the events of Maundy Thursday 1868 represented the dawn of a new age: 'Political news there [in Montevideo] are none of importance, but the excitement caused by the grand cricket match was something tremendous. Nothing of the kind has yet been seen in this part of the world, if we except the war of independence.' Buenos Aires opened a big first-innings lead of 30, which they stretched to 102 by the end of their second bat; Montevideo fell short of their target by 32, with Thomas Hogg, a railwayman from York, taking a hat-trick for Buenos Aires.

One wet game between the clubs at Palermo, during the 1873 Buenos Aires Carnival, saw a spike in the crowd on the Monday when rumour spread of a horse-whipping case to be settled at the ground. Apparently one of the parties failed to show, the affair fell through and the crowd dissipated. The clubs were crossing the Plata so regularly that on one occasion the police superintendent in Montevideo convinced himself that the Uruguayans were smuggling contraband into Argentina, and threw all the players in prison for two days.

Town played Suburbs to inaugurate Palermo's new pavilion in December 1865 – made possible by a loan from J. C. Simpson, a wealthy engineer who had co-founded the glee club and the cricket club. BACC raised the funds to level the outfield by staging amateur concerts, featuring comedic skits by one Albertus Phillips. 'The Italians and Germans harbour rather a low estimate of our musical taste,' lamented the *Standard*, 'believing we cannot appreciate or execute anything beyond ballads and comic songs.' Montevideo CC opted for statelier Italian bands, with harp and pipes, to provide musical interludes during lunch and tea intervals.

The first hat-trick in Argentina was recorded in 1866; the first century in 1867. Some of the first horse-drawn omnibuses in all South America were laid on to transport cricketers to Palermo, enticed to training on Tuesdays and Fridays by special ticket offers. The BACC even hired a professional coach, Bailey, from England, who charged an extra 20 pesos an hour to bowl at the gentleman batsmen and coach the Buenos Aires Junior Cricket Club. Dr White, the founder of the junior club, appealed for 'all nationalities to learn our national game under our auspices'.

And yet cricket's fate may well have been sealed on 9 May 1867 – the day Thomas and James Hogg founded the Buenos Aires Football Club (BAFC). It was the first soccer club in a continent that came to define the world's dominant sport. 'Today there will be a football match at Palermo,' reported the *Standard*. 'We believe it will be the first kick ever given in Buenos Ayres, and we understand that half the town will be there if the weather proves favourable.' The cricket club, unable to turn down 500 pesos, agreed to sublet the ground to the BAFC.

Rugby arrived at Palermo when Hogg re-formed the BAFC in 1873 after a yellow fever outbreak, and the new code proved even more disruptive to cricketers who found their turf carved up every October. One observer of a rugby match at Montevideo CC found it 'at the same time sublime and ridiculous . . . that young sons of distinguished families practising the games of the Anglo-Saxon in their youth and young Englishmen of blond Albion . . . in a compact mass in which one could only distinguish heads without shoulders, legs without bodies and hands without arms.' This touches on a widespread belief down the years that the contact sports of football and rugby provided visual proof that Latin Americans of every skin colour could compete with white Europeans in a way that cricket, with its careful strategies, ingrained codes of conduct and confusing Laws, could not. Plenty would refute this notion.

Brits found the time to play sport by steering clear of politics and the military: by stumping up just £60 they could avoid the draft. Descendants of the Afro-Argentines who had cheered the British invaders in 1806 were not so lucky. They were cynically sent to the front rank in the War of the Triple Alliance of 1864–70, which wiped out much of Buenos Aires's black population. In 1871, 'the yellow jack' claimed 8 per cent of the inner city, dealing another blow to their existence.

At the same time, the arrival of the Remington rifle from the US allowed the Argentine army to launch their 'Conquest of the Desert' to seize the barren lands of Patagonia from the Mapuche. The bloody campaign ended with more than a thousand Mapuche dead and 15,000 evicted from their lands. Parish wasted no time in building a railway through Patagonia, clearing the path for European settlers to turn Argentina into an agricultural powerhouse. The president who most celebrated this 'progress', Domingo Faustino Sarmiento, was made an honorary member of the BACC in 1875, and his letter of thanks to the British – in which he suggested the shared love of cricket in the Raj had staved off the Indian Mutiny – was framed and hung in the Palermo clubhouse as an eerie symbol of collaboration between *el ingles* and Argentina's ruling class. Appropriately, it is a statue of Urquiza on horseback at the intersection of the Avenida Sarmiento that looks out over the old BACC ground.

*     *     *

Fray Bentos is like most South American riverside towns – sunbathers on the banks, a central square with a bandstand ringed by palm trees, frolicking teenagers scooting around on motorbikes. As we walk up the hill to the Barrio Anglo, however, we enter a different world. There are rows of lime-coloured bungalows, unmistakeably once workers' cottages, and a gaudy mud-coloured statue depicting four bull-heads protruding out of the middle and pots of meat extract above them. It is the gateway to a post-industrial landscape as striking as any disused English colliery or Soviet missile factory. In front of the hulking El Anglo *frigorífico* are two cranes, bearing the mark of Thomas Smith & Sons of Rodley, Leeds, sitting precariously on the end of a wooden pier slowly crumbling into the Río Uruguay. This is where, for more than a century, South American beef was loaded on to steamships and bound for the gullets of Europeans.

English and Scottish farmers had in the nineteenth century imported the Hereford, shorthorn and Aberdeen Angus cattle that would become the culinary calling card of Argentina and Uruguay. The first meat extraction plant in South America was built here at Villa Independencia, in 1863, financed by the German chemist Justus von Liebig. The town was renamed Fray Bentos, after a hermitic eighteenth-century Uruguayan friar. Supplied by *estancias* on both sides of the border, the Liebig Extract of Meat Company was soon processing 180,000 cattle a year at Fray Bentos.

Jules Verne fed his astronauts beef broth from Fray Bentos in his 1865 novel *From the Earth to the Moon*. It kept French soldiers alive during the Prussian siege of Paris in 1870–1 – and would sustain troops in every major war for the next 75 years. Liebig's diversified into bully and corned beef and even forti-fied wine – not to mention the famous Fray Bentos meat pies that landed in a can on British dining tables for generations.

Fray Bentos supplied both sides of the trenches during the Great War. But after the Vestey family bought up the *frigorífico* in 1924, they sensibly sided with the Allies in the next war. This family of unscrupulous tax exiles renamed the factory El Anglo, commandeered the Oxo Tower on London's South Bank for a cold store, added Lord Hawke to their board of directors, and stapled blue and white flags on to shipments of meat sent across the Atlantic. Their treatment of their South American workers was less than generous. One British peer declared in the Lords: 'Edmund Vestey is so tight you could not get a razor between the cheeks of his arse.'

The Vesteys sold up in 1968, and the last owners ceased production at Fray Bentos in 2009. So we walk freely around this UNESCO World Heritage site, now an open museum commemorating the 'Kitchen of the World' – though in an era of evolving eating habits and social mores, retreading the fateful path of millions of animals on their bloody journey towards a metal can is not to everyone's taste. Among all the pumps, mincers and freezers, there are peculiar relics from the time, none more shocking than a two-headed calf preserved in a glass jar filled with formaldehyde.

The museum curator Diana Cerilla rummages around in a stockroom on the top floor, where British managers once oversaw operations, and digs out an oiled cricket bat, presumably shipped over from England and stamped with the mark of 'McHardy-Brown, Maipu 240', the old cricket stockist off Buenos Aires' busy Avenida 9 de Julio. The last person to wield this bat would likely have been a manager on weekend retreats to the Anglo Social & Athletic Club, welcoming teams from Montevideo and Buenos Aires for two-day games and the freshest *asados*.

Five years after Liebig built his plant, an Englishman, George Reid, began renting land over the border in Gualeguaychú, Entre Ríos ('between rivers' of the Río Uruguay and Río

Paraná), to which even 'clerks, shopkeepers and a high class of English gentlemen' were coming to get their hands dirty. The British legation minister in Buenos Aires, Hugh Macdonell, lamented these settlers as 'an idle, intemperate and worthless lot . . . gentlemen farmers who work only three hours a day'.

That left plenty of time for cricket. A carrier cart ran between Gualeguaychú and Fray Bentos twice a month, sparking up a fierce rivalry between the farmers and the meatpackers. The Fray Bentos CC secretary reported in October 1869:

> The cricket match has been postponed . . . owing to the arroyos [streams] being very much swollen; so great indeed was the flood that the Río Negro rose 20 squares in many places. The prevention of the cricket match was felt by some, but as the majority of the players are sheep farmers, and so the rain has greatly improved the camps and fattened both the cattle and sheep we imagine that the disappointment has been but lightly felt by these gentlemen.

By 1872, Entre Ríos was full with British, including the ancestors of Argentina's great writer Jorge Luis Borges. Before long, though, Reid had sailed home: 'Certainly it is an accursed country in the three years I have known it. I have seen cholera, a drought, pestilence among sheep, a war, and now a winter drought, the worst of all.'

Protestant chaplains were despatched to keep an eye on British farmhands left to their own devices in the open country. Most clergymen pragmatically dropped any opposition to the men playing cricket on Sundays, realising that it allowed them to let off steam – this half a century or more before play on the Sabbath became acceptable in England. Some clergymen would even have fielded as the cricket team's specialist long-stop, as was then the custom in village teams in England. The Revd J. T. Powell had taken the first cricket team from the 'camps' to play in Buenos Aires in 1865. When the Revd E. T. Ash became principal of Victoria College, Fray Bentos, in January 1872, his first act was to convert their open field into a cricket ground. Fray Bentos ignored a smallpox outbreak to challenge Entre Ríos CC, who lodged with the Revd Shiells in the town, to a game at their 'excellent cricket ground which commands a magnificent view of the river'. When Entre Ríos CC ventured into the capital to play Buenos Aires CC in Holy Week of 1873, they combined it with a trip to the Teatro Colón to watch *Hamlet*, billed as the first Spanish production of Shakespeare in Latin America.

Cricket made it north of the Río de la Plata to Rosario in 1867, when railwaymen on the Central Argentine Railway running between the cities of Rosario and Córdoba formed a club. Ten years later, Rosario issued a formal challenge to BACC, who caught a train north to Campaña, then boarded a boat up the Paraná River for Easter weekend 1877. When a rail line finally linked Rosario with Buenos Aires in 1886, the newly multi-sport Rosario Athletic Club secured a prime spot of land near the city centre, donated by Charles and Edward Jewell from Hampshire, who had made their fortune transporting grain down the Paraná back to the mouth of the Plata. They called this place Plaza Jewell, and unlike most of the great nineteenth-century sports clubs, Rosario AC have never been priced out of town.

Already the pestilence of downtown Buenos Aires – once christened 'fair winds' – had sent Brits scurrying out to the cleaner suburbs, where they formed new cricket clubs all along the Great Southern Railway line. Lomas CC, who found a ground in Temperley in June 1872, were quickly competing on level terms with BACC; in one match they bowled out a London Banks side for 7. Roy Gooding remembered the old ride by horse and cart to Lomas's new ground in 1893, and looking out from the top of the clubhouse to count 22 windmills on the horizon. Three years later a post and a cartload of pebbles were set down outside the Lomas clubhouse entrance, sparing members who arrived on horseback from dirtying the panel flooring.

A station on the line was named after the general manager of the Great Southern Railway, Edward Banfield. Club Atlético Banfield, now one of the biggest football clubs in Buenos Aires, first emerged as a cricket club on a pitch that took years to flatten out after cattle grazing. Quilmes Athletic Club – formed in the eastern suburb 81 years on from Beresford's landing, but before the arrival of Argentina's famous brewery – had handsome baths and their own windmill fitted. The prejudices of the *Review of the River Plate* were clear: 'If the Quilmeros could only get their train service improved as they have their cricket ground it would be to the advantage of all, but unfortunately the former is a public enterprise while the latter is private.' All this Britishness irked the French–Brazilian writer Émile Daireaux: 'The carriages and personnel are all English. The stations look like English cottages full of English families; the signals to stop and go are all in English. Travellers might well imagine they were living in a colonised country.'

There was by now a specialist stockist downtown, Gebbie & Dodds, where cricket flannels, caps and belts hung on pegs alongside Highland kilts. Head protection was a distant innovation, as one Flores batsman found out: 'A good-looking young gentleman whose name we were unable to ascertain, had a swift bowler of tremendous muscular power in front of him . . . the ground being hard, and in wretched order, the ball bounced and struck him over the left eye . . . after a few minutes he recovered sufficiently to be assisted home by his friends.'

Argentina's two great cricket arenas were relative latecomers. Belgrano AC began in 1896 on a rough patch at the English High School in the upmarket district. And the Anglo-Argentine dream of a sumptuous country club had been realised by John Ravenscroft in 1886. He named it the Hurlingham Club, after the club on the banks of the Thames. One BACC member and railway manager, Richard Hill, agreed to inject some capital if the club was built next to his lines. This encouraged the sale, for 40,000 pesos, of an Englishman's dairy farm 15 miles out of the city. In 1889 the Pacific Railway arranged for a station named Hurlingham, with one return service a day taking just over half an hour from Retiro. The town of Hurlingham sprang up around the club.

William Lacey, a former professional cricketer from Nottinghamshire, was hired to level the land, fence it off, plant the trees and build the facilities from scratch. Lacey arrived with his wife and three sons in tow, one of whom, Luis, would become one of Argentina's most legendary polo players. Over the next 31 years William Lacey turned 73 hectares of land into a sporting mecca without parallel in Latin America. Appropriately he top-scored with 22 not out in the first cricket match played at Hurlingham, in January 1890, with Hill making runs on the opposing BACC side. The teams slept the night before in a sleeper coach parked in a siding.

Evening dinner-dances at Hurlingham began as formal occasions and grew increasingly uproarious: one member, Buddy

Ross, once rode a horse on to its sumptuous panel floors, sending tables and the club's finest crockery flying. In case of breakages, the club would invoice members responsible a fee six times the value of the object; once the guilty party's hangover had worn off, it was a matter of honour to pay without delay.

A trip out to Hurlingham is still an experience for the sheer expanse of the place – the vast polo fields and the prim Victorian clubhouse looking out over the eighteenth hole of the golf course, though separate staircases for men and women are now a thing of the past. The honour of appearing on Argentina's maiden first-class ground possibly gets to one of the authors in a guest appearance for Hurlingham against the Indian Club: after successfully stopping a four at long-on, he attempts to protect his dodgy arm by underarming back into the bowler, but succeeds in throwing the ball back over his head for six. His Argentine team-mates are *simpatico* enough to console him rather than explode with indignation at this useless ringer. The club rules have relaxed enough for Hurlingham to fill out their XI with non-members such as us and, rather than suit ourselves up to dine in the clubhouse that evening in the time-honoured fashion, a waiter brings over some meat from the *asado* to the boundary's edge as dark descends.

*     *     *

Boca v. River rules all in Argentina today. But it cannot claim antiquity. The oldest sporting rivalry in Argentina has its roots in the wild cane fields of the far north.

Robert Leach – one of many batsmen dismissed by the All-England XI's 'Little Wonder', John Wisden – had done so well out of the wool trade in Rochdale that he was able to send all 11 of his sons to Marlborough College. Two of them, Walter and Stephen, played in the same side as the future England bowler A. G. Steel. In 1876 one of his sons, Roger, was sent to install new machinery for a Cornish sugar planter in Jujuy, the underdeveloped northernmost province bordering Bolivia. The Central Argentine Railway's extension to San Miguel de Tucumán, a thousand miles north-west of Buenos Aires, opened up an area rich in sugar first harvested by the *conquistadors*. Leach made the final 250-mile push from Tucumán to San Pedro de Jujuy by horse and oxen.

Decades later Roger's nephew, the noted anthropologist Edmund Leach, reflected that some fairly merciless exploitation had accounted for the family's prosperity. 'Now if you understand cricket you know quite a lot about all these brothers,' he wrote, tongue firmly in cheek.

> It develops that peculiarity the team spirit, and that entirely erroneous theory that an English public-school boy is a gentleman the world over. Eventually one of them struck gold in the Argentine . . . The team spirit prevailed – the brothers assembled from the four quarters of the globe and began to work like galley slaves. It was all cricket of course, but it lasted nearly 15 years. At the end of that time they suddenly found themselves rich and growing richer . . .

Not Uncle Roger, though, who succumbed to typhoid in 1882.

The rest of the Leaches pressed on and in 1884 reaped the first sugar harvest at their ranch, La Esperanza. As the first in the area to apply hydraulic pressure to the rollers, they took sugar production forward several decades; their cane was taller than 6 feet, towering over rival planters in the area.

The local manpower had been hoovered up by 50 other sugar factories in Tucumán. Sikh gatemen were recruited from the Punjab to guard the estate, and their families stayed until India's independence in 1947. To fill out their workforce the Leaches turned to the Wichí, the indigenous people of the Gran Chaco. Each year the company would ride out by mule to negotiate terms. The Wichí would walk up to 350 miles from their camp to the factory each season, setting off in March in an entourage led by the chieftain and his foot soldiers, followed by the women and children, and arriving in May, sustained by the liquor they made from the fruit of the algarroba tree.

As the Leach family shipped in British managers, botanists, engineers and their families, with them came diseases such as measles, causing untold damage to the indigenous population. Running water, electricity and housing were provided for their employees – except the Wichí, who preferred to live in their traditional wooden huts covered in cane leaves; the arrangement certainly boosted the Leach coffers and allowed them to expand their estate to an area the size of Surrey. The only Leach who seems to have dealt seriously with the Wichí was Walter, who took care to learn their language and customs, and earned the soubriquet *tata Gualterio* (Papa Walter). More than once he intervened to stop fighting between members of rival tribes, which would ordinarily have cost an outsider their life for causing dishonour.

The Leaches began playing cricket at La Esperanza in 1883. To the south, the growing British staff on the Northwest Argentine Railway, chaired by Robert L. Stuart, led to clubs in Tucumán, Salta and Santa Fe. After one match in 1891, the northernmost players and their families were sitting in the waiting room at Córdoba before the gruelling 600-mile train ride home to Tucumán, when the idea was hatched that they, the north of the Argentine, should take on the south. Stuart hastily despatched a letter to the BACC. Three Leach brothers from Jujuy, three players from Salta, three from Tucumán, two from Córdoba and one from Gálvez prepared to make the long journey to Buenos Aires on 12 and 13 November 1891, for the first North v. South cricket match in Argentina.

William Leach, the family patriarch and best cricketer, was the natural choice to captain North. While working in the wool trade in New Zealand, he had opened the batting for Canterbury against James Lillywhite's XI – the 1876–7 tour on which the inaugural Test match would be played at Melbourne – and the following season he was one of many victims of Fred 'the Demon' Spofforth. For all his business achievements, he said the proudest moment of his life was carrying W. G. Grace's bags.

Leach's great contemporary was James Gifford of BACC, who would go on to captain South in 10 of his 11 appearances, and hit the first two centuries in the series. Gifford was a cavalier personality who curled his moustache fashionably at the ends and introduced écarté to the Buenos Aires Jockey Club. The game had to be banned after Gifford won so much money off rival punters that they were declaring themselves bankrupt and cancelling their membership.

In the first North v. South match, William Leach caused mild displeasure at the BACC by asking if North could practise on the Palermo square to get used to the superior batting surface. It worked: Gifford was kept down to scores of 7 and 49, as Dr White took ten wickets in the match for North; William and Stephen Leach clung on at the crease to drag the visitors to their target of 44 with just three wickets intact. That was no mean feat for Stephen, who had lost part of his right foot in a skiing accident and was running between the wickets with a prosthetic limb.

The early fixtures were placed in November or December, so the northern womenfolk could combine the trip with their Christmas shopping in Buenos Aires. In the fifth year it moved to *carnaval* season in February, when it was easier to book holidays, and allowed the match to extend from two days to three. Ever since then, North v. South has been the climax to the Argentine cricket season.

Stuart drew the dividing line for selection at the southern limits of Gálvez, which threw Rosario in with South. It was an act of unfathomable bravado to think their small collection of northern clubs could sustain a challenge against Rosario and Buenos Aires; two years later the line was sensibly adjusted. That was just the start of a gradual southerly slide of the North–South divide, right down to a line midway through Buenos Aires, made inevitable by the capital's domination of the Argentine economy and its cricket.

In February 1899, William Leach made his last hundred, a classy 128, to set up North's win by an innings. But North v. South, in the shape Stuart had intended it, could not last. He had spent more time running cricket than his railway, as the Northwestern fell into financial strife and was forced into a merger, prompting the staff to move south. Stuart and a few fanatics ploughed on, trudging into schools in Tucumán to try to keep the game alive.

\*     \*     \*

The Industrial Revolution sent British expertise to Argentina in droves, and cricket in the Río de la Plata grew stronger than in most of the world's outposts. 'Young men educated at universities and public schools came out thinking that life was largely devoted to cricket, football, golf and polo,' grumbled one businessman. 'They are accustomed to saunter down to the office at ten in the morning, and leave to play cricket or tennis early in the afternoon. All the while the German clerks arrive at seven and stay all day.'

By the 1880s these Brits were demanding marled, cut and rolled wickets like at home. Run scoring went through the roof: John Garrod and Paddy Rath put on 264 for the first wicket in a 1893–4 game for BACC; Garrod racked up a record 1436 runs that season. Rath, one of the fastest of all Argentine bowlers, took six wickets in a (six-ball) over. That season he averaged below 3 with the ball, and sent one Lomas batsman's middle stump flying out of the ground; the bails were measured as flying 45 yards 10 inches. Robert Rudd, 18, struck two double centuries for the English High School against good club sides.

Some were just passing through. Hesketh Hesketh-Prichard, who had played for Hampshire in the summer of 1900, was a restless explorer in the Victorian tradition. After well-preserved remains of the mylodon – a giant ground sloth assumed to have been extinct for 5000 years – were discovered in a cave in Patagonia, Hesketh-Prichard was commissioned by the *Daily Express* that autumn to investigate rumours of a hairy beast roaming the land. He enlisted eight gauchos and 60 horses, but his 10,000-mile schlep through the barren lands and across two lakes – hunting guanacos, the spring-heeled wild llama, for their meat and fur – turned up no trace of the elusive sloth. Hesketh-Prichard grew increasingly sceptical about tales of the monster told by the local Tehuelche people, and even more exasperated with the haughtiness of the Anglos abroad. He faithfully strung out a series of articles, and luckily for Argentina's batsmen barely had time to fling down the new ball before catching the steamer home for the English spring.

Hesketh-Prichard made it on to the ship at Buenos Aires with all his limbs intact. But barely a day went by in the Plata without news of shockingly premature fatalities. In March 1897, John B. Wanklyn, son of Frederic, was shot dead on the steps on his own bank by a gunman refused a loan. 'The Wanklyn Case' was taken up with gusto by the *Standard*, who – with customary deference to the British moneyed elite – labelled his assassination 'one of the greatest tragedies the city has ever known'. A match between Lomas and Flores was abandoned when the news reached the players. In 1899 Uruguay lost one of its pioneers of football and cricket, Henry Stanley Bowles, who was playing golf on Montevideo's new links course at Punta Carretas when a whirlwind whipped off the Plata and carried away the hut in which his group had taken shelter. A few years later, Edward Moore Stanham – co-founder of the Central Uruguay Railway Cricket Club and Montevideo CC captain – took his own life in a hotel room.

The County Championship was formalised in England as late as 1890, so an Argentine national competition probably did not occur to all the ex-public schoolboys more accustomed to jazz-hat friendly cricket. It was not until 1897–8 that Banfield, Belgrano, Flores, Hurlingham, Lanús, Lomas and Quilmes got their act together to form the first Argentine Cricket Championship, played after church on Sundays. BACC stayed out, Kenneth Bridger suspecting 'possibly because they felt, like the MCC, that they were above this sort of competition'. Eventually Belgrano insisted all clubs take part or none at all, and that players appear for just one team, attempting to halt the practice favoured by BACC, who cherry-picked the best to turn out for them in the manner of MCC. Within a few years the Championship extended to two divisions, then three, plus a Saturday league. BACC were suddenly playing 50 matches a season, even when the Palermo ground was infested with mole crickets.

It proved impossible for distant Rosario to maintain a league programme in Buenos Aires, though they did try for two years immediately after the First World War. Engineers and ranchers in the pampas were often responsible for the highest-quality Argentine beef, yet many took ten-hour train rides down to Buenos Aires at weekends to play for the southern clubs and dance the nights away. J. B. Sheridan, captain of BACC, introduced cricket to his gauchos in Salto, Buenos Aires Province, as an antidote to football's violence.

In 1910 the northern clubs arranged a Camps Cricket Week for the first time, so their cricketers could gather at Rosario or Córdoba for a fortnight of trial matches leading up to selection for North v. South. Following Tip Foster's introduction of the blue England cap in 1908 and Australia's adoption of the Baggy Green, there was a timely overhaul of the North and South colours, which had seldom been worn by North, and never at all by South, as too many preferred to dust off their old school caps and blazers. 'Although I do not remember ever having seen either, I understand that both colours were distinctly ugly,' wrote the *Standard*'s correspondent. North changed to dark green on their blazers, caps and hat bands, with a palm tree as an emblem, and the letter 'N' struck through. South played in dark brown, with 'S' struck through a badge of pampas grass.

\*   \*   \*

The flow of English cricketers to Argentina peaked in 1906, when the Lancashire amateur Harold Garnett arrived to work for Hopkins & Gardom engineers. He was an unusually tall wicketkeeper and among the best left-handed batsmen in England, selected by his Lancashire skipper Archie MacLaren for a private tour of Australia in 1901–2. Garnett made a fortune in mining and shipping commodities in Argentina, and helped design Torre de los Ingleses, the neo-Palladian Big Ben replica clock tower that still dominates the Retiro square – though Argentine fury over the Falklands War led to it being renamed Torre Monumental in 1982.

Garnett's arrival was a sprinkling of stardust. Yet the man who rose above all Argentine cricketers in the Golden Age and beyond was Herbert Dorning. Like Garnett he was a left-hander at a time when it was comparatively rare – *The Times* even discussed banning left-hand batting after the First World War – and a quick left-arm bowler, forged in the hard graft of the Liverpool Competition. A strong, moustachioed man, he was known for nipping off between overs for a sip of Scotch from his hip flask.

Dorning followed his engineer father out to Argentina after school, and quickly emerged as a force with all ten wickets for 31 for Rosario against Lomas in 1893–4. He debuted for North the following season, then moved to the capital in 1902, where he would dominate for four decades, taking ten wickets in an innings three times, and five nine-fors. In the 1907–8 season, by then 33 and bulging round the waist, he sent down 429 overs, taking 137 wickets at an average of 9; in club matches, his bowling average was 4.85. In the big metropolitan derby for Belgrano against BACC in 1906–7, Dorning's remarkable 163 out of 229 featured six sixes and just one missed chance in the deep, and was proclaimed by *Golf y Cricket* magazine as '*la hazana mas grande*' ('his greatest feat').

Dorning had an insatiable appetite for runs and wickets and – much like his contemporary W. G. – did not always adhere to the niceties of cricket as idealised by the gentleman cricketers. He once forced a change of umpires in a big club game when a catch he claimed at slip was not given. When lodging at Belgrano, down from the camp on weekends, he would get up at night, quietly open the groundsman's cupboard and water the end of the wicket he would be bowling into the next day.

Even after he had hung up his spikes, Dorning loomed large: cricketers at Belgrano would glance up to the committee room to see his imposing figure staring down at them. He would pour himself a whisky from the drinks cabinet and quietly absorb everything going on in the middle.

\*     \*     \*

Rumours had been swirling since 1898 that Lord Hawke was preparing to bring a side to Argentina. Due to the payments Hawke received from sitting on various company boards, he had the time and wherewithal to arrange eight winter tours, many staging posts in cricket's development outside England. Hawke was not motivated entirely by philanthropy: he had invested considerable sums of money in Argentine railways and utilities on two previous visits.

An attempt by Argentina's best all-round sportsman, James Oswald Anderson, to cajole the 1906–7 MCC tourists to New Zealand to tack on a trip to Buenos Aires, by returning across the Pacific and around the Cape of Good Hope, fell through when the tour management vetoed the move on the grounds of exhaustion. The football codes got there first: Southampton FC in 1904 and the British Lions in 1910.

Eventually, in May 1911, Anderson, who was in England playing for Hertfordshire, persuaded the MCC committee to underwrite an unprecedented first-class tour of Argentina and Uruguay. Hawke, not long retired as a Yorkshire player and England selector, was formally invited to lead the party by Roque Saenz Peña, the president of Argentina, and his contacts were key in the MCC committee's decision to invest £5000 in Central Argentine Railway debentures.

Hawke's method for choosing tourists was to draw up a list of players, circulate it to all the candidates, and invite comment on each other's inclusion. He agreed that expenses should be paid for travel and accommodation, but drew the line at food, drink and laundry. Six past or future England Test players survived Hawke's selection process this time.

The biggest draw was Archie MacLaren. He was in some ways a surprise inclusion – perennially short of cash and prone to letting his MCC membership lapse. Then there was his famous clash with Hawke over team selection in the 1902 series defeat to Australia: 'My God, look what they've sent me,' MacLaren famously exclaimed when the uncapped Sussex bowler Fred Tate turned up at Old Trafford. Each had somewhat of a reputation for haughtiness. But MacLaren's own Test career had come to an inglorious end in 1909; he was suffering from rheumatism, and had resigned in umbrage as secretary to Ranjitsinhji, the great batting maharaja known as Ranji. As he prepared to turn 40, a rather desperate notice appeared in *Cricket* in November 1911: 'Mr A. C. MacLaren has indicated to the committee of the MCC that should there be a vacancy in the cricket team that is to visit the Argentine in January, he would be happy to go.'

The side played in Hawke's personal colours, but under the banner of MCC. Hawke called it a 'country-house sort of trip ... my eat, drink and be merry tour' – as shown by the accompanying dignitaries: Lord and Lady Farrar and Lady Agnes de Trafford. Bundled in with the party were 36 bats donated by MCC to encourage Argentine cricket. By now, at all grounds except Hurlingham, rugby was played across the square in winter, and there was some disquiet at how the clubs might foot the bill for such an illustrious party. Football and rugby were already charging on the gate, but Hurlingham were deterred by the threat of a 50,000-peso fee from the municipality.

The MCC players expected to stroll through the month-long tour, sipping G&Ts and romancing the local *señoritas* – and some surely did – but it was not so straightforward. A hail-storm had stopped play in one league game in November, yet it was hot and sticky in the Plata when the tourists arrived in February. This was not a generation that chased the sun, and Hawke's party adopted the Argentine trick of stuffing fig leaves into the brims of their boater hats to help absorb the punishing heat.

When MacLaren was assigned room 13 in the Plaza Hotel, he insisted that Kent's Lionel Troughton take it instead. 'You're a good-natured chap, I know, who won't mind, so I've just taken your room and put you in 13,' he said. 'My whole tour will be spoilt if I sleep there.' Much to Hawke's amusement, MacLaren's first four scores were 0, 0, 0 and 0.

He was all at sea against the 22-year-old quick bowler Philip Foy, son of the Western Telegraph company manager in Rio de Janeiro. When Garnett spotted his haggard old captain at a function during this barren run, he exclaimed: 'Why, Archie, you look older than 70!' At least supping the local *mate* helped soothe his weary joints.

MCC's opening tour game, against a Southern Suburbs XI at the Great Southern's ground next to their vast Los Talleres railyard, was drawn only after real drama. Hawke had enforced the follow-on, expecting an easy win. But Austen Cowper, a burly South African émigré, tore into Rockley Wilson's lob bowling. Even after Hawke put as many as five men out in the deep, Cowper flayed 182 out of his team's 235 while at the crease, including 11 sixes. Hawke dismissed it somewhat bitterly as 'a lucky innings . . . the heat rather took the vitality out of us in the field'. Cowper hit Ledger Hill's underarms into the station, while MacLaren's leg-spin was despatched into a pigsty next to the ground, from where poor Troughton was tasked with fishing out the 'odiferous ball'.

The opening three-day match between Argentina and MCC began on 18 February 1912 at Hurlingham – the inaugural first-class match in Latin America – and was billed both in England and Argentina as a 'Test match'. Hawke considered that 'an absurdly grandiloquent description considering the calibre of the sides'. Hawke won the toss with a specially minted gold coin and decided to bat. But, in humid conditions, Foy and Dorning – aged 38, but still a handful – swung and seamed the ball around, leaving MCC on the ropes at 33 for seven, before a last-wicket stand of 106 boosted the score to 186.

A dust storm whipped up and prevented play from starting on the second day, leaving the spectators to huddle under Hurlingham's green and white racing grandstand. Dorning's innings of 16 was spread across all three days. MCC were expected to bat out time for a draw, but lurched to 52 for six.

Hill was the only MCC batsman not dismissed by Foy or Dorning, whose match figures read nine for 114 and ten for 125. Argentina were left with 136 to make in an hour and 40 minutes. Garnett showed all his experience in 19 not out, including the winning run, to sneak Argentina home with one minute left and four wickets to spare. 'The delight of the spectators knew no bounds,' wrote Kenneth Bridger. 'Hats and sticks were waved and on all sides the winning team was cheered enthusiastically.' Garnett was carried off the field shoulder-high by the jubilant crowd.

For the second 'Test', MCC changed in Palermo's new pavilion, built in 1908 for 15,000 pesos after the foundations of the original had rotted away due to the constant flooding. Hawke's side clicked into gear, and ran out convincing winners by 210 runs, with Wilson – the Winchester College schoolmaster who would coach a young Douglas Jardine – taking six for 36 in the second innings.

The G. G. Brown who struck 31 in Argentina's first innings was no ordinary Anglo-Argentine. Like his mentor Alexander Watson Hutton, who had founded the English High School and started Argentina's domestic football league in 1893, Jorge Brown – as he was known in the Spanish press – was descended from Scottish immigrants. He captained the Argentine national football team and racked up 21 league titles, along with an impressive 26 hundreds in local cricket. Watson Hutton's son, Arnold, batted at number 11 and did not bowl in the opening 'Test', and was dropped from the XI for Palermo, but did take three catches as a substitute fielder.

The series came down to the third and final 'Test' at Lomas. Hawke, 51, sapped by the heat, retired from first-class cricket and stood as umpire, presiding over the toss between Lancashire pals MacLaren and Garnett. In an incredibly tight finale, MCC tumbled to 64 for eight, still 37 short of the winning post. MacLaren pushed his first ball into the hands of mid-off – who dropped it. He made no more mistakes, and edged MCC to the target with two wickets left.

MacLaren's powers were on the wane, but the glory of his Golden Age backlift and strokeplay was finally glimpsed in his 172 made against an Argentine-Born XI in the penultimate game, putting on 314 for the third wicket with Neville Tufnell.

*Cricket* reported that Hawke's team 'found the cricket around Buenos Aires much better in quality than they had expected, spoke a good word for the grounds, but a bad one for the climate, and expressed admiration for Foy, the old Bedford Grammar School boy, who did great things against them' – 26 wickets in the three 'Tests' at an average of 14.5. MacLaren declared that had they been available in England, Foy would have been first-choice pick for the Gentlemen, and Dorning for the Players. He concluded that Argentina's full-strength side would 'bustle out most of the counties'.

The experience was, said Hawke, 'the alpha and omega of my overseas cricket'. As the players tucked into the finest cuisine at the end-of-tour dinner in the Plaza Hotel, the head table was decorated in the shape of a cricket oval, the waiters dressed in cricket whites, the walls bedecked with cricket equipment, and footage from the tour beamed on a film projector. Although he kept his view private from the assembled guests, Hawke later wrote: 'I am doubtful of cricket ever taking serious root out there in an important scale. The Argentines prefer to play soccer with enthusiasm and rugger with vigour.'

\*      \*      \*

When hostilities broke out in 1914, Argentina stayed neutral. Their army had been trained and armed by Germany, wore spiked helmets and goose-stepped like the Kaiser's troops. From the 40,000-strong Anglo-Argentine community, however, 6000 joined the British forces, and 41 sports and social clubs raised money for the Allied war effort. 'Practically every fit single man playing in Argentine cricket of British birth came home to join the Army,' Harold Torre, a leading light in the rebadged Argentine Cricket Association (ACA), informed readers of the *Cricketer*.

Inter-communal amity was punctured. The Anglo-German Hospital in Rosario quietly closed its doors, and alongside editing his annual *Year Book of Argentine Cricket*, James McGough was furiously compiling *A Statutory List of Enemy Firms and Persons in the Argentine Republic* from his British Printery in the Buenos Aires suburb of Florida.

HMS *Glasgow* played a crucial role in the Battle of the Falkland Islands in December 1914, famously capturing Tirpitz the Pig from SMS *Dresden*. Before the war *Glasgow* had sailed down the Atlantic coast and visited Y Wladfa, the Welsh settlement in Patagonia, beating a Madryn XI by six wickets. When the railway had extended through Chubut in the early part of the century, Welsh settlements in Puerto Madryn, Trelew, Gaiman and Dolavon raised cricket, rugby and football teams against the railway gangs.

Three of the Argentina team who played Hawke's tourists fell in the Great War. Harry Biedermann, son of a London merchant – despite a surname to put McGough on red alert – was the hero of the last North v. South fixture in 1913–14, making 65 and a virtuoso 169 not out for North, when *el clásico* ended in a draw for the first time in 22 encounters. He left

Argentina later that year, and served at Gallipoli. He transferred to the Royal Flying Corps, and is believed to have been shot down by the ace fighter Otto Könnecke while on a routine reconnaissance mission over Belgium.

The two others died on successive days in December 1917. The patriotically named John Argentine Campbell, capped by Scotland in rugby, was a founder member of the Hurlingham Club and one of the pioneers of polo in South America. He was followed the next day by Harold Garnett, star of the win over MCC. Garnett had returned to play for Lancashire in 1914, was picked for Gentlemen v. Players at Lord's, and captained Lancashire in their final game before the outbreak of war. He was among the earliest first-class cricketers to volunteer, leaving his lucrative business in Argentina to be commissioned in the South Wales Borderers. He was wounded in 1914, then returned to the front the following year and was killed, aged 38. All three are absent from the list of cricket's fallen in the Lord's pavilion.

The wartime exodus cut BACC's membership by half. As in many cricket-playing countries, the league programme was paused, but friendlies were arranged. Several of the survivors returned to play in a poignant match at Hurlingham in 1919, for Returned Volunteers against the Rest. They faced the theoretical threat of a military tribunal for deserting their posts in Argentina, but President Marcelo Torcuato de Alvear quietly buried the issue three years later.

Foy saw more than three years' active service in the Royal Engineers, for which he was awarded the Military Cross and twice mentioned in dispatches. He returned from his post-war spell with Somerset to work on railway and bridge construction in Argentina. When North v. South fired up again in 1921,

Foy smashed 217. The match was controversially abandoned as a draw by the umpires, so unimpressed were they at the 'spectacle' of the North batsmen slashing wildly at the bowling as they set about chasing 108 to win; the innings was scrubbed from the records. Dorning was captaining South, and may have brought his imposing influence to bear.

In 1924, Foy's bowling at Palermo entranced Hugo Mackern, who was to become an esteemed rugby journalist in Argentina. 'He looked truly fearsome to my schoolboy eyes; in the second innings South were set only a hundred to win but I can recall him clean bowling the best South batsmen one after the other and in the end they lost seven wickets before getting the runs.' The atmosphere was electric when Dorning was caught off Foy for eight. 'Later on he cut down his run to seven or eight paces but he still bowled pretty fast, relying on his very pronounced body swing and follow through to produce tremendous outswingers, which I found utterly bewitching on the one occasion I had to face him.' Foy was to miss chunks of cricket due to bronchitis and heart problems, and was assigned to waterworks down in Bahía Blanca, the terminus of the Great Southern, where he was put in charge of rescue operations after harsh floods in 1939.

*     *     *

While war was raging, the most illustrious Argentine bowler of all was making his legend on the playing fields of Eton. The Gibson family had been landowners and breeders in Argentina since 1819, when John Gibson of Paisley set up shop in plush Almagro to import textiles from Britain and send meat and grain the other way. The family invested in five ranches, acquiring 60,000 head of cattle, only for drought and war against Brazil in 1827 to devastate their business and force them back to a single *estancia* in Buenos Aires Province, inevitably christened Los Yngleses by the locals. It hardly survived when General Rosas's army trampled through while putting down a nearby rebellion. To feed his 3200 troops, Rosas ordered the slaughter of 120 of Gibson's steers, offering a token apology for not saving the hides. The family cannily hid the rest of their livestock in an impenetrable swamp on the ranch that only their best gauchos dared to enter.

By 1887 there were cricket and polo fields at Los Yngleses and their smaller nearby *estancia* of La Linconia, named after the fleecy Lincoln sheep that survived in the windswept surroundings. A December 1891 match between the rival ranches, reported *River Plate Sport and Pastime*, 'numbered just five Englishmen on each side, the rest of the teams being made up of puesteros and peones belonging to the estancias. The amusement caused by the fielding and batting of those who had never seen a game of cricket in their lives may be better imagined than described.'

Through diligence and sharp business sense John Gibson's grandson, Herbert, slowly restored prestige to the Gibson name. His service on the Royal Wheat Commission, where he negotiated extremely favourable prices for the Allied war effort, made him the most respected Anglo in Argentina, earning him a knighthood from the British and the soubriquet Don Heriberto from Argentines. He was opposed to playing sport on Sundays, but had to abandon this high-mindedness once his second son, Clement, began starring with the ball on Agar's Plough, Eton.

Clement matured early, and was in the Eton College First XI for four years and captain for two, hoovering up 122 wickets at less than 11 – many of them while battling appendicitis. In the absence of any first-class programme, public school cricket was judged by the blue-rinse authorities to be the most important cricket in England, and *Wisden* editor Sydney Pardon named Gibson and four other schoolboys the Five Cricketers of the Year for their achievements in the 1917 summer. E. B. Noel noted: 'Gibson stood out by himself . . . he bowls medium to fast and starts with two great assets – a good run up to the wicket and a beautifully easy swing and action. He has a great command of length, a very good yorker, and he swerves late.' In the Eton v. Harrow match of 1919, when the fixture returned to Lord's after four years of wartime austerity, only to be marred by fighting between rival top-hatted supporters, Gibson was presented to the king after his match-winning six for 18.

Gibson went up to Clare College, Cambridge, where he spent most of his days on Fenner's sward and his evenings dressed in top hat and tails. He appeared at matches collar up, fey, almost apologetic. His team-mate and room-mate Hubert Ashton called him 'a man of great charm, tall, elegant, good-looking, immaculately-dressed . . . I remember vividly what shrewd judgment of people he had – sometimes a little barbed but never unkind'.

Even considering the press's tendency to amplify the claims of an upper-class amateur from Eton, all the evidence suggests that Gibson was a superb bowler. The *Manchester Guardian's* young cricket correspondent Neville Cardus noted how 'he has a ball which is a good imitation of Barnes's famous ball, the one that pitches on the leg stump and swings away to the off'. Others picked up on the 'wobble' he generated as the ball came down, probably not a million miles away from the great Jimmy Anderson today.

By the August Bank Holiday in 1921, the Australia side captained by Warwick Armstrong had won eight successive Ashes Tests home and away, and were unbeaten through 34 matches of their England tour. Archie MacLaren, hair jet-white and pushing 50, was asked to assemble an all-amateur England XI to take them on at Eastbourne. As a sentimental favour to his great hero MacLaren, for what was expected to be his last serious match, Cardus gave Middlesex v. Surrey at Lord's – the County Championship decider – a miss, and headed down to the Sussex coast. When the England XI were bundled out for 43 in the first innings by Armstrong and Ted McDonald, it seemed business as usual. Let Cardus take up the tale:

> I had packed my bag and sent it to the railway station; there was an express train to London at one o'clock. I went to the Saffrons once more on this Monday morning in August 1921, for sentimental reasons. MacLaren had gone in first on the Saturday evening. I wished to look on him as he faced, for the last time, an Australian fast bowler. He was bowled straightaway by the lovely panther McDonald. As MacLaren came from the wicket, grey-haired and stooping, I slowly began to walk round towards the exit gate . . . By the time I had reached the exit gate, I had seen enough. I retraced my steps a little; I got on a bench facing the pavilion. I did not go to London that day. Or the next. I stayed at Eastbourne. I saw [Aubrey] Faulkner and Hubert Ashton make a great stand. I saw Aubrey Faulkner's last great innings. And next day I saw C. H. Gibson of Cambridge University skittle out the Australians; MacLaren won by 28 in a scene of heartbreak and shouts.

The moment that started the slide was 'a glorious ball' from Gibson to the left-hander Warren Bardsley, which pitched on off stump and broke back through the gate to take out leg. When Gibson bowled McDonald to seal it, the crowd charged the field and Gibson was carried into the pavilion.

Gibson was on the cusp of Test cricket. But the war effort had taken up much of Don Heriberto's time: he had over-invested in property and livestock, and the family's entire grape crop in Mendoza was lost to hail. Clem dutifully sailed back that winter to head up the offices of Gibson Brothers at 296 Calle San Martín, and his departure from first-class cricket was later mourned by Fenner's stalwart Jack Davies as a 'casualty of the great British mercantile tradition'. Gibson could still spare the time to turn out once a week for Hurlingham, and in his first classic he took six for 16 as he and Dorning swept through North for 39.

Gibson did clear time in his diary 12 months later to join MacLaren on an MCC non-Test tour of Ceylon, Australia and New Zealand. His haul of wickets was second only to Tich Freeman, and he took 57 at an average of 17 on the New Zealand leg.

He had not played county cricket for four summers, but on Archie MacLaren's recommendation – and presumably that of his old Cambridge mucker and Sussex captain Arthur Gilligan, who was in charge of the tour – Gibson was chosen for the 1924–5 full Ashes tour, as a new-ball partner for another Sussex man, Maurice Tate. MCC secretary Francis Lacey fired off a telegram to Gibson's office in Buenos Aires: 'SELECTED FOR AUSTRALIA TEAM LEAVES ENGLAND SEPTEMBER THIRTEENTH ARRIVES ADELAIDE NOVEMBER FOURTH LACEY'. Gibson agonised, then turned down the invitation. It was reported that 'business interests' had kept him back in Argentina; some suggested his father put pressure on him to stay at home.

His youngest son, Thomas Gibson, now in his seventies and speaking from his art gallery in Mayfair, London, says the sheer isolation of Argentina was the reason: 'He just didn't think he could justify the risk. He worked out that in order to get to Australia he would have to leave immediately for Chile, then catch a freight boat to New Zealand, where he could take a passenger boat from Auckland to Sydney – and if all the timings went absolutely right he would arrive the day before the opening Test at the SCG.' England ended up badly lacking in pace options and lost 4–1.

Stung by missing out on an Ashes tour, Gibson, then 25, sailed over in April 1926 for one last stab at the big time with Sussex. Gilligan was no longer England captain, but he was Sussex skipper and on the national selection panel. Gibson wrote to him from Buenos Aires: 'Cricket here is confined to one day a week, but that has been enough to keep my muscles loose.' The return of the Eastbourne slayer was the talk of the papers, prompting feverish talk of a Test call-up, and it reached a crescendo in mid-May when Gibson clean-bowled the great Jack Hobbs in both innings, helping inflict Surrey's first Championship defeat at The Oval for six years. The Master walked off second time, admitting to Gibson that he had beaten him all ends up by a ball that had pitched on middle and seamed away to hit off. 'Only "W. G." in his prime could have stopped it – or perhaps "Ranji",' gushed the *Daily Mail*. Gibson then smacked a merry 54 batting in a long-sleeve sweater, took it off and edged Bert Lock's next ball behind.

Gibson was the pick of the South of England's bowlers against the Australians at Bristol. Pelham Warner's selection panel chose him for The Rest against England in the Test Trial at Lord's . . . only for Gibson to pull a fetlock beforehand in a friendly outing for Free Foresters at Fenner's. His replacement, Worcestershire's Fred Root, went on to play in three of the Tests, and was a practitioner of leg-theory bowling; Harold Larwood, who would turn it into 'bodyline' in 1932–3, was another debutant in 1926. Gibson's bowling tailed off and he sailed back to the obscurity of South America, his name but a footnote in the history of English cricket.

*    *    *

Gibson returned to a Buenos Aires scene of 12 clubs playing across two divisions on Sundays, and five playing shorter matches on Saturday afternoons, plus midweek works leagues for the obsessives. Quilmes were bowled out for 6 by BACC in 1919. They did, however, put out a women's team, who played in blouses, sunhats and three-quarter-length skirts, and were front-page stars of the *Anglo-American Review* in 1923.

There were some very influential figures with business interests in Argentina, and cricket did not struggle for support. The Argentine Cricket Association's well-connected secretary and treasurer E. W. S. Thomson wasted little time in asking the proprietor of Bovril, George Johnston, Baron Luke of Pavenham, and other British tycoons with interests in the Plata to represent the association in London, as much in the corridors of the Argentine Club in Piccadilly as the Lord's pavilion.

A fat and jovial cricket nut born in Wellingborough and schooled at Bedford, Ernest Thomson would open up his breast pocket every lunchtime to offer cigars to the players, then tuck into his favourite tipple, 'pink gin . . . *poco de pink*'. He served on the ACA committee from 1905 until leaving to join the Home Guard in England during the Second World War. His fortune amassed in the Argentine shipping industry allowed him to organise tours to England every summer from 1924 to 1929, under the banner of Anglo-Argentine XIs. The 1926 and 1928 tours included grand days out against MCC at Lord's.

Thomson also led Buenos Aires teams on 36-hour rail trips up to the Leach estate. For them it was a holiday where tennis, golf, swimming and race meets could be indulged alongside the more serious business of cricket, on a field next to the Bachelors' House. After play they would adjourn to the billiards room, where the evenings morphed into jazz dances. The presence of the Wichí appears to have been little more than a curiosity. 'This semi-tropical district has been the scene of many enjoyable games of the country house nature . . . and are particularly interesting during harvest time, when the Indians come in from far distances to work in the sugar canes,' wrote Thomson. 'The amateur book-makers are splendid and the keenness shown by the Indians lends great fun to the proceedings.' On the Easter 1922 trip Dorning and Gibson were overshadowed for once as J. H. 'Toby' Paul – the crack bat in Rosario – struck a phenomenal 166 out of the ACA's 234, with no other team-mate passing 16.

After almost a century of play, the strength and breadth of Argentine cricket was impressive; the depth less so. With the benefit of hindsight, this interwar period was crunch time if cricket was to catch on among the locals. But one correspondent betrayed the prejudice of many Anglo-Argentines: 'The foreign element in B.A. despises any exercise more exacting than a walk to the promenade.' This does not square with their love of football and rugby.

The locals were variously damned as either too lazy or too excitable. Philip Foy, writing for the *Cricketer*, took a defeatist attitude: 'The game is too slow for the Latin temperament to accept spontaneously and there are no Argentine public schools where it could be taught. There is undoubtedly, however, a large element that would take to the game and play it well if facilities and education afforded.'

Joseph Kelly worked at the Anglo-South American Bank, which had their own sports ground within view of the Plata. He was taken aback by the way life was stratified along racial lines. 'The British lead an insular social life and, outside of business, come little into contact with the natives and other foreign residents . . . We tend to glare at each other . . . For some mysterious reason conditions here seem to make for snobbery, and anything which may tend to alter this would be greatly welcomed.'

Even Belgrano, one of the less exclusive set-ups, had started charging for attendance in an attempt to 'keep out undesirables', following other clubs who for decades had sought to 'avoid the mob of "non-distinguidos" who are found to be spoiling the pleasure of events'. Lomas had stationed a gateman to charge entry in 1909, and engaged the services of a 'vigilante' to enforce good behaviour. Hurlingham were a strictly British-only club and would never have allowed a *peon* through the gates unless he was a cleaner.

One teacher, ruminating in the *Spectator* on his years in Argentina, remembered heading out at the same time as Guy Halkett, the new headmaster at Belgrano Day School:

It was not so much that he disliked Argentina as that he did not see it. He dropped instantly into the British community, became popular in a dozen homes, a leading figure in amateur theatricals . . . a bulwark of the local cricket team [Club Atlético San Isidro]. He treated Argentines rather as he would have treated the more educated Indians, and behaved much as though the whole country were a colony of ours . . . I can see him now, his tall lank figure erect and his chin high, walking down the centre of an Argentine street, his pipe in his mouth, his dark grey flannels and sports coat as the insignia of his type, quite oblivious of the amused stares of the dapper Argentines, to whom he was a good example of an *ingles seco*. He bothered little about the language, and reproved all menials in savage English – a most effective method. I can hear him snapping, 'Get out of my way, can't you!' to a group of dirty children crawling on the pavement before him. He was always courteous, but he expected, and obtained, respect from what he called 'native' working people . . . I remember the easy way in which he gave orders to everyone [including] the youths who tried to interfere with the English boys' games at the Athletic Club.

In spite of Halkett, CA San Isidro, up in the northern suburbs near the Plata, were renowned for casting their net wider than most. In February 1915, they fielded a side domi-nated by Latin Spanish-speakers: Arbelaiz, Bunciaz, Casserly, Gallerdo, Pendola, Strada, Tiberio, Torres and Yanon – many of them posing in their batting gear for portraits in *Mundo Argentino* magazine. Eight years later San Isidro shocked the cricket scene by lifting the second division title. 'Our most hearty congratulations go out to the new champions,' declared the BACC, 'since several members of their team are pure Argentines, to whom the game is yet in its infancy.' When San

Isidro turned over Belgrano on 16 December 1922, the *Anglo-American Review* carried a photo of Belgrano's H. H. Vignoles, a white man, at the toss with the dark-skinned San Isidro skipper E. Arbelaiz, who was standing in for R. E. Jones. Arbelaiz hit 60 in one match, and Yanon took a hat-trick as San Isidro closed in on the title in February, finishing on 37 wickets at the price of 10 over the season. The Talbots of Rosario were dark-skinned but able to conceal their part-Latino heritage behind the surname of a British father. G. Tosetti, a prolific century-maker, must have had *some* British blood, or he would not have been admitted as a Hurlingham Club member.

McGough's fastidious archiving shows that several Latin Argentines had raised their bats to salute centuries. Among them were A. Leunda, who scored 132 for San Isidro v. Barracas in 1903, and A. Camacho, with 123 for Club Ferro Carril Oeste v. Buenos Aires Grammar School in 1909.

Many Spanish speakers had learned the game at schools across Buenos Aires and were able to read about cricket in their own language. As far back as 1881, J. W. Williams of Buenos Aires had published the first Spanish-language cricket instruction book in the world, *La Tranca: juego atlético*. The title itself refers to the pitch, though as with 'wicket' in English, *tranca* has multiple meanings in Spanish. In Argentina if a batsman looks like getting out to a rash shot, his partner might walk down to say '*tranca*', as in *tranquilo*, to calm down and bat long. *La Tranca*'s glossary included *resbala* (slip), *intruso* (lbw), *bola-punzadora* (shooter) and many terms that survive in Argentine cricket today. Tellingly, a run is *punto* – literally a point. The country's leading conservative papers, *La Nación* and *La Prensa*, reported on Test matches and County Championship action as well as the Argentine scene, while the dramatic 'Fowler's Match' of 1910 between Eton and Harrow earned a photograph and extended report.

*　　*　　*

The earliest editions of Pelham Warner's *Cricketer* came decorated with slogans reflecting the great game's reach: 'Everywhere Under the Sun' and 'The Sun Never Sets on Cricket'. Subscribers could be found in Buenos Aires, Lima, Montevideo, Port Stanley, Rio de Janeiro and Valparaíso. The family of Warner's mother, Ella Rosa Cadiz, came from Venezuela. That he would take a cricket team to Latin America was written in the stars.

Although Percy Chapman led England to a win at The Oval that claimed back the Ashes in 1926, the conflict of interest between Warner's dual roles as an England selector and cricket journalist came to a head, and he was dropped from the panel. The captaincy of an MCC tour to South America may well have been the compensation.

The party he enlisted was blue-blooded even by MCC standards: three army captains, a lord who would be a Tory prime minister, and three future England Test captains. The reunion dinner in May 1927 was held at the Conservative Club in London. Naturally, President Alvear and General Agustín Pedro Justo – who three years later launched a military coup in order to seize the top job for himself – came by to watch play and greet the teams in the 'Test' at Hurlingham. Somehow the president mistook the stooping, balding Warner for a famous bullfighter, though it's possible he was joking. 'President Alvear liked the English and tried to accommodate their wishes,' reflected Andrew Graham-Yooll. 'A strike in 1920 at the British-owned tannine producers, the Forestal Land, Timber and

Railways Company in Santa Fe, had been crushed by the army . . . And the powerful railway unions had also been demolished. In Patagonia, a strike organised by expatriate European anarchists at British-owned sheep farms had been ended by the army, with the execution of the ring-leaders who fell riddled with bullets into the graves they had dug.'

The players' average age was a long-in-the-tooth 36, dragged down by Alec Douglas-Home – then marked in the scorebook under his courtesy title, Lord Dunglass – and Gubby Allen, both in their footloose early twenties. The bushy-chested Gerry Weigall, 56, was a notorious bounder, famous for his aphorisms and for being regularly chucked out of social events for droning on. One morning in the Parque Hotel at Montevideo he pottered down for a pre-breakfast dip, stripping down to everything but his trunks. As the assembled ambassadors' wives scurried for the exits, Weigall rubbed his chest vigorously, hollering 'Virility! Virility!' At a Jockey Club ball, Weigall sauntered up to a beautiful woman clad in black, leaned over and whispered to her: 'Always wear black with pearls, ma'am, you look magnificent.' It turned out that she was the wife of a prominent gangster, and Weigall got out of the club alive only because of the eminence of the MCC name.

Thomson had made arrangements for a party of 14 – all expenses paid, free passes to the Jockey Club and golf clubs, and train fares covered for up to 3000 miles. When MCC sent just 12, he worried the intense heat and humidity would knock the stuffing out of the ageing English gentlemen. Perhaps the most important individual during the 'Test' series against Argentina was not a player, administrator or umpire, but the driver of the ice wagon stationed on the sidelines day after day. Sure enough, in one match MCC were left with nine men standing. Warner gave Thomson space to vent his grievances in the *Cricketer*, in which he declared himself 'bitterly disappointed, and perhaps annoyed . . . having raised some £3,000 to defray expenses'. To help fund the tour, Jorge Brown ran a competition in conjunction with the *Buenos Aires Herald* to guess the highest individual score and scorer in the 'Test series'.

Gubby Allen, young and distinctly quick, sent down plenty of overs – and was exerted more than he might have been due to the Argentine umpires' proclivity for no-balling him due to differing interpretations of the 'dragging' Law. (It has long been rumoured that Allen was Warner's son, conceived out of wedlock. Allen, however, was born in Sydney in July 1902, when Warner seems to have spent the previous winter in Paris.)

'The tour was unique in that not a single game was played within the British Empire,' gushed Warner, strangely ignoring Hawke's tour of 15 years earlier. This was a time when West Indies, New Zealand and India were all ascending to Test status, and the stream of cricketing news from the Río de la Plata created excitement about the possible emergence of a Test power in the New World. It would have needed the subverting of the Imperial Cricket Conference's constitution: not until 1965 was ICC membership available to countries outside the Commonwealth. But if anyone could pull some strings at Lord's, it was Warner.

The SS *Andes* came into port at Montevideo on Christmas Eve 1926 with the egg-and-bacon MCC flag flying from the yardarm, a suggestion apparently made by the ship's captain. 'Never before had a cricket flag been flown on any ship on any sea,' beamed Warner. They were a day late and, after a quick lunch at the Parque Hotel, were thrust straight into a two-day match at La Blanqueada. Dorning spent *Navidad* taking the ferry across the Plata – a distinctly less picturesque journey than it sounds, and a more industrial one back then – to compile a dossier on his opponents.

In an intra-club trial match between South American Born and Foreign Born, Montevideo CC's best Latino players, the Peña brothers José and Juan – sons of the groundsman at La Blanqueada – captured all 18 wickets for their side. But, in the long awaited Montevideo CC v. Marylebone CC clash, old connections seemed to tell: just Juan donned the dark blue and orange Montevideo cap, and he batted at number 11 and bowled just five overs. The side also contained Charles E. Cat, founder of the Unión de Rugby del Uruguay – whose great-grandson Juan Manuel Cat would score one of Uruguay's tries in their landmark win over Fiji in the 2019 Rugby World Cup. Montevideo batted against new sightscreens erected specially for the occasion, but were bamboozled by Jack 'Farmer' White's slow left-arm variations in a spell of seven for 27. No wonder: White would be England's leading wicket taker in the 1928–9 Ashes.

Before the side had even arrived in Buenos Aires, the War Office sent a telegram to the Plaza Hotel insisting that Captain R. T. Stanyforth, MCC's wicketkeeper, return home by 2 February 1927 to report for duty with the 17/21 Lancers. Someone must have put in a word as, within a week, the War Office granted him extended leave up to 4 March to complete the tour. Twelve months later Stanyforth was named England Test captain for the tour of South Africa – much of it on account of his oratorical skills in South America. He remains the only man to have led England in a Test without playing county cricket first.

This was the first time Dunglass, the future prime minister and foreign secretary, had been abroad. He was on his way down from Oxford, where he had scraped a third-class degree in Modern History. Embarrassingly his portrait in the *Herald* came accompanied with the caption: 'The first M.C.C. player to suffer the effects of the intense heat in Argentina', and he spent much of the tour on his sickbed with heatstroke and appendicitis. Warner showed no mercy, shoving the future PM in at short leg, in the days before protective equipment, and Dunglass broke down 20 minutes into the first 'Test' at Hurlingham.

Argentina produced their best batting in this 'Test', with Henry Marshal – rated by Warner as the best batsman in South America – stroking 105, which would be the only century of the series, thus making him the surprise correct answer in Jorge Brown's competition. The only first-class cricketer to have been born in Colombia, Marshal was sent from the family ranch to Oundle School before venturing south to make his career in Rosario. 'He watched the ball closely,' judged Warner, 'and seemed more at home when the ball was turning than any of his companions, and as a mid-off he is in the front rank.' Argentina managed 327 – no mean feat against an attack of Test quality in Allen and White – in a draw.

MCC easily won the second 'Test' at Belgrano, though Warner was relieved when the clouds came over, giving the ageing Englishmen some respite from the sun before a final charge with the ball. 'Even the strongest are exhausted,' said Warner. White – or 'Señor Blanco', as he was christened by the Belgrano dressing-room attendant – had to change his shirt four times over the course of the day. Warner paid tribute to the attendant: 'A prince of couriers, a Chesterfield in manners, ever ready with "whiskey soda" or "gin tonic" to quench the thirst.'

Much like Lord's at the time, the venerable BACC did not translate to pristine batting surfaces. Palermo's high water table and sandy surface made for devilishly difficult batting in wet weather in the third 'Test'. The pitch – re-dressed a few years earlier using wagonloads of black earth donated by the Pacific Railway – had been marled, but it crumbled after a thunderstorm. Warner made the mistake of letting the Argentines bat when the pitch was freshest, and their 134 proved the highest total of the match. Dorning, one of the spearheads of the win over Hawke's side 15 years before, was now into his fifties, but the English found him unplayable. Warner reflected: 'He is now on the slow side, but still commands the respect of the best batsman. He can spin the ball, and make it swerve and go with his arm.' He took seven for 38 as MCC folded for 89. Twenty-year-old Dennet Ayling's off-spin mopped up with six for 32 in the second innings in an Argentine triumph.

Warner, ignoring the golden rule of cricket tours – never offend your hosts – was so irked by the defeat that he strong-armed Thomson into squeezing in an extra 'Test' at Belgrano. It forced the Argentines to arrange more time off work, which may explain why Marshal refused to leave the crease after treading on to his own stumps. The umpires, R. W. Rudd and 'Curly' Roberts, the Sussex professional coaching in Argentina, claimed not to have seen it, and let Marshal bat on. But MCC ran through Argentina for just 101 in the second innings, winning with five minutes to spare, and Warner had his series victory.

It was on to Chile, though not by mule this time. The Pacific Railway laid on the train decked out with marble baths and sitting rooms that the Prince of Wales (the future King Edward VIII) and brother Albert (King George VI) had used to travel around Argentina and Chile in 1925. The ruddy-cheeked

White liked a hand of poker, but as the team were passing Aconcagua on the Transandine Railway, he was beaten by two royal flushes from Tom Jameson, and threw the only pack of cards the touring party had out of the window and on to the slopes below.

*     *     *

Arriving half an hour late at San Isidro station, we turn right to walk towards the stationhouse, assuming we have to pass through ticket barriers. Wrong. Our lift, Ronnie Scott is spitting feathers at the other end of the platform, and clearly expected better from two British journalists. He is dressed impeccably in board shorts and fashionable shoes, muttering about how useless the British are these days. He marches us off to his car, and the 99-year-old drives us and the doyen of Argentine cricket, David Parsons, to lunch in a German restaurant, swearing all the way in clipped tones about the dreadful Argentine driving. He turns out to be great company and a fascinating man.

Scott was one of 400 Argentine pilots who flew for the Allies in the Second World War. His role was to stop the V-1 bombs bound for London. He returned home at Christmas 1946 to a rude awakening. 'I was told fairly promptly, "You're not a Peronista. You'd better become one."' Luckily, he and other Argentine RAF veterans were gratefully snapped up by Aerolinias Argentinas, the new national flag carrier, who were to become a loyal sponsor of the Argentine Cricket Association. When the first long-haul flights began from Buenos Aires to New York, they would stop over in Trinidad, which allowed Scott to slope off to watch Sonny Ramadhin and the rest in

The oldest-known cricket-related photograph from Argentina. The Scottish ranch of Adela, Buenos Aires Province in 1869, with a man padded up and leaning against his cricket bat. *(Universitario de San Andres)*

CRICKETERS

ín del "F. C. Sud".—L. Tintoré Ro dríguez, V. S. Gallardo y C. Bincas, del "San Isidro"
H. L. Gibson, capitán del "Lomas A. C."

Photographs of Latin homegrown cricketers, often CA San Isidro players, posing with their gear were commonplace in Argentine magazines before the First World War. *(Mundo Argentino)*

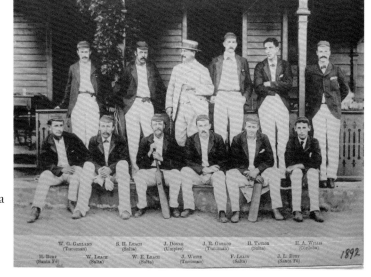

The first North of Argentina side which travelled hundreds of kilometres to Palermo in early 1892. *(Cricket Argentina)*

W. G. Garland (Tucuman). S. H. Leach (Salta). J. Donne (Umpire). J. R. Garroo (Tucuman). H. Taylor (Salta). H. A. Willis (Cordoba).
H. Bury (Santa Fé). W. Leach (Salta). W. E. Leach (Salta). J. White (Tucuman). F. Leach (Salta). J. L. Bury (Santa Fé).

1892

Players watch a game unfold from Buenos Aires Cricket Club's pavilion. It would be burned down by Peronistas in 1947. *(Archivo General de la Nación Argentina)*

The Planetario Galileo Galilei now stands on the site of the Buenos Aires Cricket Club. *(Jeffrey Greenberg, Universal Images Group/Getty Images)*

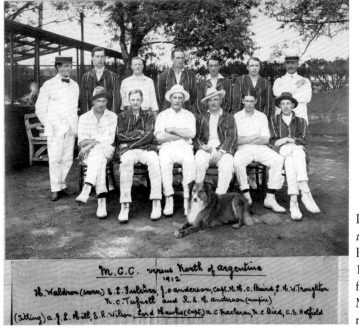

M.C.C. versus North of Argentine
1912
H. Waldron (score) E.L. Sulivan, J.o anderson, Capt. H.B.C. Baird, F.H.W. Troughton
H.C. Tufnell and I.E.H. anderson (umpire)
(Sitting) A.J.L. Hill, E.R. Wilson, Lord Hawke (Capt) A.C. MacLaren, M.C. Bird, C.S. Hatfield

Lord Hawke's MCC XI and *un perro* as 12th man at Rosario Athletic Club, 1911–12. Hawke is sitting third from the left, with Archie MacLaren immediately to his right. *(Rosario Athletic Club)*

A women's cricket team was formed in Argentina in 1865, giving them a claim to the oldest women's club in the world. The *Anglo-American Review* celebrates women players from Quilmes on its front page in 1922.
(Anglo-American Review)

Pelham Warner's 1926–7 MCC tourists in front of the racing grandstand at Hurlingham – which still stands today – before their 'Test' against Argentina.
(Roger Mann Collection)

Plum Warner, captaining MCC, and Clement Gibson, leading Argentina, shake at Hurlingham, 1926–7. Gibson had turned down an Ashes call-up two years earlier. *(Thomas Gibson Private Collection)*

Argentine daily *La Nación* gives the South Americans a front-page send-off ahead of their unprecedented 1932 tour of Britain, where they would play six first-class matches. *(La Nación)*

The great English swing bowler Maurice Tate, hospitalised by a septic foot on Sir Theodore Brinckman's first-class tour of Argentina, 1937–8. He is seen off from Plaza Constitución station by a group of Argentine cricket enthusiasts. *(Martin Chandler)*

Brazil might hold the bragging rights in men's football, but Argentina's men have not lost to their biggest rivals in cricket since 1994. Here they go on the attack during the South American Championship. *(Cricket Argentina)*

The view from Belgrano AC's clubhouse as Argentina's bowlers struggle to take wickets against the Cayman Islands in 2017. *(Timothy Abraham/James Coyne)*

Jorge Mario Bergoglio blessed a cricket ground in his hometown of Buenos Aires before he became Pope Francis. The players of the Cricket Sin Fronteras project were invited to the Vatican and presented him with a bat which he keeps in his office. *(Cricket Sin Fronteras)*

Gilberto Casey, a descendant of one of the original colonists of Nueva Australia, Paraguay, shows us some of his family history. Cricket had long since died by the time we visited. *(Timothy Abraham/ James Coyne)*

CAMPO GRANDE, SAN SALVADOR.

A sketch by John James Wild of a match between HMS *Challenger* and Bahia Cricket Club on the Campo Grande, Salvador in Brazil. The woman to the right of the picture wears clothing typical of those who follow the Candomblé religion. *(Alamy/John James Wild)*

A bird's-eye view of the seaside location of Santos Athletic Club, Brazil. *(Miguel Betti)*

Beach cricket was a formal affair for Santos players in the 19th century with blazers, a rolled pitch, afternoon tea and labourers to transport the mat by mule. *(Santos Athletic Club)*

Brian Johnston, standing centre wearing a jazz hat, along with his team-mates at Santos. Johnston would keep wicket in the State of São Paulo v State of Rio fixture. *(Barry Johnston Private Collection)*

Prince Harry plays the Brazilian game of *taco* – a street game derived from cricket – with youngsters in a Rio de Janeiro favela. Matt Featherstone, the inspirational president of Cricket Brasil, is about to stump him. *(Arthur Edwards, Pool/Getty Images)*

Brazil women won their fourth South American Cricket Championship in 2019. Handed central contracts by Cricket Brasil, they look primed to make waves in the women's game. *(Juliana Anwar)*

Nieuw Nickerie cricket chief Richenel Small poses in front of a scoreboard with his prized black picolet used for big matches in Suriname's bird-singing contests. *(Timothy Abraham/James Coyne)*

Test or Shell Shield matches. He played rugby for Belgrano and cricket for San Isidro, and is the oldest surviving player from the North v. South series. San Isidro stuck to their guns and were the one cricket club who refused to hang a portrait of President Perón in the clubhouse. San Isidro didn't need any inspiration from 'Johnny Sundays' anyway – they had the Ayling brothers.

Guy Halkett did at least one unequivocally good thing for Argentine cricket. As captain of San Isidro, he persuaded Ernest Ayling to allow his teenage sons, Cyril and Cecil, to come into adult cricket. Their older brother, Dennet, had already debuted for Belgrano, and walked down the aisle with a black eye, having been struck in the face by a BACC quick bowler, an injury that his brother-in-law witnessed behind the stumps. Dennet's reason for not joining his younger brothers at San Isidro was a bet with his best man, Jack Goodfellow. 'Jack,' he promised, 'I will join San Isidro when *you* get married.' Goodfellow, a bit of a playboy, delayed getting hitched until 1933, and when he did – to a voluptuous Swedish-Argentine woman – Dennet kept his word, moving that season to San Isidro. With all five Ayling brothers in the side for the first time, San Isidro won the title, with the family accounting for almost three-quarters of all the runs scored and wickets taken.

Ernest Ayling had arrived in Buenos Aires in 1900 to work for the River Plate Trust Loan Company. He himself was no bad player, scoring 171 not out for Belgrano against Hurlingham, and representing South four times. His five sons grew up playing cricket in their back yard at Sucre y O'Higgins in Belgrano. They learned to bat with a broomstick to fend off hard green oranges, and a salvaged kerosene tin for stumps. They played cricket at every opportunity and introduced their Latino neighbours to the game. The Aylings were to suffer agony in 1933, when their sister, Rowena, an accomplished Spanish dancer, died of peritonitis aged just 13. As part of the grieving process, Ernest took the boys off to Brazil . . . where the brothers still managed to fit in a couple of guest appearances in Rio.

Dennet Ayling was at his peak when Sir Julien Cahn, the eccentric furniture magnate from Nottingham, bankrolled a party of 30 to Argentina in early 1930. Cahn had embodied the country-house cricket of the Jazz Age – building his own grounds in West Bridgford on the outskirts of Nottingham and Stanford Hall in Leicestershire, and providing jobs for first-class cricketers in exchange for turning out for his team in summer and winter. He brought along his family, the Trent Bridge dressing-room attendant George Shaw and his personal Russian barber, Louis Dubnikov.

On the boat journey out, the *Avila* of the Blue Star Line – the shipping company owned by the Vesteys, which advertised deck cricket to passengers – Cahn dressed up as Neptune to dunk the heads of his players in the sea when they crossed the Equator. Cahn was an obsessive hypochondriac, and to guard against bruises or broken bones – or perhaps to ensure that his frequent plays and misses picked up runs from leg byes – he went out to bat in giant inflatable pads, and was carried to the crease by his minions in a bathchair. John Gunn, the former Nottinghamshire opener and Cahn's umpire, reportedly never gave his boss out lbw. Although Cahn was nominally the captain, he was 'consulted on strategy' by Walter Robins, and limited his tactical input to adjusting the direction of the tail on the wooden fox that he pitched into the ground near the pavilion: when the team was doing well, Cahn would raise the tail; when things went south, he would point it to the earth.

Dennet picked up three wickets in four balls – Peter Eckersley, Cyril Rowland and Fred Nicholas (grandfather of the broadcaster and former Hampshire captain Mark) – to help the Northern Suburbs thrash Cahn's XI by an innings. But in Cahn's party were two fine leg-spinners: Middlesex and England star Robins and Len Richmond of Essex. Even Cahn, who bowled dreadful lob-ups, took his one first-class wicket, when Dennet ran down and missed one at Belgrano.

The 'Test' series, won by Cahn's XI 1–0, marked the last competitive action for Dorning, who captained Argentina at the age of 55. He did so wearing the guanaco on his cap for the first and only time. In March 1928 the ACA had adopted the guanaco as its emblem – intended to evoke the fleet-of-foot Argentine fielder – which took pride of place on dark blue Argentine caps, blazers and letterheads for the rest of the century. Dorning retired to Perranporth on the north Cornwall coast, and on his death in 1955, the *Buenos Aires Herald* declared him 'the W. G. Grace of Argentine cricket'.

*　　*　　*

It came too late for Dorning, but in April 1932 ten Argentines, three Brazilians and two Chileans set sail for the old country to mark the centenary of cricket in Buenos Aires. This unique South American combination, never attempted before or since, wore sky-blue caps and blazers, with a yellow badge incorporating the Argentine guanaco, a Brazilian palm tree and the star of Chile.

The financial ripples caused by the Wall Street Crash had put a halt to Thomson's private tours, and the great organiser of Argentine cricket may have viewed this as his grand farewell.

*La Nación*'s front page led with a preview special penned by tour manager Thomson, and headshots of the Argentine contingent. Dennet and Cyril Ayling made the cut, but 20-year-old Cecil was deemed too young, despite having scored a century in a North v. South match. He and his father made the trip to England in support of Dennet and Cyril.

For Gibson, the touring captain, it was his last hurrah on the English stage – both in cricket and the high life as a distinctly eligible bachelor. By now his father was heading Gibson Brothers, on the board of Liebig's, chairman of the British Chamber of Commerce, chair of the Great Southern Railway and tasked by the Prince of Wales with overseeing the Empire Trades Exhibition in Buenos Aires – for which he was made the first overseas baronet.

On the eve of the tour, Gibson had announced his engagement to Marjorie Anderson, scion of the famed Buenos Aires sporting dynasty. Where Clem was quiet and taciturn, Marjorie was fiery and dogmatic. In February 1933, Sir Herbert found Clem 'sadly upset and broken by what had evidently been a stormy time with Marjorie . . . as time goes on he finds he has nothing in common with her, but he feels duty-bound to go through with the marriage.' They were wed, in a small civil ceremony attended only by close family, that June, but it was a tough marriage. The family were to grow up in England while Clem worked back on the *estancia*.

On the first morning at Canterbury against Kent Second XI, the teams pioneered an experiment with brass stumps and bails painted khaki. It was a trial for an alternative to ash, which broke too easily in the hot and humid Americas. But the metal bulged to a ridiculous size when the ball started hitting the stumps, and the experiment was abandoned at lunch on the first day. Kent, featuring the young leg-spinner Doug Wright, won by six wickets.

*The Times* sent their cricket correspondent Richard 'Beau' Vincent to report on the South Americans against MCC at Lord's. The tourists were staring at the follow-on before Cyril Ayling launched a superb comeback. He picked up five for 72 in the first innings – swinging the ball both ways and finding pace off the pitch – as MCC racked up 338. Cyril was at the crease by the end of play as the tourists stumbled to 92 for six. The MCC side – containing four Test cricketers – might have imbibed a little too readily at the gala dinner in the Long Room, as next morning Cyril came out and struck a superb 95 not out, with eight fours and not a chance offered, earning a standing ovation as he walked back into the pavilion.

In the South Americans' ten-wicket win over Oxford University in the Parks, Marshal struck 153, and was assisted in a stand of 159 by teenage George Ferguson, 'who used his reach in powerful driving, and pulled and cut well', reported *Wisden*. The South Americans' only other win came at West Bridgford against Cahn's XI.

On the whole, though, the British press were sniffy about the South Americans. It did not help that, at Leicester, Toby Paul twisted his ankle in the wet conditions and was ruled out of the tour. By 1932 the cattle rancher was 44 and short of practice, yet still struck 110 against Richmond CC and 92 against the Gentlemen of Somerset. The *Daily Herald*'s man compared Paul favourably with the England captain about to lead his side to Australia: 'He gives me far more pleasure to watch than D. R. Jardine.'

\*     \*     \*

As the rural economy stuttered, northern ranchers moved en masse to Buenos Aires or left the country altogether. In 1929, E. F. 'Pancho' Sylvester, chairman of the North committee, cabled Buenos Aires to inform them that, for the first time except in case of war, the old classic would have to be cancelled. Nonetheless, North scrabbled together 11: Paul rushed to Belgrano straight off the boat from England to find the game already three hours old, and struck an unbeaten 207 not out – just ten short of Foy's record.

To McGough's disgust, the North committee was disbanded in 1932, Camps Cricket Week cancelled in 1934 and the responsibility for selecting both sides passed to the Buenos Aires clubs. The city's journalists, feeling that *el clásico* was no longer fit for purpose, floated alternative fixtures that might better reflect the country's cricketing divisions: Argentine-Born v. British-Born; Capital v. Country. 'Many times through the years North v South has been on the point of folding up or changing its name,' wrote Bridger. 'Wiser councils [*sic*] have always sought ways and means to keep it going.'

Sir Theodore Brinckman, a Yorkshire baronet, brought the last first-class touring side to Argentina, in 1937–8. Bob Wyatt had played his final Test at Melbourne the previous March, on England's first Ashes tour after Bodyline; Andy Sandham and Maurice Tate had just called time on their county careers; the leading umpire of the era, Frank Chester, who had lost his right arm in the Salonika campaign in 1917, made for a stirring figure as he signalled to the scorers with his white jacket flapping against his black prosthetic limb. Tate would have been the finest bowler ever to send one down in Argentina, but he suffered a bizarre injury when he cut his foot playing golf on the stopover in Lisbon. The wound turned septic, and there was concern he might lose the entire foot. On docking in Montevideo, 30 hours late due to storms, he was diagnosed with pneumonia, and spent almost the entire tour, including Christmas, in bed in the British Hospital, as Brinckman's XI drew the series 1–1.

\*     \*     \*

Argentina's generals assumed Germany would win second time round. Most of the German and Austrian workers on the British-owned railways quietly slipped away once Britain declared war on 3 September 1939. Around 4000 Anglo-Argentines answered the call this time, and the RAF No. 164 Squadron was turned over to a combination of Polish and Argentine volunteers; Philip Runnacles of CA San Albano was in Stalag Luft III when a group of British prisoners launched their 'Great Escape' in April 1944.

The highest-profile engagement in South America came early, in December 1939, with the Battle of the River Plate. HMS *Exeter*, *Ajax* and *Achilles* shadow-boxed *Admiral Graf Spee*, a prolific sinker of Allied boats, into the port at Montevideo, causing its captain, Hans Langsdorff, to scuttle the ship. Later in the war, the *Ajax* crew played at Belgrano where Roy Gooding, who scored 64, took the field for an ACA XI alongside Clem Gibson, still a formidable bowler in his mid-forties. 'I remember thinking that putting him in the side was a bit unfair on the sailors. I watched him practising his bowling and he somehow seemed to get a lot of speed out of his hand in relation to the speed of his action.' Lomas AC, in the midst of a run of three wooden spoons, were visited seven times by British naval ships, and made ten officers and clergy honorary members.

BACC scraped through the 1941–2 season using just 12 new balls, but shelled out 2350 pesos for a mechanical mower, which finally consigned the Palermo horse to the knacker's yard. MCC are said to have smuggled bundles of bats and balls into relief packages bound for Buenos Aires: some sunk by German U-boats; some which made it through; some sent on to the Falkland Islands. Eventually the ACA suspended the Championship and North v. South, and made do with friendlies. These fixtures were not universally popular in Buenos Aires, and the ACA were forced to defend themselves in the press for organising matches to raise funds for war donations or local charities.

Even in war, Argentina was a society preoccupied with class and colour. Belgrano shocked 'snooty Hurlinghamites' by turning up to play them wearing rugby socks pulled up over their whites. Belgrano considered themselves a cut above San Isidro, who played in the shadow of a utilitarian concrete rugby grandstand, still there to this day. 'It was somehow a bit off-putting,' said Gooding. 'Monumental in its poor taste, it dominated the field. I seldom seemed to have much success at San Isidro, and there was a crowd of "Argentine" boys playing there at that time, who, horror of horrors, beat us quite easily.' One inhabitant of the San Isidro suburbs was Ernesto 'Che' Guevara, a medical student, who played rugby for their local rivals San Isidro Club.

For away days, Belgrano boys would clamber into O. H. 'Papoosa' Rendtorff's open car, which had 'a dickey at the back, and a rubber "claxon" horn on the windscreen'. Confusingly, all the males in the family were christened O. H. Rendtorff. James McGough's ears would have been pricked by their German surname – a candidate for round two of his statutory lists of enemy persons. Indeed, Stalin had been so paranoid about Nazi operatives in Buenos Aires that he ordered Soviet operatives to burn down the city's German bookshop. But McGough died in July 1942, too soon to assist in tracking down the Nazis who would escape to South America. He would not have had to go far: at one stage Josef Mengele lived just around the corner from his house in Florida.

One intervention by an Argentine cricket acolyte did help the Allies turn the tide. In 1943, Harry Martin, a chartered accountant and a former BACC secretary, dined out on steak with László Bíró, a Hungarian Jew who had escaped to Buenos Aires. Bíró hoped to license his ballpoint pen invention in Argentina. Martin raised the idea with the RAF, as fountain pens did not work reliably above a certain altitude, and persuaded the British government to sanction the production of Bíró's pen. Martin had already bought 13 hectares of land in Pilar, 'the polo capital of Argentina', with the intention of running a dairy farm. But he accumulated enough wealth from Biros to build the sumptuous Martindale Country Club there, complete with a cricket ground. For three decades, Martin would clear out the club at weekends for the ACA to bring up hundreds of Argentine youngsters for cricket festivals.

Once the war was over, the writing was on the wall for the British in Argentina. The Truman administration in the United States made it clear to their closest ally that outright sale of the Argentine railways was the only acceptable option. So, after years of negotiation, on 1 March 1948, 16,000 miles of rail network encompassing 11 British-owned companies all passed into state ownership. Argentina paid Britain £150 million, wrapped up in a meat agreement up to the end of 1949. On the same day, the remaining British-run railways in Uruguay were transferred to their government. Perón announced his deal to a gathering of a million in Buenos Aires. '*Perón cumple*' ('Perón delivers!'), '*Nuestro, gracias a Perón*' ('Ours, thanks to Perón') declared posters on stations and trains. Winston Churchill, the leader of the opposition, quipped that the Attlee government had sold the railways to pay for Britain's false teeth – the NHS.

Generations of Anglo-Argentine railwaymen and cricketers were suddenly serving new masters. Gone were the reduced fares for cricket teams; entire sports clubs fell away when the railway and utility manpower that supported them disappeared overnight. In August 1948, two directors of Leach's Estates were called in by the Argentine ambassador in London and asked to hand over millions of pesos to his government there and then, without receipt. Their vast estates in Jujuy were soon nationalised.

Foy, a lifelong bachelor who had plunged his time into teaching English and coaching cricket, had his ashes scattered at Hurlingham in 1957. With him died the annual fixture between the Argentine branches of the Old Bedfordians and Old Alleynians, which had endured at Palermo or Hurlingham since the late nineteenth century.

Geoffrey Brooke-Taylor – uncle of comedian Tim of *The Goodies* fame – had played for Cambridge University alongside Clem Gibson and for Derbyshire before sailing out to make his fortune in the 1920s, becoming assistant manager of the biggest wine merchants in Argentina. In September 1948, a box of rifles and 1000 rounds of ammunition were discovered in his stockroom. Brooke-Taylor was arrested and spent four days tied to a chair being interrogated. He insisted the case of rifles had been passed on by a bankrupt company subsumed 14 years earlier. Some of the press jumped to the conclusion that the guns were linked to a recent assassination plot on the Peróns. A few weeks later, shots were fired into Brooke-Taylor's house, and he had to beat out petrol-soaked burning rags blazing at his doors and windows.

Meanwhile, the Argentine Congress offered BACC a sop of 150,000 pesos to rebuild their charred pavilion. But the committee considered it too precarious to build on rented land. After a season of wandering, able to field just one side, BACC took up an 'offer' to merge with their old tenants the Buenos Aires Rugby Club and move to their ground at Don Torcuato. There was no cricket pavilion, rugby dominated the square and they were 20 miles out of sight of downtown Buenos Aires. The BACC literally sank into a quagmire. Although the municipal authorities offered Palermo back after Perón was deposed, the asking price was astronomical.

In 1953 the Jockey Club was burned down by a Peronist gang. Clem Gibson and three friends dashed there with shotguns to guard the entrance, but a waiter let the arsonists slip through the back. The library containing 50,000 books and some priceless works of art, including an original Goya, went up in the blaze. When the fire brigade was called, the plaintive reply down the phone was: 'We have no instructions to put out a fire at the Jockey Club.' A fire truck turned up, but the *bomberos* were reportedly held back by the police.

When Liebig's was nationalised, Gibson took up a senior directorship at Quilmes brewers. He too was approached to pay a backhander. When he refused, Evita put out a hit on Argentina's most illustrious cricketer. Gibson fled to the family's northernmost ranch in the Chaco. 'My father took this threat to his life rather casually, I thought,' says his son, Thomas. 'Our gauchos would all carry a sidearm, and the Indian gauchos used to ride in bare feet and spurs. Imagine that? They all loved my father – he was a calm, gentle man who seemed to command adoration. I was told that two sets of hitmen were sent up by Evita to bump him off, but they never made it back to BA . . .'

Gibson's real sadness was being unable to travel back to London to see his other son, Clem Jr, follow him in representing Eton at Lord's. 'In those days they used to give the Eton v. Harrow score on the BBC, so he was huddled around the wireless on the ranch every evening listening to the World Service.'

Montevideo CC were themselves pushed out to the suburbs at Carrasco, into a partnership with the British School. In a bizarre case of self-harm, the kind in which cricket excels, even after Perón's travel restrictions were lifted Montevideo's application to join the Argentine Championship as *extranjeros especiales* was rejected by the ACA. It was the killer blow to Uruguayan cricket – in the 1960s the Montevideo Cricket Club became a rugby club first and foremost, with cricket little more than a word in the title.

The Anglo-Argentines who ran cricket believed they had something special to protect; not all grasped they needed to adapt to new realities. 'The game is more "acriollado" than before the war,' reflected Gooding.

There are few Public School blazers on show now and Spanish words are liberally intermingled in the cricket jargon. The midday pre-lunch drink session on Sunday, with a few rounds of 'liar dice' has become much reduced, largely because of the expense. Even the sit-down lunch itself, with *milanesas*, salads, ice cream and coffee, is threatened with being replaced by sandwiches, but thank goodness this has not yet happened at Hurlingham . . . In most other respects we, basically, perpetuate the scene as it has always been, and I suppose to the outside world our way of doing things would appear amateurish, archaic, anachronistic – and expendable.

\*       \*       \*

In March 1958, Lt-Col. R. T. Stanyforth received a tip-off from Clem Gibson: Argentine cricket was in a bad way. ACA membership had tumbled to less than 500; the playing numbers were half that. It seems that many clubs were still not open to a wide spectrum of Argentines. Stanyforth dashed off a letter to MCC secretary Ronny Aird: 'All agree they want an MCC tour out at once. It is in the nature of an SOS. They say their cricket is at the crossroads. Their good players are old, the young Britishers have had no encouragement, as also the Argentines who have only recently taken up cricket. They say that never before had Spanish been spoken in the nets. Personally, I think we [MCC] have always treated them badly.' MCC issued invites for just their second non-Test tour since the war and one of the last all-amateur jaunts before the status was abolished in England in 1962, though the Essex professional Micky Bear, who was coaching in Argentina that winter, was allowed to tag along (and presumably share the same dressing rooms).

Air travel was the game changer. England's 1953–4 trip to the West Indies was the first time an MCC side had flown out on tour. By 1970, the New Zealand Ambassadors flew from Auckland via Easter Island and Tahiti to Santiago, and were able to visit six countries of South America in a month. Some things didn't change: they were still fed roast beef and boiled vegetables, followed by apple pie, on arrival in Buenos Aires.

The young Warwickshire captain Mike Smith knew the country from an Oxbridge rugby tour of South America two years earlier. He had good reason to return with MCC: at the Hurlingham Club he had met Diana Leach, a charming primary-school teacher, and the granddaughter of Frank Leach, one of the cricketer-pioneers in Jujuy. They fell in love, and married within three years.

Hubert Doggart's MCC tourists rang in New Year on a DC-6 somewhere over Uruguay in the company of a singing padre, who 'conducted seasonal community singing . . . using a champagne glass for a baton'. The English cricketers countered with a bawdy take on Cole Porter's 'You're the Top'. In the heat, MCC sensibly relaxed their jacket-and-tie dress code to an open-necked shirt, white blazers and khaki shorts, which confused the Kent fast bowler David Sayer. At one cocktail party, he tapped a man in a white tuxedo on the shoulder: 'Hey, maestro, how's about a glass of *vino*?' It turned out to be the British ambassador. An awkward silence ensued.

With ball in hand, MCC were deadly serious. In their opening match, at Hurlingham, an Argentine Colts XVI were bowled out for 42. A senior ACA XI were so desperate to meet top-class opposition, after a gap of more than 20 years, that they waded through a submerged outfield to play MCC at Lomas, only to be blown away for 16 by Sayer and Essex's Jack Bailey. Sayer's pace and hostility had not been glimpsed in Argentina for a generation. He was called up as a late replacement only after Ted Dexter was promoted to the more illustrious MCC party in Australia for the Ashes. Doggart told his team-mates that Cyril Ayling had bowled an over at him as good as any he had ever received in England. But he couldn't bowl from both ends. The pair of two-day 'Tests' ended in withering defeats.

From the removal of chilly England, Roy Webber grumbled in his statistician's column for the *Cricketer* that MCC had dropped first-class status from the 'Tests' 'in direct conflict with the past'. But no one could make a serious case for the Argentines being up to first-class standard. It did not stop the Association of Cricket Statisticians & Historians from debating if the full record of North v. South matches should be made first-class – though the proposal was blocked.

With Cecil Ayling bowing out in 1959–60, San Isidro won their last Championship. He finished with 70 centuries in all cricket, and 2563 runs in 26 North v. South encounters – both Argentine records. Five years later Cyril – with 35 hundreds among all his wickets – turned down the chance to play in *el clásico* after 25 consecutive appearances. For the first time in four decades there was no Ayling in the fixture. He came out of retirement one last time to face the New Zealand Ambassadors in 1970, bowling 28 consecutive overs in heat nudging 37 °C. San Isidro could not cope with losing them, and their cricket section limped on for just a handful of years before folding. Cyril retired to concentrate on his manufacturing company Cirilo Ayling, whose bank transfer machines live on under the nose of Argentines in branches across the nation. Regrettably few of the Argentines carrying out their transfers or processing their IDs would realise how he felt coming within one boundary of achieving a century and five wickets in a match at Lord's.

MCC teams led by Doggart and then A. C. Smith in 1964–5 tried to resuscitate cricket in 'the camps'. Porteños would head up from Buenos Aires and congregate in the Churchill Club of Venado Tuerto at 8 p.m. on Friday nights, and drink while they waited to be billeted in the *estancias*. 'The "camp" people were always very critical of the form,' remembered Gooding, 'and the game was played very seriously beneath a surface appearance of light-hearted gaiety.' One of the Churchill Club members and cricket watchers just after the war was Col. Charles Davison, father of the singer Chris de Burgh, who was born in Venado Tuerto in 1948.

The young Glamorgan batsman Tony Lewis looked on absorbed as players and spectators rode up on their steeds, likening the spectacle, in a polo field stretching miles, as 'reminiscent of scenes from *Lawrence of Arabia*'. Lewis noticed a pair of yellowing pads in the corner of the Churchill Club, dating back to Hawke's time. 'There I truly appreciated what cricket meant here. They live on cricket memoirs and the written word.' Some of the ranchers were flabbergasted to learn that amateur status had been abolished in England, and when Lewis lodged with Rupert Cran-Kenrick, the Old Reptonian spat out his wine when he found out that such a fine cricketer had been schooled at humble Neath Grammar. An MCC side donned helmets for the first time – colonial-style planters' hats, actually – to combat the lethal 22 yards and the unforgiving sun at Venado Tuerto.

Doggart had been enchanted by the strokeplay of Maxie Dumas, 'a charming Argentine 17-year-old with no English blood'. Juan Arroyo – inevitably known by the English translation, 'John Brook'– was a renowned tap dancer who was as good at cricket as most Anglos. Pardo Bazan walked out against Doggart's side with an oversize bat a foot wide, obscuring all three stumps, then asked the umpire for a guard of 'three legs', but he proved he was no mug with a proper bat, and top-scored against A. C. Smith's side.

A mangled cricketing Spanglish took root as more Latin Argentines came into the game. Cristóbal Nino, a prominent player at Belgrano, sets the scene after a visiting batsman had just been given out to an overzealous lbw appeal. The Belgrano players gather round to discuss the decision:

'*Para mi no estaba.*' ('For me it was not out.')

'*La jugó bien afuera.*' ('He got a good stride in.')

'*La pego muy arriba.*' ('I hit him very high.')

'*La jugo across.*' ('He played across it.')

'*Estaba plumb.*' ('It was plumb.')

'*Estuvo bien dado el elebee.*' ('The lb was given correctly.')

Nino's team-mate Pedro Jordan captures the challenge of being a thoroughbred Argentine in a sport with peculiar English customs: 'Your captain waves at you as though he were swatting flies and makes you feel rather unwelcome as he says: "*¡Junto a la raya, entre medio de los dos arboles y atento que las casca todas y la mayoria para ese lado! ¡Ojo! y a no arrugar.*" ('Next to the boundary, between the middle of the two trees and watch out because he smashes it! And try not to shrivel.')

'Your bowler adds: "*¿No, tanto, venite un poco mas para la izquierda y no tan lejos, pero jugate, eh?*" ('Not too far, come a little more to the left, but give it a good go, eh?')

' "*¿Vista la que esta tomando sol en el septimo piso?*" ('Did you see the one sunbathing on the seventh floor?')

The ball inevitably flies out to Jordan, who lets it through his hands. He scrambles around for the ball to throw it in; meanwhile the batsmen run three. He expects a volley of abuse from his fellow players.

'This is the moment when you realise what a magnificent crowd cricketers are: "*Well stopped! Bien negro, y la vas a agarrar.*" ('Well done, "darkie", and the next one you'll grab.')

' "*¿Viste que no es facil? ¿Te lastimante?*" ('See that it isn't easy? You hurt?')

'And your captain says: "*¡Cumpliendo! Ponete donde yo te digo.
No te distriagas. La proxima sera. ¡Vamos Belgrano! ¡Apretando!*"
('Well done! Stand where I tell you. Don't get distracted. Next
one. Come on Belgrano! Squeeze!')

\*     \*     \*

'Things got hot here in the 1970s,' says David Parsons, pursing
his lips and wiping his mottled head as he recalls the paranoia
of the time. In 1969, the Ejército Revolucionario del Pueblo
(ERP), a Guevarist group, launched a guerrilla campaign
against the military junta. Brian Adams, touring in Buenos
Aires with the New Zealand Ambassadors, noted that his digs
had three sets of shutters and two Alsatians to guard against a
break-in.

In May 1971 the ERP doorstepped Stanley Sylvester. He was
the British consul in Rosario, the energy behind cricket at the
Athletic Club and the manager of the Swift de la Plata meatpacking plant. The kidnappers demanded better working
conditions, and the distribution of $60,000 of food and cloth-
ing to the poor. After a few days, their demands were met, and
Sylvester was released without harm. The case was Graham
Greene's inspiration for *The Honorary Consul*, though Sylvester
would hardly be flattered by allusions to the hapless title char-
acter Charley Fortnum, a divorced Anglo-Argentine consul in
Corrientes who the kidnappers mistake for the wealthier US
ambassador.

In 1973 the ERP took its rural insurgency into the Andean
highlands, inspired by the Viet Cong and funded by Castro's
Cuba. So Anthony Paine was swimming against the tide when
he breathed life back into cricket in far-flung Tucumán – 'to

prove there was more to it than sugar and guerrillas'. Paine had moved north to work for ICI, and wanted his cricket fix. From the old cricketing strongholds of Tucumán, Salta and Jujuy he tracked down two Leaches, some keen youths and 'three full-blooded Argentines rejoicing in the names of Zaeferer, Pasquini and Migliabacca, none of whom had heard of the game' to make the 400-mile journey to Sierras de Córdoba – dubbed 'the elephant cemetery', for the abundance of wealthy retired Argentines living there. In spite of a military coup, Tucumán CC honoured their return game against Córdoba in 1976. They went to the extent of driving a cast-off motor-mower up from Buenos Aires to cut the wicket at the sports ground belonging to Johnson's Wax. Even more remarkably, Paine succeeded in persuading the first division football club not to train on the square.

Things turned truly nasty when the army launched a counter-insurgency to crush the far left, marking the start of Argentina's Dirty War. Although he seemed to have little time for the place, the British–Trinidadian novelist V. S. Naipaul visited Argentina frequently in the mid-1970s to see his mistress Margaret Gooding, reporting for the *New York Review of Books* on the chilling 'killer cars' driven around by the plain-clothed security services. Margaret had spent her life in the cloistered environment of Catholic girls' boarding schools, and had little time for the clubbable, sporting world inhabited by her husband Roy. The affair carried on for 24 years, but Naipaul was on good terms with Roy for a while, even interviewing him for background on the country. 'Roy was a very intelligent man,' he wrote. 'He had well thought-out views about Argentina.' The Goodings' son, Alex, represented Argentina in three ICC Trophies.

Amnesty International estimated that up to 20,000 Argentines disappeared in seven years. Some bodies were dropped by state-sponsored death squads from helicopters into the Plata; others dumped in an alleyway around the back of the Hurlingham Club. The insurance premiums kept creeping up, not that it deterred the Leicestershire wicketkeeper Roger Tolchard. Left out of England's 1977–8 winter touring team, he took up a coaching position in Buenos Aires. He was coaching at Colegio San Albano when shooting broke out between police and urban guerrillas, and the school was put on lockdown. Tolchard still fell in love with Argentina, and was due to go back in 1978–9 until he was called up for the Ashes, passing the placement on to his younger brother Ray.

The league programme carried on as if nothing was happening: Belgrano and Lomas B took their obsession to extreme lengths when one game finished in a dust storm. The visibility was almost nil when the final over came round with Belgrano needing 11 to win. A shot was struck direct to a fielder, but his return missed the stumps and no one could find the ball. The batsmen gleefully ran down the 11 runs, and incredibly no fielder shouted '¡Bola perdida!'

It was a brave time for D. H. Robins to bring a team to Argentina. The ACA – who had convinced themselves they could still ascend to Test status – insisted on playing a three-day 'Test' instead of three one-day matches. The game was all over in a day, and by the second scheduled day the young English players were all playing golf at Hurlingham. The assistant tour manager, Henry Blofeld, penned a guest column for the *Buenos Aires Herald* in which he praised the values upheld by the Hurlingham Club and contrasted it with Kerry Packer's pursuit of profit in Australia, which he had covered for the *Guardian*. But he tackled head-on the elephant in the room: 'It is extremely important that if the game is to survive as a healthy pursuit rather than a geriatric attempt to preserve the past, that local players must be recruited and enthusiasm kindled.'

Blowers was quite taken by the performance of 23-year-old Martín Martínez for the ACA Colts at Belgrano. 'It was the bravest innings played against the tourists thus far in South America . . . I have no doubt there are many more like him in Argentina who could play cricket with equal skill.' Blofeld called on the ACA to select Martínez for the first ICC Trophy in England the following summer, and for MCC to grant Argentina a match at Lord's so that he could have the chance to appeal 'long, loud and clear in Spanish'. He signed off with a triumphant Blowerism, which could easily have come from one of his *Test Match Special* commentaries: 'The windows of the hallowed Long Room might rattle momentarily in disbelief, but what a tremendous moment it would be for cricket.'

*     *     *

'Antarctica is the only continent not sending a team to compete for the International Cricket Conference Trophy starting in the Midlands,' wrote Scyld Berry in the *Observer* in May 1979. 'From every other continent cricketers are coming, of multifarious races and creeds: Muslim wicketkeepers, Buddhist batsmen, Jewish medium pacers. Over 200 players from 14 countries will be speaking in Dutch and Danish, Hindi and Spanish, Bengali and pidgin. The two hotels in Birmingham where they are staying will be towers of Babel.' The intrigue over the

Spanish speakers went up a notch when the *Daily Telegraph* reported – wrongly – that Evita Perón had tried to ban cricket altogether.

World Cup qualification was the prize on offer for the two ICC Trophy finalists. The Associate teams brushed shoulders with the six Test nations at the Changing of the Guard and a photoshoot of all visiting teams on the Lord's outfield. The short, podgy Argentines filed into Buckingham Palace to meet the Queen and the Duke of Edinburgh right after the towering West Indians, who went on to lift the World Cup trophy later that summer.

Little did they all know it would be the wettest May in Britain since 1722. The Argentines lapped up one day of uninterrupted sun, in a friendly at Outwood CC, less than 24 hours after landing at Gatwick. Cristóbal Nino won one toss out of 12. 'Even that was a tie,' he laughs. 'The coin got stuck in the muddy pitch and the home captain gave me the benefit of the doubt.' It was soon clear how seriously some of the other nations were taking it, when, in the first game, Singapore ran out Argentina's Dougie Annand backing up without a warning. Trust a Mankading to expose a cricketing culture war.

All the World Cup teams were assigned individual buses to get around the club grounds in the Midlands; the Trophy sides had to share. After one club friendly, the Argentines were keen to stay and drink in a local pub to socialise with the locals; the more focused Sri Lankans, keen to claim Test status by winning the tournament, just wanted to get back to the hotel.

The Argentines took in riotous nights out alongside the Fijians, Canadians, Dutch and Danes – all trying to outdo each other with sing-songs in their native tongues. Nino gave every opposing team a woodcarving of a gaucho furiously pursuing a cricket ball. Their Fiesta Patria on 25 May was called in with an *asado* at the farm of the Middleton family, who also had an *estancia* near Rosario.

Alas, Blowers's dream for Martín Martínez never material-ised. Argentina did not get their fixture at Lord's, and he was given just one outing in the Trophy proper, though he did make 37 not out in a friendly. Argentina's permitted overseas player, the Essex opener Brian Ward, had coached out in Buenos Aires, later married an Argentine and moved to Uruguay. He was a useful tactical sounding board for Nino, but he struggled for runs. *Los Guanacos* lost every Trophy match.

Ahead of the next ICC Trophy in 1982, the Argentines prac-tised diligently at Hurlingham, where the soft wickets best resembled a green English seamer. But before they could fly over, events in the South Atlantic took a turn for the worse. Bob Evans, the tournament organiser, solemnly had to inform the ACA that 'the clubs and sponsors have said they can no longer welcome Argentina following the crisis'. Stanley Field, the cricket ground on the Falkland Islands, had just been bombed in the Argentine advance. 'I was studying in London at the time,' says Mike Ryan, an Irish-Argentine all-rounder in the squad. 'I woke up in my hotel room and turned on the radio. The second item on the news, after leading off on a summit between Reagan and the Soviet Union, was "Argentina cricket team pulls out of this summer's ICC Trophy".' The tournament began two days after the British retook Port Stanley, ending 74 days of war.

Incredibly, it was not long since Argentines had played cricket on Stanley Field themselves. Club Ferrocarril San Martín – the Pacific Railway AC, before the railway was nationalised – had

ventured to Islas Malvinas in the 1960s. They followed the path
of the Scottish-Argentine farmers who had long taken the SS
*Darwin* between Montevideo and Port Stanley, carrying British
materials, including cricket equipment, to the Falklands, and
wool back to Uruguay. The wealthiest Kelpers, as Falkland
Islanders are called after the seaweed beds off their shores, sent
their sons to board at private schools in Buenos Aires, where
government inspectors took particular pleasure in making the
Anglos sing the Argentine anthem on the Day of the Islas
Malvinas. Dr Roger Diggle, former chairman of the Falkland
Islands Cricket Association, was told that Stanley CC even
visited for matches in Buenos Aires in the 1960s and 1970s. The
scorecards have conveniently gone missing.

In the feverish anti-British atmosphere of the early 1980s,
the ACA sounded a note of trepidation at cricket being viewed
as an English sport: 'This is our first "post-war season" and it is
still not certain to what extent debris will continue to fall and
how this might affect cricket. In the event only two players
were not involved as a direct result of the conflict.'

One was 19-year-old Miguel Savage, a member of the Old
Philomathian Club, which had already been nudged into
renaming themselves Club San Albano. An ancestor on his
mother's side had donated land for the first Presbyterian church
in Chascomús; his grandfather had fought against Nazi
Germany as an RAF intelligence officer in the Allied advance.
'He probably suffered the most,' said Miguel. 'He was born in
Argentina but in some ways was more British than the British,
and now they were fighting his country, and his grandson was
on the frontline.'

Miguel, serving in the 7th Regiment La Plata, spent two
months in the hills waiting for the British to attack Port Stanley.

'We were around one hundred and fifty men, two officers and maybe ten NCOs, and the rest of us just badly trained civilians. We had *mate cocido* for breakfast, never any bread, and we only had one meal later in the day – watery soup and nothing else.' Of 53 packages sent to him by friends and family, Savage received just one. Argentine soldiers were forced to steal supplies to stay alive. Once a corporal caught Savage stealing a tin of meat. 'The punishment was *estaqueo* – they would peg you to the ground and leave you crucified for hours, with minus-twenty degree temperatures, rain and even shelling,' he said. 'He made me kneel down, pointed his gun on my head and I was crying and begging for him not to shoot. They were our worst enemies, torturing us physically and psychologically.'

Margaret Thatcher was advised of possible danger to Anglo-Argentine civilians on the mainland, but they were either too important to the economy or so well integrated they could not be identified by the secret police. Hurlingham dutifully took down their picture of the Queen after receiving several threats to burn down the clubhouse. When ARA *General Belgrano* was sunk to the loss of 323 Argentine lives outside the officially declared war zone, it was to the horror of many Anglo-Argentines: one volunteer, proud of his 'pure Anglo-Saxon ancestry' linked with 'chivalry, fair play and honesty', lost faith at that moment. The atmosphere was sombre indeed at Belgrano AC, who shared their name with Argentina's *libertador* Manuel Belgrano. The whole conflict focused the minds of Anglo-Argentines, and most of the younger generation at least chose to back their Argentine future rather than their British heritage.

Their English trip cancelled and General Galtieri deposed, Nino's men went off to tour apartheid South Africa instead.

The ACA had links there, as a Junior Guanacos team had toured in 1980. Argentina, as one of the few cricketing nations outside the Commonwealth, were not signatories to the Gleneagles Agreement, which discouraged sporting contact with South Africa. Luckily the ACA's representative at Lord's, the former Middlesex leg-spinner Charles Robins, had already secured Argentina's place as an ICC Associate Member in 1974, and there were no concerted efforts to remove them.

Diplomatic relations between Britain and Argentina were patched up in 1990, at the Madrid conference between the British, Argentines and Falklanders brokered by Barney Miller, the chairman of the Anglo-Argentine Society in London. Miller makes light of the Falklands fissure every year with a cricket match between Hurlingham and the British Embassy in which they compete for a sheep's limb dubbed the 'Bone of Contention'.

MCC were advised by the British government to stay away from Argentina; Miller feared cricket might wither on the vine. In 1986 he phoned Brian O'Gorman, the head of English and master-in-charge of cricket at St George's College, Weybridge. His son, Tim, was on the staff at Derbyshire. Brian tells us: 'This chap Barney Miller introduced himself: "I want to take a side out to the Argentine. And I think you're the man to captain it." "Sounds great," I thought. Before I had the chance to accept, he added: "Oh, and by the way, is your son available?"' Luckily, father and son both agreed, and they snapped up an opening bowler in Tim's Derbyshire team-mate Martin Jean-Jacques, along with Roland Butcher of Middlesex, Surrey's Trevor Jesty and Neil Smith of Warwickshire. As the son of Mike Smith and the great-grandson of Frank Leach, the trip was especially meaningful for him.

Miller and two other players, who had all been in the Cambridge Footlights, performed revues for charities and clubs – lent some class by his wife Diane's singing voice; Brian O'Gorman's father Joe – who played for Surrey – and uncle Dave had been popular music hall entertainers between the wars. So O'Gorman suggested naming the touring side 'the Troubadours', in homage to the musical performers of the Middle Ages who travelled around spreading goodwill. One of their more risqué sketches was a ditty about Diego Maradona's handball against England, committed just a few months earlier in Mexico City. 'I barely got away with that one,' Miller says.

No cricket had been played at the Media Luna Polo Club, Ameghino, since 1939, as most of the local ranchers never returned from war. Miller's son-in-law, John Hosken, remembered: 'We brought the wicket with us in the bus – a strip of matting bought a couple of days earlier from a surprised carpet salesman in Buenos Aires, who couldn't imagine a room 26 m long and 1½ m wide. When we finally had it rolled out, we realised we hadn't brought any stumps, so an SOS went out to all the *estancias* within 50 km, which produced no less than 12.' The Troubadours batted first and made 227 for seven declared. John Sylvester, son of Stanley, drove 400 miles for the chance to pull on his whites for the first time in decades. He bowled four balls, all with a lovely action, until he ruptured his Achilles and had to be hoisted into an *estanciero*'s pick-up truck.

Wickets started falling in the Ameghino reply, and the complexities of padding up became apparent: the walk from the pavilion to middle was a 15-minute trek across a golf course and two polo fields. Had the Laws been applied strictly, there would have been a few timed out. 'The call went out on radio for another *bateador* who could spare time from the harvest,' said Hosken. 'A few minutes later, a cloud of dust would appear at the gate and move speedily up the driveway to the polo field. A pick-up would screech to a halt, and a new batsman, resplendent in gleaming white *bombachas* or shorts . . . would stride out, usually scorning pads or gloves, but almost certainly wearing his club cap or school beret. He would arrive at the wicket, brandishing his bat, sometimes at the right end . . . He would take guard, which would take a bit of time if he wasn't clear about the possible meaning of middle-and-leg. He would receive a bit of coaching and encouragement from the other batsman – in Spanish, of course. The bowler would bowl. Bat would miraculously make contact with ball and elude the field. Time for decisions. "*Dos, dos!*" "*No, no.*" "*Vamos.*" The wicket would fall. And the process would begin again.' Eventually 22 *estancieros* were dismissed for 154. O'Gorman went on to teach at St George's College, Quilmes, for some years, but in the night of revelry that followed at Ameghino he encountered for the only time open hostility to the British role in the Falklands, from an enraged local who had lost his son in the war.

Two years later, the Troubadours returned, taking with them the Kent pair Danny Kelleher and Simon Hinks. One of the party, Charles Fellows-Smith – who worked in the opaque world of Swiss banks in Latin America – remembers Kelleher as jovial, lapping up the night-time revelry. But, after he was released by Kent in 1991, his actor girlfriend walked out on him and he sank into depression. The ACA offered Kelleher a coaching stint in 1994, but he was still unhappy, and flew back to England on Christmas Day. His father, John, said that Danny was 'a shy lad who hid it under an extrovert bravado'. After two failed suicide attempts, he overdosed fatally within a year.

The professionals hired from overseas could never be quite sure what they would find in Argentina. Rupert Gomes, a Guyanese all-rounder who had emigrated to the Netherlands, attempted to liven up the legendarily docile Hurlingham square by relentlessly cutting, rolling and watering for two months, so that come the 1986–7 North v. South fixture it looked like the Belgrano wicket of old. Alas, it rained beforehand, and the pitch reared up worse than ever. Hurlingham stalwart Nick Ulivi remembers Paul Smith, the free-spirited Warwickshire all-rounder, arriving direct from the swimming pool at Belgrano to conduct cricket nets in his Speedos (and nothing else); the ACA sent him home after four weeks. He spent an inordinate amount of that time socialising with Pablo Escobar in Buenos Aires's infamous New York nightclub. Smith's county team-mate Andy Moles ventured out to Argentina in 1992. 'He was the one who started all the sledging here,' sighs Ulivi.

Moles was trying to prepare Argentina for the varied and competitive new world of international competition made available to ICC Associates. Argentina had the grounds, infrastructure and heritage, though not the playing numbers of rivals who grew strong on the back of immigration from the Indian subcontinent. In 1990, delirious at beating East & Central Africa for their first win in four ICC Trophies, the Argentines drove the team minibus direct into the hotel foyer in Amsterdam. After repeating that win four years later in Nairobi, through star performances from Lorenzo Jooris and Christian Tuñon, the entire team jumped fully clothed into the hotel swimming pool.

In 1995, Italy toured Argentina and played a multi-day international at Belgrano. All seemed fine as Italy batted first, scoring 160; Argentina were bowled out for 205 just before the close. Then, at 7 a.m. ahead of the second morning's play, the computerised sprinkler system went off by accident, soaking the pitch beyond repair. The groundsmen rushed to prepare a new strip, but the Italians refused to commence their second innings in protest. Instead of seeing the game abandoned, the stocky home captain Donnie Forrester offered to go out and bat on the wicket himself; Argentina had effectively followed on with a first-innings lead of 45. Guillermo Kirschbaum ended up on his backside, run out in the slippery conditions as the two teams played out a draw.

Kirschbaum, a swashbuckling all-rounder with a flowing blond mane, captained the Argentine Colts to a memorable win over Paul Parker's MCC tourists in 1989–90. There was a moment of gallows humour at the following summer's ICC Trophy in the Netherlands when Stanley Perlman, Israel's captain, bounded up to young Kirschbaum to commend him on his batting performance, hoping to bond with a fellow cricketer in the Jewish diaspora. Before Perlman could go too far, Kirschbaum had to break it to him that his grandfather had flown in the Luftwaffe. In 2003 the inspirational Kirschbaum, Argentina's leading scorer in ICC Trophies, died, aged 35, from complications after a severe asthma attack. A tree was planted in his memory and his ashes scattered next to the stand at Belgrano.

All this rough and tumble was matched in the boardroom. At 1992's ICC annual meeting, Spain prepared a detailed case for membership, seconded by Denmark and Argentina. Gibraltar, however, vowed to vote down the Spanish application, apparently in retaliation for the banning of a Gibraltarian boxing referee from that summer's Barcelona Olympics. At a heated meeting chaired by Colin Cowdrey, Miller, representing

Argentina, managed to persuade other members to back Spain, who got through on the nod. 'Buzaglo of Gibraltar abstained, and I don't think we ever spoke again,' says Miller.

Argentina were on the other side of the ledger in 2007, when the Falkland Islands' ICC membership came up. The ACA abstained, apparently under pressure from their neo-Peronist government, but the Kelpers were voted through. The Falklands now play at RAF Mount Pleasant, on a pitch so exposed that matches are often abandoned as 'winded off'. The Falklands expressed their interest in competing in the next South American Championship and were marked down as first reserve in case of a withdrawal. But with the Peronists back in charge in Buenos Aires – during the coronavirus crisis President Alberto Fernández donned a facemask with a silhouette of the Malvinas over blue and white – the chance of an Argentina v. Falkland Islands fixture would surely lead to a diplomatic storm.

David Parsons was still faithfully reporting every cricket happening in the *Herald*, but elsewhere attachments to this 'English' sport were loosening. The Buenos Aires branch of Harrods, the only one anywhere outside London, closed its doors in 1998, and the English Club was forced to shut when it emerged during the Argentine economic crisis that they had been paying no tax for ten years.

Harry Thompson, the inventor of *Have I Got News for You* and author of *Penguins Stopped Play*, was on the receiving end in a game at Hurlingham with his Captain Scott's XI. When Lucas Paterlini sent an off-drive roaring past Thompson's opening bowler, he pursed out of the corner of his lips: 'Go fetch your sheeeet, Engleeeshman.'

\*　　\*　　\*

Argentina were leaning on a small, well-honed nucleus of cricketers when the ICC formed the World Cricket League (WCL)
– a 50-over pyramid for the Associate and Affiliates in 2007. By
now, Argentina were represented almost entirely by Spanish
speakers, some with British heritage, leading to such colourful
scorecard entries as Diego Lord, Hernán Fennell and Esteban
'Billy' McDermott. *Los Guanacos* introduced a tradition of
giving every newcomer a buzzcut ahead of their debut. 'You
had the option to go to get it done professionally at the hair-
dressers, or entrust the job to one of the lads with a rusty razor,'
remembers Lautaro Musiani, who had his flowing teenage
locks removed at 15. 'Mine looked appalling.' The line was led
by Lord, an amateur dramatist and wrestler, whose bald head
and heavy build gave him an air of Tony Lock, though with a
fast bowler's mentality. 'I smell a wicket!' he would snarl with a
thespian's sense of theatre, though his bowling was steady
enough for wicketkeeper Alejandro 'Alé' Ferguson to stand up
to the stumps.

The highpoint was 2007 WCL Division Three, when one of
USA's many suspensions from the ICC handed Argentina late
entry. They beat Papua New Guinea, Fiji and the Cayman
Islands in reaching the final against Uganda and promotion to
Division Two.

No one could then have foreseen Argentina going on a run
of defeats to rival the hapless Scottish footballers of Bon Accord.
Across four WCL tournaments in five years, from Windhoek
to Buenos Aires to Bologna to Singapore, Argentina lost 23
matches, won none, and tumbled down from Division Two to
Division Six, where they suffered a fifth consecutive relegation
and slipped out of the WCL. They are now stuck in the
Americas region, unable to overcome the Caymans or Bermuda.

When Argentina met Afghanistan in Buenos Aires in WCL Division Three in January 2009, ships were passing in the night. The Afghans had learned their cricket on the scarred earth of the refugee camps of Pakistan in the 1990s, war raging around them, with barely any equipment to scrape together. Here they were flying through the WCL in the other direction, on an improbable charge to World Cups in 50 overs and T20, and Test status.

Afghanistan lost to Uganda in their opening game and were under real pressure when they met Argentina at Hurlingham. Some of the more devout Muslims among the Afghans had been left on edge by a particularly raunchy tango performance put on for the teams at their hotel. Both sets of players changed nervously on opposite sides of the pavilion where Plum Warner and Gubby Allen had showered two lifetimes ago. Lord invoked some of Hurlingham's heritage by removing 21-year-old Asghar Afghan (then known as Asghar Stanikzai) who would go to lead his country in their maiden Test match in 2018 – for 11, and 24-year-old Mohammad Nabi – the future IPL and Big Bash star – for 17. The best news story in world cricket were kept down to just 164 on a docile surface. When Hamish Barton and Matias Paterlini took the Argentines to 56 without loss in the first 15 overs, the Afghan dream looked dashed. Then Nabi removed Paterlini for 35, and the match turned. Argentina needed 21 off 20 balls with the last pair at the crease. Lord hoicked across the line, was dropped by short third man running round, but he got up and flung the ball in. Lord was run out coming back for the second, when his bat bounced up as he dived for his ground. Pandemonium for the Afghans; dejection for the Argentines.

Afghanistan went on to win the tournament, but only due to some ICC largesse which has been left out of the Afghan fairy tale. They were heading for defeat in their pivotal last-round game against the Caymans at San Albano when rain arrived to wash out their match and Argentina v. Uganda across town at Belgrano. Under ICC rules, the points should have been shared, and Uganda and Papua New Guinea sent through. But the ICC decided to scrap the usual play-offs, and replay the last two group games the following day. Afghanistan and Uganda won, meaning they, and not the Papuans, carried on their meteoric rise towards the game's elite. Argentina, once the standard bearers for Associate cricket, are waiting for the spark that will take them back up there.

# 10

# Paraguay

## *Down Under with the Nazis*

'G'DAY MATE,' RODRIGO 'Roddie' Wood says with a curious hybrid accent and a broad toothy grin as he administers a crushing handshake. 'Suspect you're both looking forward to a few jars and some tucker.' Roddie is a barrel-chested Paraguayan with square shoulders and strong arms. His imposing stature is offset by a kindly face, gold-rimmed glasses, neatly parted thick grey hair and a mischievous smile. We meet at a monthly lunch gathering of the Stranger's Club at the 'English-style' Hotel Chaco in downtown Asunción. The hotel building itself is an unremarkable nine-storey concrete monstrosity where tired red carpets, wood panels and candy-striped tablecloths provide the supposed appeal to Anglophiles. The 50 or so guests are a curious assortment of silver-haired Paraguayans with Commonwealth connections. Conversations flit between Spanish and English.

Roddie enthusiastically devours his beef with *chimichurri* sauce and vegetables, supping from a glass of imported Guinness while speaking with the charm of a fair-dinkum Aussie, in tones part-Queensland, part-Paraguay. After lunch, the Stranger's Club members listen to a guest talk by a retired economist before filtering their way out into the sunshine to sleep off the excesses in the late afternoon. Roddie remains among the stragglers, along with Peter Logan, a softly spoken Paraguayan of Welsh ancestry.

Logan was one of the founders of the Asunción Rugby Club and, in the spirit of his playing days, uses our full stomachs as an excuse to throw as many bottles of Paraguayan pilsner down our necks as time permits. He turns to the subject of Paraguay's national rugby team, briefing us on the fortunes of *Los Yakares* – the Alligators – before Roddie offers a revelation. It has been a few years since he last picked up a bat and ball in anger, but Roddie is the last bona fide *Nuevo Australiano* to have learned and played all his cricket in Paraguay.

*       *       *

The lunchtime bus from Villarrica to Coronel Oviedo is hot. Stifling, in fact. Sweaty bodies lean to catch a bit of a breeze from the window as it rattles along. Children pick the stuffing out of the worn seats, teenagers in starched school uniforms giggle and take selfies, while old women gossip and grumble. Like most of Latin America, every time the bus stops it is punctuated by the arrival of people of all ages selling everything from bottled drinks and *empanadas* to pirated DVDs and, on this occasion, plastic dinosaurs. They are permitted on, without a fare, for a few stops, before repeating the journey in the opposite direction.

Armed with a few names and a rudimentary map, scribbled on the back of a serviette by Roddie Wood at the Stranger's Club lunch, we are heading into deepest Paraguay. After an hour the bus wheezes to a stop at a motorway tollbooth, and only frantic shouts to the driver prevent him from completely whizzing past our destination.

Once the exhaust fumes clear, a white sign overhead comes into view with the words: '*Bienvenidos a Nueva Australia – distrito de Nueva Londres*'. On the right of the sign is one side of the flag of Paraguay – the only national flag in the world that is different on the obverse and reverse. Next to it are the instantly recognisable stars of the Commonwealth and Southern Cross on the flag of Australia. As we make our way through the entrance the concrete of the main road quickly fades into a Mars-coloured dirt track. The midday sun beats down intensely from a cloudless sky. Teleport any Australian here, and they would swear it was the Outback.

The concept of an Australian colony in Paraguay had been the brainchild of an Englishman. William Lane was born in Bristol on 6 September 1861, and at 14 emigrated to Canada then the US. It was here that Lane forged a career in newspapers, becoming a reporter for the *Detroit Free Press*, where he met his wife, Anne. They married in 1884, and a year later briefly returned to England before moving on to Brisbane, Australia.

Over the next few years Lane established a reputation in Queensland as a partisan newspaper columnist with staunch socialist views. He became an influential opinion maker and fraternised with figures in the labour and trade union movements. He wrote articles hostile to the British Empire, business, the government and Chinese immigrants.

The failure of the 1891 Australian sheep shearers' strike – over pay, working conditions and use of cut-price labour – spawned the growth of the Australian labour movement, and inspired Banjo Paterson to write 'Waltzing Matilda'. It persuaded Lane the society he and other like-minded agitators yearned for could not be established in 'old' Australia. A 'new' Australia where they could lead their socialist cooperative life had to be found.

Lane was influenced by the Icarians, a French utopian socialist movement. 'We must go where we shall be cast inwards,' he wrote. 'Where we shall be able to form new habits uninfluenced by old social surroundings, where none but good men will go with us.' Hopes of creating a settlement elsewhere in Australia had reached a dead end, and Lane cast admiring glances at South America.

At this time Paraguay was emerging from the War of the Triple Alliance, when obese despot president Francisco Solano López – fuelled by the whims of his furtive Irish mistress-turned-wife Eliza Lynch – led the country into a disastrous conflict with Brazil, Uruguay and Argentina. From 1864 to 1870 the war devastated Paraguay's population from 450,000 to fewer than 150,000, of which only 28,000 were men. Paraguay's government passed a law in 1881 that permitted colonisation of land by foreigners to boost the number of inhabitants.

A German socialist group led by Bernhard Förster, who was married to the sister of Friedrich Nietzsche, had already founded Nueva Germania in north-east Paraguay in 1887. Three of Lane's acolytes, assisted by Spanish-speaking Englishman Arthur Tozer, travelled to Paraguay and were impressed by the land. The New Australia Co-operative Settlement Association were eventually given 463,100 acres completely gratis, on the proviso that 1200 families were settled there within six years. Cash was raised from members and they purchased the *Royal Tar*, converted it from a freighter for passenger use and, on 16 July 1893, the first 238 utopians set sail for Paraguay.

Lane's socialist utopia of Nueva Australia was to be underpinned by a number of strict beliefs. Teetotalism and communism were the cornerstones. There was also a 'brotherhood of English-speaking whites', and preservation of the colour line via life marriage. Lane noted Paraguay had an 'Aryan climate', which would enable the colony to 'be white, to keep our white civilisation'.

Early life in the new colony, however, was tough and unforgiving; poor living conditions, disease and internal dispute beset Nueva Australia from the beginning. 'Many of the colonists left good and comfortable situations in Australia and came to Paraguay expecting to find a land flowing with milk and honey,' said the *Rio Times*. 'And had a rude awakening to the discomforts and hardships inevitable in opening any new colony.' Lane clashed with the other settlers as the colony became split between those loyal to him and a growing number of dissenters. Many despaired of his leadership, especially a zero-tolerance approach to alcohol and fraternising with local women.

The British residents in nearby Villarrica viewed their English-speaking colleagues in Nueva Australia with a mixture of bemusement and curiosity. Many of the British had come to Paraguay as engineers and workers on the country's railways, bringing cricket with them. A bat-and-ball game resembling it is still played by Paraguay's indigenous Guaraní along the old railway route. Relations with the Australian colony were cordial enough to challenge them to a cricket match.

Colony divisions were temporarily put aside in March 1894 as a team representing Nueva Australia went off on horseback to play the English in Villarrica. The hosts' cricket team was assembled by the physician Dr Bottrell, who would deliver the first babies born in the Aussie colony. We had seen a town named after him, albeit with his name incorrectly spelled, en route to the colony. The team's arrival caused much confusion to Villarrica's Paraguayan residents, who assumed it must have been the start of a revolution so bolted their doors. Updates on the score in this unlikely Ashes contest played in a 'large untidy plaza' were telegraphed to Asunción at the end of every innings.

In the first innings the English XI had made 63 to the Australians' 56, and the players of both sides then sat down to an 11-course dinner at Villarrica's finest hotel. 'After dinner,' wrote Frank Birks, one of the Australians, 'we had songs and boxes of cigars which are very cheap. As we New Australians couldn't get drunk on wine, we tried on ginger ale and iced lemonade leaving the wine to the Englishmen who were not slow in putting it away.' The Australians benefited from their abstinence in the second innings and scored 71, then bowled out their opponents for 63 to secure a one-run victory.

On their return to Nueva Australia the colonists found the Río Tebicuary swollen after heavy rains and needed a boatman to get their horses across the water. They then got lost in the darkness and had to enlist a guide to get them home. 'Tree ferns of a dozen different kinds met over the path and sprinkled dew over us as we passed under them or pushed them aside,' wrote Birks. 'The moonbeams which managed to come through the thick roof of trees, and creepers, here and there, were no small addition to the lovely scene. It was fairyland pure and simple.'

The detente of the cricket match at Villarrica, and the hypnotic night under the stars, were quickly forgotten. Lane met with one of the main dissenters, Gilbert Casey, who was in favour of an elected board running Nueva Australia's affairs. Casey was a former union leader keen to end the ban on alcohol and let the colonists marry Paraguayan women. When it came to a vote Casey's board idea was passed by 106 votes to 4, with Lane's supporters abstaining. The split in the camp had become irreconcilable, and Lane went off to lick his wounds with 63 of his loyal supporters. They trekked some 30 miles away to start afresh, at what became Cosme, on a new piece of land bought from the Paraguayan government.

Casey's house is one of the first we encounter after walking about a mile up the road from the entrance to Nueva Australia. His great-grandson, Gilberto Jr, holds back barking dogs as we open a creaking wooden gate leading on to the family land, and beckons us through the soft mud and up to the house. His wife clings on to their fair-haired young children, while Gilberto Jr digs out a crinkled printout from Wikipedia on Gilbert Casey, and a picture of his father, also called Gilberto, in a cracked glass frame. 'Of course we know a little bit about our Australian heritage, but we've never been there,' he says with the overriding sense of being underwhelmed by our appearance at his front door. 'It's a place we have nothing to do with.' Gilberto Jr shrugs his shoulders when we ask about cricket.

Today the area has two small communities called Nueva Australia and Nueva Londres. A descendant of the original settlers, Juan Kennedy, had wanted to name the second of these New Canberra, and sent a letter to the Australian government to ask for permission. He never received a reply, so New London was chosen instead. There's little to connect the place with England's capital city, although the local ice-cream man does pedal around on a bicycle playing 'London Bridge is Falling Down' from a tinny speaker.

319

Stephanie Edwards, a US Peace Corps volunteer working with children in the old colony, is the only foreigner living there. 'Occasionally you might get an Australian tourist visiting,' she says. 'But we are very isolated and hard to find here. There is no internet, for example.' We speak to a few more families with English surnames but they know nothing of cricket, or where it was played. There is no Australian Embassy in Paraguay and the connection with the homeland of their ancestors appears weak to non-existent.

Stephanie introduces us to Juan Kennedy's niece, Iris, who is in her late seventies and wears a sweatshirt with 'Greenland' emblazoned on it. Iris runs a small stationery shop. Her grandfather was a Scottish farmer from Ayrshire who came to Nueva Australia after running off with the maid. 'I still make scones, biscuits and blood sausage from original family recipes which have been handed down,' Iris tells us. 'I remember the older generation talking about cricket, but I've never seen it played in my lifetime here.'

After those early games cricket did continue in Nueva Australia, although with Lane now out of the picture the colony succumbed to more worldly temptations. 'Some of the colonists have intercourse with the native women and natives of both sexes attend their balls and socials,' wrote Tozer. 'The old rules are ignored and drinking common. At a recent cricket match with the English residents many got drunk and even boys were carried off the field in a state of intoxication.'

The light is starting to fade and we ask Stephanie about a hotel in Nueva Australia to spend the night. 'There isn't one,' she says, laughing. 'There aren't any buses either, you'll have to hitch a lift to the main entrance.' An hour of standing near the town's shop with our thumbs out draws a blank before Stephanie takes pity on us and coerces a couple of teenagers with scrambler motorcycles to help out.

A few minutes later we're holding on for dear life. *The Motorcycle Diaries* this isn't. Having led relatively sheltered lives, being on the back of a motorbike for the first time, without a helmet, at dusk, in the hands of a Paraguayan not yet old enough to vote, gets the heart pumping. After a few near misses with potholes and a cow bedding down for the night, we make it safely back to the main road, breathe a sigh of relief, and catch a bus back to Villarrica.

*     *     *

'Hard luck. But you'll find more on cricket in Cosme,' reads a text message from Roddie Wood next morning. 'Ask for the Woods when you get there and tell them Roddie sent you!' Getting to Cosme proves tricky; it's not on any maps, nobody in the tourist office at Villarrica has heard of it and even when we get to the bus terminal in nearby Caazapá, on Roddie's advice, people scratch their heads. Eventually, a taxi driver in Caazapá overhears our conversation and asks, almost whispering: '*¿Quieres visitar la colonia?*' A haggled fare later and we're bumping up and down on the red dirt road in a clapped-out Honda into the *campo* where cattle roam free and fertile farmland is lush and green.

Roddie's grandfather Bill Wood, a sheep shearer and union secretary, and his wife were among a second batch of settlers to arrive at William Lane's breakaway Cosme colony from Australia in May 1895. They got there in time to celebrate the first anniversary of the foundation of the colony, which included 'a minstrel show, cricket match and much dancing'.

Norman Wood, Roddie's late father, also grew up in Cosme and spoke English with an even broader Aussie twang, though he never visited Australia either. Roddie's own curious accent came about when he conversed in English with family members, listened to Slim Dusty and went to New York to study. Since then he's taken holidays to Australia but, while there is a pull to move Down Under, his grown-up children don't feel the same connection, so it's Paraguay for the time being.

After 45 minutes we make it to Cosme. It's a warm, lazy Saturday afternoon and the echo of closing the doors on the taxi sends startled birds flying out of trees lining a lush green patch of land. In red writing painted on a wooden sign on the field are the words: '*Plaza 25 de XII – Fdo – 1894 Colonia Cosme*'. An elderly Paraguayan woman with a kind face approaches, and when we ask '*¿Donde vive la familia Wood?*' she points us in the direction of a wooden house on stilts behind some trees.

As we edge closer an impressive two-storey building with a balcony comes into view on a dusty piece of land. Built in an Australian architectural 'Queenslander' style, it is more striking than other houses in Cosme. Roddie's uncle Francisco ambles out to greet us, ushering away various roaming farm animals before assuring us it is safe to venture through the gate on to his property. We sit down on some plastic garden chairs, drink a cup of *mate* and begin to chat.

Francisco has a basic grasp of English but nods approvingly when we mention cricket. 'We have an old bat somewhere,' he says, but after momentarily rummaging around under the house is unable to locate its whereabouts. Francisco tells us his brother Patricio avidly followed cricket when he moved to Australia in the 1970s, where he lived and worked for nearly 30 years, and his hero was Dennis Lillee.

Bill Wood, who had been a friend of Australian writer and bush poet Henry Lawson, was an active member of Cosme's cricket team. One of the few surviving photographs of Cosme's cricketers shows him sitting on the front row. He has a handsome face, jet-black hair and a thick moustache. Bill longed to return to Australia but died in Paraguay in 1935.

Cosme's early inhabitants made light shoes and slippers from monkey fur, and raised money by exporting everything from alligator skins to armadillo shells. Sourcing the wares for their matches, typically played on a Sunday, was not beyond them. 'We can make all cricket tools on Cosme excepting balls,' said the *Cosme Monthly Notes*, which documented much of life in the breakaway colony, 'though the locally made bats are not of first-class quality.' The white willow tree, with its draping green leaves, contains the ideal wood for cricket bats, but unhelpfully it is not native to South America.

The pride and joy of Cosme was its cricket oval. Time was set aside to enlarge, plough, harrow and roll the land not long after they left Nueva Australia. Eventually it was sown with English grass seed, enclosed by a smart two-railed morticed fence and a small wooden pavilion erected for the players and spectators to wider approval: 'Though the ground cannot be compared to a billiard table, some most enjoyable games are played there.'

Cosme continued the rivalry with teams of English residents in Paraguay, and these 'Ashes' contests were relished by both sides. After a defeat by the English at Villarrica in April 1896, when they were undone by the excellent bowling of W. J. Holmes, the British consul, the first match at the Cosme Oval in August was an altogether more one-sided affair. The Englishmen found Frank Birks unplayable: he took seven for 4 as they were rolled for 14 and 29 in a 90-run thrashing.

The *Cosme Monthly Notes*, printed on yellow packing paper, even produced a droll article with the headline 'Advice for Cricketers' ahead of the next fixture:

Always make a point of grumbling at the light and the wicket. Don't hold the bat as though it were a chisel, even though you do cut with it. If you should happen to hit a ball on the proper side of the wicket, apologise by saying that modern cricket sometimes allows it, this will at once explain why you pull, and will make good cricketers feel awkward and old-fashioned. Strict attention to these little matters will build a reputation sooner than a dozen centuries. When fielding never appear to get out of the way of a swift ball, good cricketers always let it go by accidentally like; you cannot always blame the ground. If you must stop it, do so with your foot, that is if you have boots on. It's a good plan to have three excuses ready for not stopping a ball, but no less than six are needed for buttering a catch. After taking a catch it's a good thing to tumble down, but don't do it if the ground is wet and slippery, and you have white pants on, and your laundress has a shortish temper and charges you for the soap. You should not run to a catch as though going to embrace your best girl; you should reserve that attitude for recitations, it is graceful but not appreciated in the cricket field.

The 'Ashes' matches the following April were the most eagerly anticipated in Paraguay's cricket history. Cosme's players trained four evenings a week, and held trial matches in the build-up to select their XI. 'While the Britishers had been cricketers in their youth and, though quite out of practice, were expected to show public school form,' read a preview of the match. 'Six of the Cosme team were bowlers, their sheet-anchor being Rod Lewis, its youngest member – Australian born – whose bowling thought good enough to dismiss the craftiest batsmen.'

The challenge had been issued by Patiño Cué-based Thomas Blackmore, brother of Richard Blackmore, author of *Lorna Doone*, and he 'spared neither labour nor expense' on a ground at Tacuaral, a village on the railway line, near Asunción. The *Cosme Monthly Notes* reported: 'Flooded roads and rivers made the getting from Cosme to the railway line a very wet undertaking. On arrival the Cosmans were warmly welcomed and as guests of the Britishers were provided with snug quarters and entertained most hospitably. A flat meadow was prepared as a ground, and a bough shed erected as a pavilion. In out of the way corners of the country hide balls and impromptu bats served to revive the national game.'

In the first match Cosme won the toss and took advantage of showery conditions and a damp pitch to skittle the Englishmen, without star turn Holmes, for 34 before compiling 48 themselves. The lead was small, but Cosme dismissed their opponents for 33 before knocking off the runs to win by seven wickets. The next day's single-innings game commenced in fine weather conditions. William Lane's brother John, who skippered Cosme, scored 69 in their total of 147 with the English undone by Lewis, who lived up to his hype with seven for 21 in a 95-run victory.

Despite his differences with William Lane, Gilbert Casey wanted to build bridges between the two colonies. He asked Harry King of the New Australia Cricket Club to write to their counterparts in Cosme about a match, but received a curt reply.

'I'm instructed to inform you that we will be unable to play you,' came the terse response from Frank Birks, doubtlessly under duress from Lane, who had a reputation as a man who held a grudge. Before he died, Riccardo Smith recalled to Anne Whitehead in *Paradise Mislaid* there were in fact 'two or three cricket matches' played between the colonies in later years. But afterwards 'through bad communications they didn't visit each other. There were hardly any visits from one colony to the other. There was still bad feeling.'

While cricket was embraced in Lane's socialist utopia, the man himself, unlike his brother, was not much of a player. Lane was short, fragile, had poor vision and required the use of a walking stick. His own relationship with cricket was forever tarnished by a heart-breaking incident.

In May 1895, Lane's eight-year-old son Charles was sent to the settlement barber by his wife Anne, but was persuaded to join a knockabout game on the Cosme Oval. While batting, a delivery from another youngster, Wally Head, struck Charles on the heart. He dropped his bat, slumped at the crease and was dead within minutes. Of the incident, Tozer wrote: 'There was no bruise to indicate that the ball struck him with any great force and the boy bowling is hardly old enough to do any damage.' It was a cruel blow for the Lanes, and many saw it as a portent of what was to come for the colony. Anne Lane wept and cried: 'Oh, Cosme, Cosme, I'll never love you anymore'.

Four years later, depressed and disillusioned at the continuing failure of his socialist project, Lane and family left Paraguay, never to return. Many others would follow, if they could afford to. The Woods are the only people with Australian heritage who remain to this day. Cosme's original ground, so lovingly constructed, is now a field with knee-high grass. The green sward we saw on arrival in Cosme also formerly staged cricket matches, having been built next to an orange grove a six-hit from the Wood family residence. Its pasture is now used only for football. As we left Cosme it dawned on both of us: it would not be long until the last dying embers of cricket remembered by the descendants of Australian colonists in Paraguay would burn out. Except this time forever.

\*     \*     \*

A framed oil portrait of Norman Langer is hung up at every Stranger's Club lunch, held in Asunción on the first Friday of every month. In the picture Langer, the club's founder, has brown hair brushed back, bushy eyebrows and a pointed nose, which emphasises a pensive expression. He wears a thick blue sports jacket with the kind of white polo-neck jumper favoured by Captain Birdseye.

Born to Anglo-Argentine parents in Villarrica, Langer led a colourful yet hapless existence, and was likened to a cross between Basil Fawlty and Del Boy Trotter. 'He inherited some money from an aunt and decided to build Paraguay's first ever squash court,' recalls Peter Logan, his long-time friend. 'Then spent most of the time denunciating the Irish folk here of stealing the equipment. In another venture Norman opened a restaurant. He was struggling to make ends meet but his snobbish attitude meant he would still turn certain customers away if they were not his sort of clientele.'

Langer, who had a penchant for club ties, blazers and old-fashioned England rugby shirts, lurched from one scheme to the next as he tried to keep his head above water, and fellow members of the Stranger's Club frequently had to bail him out.

A lifelong bachelor, Langer was thought by friends to be gay –
but Paraguay, during the longest dictatorship in modern South
American history, was not the kind of place where LGBTQ+
people could openly lead their lives.

Alfredo Stroessner came to power in 1954 when he won an
election in which he was the sole candidate following a coup.
The son of a German brewery accountant father and a wealthy
Paraguayan mother, he would go on to rule for 35 years. For
the Paraguayan people the wounds of dictatorship are still raw,
and a few hours after our extended luncheon at the Stranger's
Club we would see Asunción's streets descend into violent
chaos. President Horacio Cartes was attempting to change the
constitution so he could stand for re-election. Under the
current arrangements, introduced in 1992 after the dictatorship, the head of state may serve only a single five-year term.
We were to witness pitched battles between protestors and the
police as the smell of tear gas filled the night air. It would
culminate with hundreds of people invading Paraguay's parliament, tearing down signs, and smashing up doors, windows
and computers before setting it ablaze.

'It's a pleasure to be in a country that isn't ruled by its people,'
Prince Philip had quipped on a royal visit to Stroessner's
Paraguay in 1963. It was a wholly accurate, if somewhat insen-
sitive, comment. Political opponents to Stroessner's Colorado
Party were imprisoned, tortured and killed. The country was
kept in a near-constant state of siege for the majority of his
regime.

For the most part the British community, provided they kept
their noses out of domestic affairs, could go about their business with cricketing activities unhindered. 'Regarding general
political guidance on subjects which may possibly be raised in

your conversation with your friends and acquaintances here,' Sir Leonard Scopes, British ambassador to Paraguay in 1967, advised in a newsletter circulated to the English-speaking community. 'I think that by and large it probably helps better to lie fairly low. It is very difficult indeed to have the last word in a Spanish-speaking area.'

Cricket was played way before Stroessner's regime at a ground on the Liebig's meat-processing factory in Zeballos Cué on the outskirts of Asunción. Liebig's had an established presence in Paraguay since 1898 and around this time Dutchman William Paats, a sports instructor, had tried to introduce cricket in the capital without success. Paats enjoyed more luck with football and became the father of the game in Paraguay, being renowned in the early days for walking the streets of Asunción bouncing a ball and kicking it in the air to generate interest.

One inquisitive visitor to Paraguay in 1932–3 was the Essex wicketkeeper Roy Sheffield. At the end of the English county season he decided to spend the winter gallivanting around South America. While England's players were embroiled in Bodyline, Sheffield was ruffling feathers in Paraguay, where he was arrested on suspicion of being a Bolivian spy. Sheffield had been working as a *gaucho* in Argentina, where he umpired North v. South, before he decided to paddle up the Río Paraguay in a canoe to Asunción, only to arrive with the country in the midst of the Chaco War.

The Paraguayan authorities were seemingly confused by the occupation 'professional cricketer' on his official papers and, armed with only a few words of Spanish, Sheffield was put behind bars until British officials intervened. He also lived with indigenous people in the Mato Grosso and caused a stir in the then-conservative Brazilian city of Curitiba with his dress sense.

Teddy Roosevelt had considered the city's formality to be ridiculous, and Sheffield 'caused displeasure by walking about in a cricket shirt and grey flannels, a sensible enough attire for Bond Street if the weather is hot enough, but not for Curitiba'.

Cricket matches were played biannually at Liebig's after the Second World War, with the company donating equipment and mouth-watering *bife lomito* for the post-match *asado*. Even when the number of British staff dwindled in later years the cricketers knew how to keep the company sweet. When Ian Martin, the manager of Liebig's, was taken hostage in 1973 and put inside a wooden box, Logan volunteered to take the suitcase full of cash to pay off the kidnappers.

From 1945 Paraguay became a haven for Nazis on the run and though many kept a low profile in the countryside they occasionally ventured into Asunción. 'I never encountered Josef Mengele, or "José" as he became known, when he lived in Paraguay,' Logan says. 'But I remember playing against a guy at the chess club who we later found out was an escaped Nazi. Very occasionally a German-speaker would join in cricket matches, and while you may have suspected something ... well, you never quite knew.'

Liebig's closed its doors in 1980, and turned Zeballos into a ghost town overnight. Paraguay's cricketers mourned its loss and were temporarily homeless. Asunción's Botanical Gardens and Zoo briefly staged matches before Langer buttered up Antonio Zuccolillo, who had previously served as the Paraguayan ambassador to Britain. A wealthy businessman, Zuccolillo was made an honorary life member of the Stranger's Club, and freed up land on a nature reserve and country club he owned in Surubi'i, on the outskirts of the capital, for cricket.

The Turtles XI, made up of old boys from cricket-playing schools in Buenos Aires, made the first of four annual trips north to Asunción in May 1984. 'The Gentlemen of Paraguay, or President Stroessner's own?' wisecracked the *Buenos Aires Herald*. Langer top-scored with 24 as a Stranger's Club XI were dismissed for what appeared a paltry 70, having made first use of a 'cabbage patch' pitch at Surubi'i. But they then bowled out the visiting Argentines for 42 and sealed a surprise victory. 'Whether the *milanesas* and *mandioca* or the native gin tonics had a hand in what happened on the pitch will remain forever in the minds of the contestants,' wrote Langer in his report of the game. In classic Argentine cricket fashion, the Turtles insisted on playing an unscheduled match the following day, and promptly chased down 43 for the loss of two wickets to ensure they went home with their pride intact.

The Stranger's Club XI now boasted a bona fide Paraguayan *Nuevo Australiano*, as Roddie Wood acquired some cricket whites, learned the rudiments of the game and turned himself into a hard-hitting batsman and seam bowler. Cricket had long since disappeared from Cosme, but Roddie insisted the game was 'in my blood'. He also took on the arduous task of looking after the ground at Surubi'i, driving out on weekday evenings to prepare a pitch and mow the outfield.

When Langer invited the Turtles back the following year, Wood was in the Stranger's Club XI as the sides played a two-day match for the Surubi'i Trophy. The match, which ended in a draw, is fondly remembered for Ricardo Lord of the Turtles smacking sixes on to the rooftops of surrounding houses, which created an almighty din. The Asunción constabulary arrived at the ground under the misapprehension something more sinister was occurring.

In 1989 the minutes from a British Council meeting cryptically noted: 'Norman Langer does not know the whereabouts of the cricket kit.' In the following decade Langer switched his attention to tenpin bowling. He represented Paraguay at a South American tournament, and took part in the World Masters Games in Australia, leaving others to keep cricket going. In December 2000, a time when the ICC were throwing money at globalising cricket, Langer's interest resurfaced. He founded the Asociación de Paraguaya de Cricket and appointed himself chairman. Umpiring and filing updates for *Wisden* was all Langer could manage at this point. An Ambassador's XI v. Lloyds Bank became the only regular fixture, played on a bumpy piece of land near an airstrip owned by the Paraguayan Air Force.

Langer's final cricketing gig before his health began to deteriorate was his tour de force. For the first and only time, a cricket team claiming to represent Paraguay took to the field. Australian Allan Boyd, president of the Galah Cricket Club in New South Wales, had fired off a speculative email to Langer in 2002 to include Paraguay on their South America tour. A year later Boyd and his nomadic team of veteran Aussie 'cricket tragics' were nervously being ushered by Langer across the Puente Internacional de la Amistad, the tripoint border with Argentina and Brazil near the Iguazú Falls, into the bustling chaos of the free-trade zone of Paraguay's Ciudad del Este. 'Without visas to enter Paraguay we were informed by Norman that we had to leave our passports at the border check and collect them on our return later that night,' Boyd tells us. 'Apprehensively, we obliged.'

A stone's throw from the Itaipu Dam, which provides 90 per cent of Paraguay's electricity, a Flicx matting was laid at the

Alto Paraná regional football ground. For the one-off match Langer pulled out all the stops. Temporary sightscreens were erected, while the British ambassador was on hand for ceremonial duties. In the post-match dinner Langer presented a commemorative plaque and Paraguayan harp, a traditional wooden Guaraní instrument with strings made from catgut, which requires long fingernails to play. Langer had won the Flicx pitch for the match in an online competition but its whereabouts in later years became a mystery. 'The Flicx was donated by the MCC,' adds Galah president Boyd. 'A week later we played in São Paulo and the story goes we played on the same pitch – Norman had sold it to the lads at Clube AB in Cotia.'

The Paraguay XI – who finished on 100 for nine in valiant pursuit of Galah's 168 for nine – wore white T-shirts with red sleeves. Langer had wanted the team kit to match the red, white, and blue of Paraguay's flag so he insisted players finished the look with blue tracksuit pants. The trouble was that most of the Indian players who made up the side didn't own a pair. They had to improvise with whatever blue trousers they had in their wardrobes, which unwittingly ensured another international cricket first – surely the only time a national cricket XI has taken to the field with the majority of the players sporting blue denim jeans.

# 11

# Brazil

## *Johnners at play*

'*O QUE É ESSE esporte?*' asked one Paulista.
'*Com que bola vamos jogar?*' asked another.
'*Eu tenho a bola . . .*' answered Charles 'Carlos' Miller.

It was a cool afternoon in 1895 during what loosely passes for autumn in São Paulo. The cricket season had finished a few weeks before, and São Paulo Athletic Club, including Miller, had rounded it off with a victory in Santos. Miller gathered some of his cricket friends together at Várzea do Carmo, a stretch of public grassland, and tried to convince them of the joyful exuberance to be found in another sport growing in popularity in England. His acquaintances had heard or read about it, but none of them had played it. The *bola* he held in his hands was a football, and it would change the course of Brazil forever.

'On the quay at Santos, solemn, as if he were at my funeral, my father was waiting for me to disembark holding my degree certificate,' Miller said in an interview in his fifties. 'In fact, I appeared in front of him with two footballs, one in each hand. The old man, surprised, enquired: "What is this Charles?" "My degree," I replied. "What?" "Yes! Your son has graduated in football!"' Miller had embellished the story a little – his father had died in Glasgow several years earlier. But part of the yarn was true. He had returned with two balls, a pump and a copy of the Laws of Association Football.

Contrary to popular belief, Charles Miller was not the first person to introduce 'the beautiful game' to Brazil. Yet his passion and influence established foundations on which it would flourish. After several training sessions Miller organised an 11-a-side football match – between teams representing the São Paulo Railway (SPR) and the London Bank, two of Miller's employers, and the Companhia de Gás – on Sunday 14 April, 1895. Miller's Anglo-Brazilian friends were still sceptical. Six players were too fatigued to complete the game and felt the slower nature of cricket, like in much of the British Empire, was more to the tastes of Paulistas. 'The name "football" itself was a novelty,' Miller would recall in *O Cruzeiro* years later. 'Since at that time only cricket was known.'

By 1904, however, there were around 70 football clubs in São Paulo, and big matches had started to pull in crowds of 6000 fanatical Brazilians. 'Unlike cricket, this was a game that other people actually wanted to play,' is Josh Lacey's sobering assessment in *God is Brazilian: Charles Miller*. 'No-one but the British could see the thrill of three stumps and two bails shattered by a spinning ball. The locals showed a willingness to stare at cricketers and laugh – the game nicely confirmed the British as lunatics – but refused to join in.'

Miller was on the short side but a fine footballer. An intelligent winger, he had played to a high standard in England, representing the famous Corinthian club alongside C. B. Fry, St Mary's (the forerunner to Southampton FC) and Hampshire County. Less well-known, particularly among the Brazilians

who revere him as one of the country's football founding
fathers, was his gracefulness at the crease. Miller was also Brazil's
most distinguished cricketer.

Charles William Miller had been born in the São Paulo
district of Brás to a Scottish father and an Anglo-Brazilian
mother on 24 November 1874. Miller's father had left Ayrshire
to work for the São Paulo Railway, but insisted young Charles
receive a British education so when he was ten packed him off
to Banister Court School in Hampshire. He went on to become
a key player for their First XI, prominent in the batting and
bowling averages, and an unbeaten 107 and six for 12 in one
match secured a place in the county's notable cricket achievements for 1894. That same season Miller was drafted into the
MCC & Ground XI against Hampshire, where he lined up
alongside future Surrey and England captain H. D. G. 'Shrimp'
Leveson Gower.

São Paulo Cricket Club was founded in 1872, two years
before Miller was born, and *Correio Paulistano* announced its
inaugural match against Wanderers on St John's Day – 24 June
– at a ground 'behind the house of correction' near St Paul's
Anglican Church. This was a short distance from Estação da
Luz, where British workers for SPR had played since 1860.
According to Robert Brooking, the diligent chronicler of
Brazil's early cricket history, the ground 'more or less resembled
a brick field'.

To the north of São Paulo, fixtures were arranged against
SPR staff living in Campinas and Jundiaí, the gateway to the
Mogiana coffee region. In a colourful report from 1882 Peter
Miller, Charles's uncle and one of São Paulo CC's founders,
recounted a trip to face Campinas. 'The field was quite inspir-
ing ... A long tent with tables, decorated with flags and

streamers. There were swings, seesaws, Brighton donkeys disguised as horses, bands of music and on a level piece of ground three sticks stuck in the ground placidly contemplating another three sticks 22 yards away.' When play began Miller was cut little slack by Campinas, a side dominated by Scotsmen. He made 52 on 'lumpy ground', but was struck in the eye, suffered broken fingers and was covered in bruises in a 46-run win for São Paulo. The highlight of the post-match festivities was a pig hunt – where a swine was 'buttered' and chased around the ground by the cricketers. 'They took the monster and placed it in the middle of the plain, gave him a start, and went for him,' Miller wrote. 'Mr Putney would insist on hugging the pig, the pig taking quite naturally to him, and that was not fair to the other fellows you know!'

Many railway workers lived further down the line, between São Paulo and Santos, at the Paranapiacaba workers' village. Based on designs developed by Jeremy Bentham, the founder of modern utilitarianism, it became an enclave of 4000 British. We leave the frantic melting pot of São Paulo by bus and arrive in deserted Paranapiacaba at dusk. As the mist floats down from the green treetops we see rusting train carriages near the original *estação ferroviária* below. The next day we find the Victorian-style architecture remarkably intact: the old bakery, dance and music hall, clock tower and immaculate wooden house of the chief engineer, now a museum.

The São Paulo–Santos line was one of the world's most spectacular stretches of railway when it opened in 1867, zigzagging 2625 feet in the space of just five miles. The steep slope between Piaçaguera and Paranapiacaba presented the greatest challenge during construction and was solved by hauling the train carriages using a series of funicular-style cable inclines powered by stationary steam engines. Only the wagons were pulled up the steep escarpments, with locomotives waiting at either end. The amount of traffic on the line meant a second cable incline, parallel to the existing one, was opened 28 years later. 'An extraordinary feat of engineering,' gasped Sir Julien Cahn when he took his private XI to Brazil in 1929–30. 'Although less nerve-wracking than the outward car journey . . .'

West of São Paulo, cricket surfaced in the city of Sorocaba and the neighbouring town of Votorantim, where textile mills had sprung up to feed the cotton shortage caused by the American Civil War. 'The train brought many spectators including an Italian band which enlivened proceedings as each wicket fell,' read the report of one visit by São Paulo. Visiting teams were given guided tours of the mills.

As São Paulo's population swelled, Brazil-born stockbroker William Fox Rule, ably supported by Peter Miller, established a new sports club, which swallowed up the old cricket team. São Paulo Athletic Club, colloquially known as SPAC, was formed on 13 May 1888 – on the same day the *Lei Áurea* was signed by Isabel, the Princess Imperial, abolishing slavery in Brazil. SPAC made their home in Bom Retiro, at a private farm called Chácara Dulley. The grounds, owned by the American Dulley family, were in an industrialised working-class area with a bustling mix of Italian, Greek and Jewish immigrants. It was here where Charles Miller threw his energies into Brazil's early football scene. It was also where he forged a reputation as Brazil's first cricket star.

The 1898 season was Miller's *annus mirabilis*. He topped batting and bowling averages with 629 runs at 44.9, including a chanceless 125 not out against Sorocaba, and claimed 52 wickets at 5.8. 'Miller is capable of scoring fast against any bowling,' purred the *Rio News*. Miller's finest knock came the following season for SPAC at the inauguration of Santos Athletic Club's new *campo* in May 1899 when, aged 24, he crafted a spellbinding 106. It was declared the 'best innings ever seen in Brazil' by the *Rio News*: 'Miller began steadily but soon warmed up to his work and played beautiful cricket. His cutting and placing as well as his strokes on the leg were magnificent and his timing perfect. He received quite an ovation on returning to the pavilion . . . pleased to see it was Charlie Miller who made the first century on the Santos ground. No more popular man plays cricket in Brazil. Miller is a true sportsman thorough in everything he does and modest.'

The first tussle between sides representing Brazil's two pre-eminent cities occurred in 1875, when the São Paulo Cricket Club hosted Rio's Anglo Brazilian Cricket Club. *A Província de São Paulo* prophesied the match would 'develop among us the taste for the game adopted in the main schools of England and Germany for the hygienic advantages that come with it'. The Paulistas took the bragging rights with an 11-run victory.

By 1898 these matches had assumed the lofty title of State of São Paulo v. State of Rio de Janeiro. From 1908 the sides battled for the Conde de Selir Trophy, named after Portugal's minister to Brazil: it had a scalloped rim made out of old coins, and was consequently 'a bit awkward to drink out of'. In the main, State of São Paulo drew from a pool of cricketers from SPAC, São Paulo Railway and Santos AC. Rio pulled their players from the city's two main clubs – Rio Cricket & Athletic Association and Paissandu – plus the best of the rest from banks and company teams, including Bangu, a team of textile workers on the outskirts of Rio who played at a ground owned by

Companhia Progresso Industrial do Brasil, overlooked by a giant brick chimney.

The interstate fixture briefly challenged Argentina's North v. South as the continent's premier domestic fixture when it became a three-day affair in the 1920s, and Rio's Harold Morrissy and São Paulo's Oliver Cunningham, both classical batsmen, would go head to head. Morrissy was part of a family with strong roots in Brazilian cricket and they had been in the country for a century. They once turned out an entire XI made up of family members. Cunningham, dubbed 'Boy' on account of having a twin sister, had been born in Buenos Aires, worked in meatpacking and featured for Argentina against Pelham Warner's MCC side on their 1926–7 tour. Boy's father, Ernest, once promised to buy him a car if he could score 200 runs across both innings during the North v. South match in 1925 – he fell 21 short.

*       *       *

The intense football rivalry between South America's two powerhouses began in 1914, but cricket relations between Brazil and Argentina were struck up some years before. In December 1888, a Brazilian XI lost a two-day match to Buenos Aires Cricket Club at Palermo – bowled out for 90 and 30 in response to BACC's 135 and 138. Argentina visited Rio two years later, and suffered the surprise of a 7-run defeat before the frustration of a trip to São Paulo in 1892. The Argentines arrived in a downpour, and headed out to the São Paulo ground, at this time located at Ponte Pequena beyond the River Tietê, accessible only by one-mule tram. 'It rains today. No problem, tomorrow the sun will come out,' said the optimistic Argentine captain. After 12 days of constant rainfall, and with the ground a huge swamp, his mood was less upbeat as they sailed home.

Charles Miller was elected Brazil's captain on board the RMS *Danube* en route to Buenos Aires when the first combined Rio and São Paulo XI travelled to Argentina in November 1902 – the tourists lost three matches and drew one. Miller acknowledged his side had a 'very weak bowling' attack, but the 'vast difference' was Argentina's greater experience of grass wickets. The Brazilians, due to more rain in their climate, always had to play on matting.

Miller had just turned 47 by the time Brazil and Argentina next met on the cricket field, in 1921. There had been a near two-decade hiatus because of a period of tense relations between the countries, with Argentina fearful that Brazil's territorial ambitions might stretch to an invasion. Although past his peak, Miller was still churning out the runs for SPAC and, despite greying at the temples, far from disgraced himself on the tour against a strong Argentine attack. Miller averaged 20.11, bettered only by John Naumann (24.54), a Cambridge Blue who represented Sussex, and young Morrissy (24.27). Argentina convincingly won 2–0 on home turf over the Christmas and New Year period, with the last match drawn, in what were deemed official Tests by the Argentine Cricket Association (though not Lord's).

The series was covered widely on both sides of the border, though in Argentina the *Anglo-American Review* poked fun at *La Nación's* misinterpretation of no balls as 'notable balls' and their tendency to misinterpret runs as points. 'Let us, from the very outset, remark that we are extremely pleased that our Argentine colleagues are paying some attention to cricket at last . . .' chortled the *Review*, 'but we must say that these early reports have caused many of us to smile somewhat broadly.'

The sides were more evenly matched when they met in Brazil six months later. Miller's gritty 50 at Santos in July 1922 helped Brazil secure a draw in the first 'Test', and the second in São Paulo also ended in a stalemate. Fingernails were bitten to the quick under the thatched pavilion roof in the Rio decider as Argentina scraped home by one wicket. 'Charlie Miller was, in his heyday, a beautiful bat and a contemporary of Herbert Dorning,' wrote Kenneth Bridger, Argentine cricket's historian. 'He was for many years the outstanding batsman in the State of São Paulo – and perhaps we are not far wrong in saying Brazil.'

Miller passed the baton to Richard 'Dick' Latham, another Paulista. Latham was a wiry 19-year-old opener when Brazil headed for Buenos Aires in December 1927 on the RMS *Arlanza* with their strongest-ever team. The tourists' optimism was quickly dashed in the opener at Saenz Peña as they were thrashed by eight wickets. Latham's 35 on Christmas Eve, the highest score by any Brazil player in the match, caught the eye of the *Buenos Aires Herald*: 'He possesses an easy and confident style. His carpet drives especially being the most attractive.'

Latham began 1928 with a hundred in the second innings of the second 'Test' at Belgrano. 'Latham, the batting ace,' Brooking, trademark fag in mouth, whimsically penned. 'He made a bigger hit with the crowd than Hamlet would had he played with Romeo and Juliet, the Siamese Twins in the Comic Drama, "Homeless Sherlock". His innings of 116 was like an awning – it put them all in the shade.' The next day Latham woke at Buenos Aires's Plaza Hotel to a pile of telegrams from well-wishers, including a simple 'Congratulations' signed by the mysterious 'FattyMac Jimmie'. Dennet Ayling's 191, however, in Argentina's first innings, a record between the two sides that stood for 33 years, proved the difference as the Argentines took an unassailable 2–0 lead in the series.

Brazil had built up a head of steam by the third 'Test' at Hurlingham. W. A. Bond's seamers and cutters flummoxed Argentina as they were bowled out for 287, and he finished with five for 95. Brazil then racked up 534 – the highest-ever score in an international match against Argentina, with Morrissy's 163 a record for a Brazilian. Argentina looked on course for a draw on the final day at 203 for four, but the tireless Bond (four for 54) sparked a collapse to skittle the home side for 211. Brazil had humiliated their more illustrious rivals by an innings and 36 runs.

The letters bags of the *Buenos Aires Herald* and the *Standard* bulged in the days that followed as the fallout reached fever pitch. Angry correspondence lamented the absence of Clem Gibson, called for a root-and-branch reform of school cricket, and lampooned the selectors. It would be Brazil's only 'Test' victory on Argentine soil and their greatest cricketing moment. Their only other away win, in men's senior cricket, would come in a single-innings match at Belgrano in January 1978, when Boy Cunningham's son Gerry kept wicket for Brazil. 'There was a long delay in the match that day,' Gerry tells us. 'Argentina had been so confident of winning that four of their players had taken off to the tennis courts for a game of doubles and had to be beckoned back to bat. They were given a dressing down by ACA president Donald Forrester in the post-match dinner when he accused them of not having any *cojones*!'

When Argentina next travelled to Brazil, in May 1929, Latham would write his name into cricket's history books. SPAC had recently inaugurated a new ground at Pirituba after SPR superintendent Col. Eric Johnston found them a site next to a railway station. 'Hills and swamps have been filled in and drained, springs have been side-tracked and rough places made smooth,' said the *Anglo-Brazilian Chronicle*. 'The result is what was once a useless piece of waste *mato* is now a beautiful cricket ground complete with pavilion, stands and rustic sheds to say nothing for the bowling screens.' Johnston's grave concern had been the passing trains clicking and clunking their way into the batsman's eyeline, so he invested in substantial sightscreens – when Cahn brought his XI later that year, he reckoned them the biggest in the world. 'They were a sight to behold,' Gerry Cunningham remembers. 'They must have been thirty feet high and nearly a hundred and fifty feet wide.'

Latham could have batted with a blindfold in the first match against Argentina. His timing, judgement and finesse were impeccable as he made 105 and 100, becoming the first player from a country without official Test status to make centuries in each innings of an international match. Brazil crushed Argentina by 186 runs. 'Latham. A revelation!' the home press bragged. Argentina were wounded lions, and roared back easily to win the next two Tests and the series 2–1.

Latham was a late inclusion for the South Americans' tour of England in 1932. 'A steady bat with a strong defence and powerful strokes in front of the wicket. He should be a success,' wrote H. D. Swan, said to have managed more MCC out-matches than anyone in history. Initially it looked like Latham was carrying some kind of Amazonian hex. In the opening match against the Affiliated South American Banks at Teddington, two separate deliveries hit Latham's stumps without dislodging the bails. His personal highlight in five first-class matches was a half-century against Scotland. At 24, the big cricket break he craved had gone. Three years later he moved to Rio, and that season would make 1497 runs in 25 innings at an average of 99.80.

Relations soured again in the years after the liberal revolution of 1930, which overthrew Brazil's coffee-growing oligarchy. Neither Latham nor Miller would be around to witness Argentina and Brazil's next meeting in October 1953. They died within three months of each other earlier that year. Aged 78, Miller had been in poor health, and his death was expected. His contribution to football filled newspapers in Brazil and around the world. Latham's passing a few months before was more of a shock. He was only 43, but slipped away without a mention, and outlived by his father. A tattered scrapbook of Latham's that we discover in a plastic box buried in the offices of Rio Cricket & Athletic Association helps us piece together his story.

*　　*　　*

The benevolent Anglophile leanings of Prince Regent João of Bragança brought the first cricketers to Rio de Janeiro. Bragança, dubbed 'The Clement', and the Portuguese court were escorted by the Royal Navy out of the clutches of Napoleon's armies and to the relative comfort of Brazil in 1807. He repaid the favour by opening up its ports to the British, who received generous trade terms and lower import duties. 'By the free intercourse which was permitted with England, many of our arts and some portion of sciences were introduced,' Maria Graham wrote in *Travels in Brazil*. 'England, though not a parent state, became in a great degree, the metropolis of Brazil.'

By the 1820s taverns called the Red Lion and Jolly Tar popped up in Rio to quench the thirst of British sailors, some partaking in Brazil's national drink *cachaça* – a sugary rum today used in caipirinha cocktails. Cricket kept some away from the decadence of the alehouse. Diaries kept by Rear-Admiral Graham Hammond, who had escorted British ambassador Charles Stuart aboard the HMS *Spartiate* in 1825 to mediate Portugal and Brazil's divorce, recounted the first matches. 'I find there is a cricket match today in the neighbourhood of São Cristóvão which I am sorry I was not informed of before I invited a party to dinner,' he wrote on 8 September 1836. 'I fear there will be a clashing of interests which I shall regret very much.' In his next entry Hammond added: 'The gentlemen cricketers report favourably of their game. One of the young men has most credit for his play, having I suspect had no inconsiderable practice in that way in his last ships.'

A team representing Rio beat the officers of HMS *Southampton* in 1842 in unbearably hot conditions, though claims the 'thermometer on the day of the match was at 132 degrees Fahrenheit [55 °C] at noon' were an exaggeration. From 1854 the British Cricket Club played regularly at the Campo de São Cristóvão. The descendants of Swiss settlers in Nova Friburgo – 85 miles from Rio – also found cricket on the school curriculum when British teacher John Henry moved there.

In Rio it was an almost entirely British affair. Brazilians were not encouraged to join in or, as the poet Francisco Otaviano scornfully claimed at the time, they were unwilling: 'The present generation was born with rickets: lives spent with the old who had had their youthfulness stagnated; effeminate lives; excitement being derived from playing lansquenet; oysters dipped in port wine; reading some serial or erotic poetry.' The Artisan Amateurs Cricket Club, made up of cobblers, carpenters and other craftsmen, and the Rio Amateur Cricket Club were short-lived affairs.

Brazil was ruled at this time by Emperor Dom Pedro II who, as a timid and reluctant 14-year-old, assumed full responsibility of the country's monarchy in 1840. Despite his feeble health Pedro II grew into a statesman of stature. Partly through unswerving dedication to his duties for the betterment of Brazil, and partly because of insomnia, he worked from 7 a.m. until 2 a.m. Known as Dom Pedro 'the Magnanimous', he championed education, science and culture. He exchanged regular correspondence with Richard Wagner, Alexander Graham Bell and Friedrich Nietzsche. What little free time Pedro II had was spent reading, studying and learning a multitude of languages. The Brazilian emperor also developed a soft spot for watching cricket.

A penchant for Parisian grandeur influenced Pedro II to embark on a programme of beautification in Rio. This took in the creation of new parks, and the area in front of the house of his daughter, Princess Isabel, in the Laranjeiras district, was turned into an idyllic green space. The setting, at the foot of a stone quarry, proved an irresistible spot for Rio's cricketers. What captured Pedro II's interest in cricket is not clear. Viscount Eugenio Tourinho was only one of a handful of Brazilians who had played in this period. Pedro II may have seen cricket in England on a six-week tour, while Gall Abbot, an American physician and a trusted confidant, might have played a key role. When Abbot complained that sports were lacking in Brazil, Pedro II relaxed customs duties on sporting goods.

Pedro II, Isabel and the rest of the family were such frequent spectators that a special stand for the comfort of the imperial party was constructed on the centre of the Rua Paissandu boundary. Interestingly, cricket was played there not long after Anglo-Brazilian diplomatic relations were severed following a brouhaha between Pedro II and British Consul William Christie. Pedro II's permitting play in front of Princess Isabel's house either hinted at a love of cricket that transcended politics, or was a smart way to mend the fences.

Rio Cricket Club were founded in 1872. They initially played at a ground in Fifés, on Rua Berquó in the district of Botafogo, a popular residential spot for the British, just over a mile away from Copacabana. The world's most famous beach was, at this time, a relatively unspectacular thin strip of sand where the sea lapped up against the promenade when the tide was in, though it was still the first night-time stop for the MCC tourists of 1958–9. It was not until a landfill project in the 1970s, which saw the sandy area increased, that it become the iconic beach we observe while in Rio, packed with peacock-strutting sun worshippers, surfers and beach footballers.

Rio CC made Palácio Laranjeiras their home in 1880 but nine years later Brazil became a republic, the weary Pedro II deposed by a military coup. The palace land was expropriated by a bank, and Rio CC were forced to share it with a team made up of Brazilian nationals, which later became Paissandu CC. In 1893 the Brazilian navy launched a bombardment on the city during a match. Nobody was injured, although Henry Watmough, a clerk who opened the batting for London & Brazilian Bank, was not so fortunate a few days later, killed by shelling while eating lunch at a hotel.

George Cox, Rio CC's secretary, grew tired of the club not having a home to call their own, and vowed to find a new ground in 1896. They tried and failed to buy the land in the grounds of the palace, so Cox spearheaded a move to a site across the bay to Niterói, reached by a Mississippi-style paddle-wheel ferry. In August 1897, the club changed its name to the

Rio Cricket & Athletic Association (RC&AA) – 'cricket' inserted to indicate its seniority over other sports.

Cox's son Oscar, meanwhile, had returned from schooling in Switzerland, bringing with him Rio's first leather football. Like Miller, he would play an integral role in growing football in his city, but unlike his São Paulo counterpart he only fleetingly played cricket. Oscar dedicated his efforts to Fluminense FC, which he founded in July 1902. They played their first football matches on Paissandu's cricket ground.

We get off at the Flamengo Metro stop, and stroll the short distance to the heavily guarded Palácio Guanabara. Princess Isabel's beautiful neoclassical old home is now the headquarters of the government of the State of Rio de Janeiro, and was the subject of a legal battle lasting over 123 years from her descendants, who claimed ownership, before the courts ruled against them in 2018. A few of the tall palm trees we had seen in photographs of matches are still there, but the cricket ground itself is now a car park for government workers. Next door is the Estádio das Laranjeiras, home to Fluminense's museum, where there is a bust of Cox Jr and the club's striped blazer.

A cricket XI representing Fluminense played Paissandu in June 1910, and the same year Corinthian FC, which would inspire the football club of their Brazilian namesake, arrived from Britain on tour. As well as playing Fluminense at football, Corinthian met Rio in a cricket match. Corinthian boasted a strong line-up – Samuel Day (Kent), Charles Page (Middlesex) and Robert Braddell (Gentlemen of England) – but Rio clung on for an admirable draw.

After a brief visit to Paissandu's swish downtown club, which sits on the shores of Rodrigo de Freitas Lagoon, we make our way to RC&AA. The club is still based at the ground in Niterói, a chugging 20-minute ferry ride across Guanabara Bay from Rio. En route we thumb a 1920s copy of the *Anglo South American Bank Magazine*, which gave a dewy-eyed description of a corner of a foreign field forever England:

> The scene on the occasion of a big match brings up memories of enjoyable cricket weeks in the Old Country. The pavilion and seats are ranged along one side of the ground in the shade of a tree-clad hill. In front stretches a broad expanse of green against which the players and the bowling [sight] screens stand out in dazzling white. Overhead a deep blue sky and great masses of cumulus top the distant hills. From the tall mast by the pavilion, the Union Jack floats lazily. The sun beats fiercely down, but one has the comforting knowledge that there is plenty of ice under the thatched roof at the back. A day like this, on an English ground, surrounded by English-speaking people, and watching or playing the English national game, makes the exile forget for a while that he is in a foreign land, five thousand miles from home.

Marcelo Fellows, whose British grandfather George was a leading cricketer, greets us on arrival outside the green gates of RC&AA. The bar in the renovated 1930s pavilion is adorned with the shirts of AC Milan and Brazil worn by Leonardo, who played for the *seleção* from 1990 to 2002 and witnessed cricket being played in Niterói as a junior in the early 1980s. Fellows recalls the slight midfielder was nicknamed 'Mouse'. Next to the changing rooms we find a framed Union Jack given to the club by Ernest Shackleton when he visited RC&AA in December 1921, shortly before the Shackleton–Rowett Expedition. Shackleton was a cricket enthusiast who had played at Dulwich College, but was in no fit state for a game at Niterói – his health had started to deteriorate, and in January 1922 he died aboard the *Quest*.

Among the meagre early cricketana held in the club offices, much of which we find in poor condition, is a handful of musty old pamphlets and handbooks. In gold letters, embossed on the forest-green jacket of one pocket-sized booklet, are the words 'Rio Cricket & Athletic Association – fixture card – season 1928'. Leafing through the faded pages, past the list of members and various committees, to the cricket fixtures we find one match immediately stands out among the rest, so shocking and offensive it is: 'August 26th Sunday 10am . . . Niggers v Whites.'

The *Rio News* acknowledges, striking a curious matter-of-fact tone, the intra-club match is 'facetiously termed' and takes place 'between those born in South America and the Rest'. The match was first played by the old Rio CC in 1892, continued until the late 1930s, and also appeared on the fixture lists of SPAC and Santos. In 1902, Brazil-born Charles Miller made a century in one of the matches. Brazilian cricket was not alone in this regard. Imperialist posturing, a sense of superiority to reinforce the hegemony of white 'Englishness', was found in clubs wherever the British set up shop in Latin America.

In the same booklet, at the top of the list of the club's honorary members, we discover the name of Rudyard Kipling. He made a sojourn to Rio to recover from pneumonia, having long wanted to make the trip, writing in *Just So Stories*: 'I'd love to roll to Rio, some day before I'm old.' Kipling took in Rio's *carnaval* and spent time at RC&AA, where he curiously observed:

Another gathering was made up of some of the English men, women and children at ease after the day's work in a beautiful club. Here one seemed to come a little closer to hints and half-confidences of life. But convention – more's the pity – forbids cross-examining people as they pass and asking them: 'How do you truly live?' 'What do you think about things here – business, marketing, servants, children's ailments, education, and everything else?' So the river of face flows placidly enough and one can only guess at what underlies the ripples and dimples.

Kipling was not a cricket lover, despite claims he turned out for J. M. Barrie's literary cricket team alongside H. G. Wells, Arthur Conan Doyle and P. G. Wodehouse. A school chum of Kipling said he shuddered 'at the mention of W. G. Grace's name' and he famously later wrote of 'flannelled fools at the wicket'. But he hardly baulked at the offer of honorary membership. RC&AA's members doubtless would have grasped, in later years, what he meant when posing: 'What do they know of England, who only England know?' All of which seems drastically at odds with the cosmopolitan make-up of Brazilian cricket today.

*     *     *

Every Sunday morning a thousand black men, women and children would gather in the compound in front of the Casa Grande at Morro Velho for a *revista*. The men would be dressed in white shirts, cotton trousers and red caps. In front of them the women would wear white petticoats with a red band around their lower third, blue and white striped shawls, and a red handkerchief. A roll call would be taken before the superintendent of the St John d'el Rey Mining Company and his senior colleagues, including two medical officers, would walk down the columns of people, taking a moment to inspect each individual.

They would then all be marched en masse, in their Sunday best, off to church. 'A peculiar sight,' the great adventurer Richard Burton wrote in *Explorations of the Highlands of the Brazil*. 'Both sexes were bare-footed – everywhere in Brazil a token of slavery.' Burton sat on a hill above the compound in 1867 and sketched *The Fortnightly Slave Muster*. Slaves would be presented with medals, ribbons or merit awards for good conduct, which would count towards their freedom in the *revista*. It was, however, also a ritual designed to strengthen the hand of slave masters.

The remainder of Sunday was 'free' for slaves to wander throughout the mine's estate where they could visit friends and family, or, as Burton noted, 'lie in the sun and, if they can, drink and smoke hemp'. The British workers, meanwhile, could put on their cricket whites and head to a flattened field on a hill above the Casa Grande on the Morro Velho estate. The turf would be cared for during the week by elderly slaves no longer physically capable of working in the mines. Slaves would watch from afar. They were never permitted to join in with what was then an exclusive whites-only pursuit.

The early players were mostly Cornishmen, numbering some 350 during Burton's visit, who lived in single-storey whitewashed buildings with cottage-style gardens in the Colônia Inglesa, segregated from an area dubbed 'Timbuctoo', where the slaves lived in trying conditions. The two groups rarely fraternised, although in the company archives we unearth records of workers dismissed for having sexual relations with slaves. Cricket doubtless served to emphasise the racial divide between the white middle management and engineers, and the slave workers.

São João d'el Rey in Minas Gerais was first mined by the St John Company in 1830, before operations moved, four years later, to a more lucrative site at Morro Velho. Near the town of Nova Lima, it was once the deepest mine in the world, and the most profitable of all British investments in Latin America in the nineteenth century. A key factor was the slave workforce. Morro Velho was the largest single British slave-holding organisation in Brazil, and slaves were made to work 12 hours a day underground in the most atrocious environment. Slavery in British colonies was abolished in 1833, and Morro Velho dubbed a 'monstrous incongruity' by the anti-slavery press. It was not until 1882 that the last slaves at Morro Velho were freed, although many chose to remain as paid labour where they had put down roots.

It was against this backdrop that George Chalmers, a 28-year-old Cornishman, came to Morro Velho after being appointed superintendent in 1884. Two years into the assignment disaster struck when the mine collapsed. Chalmers returned to London, and convinced the company's board the mine could be rebuilt and turned it into a profitable enterprise again.

Cricket in Morro Velho, up to this point, had been confined to matches on the company estate or at Quintas da Boa Vista, a nearby farm where the British grew their cauliflowers, potatoes, peas and turnips. It was during Chalmers's time as superintendent that the Morro Velho Athletic Club (MVAC) was founded, in 1896, in the district of Quintas.

A smallpox outbreak in Morro Velho delayed a match against Rio's cricketers, to inaugurate the ground, until 1898. 'The journey was most arduous,' wrote Robert Brooking. 'The gauge change had to be made in the early hours of the morning. When we arrived at Honorio Bicalho there was a long ride on mule-back to our destination. The ticks or *garrapatas* must have been informed of the journey as we got covered in bites.' With just 70 Englishmen working at the mine during the rebuild, MVAC were weak opponents and Rio cricketers brushed them aside. A lavish ball held on the evening after the first day did not prevent Brooking from taking 10 wickets in the match.

In later years, visiting teams would take a tour of the mine, including the sorting room where the gold dust was weighed before being turned into gold ingots. There the manager would open a large safe and pull out a gold bar, and challenge players to pick it up with one hand. If they could do so, the bar was theirs to keep. 'In anticipation we all lifted weights the weeks before!' recalls Gerry Cunningham. 'But it was too heavy and slippery to grasp. To rub salt in the wounds, the manager would call in a Brazilian colleague who calmly picked up the bar one-handed and returned it to the safe.'

The prize possession in Morro Velho's museum is a bone-china tea set, coloured light blue, decorated with the crest of the three lions and with a note from the Football Association thanking the mine for their hospitality during the 1950 World Cup. England's players under Walter Winterbottom had based themselves at MVAC before their match against the USA, 18 miles away in Belo Horizonte. England's squad included Yorkshire's Willie Watson, who would become a dual international the following year when he made his Test debut against South Africa. A cricket match against the travelling press corps at MVAC allowed Watson to keep his eye in, and in his first County Championship innings after the World Cup the Yorkshire left-hander hit 122 in a victory over Somerset.

At this time the mine boasted 2000 British staff, who did a Klondike rush along miles of mountain path to get to Belo Horizonte and support England. 'We ain't got a chance,' Scotsman Bill Jeffrey, USA manager, said on the eve of the game. 'But we're going to fight to keep down any cricket score.' England had Tom Finney, Wilf Mannion and Stan Mortensen, so were expected to win easily, but a solitary goal from Haiti-born Joe Gaetjens gave the USA their 'Miracle of Belo Horizonte'. Local legend persists to this day that England's players enjoyed themselves too much during their stay in Morro Velho and were relaxed to the point of being horizontal. On the same day, 29 June, England's cricketers lost a Test to West Indies for the first time on home soil. The British sporting press went into meltdown.

Little has changed at the ground, now under the auspices of Clube Das Quintas, by the time we make a steep uphill walk from downtown Nova Lima. The turf is as immaculate as when England's footballers visited, the view of the surrounding hills barely obscured by urban development and the original white wooden benches for spectators lovingly maintained. For many years Brazilians in Nova Lima were scarcely admitted, and the club was a reminder of unwanted foreign dominance. Morro Velho is now the world's oldest continuously worked mine, employing 3000 people, but there is barely a cricketer among them. 'We no longer have any British members,' Quintas secretary Júnior Souza tells us. 'But the cricket bats, balls and photographs are reminders of the history.'

Round the back of the pavilion is a row of smart English-style houses where we are told a few British families in Nova Lima retired. John Hislop answers the third door we knock at. He is 85 and worked at the mine for 45 years. 'We dropped the

"V" and called ourselves MCC but, overall, the quality of the cricket here wasn't that great,' he admits. 'Some, such as mine superintendent A. L. Yarnell, a former army man and a good cricketer, would help us give Rio a game.' Yarnell was once unable to get away to play against Argentina because of a strike at the mine.

John's wife Vivian shuffles into the living room, wheeling in a trolley, and for the only time during our stay in Brazil we are served, unprompted, tea with milk. 'It's one of the few traditions left over from the British presence here,' Vivian says, chuckling. 'If you ask for tea anywhere else in Brazil they serve it without milk, but everyone in Nova Lima prefers to drink it *com leite*.' The town is also famous for its Christmas cake – *queca* – made to a traditional British recipe and not found anywhere else in Brazil.

\*   \*   \*

A few weeks after his twenty-fourth birthday, in July 1936, Brian Johnston trudged off the RMS *Almanzora* as a roaring tropical thunderstorm battered the port of Santos. After disembarking, Johnston, drenched from head to toe, was driven to a beachside house where he sat glumly on the veranda, watching the rain fall, feeling miserable and homesick. The next day he stood in some dog muck and boarded a train for Brazil's interior to sort out his immigration papers. The smell stank out the carriage of the train for hours.

Ten years before 'Johnners' joined the BBC, launching a cricket commentary career that would span six decades and turn him into a national treasure, he had been despatched to serve an apprenticeship in the family coffee business in Brazil.

Johnston had been reluctant to do so after Eton and Oxford, leaving behind cricket and his busy social life in London.

The Johnston coffee empire had been founded by Brian's great-grandfather Edward, who ventured to Brazil – then a Portuguese colony – in 1821, aged 17. Edward worked for a number of companies, married a Dutch woman, Henriette Moke, whose father owned a coffee *fazenda*, and in September 1842 established Edward Johnston & Co.

Coffee became Brazil's number-one export, and its profitability owed much to slavery. Around 1.5 million slaves were brought into Brazil from Africa in the first half of the nineteenth century. Gaspar da Silveira Martins, one of the country's senators, in 1880 asserted '*o Brasil é o café e o café e o negro*' – Brazil is coffee and coffee is the negro. Slaves worked 17-hour days, slept in cramped wooden dormitories and faced brutal punishments. Life expectancy on arrival in Brazil was seven years.

The presence of British companies in Santos provided landmark sporting impetus in the late 1800s. The beach in front of the Boqueirão Hotel was the venue for cricket, and there was not the merest hint sartorial protocol would be relaxed even on the sand and in the heat. A rare photograph of Santos's early cricketers on the beach shows almost all of them formally attired with striped blazers and cricket whites. In the background a horse pulling a roller is tended to by three men.

On more than one occasion matches were abandoned after being planned around the wrong tide. 'How many times has the writer seen cricketers carrying out their matting and preparing a pitch on the sand for a game?' reported the *Rio News*, incredulously. 'And how many times, just as everything was prepared and the game ready to start has seen a big wave of the sea wash completely over the pitch?' The Johnston brothers were among this group of beach-cricket enthusiasts, as Brian discovered in Santos nearly 50 years later. 'I see quite a lot of an old Mrs Julia Ford who knew all the family and used to supply the teas on the beach,' he wrote in a letter to his mother in 1936. 'GrannyPa [Reginald Johnston] was very shocked at cricket on Sundays, but later became keen on it.' Coffee Houses v. Rest of the World was a regular fixture, while E. Johnston & Co. had enough staff to put together a company XI.

In August 1889, at the offices of Naumann, Gepp & Co., a meeting was convened by Australian exchange broker Alexander Kealman to found the Santos Athletic Club (SAC). Santos at this time was rife with disease, and plenty of fixtures between SAC and SPAC were postponed because of illness and quarantine. Santos kept their spirits up with matches between themselves, to the approval of the *Rio News*: 'The fact playing was well up to the mark shows the English colony is not yet demoralised by the discovery of the dreaded bubonic pest. Authorities say we should keep up our regular modes of life, and that means keeping up cricket.'

In reality it was yellow fever, rather than the bubonic plague, which was the scourge of Santos – 10 per cent of the city's 20,000 inhabitants perished from the disease. The Johnston family in Santos were not immune, and it claimed the life of Bertram, the grandson of Edward Johnston. Andrew Miller, the secretary of SAC and uncle of Charles, wrote to *Cricket* in 1894 and touched on its impact:

Cricket is carried on in these warm regions by the 'balance' of the English and Americans left over from the ravages of the 'Yellow Jack'. Our club . . . is not a very old institution, but there is plenty of enthusiasm, cricket being looked forward to as only Englishmen can look forward to it, even with the great difficulties we have to overcome. We are obliged to play on the sea beach, which is luckily very hard and makes a really good and true pitch with coconut matting laid down.

Behind Santos's original beach cricketers, in the photograph, are the *Illha das Palmas*. They became known as 'Johnstons' Islands' after the family built quarantine barracks for visiting sailors. The legacy of the disease was also reflected in the colours adopted by SAC in January 1898, which remain to this day: blue represents the sky, yellow the fever, and black for the mourning over those whose lives it took.

Shortly before the turn of the century, Kealman and Alfred Sell, manager of the Santos branch of the Western Telegraph Company, purchased a site for the club at the foot of José Menino Hill. 'The area was an actual vegetable patch before being turned over to the club,' Kealman's elderly but glamorous granddaughter Isabelita Randolph recalls over glasses of *limonada suíça*, Brazilian lemonade with lime peel, at SAC. 'In the early days the players changed behind a tree, although supporters were able to watch matches from magnificent wicker chairs. They used to have a mule to pull the roller on the pitch. I used to feel so sorry for that poor mule.'

SAC's first pavilion faced the sea in order to catch the breeze, and in 1912 influential Brazilian polymath Ruy Barbosa dropped by for a visit. Tall and striking palm trees now line the ground at what we discover Santos locals still call the *Clube dos Ingleses*. We can taste the sea salt in the air, but annoyingly modernist high-rise flats obscure the ocean vista. Much of the cricket history from the club's archive was washed away 17 years ago in an exceptionally high tide. A heavily oiled Gradidge 'Imperial Driver' bat signed by the 1958–9 MCC tourists in SAC's English-style pub is the only surviving relic.

We find the Johnstons are fondly remembered in Santos. Tales of Brian's time have survived the years. After all he was, by his own admission, pretty useless when it came to the coffee business: 'I could never tell one bean from another, nor taste the difference between various types. So it was not surprising I was never given a job with any authority or responsibility. I hated my work and was trying to escape from it into something I could enjoy.' Johnston did, however, throw himself into cricket for SAC. His wicketkeeping impressed the selectors sufficiently to earn him a place in the State of São Paulo side to face the State of Rio de Janeiro.

Johnston once played a game up the coast in São Sebastião, where SAC visited the Caraguatatuba fruit farm. 'I was violently sea sick – the only one, which was bad,' he wrote in a letter to his mother of the boat trip. 'We lost. I stumped three men, made top score with 14 so you can imagine how many we made. I hit a ball on my nose and it's still sore and swollen.'

Operated by the Lancashire General Investment Company, part of the Vestey business, between 1927 and 1939 the farm met the growing demand in Britain for bananas and grapefruit. The *Fazenda dos Ingleses* had its own 75-mile internal railway, docks, stores, church and, of course, space was found on the 4000-acre farm to carve out a ground for cricket and polo. Production continued until the 'Catastrophe of Caraguatatuba' in 1967, when an incredible deluge brought about mudslides that destroyed crops, roads, buildings and claimed the lives of 437 people.

Johnston, and no doubt many other British in the managerial class, rarely mixed with Brazilians, although when *carnaval* came around in February 1937 he was prepared to throw off the shackles of British stuffiness:

> The Brazilians go quite mad and dance in fancy dress in the streets and cars for three days and end with an enormous ball at the big hotel which literally never stops from 11pm until 6am as they have two orchestras which pick up the time from one another. They only play about five tunes all evening and people just rush around doing this queer Brazilian dance, just like gallop in England but with sort of a tango rhythm. We enjoyed it frightfully. We went through the streets in an open car, 12 of us throwing streamers etc, it really was great fun.

*Carnaval* in Brazil is an outrageously colourful national event, which gyrates its way through streets of every village, town and city, most famously in Rio, where the costumes, spectacular floats and week-long parties bring two million people on to the streets and draw visitors from all around the world. The origins of Brazilian *carnaval* trace back to Portuguese Catholics in the seventeenth century, who celebrated the period before Lent with formal balls. Afro-Brazilians responded with their own kind, the fancy-dress element initially their way of mocking Brazil's white elite. It morphed into an event bound up with the country's identity and infused with samba beats. The rest of Latin America loves *carnaval*, though not with quite the same zeal as Brazilians – it is said the calendar year does not really start until the clean up.

Johnston's half-hearted attempts to learn Portuguese became an endless source of amusement for his colleagues, and Fred

Duder, a fellow cricketer and his best friend in Santos, remembers his Portuguese accent was 'atrocious'. Legend has it he still managed the odd dalliance with local women. There was a shortage of appropriate unmarried ladies in town, and a number of European bachelors, so Santos boasted countless *bordellos* at the time, and Johnston was reputed to be an enthusiastic customer. His biographer, Tim Heald, generously concluded that he visited them for the music rather than anything else on offer.

Letters sent home by Johnston included observations on the latest Test matches based on BBC World Service bulletins, updates on his own cricket performances, plus requests for copies of the *Cricketer* magazine and newspapers to be posted out to Santos. Other than sport it was to amateur theatricals that Johnston dedicated himself to alleviate the humdrum world of coffee. He is even said to have brought several pairs of tap-dancing shoes with him from London, and taught staff during break times. The highlight was a two-act revue entitled *Nuts in May*, which he produced and also appeared in a number of sketches, including playing the Mystery Man from Newmarket in the skit 'I've Got a Horse'. 'It was a great success and the funniest show they'd had at the club,' he said. 'It was fun but very exhausting. We had a good run at the end where a chap and I threw puddings, eggs and flour at each other.'

While in Santos we heartily tuck into Brazil's national dish *feijoada*, a delicious bean and meat stew served with rice, washing it down with a glass of Antarctica lager, one of the country's most popular and distinctive brews. Johnston, typical of the less-than adventurous British living and working in Latin America during this era, shunned the local food, which did little to foster relations with his Brazilian colleagues. He even had an aversion to the region's sumptuously fresh tropical fruit and vegetables.

Johnston's diet saw him became gaunt and stick thin. Shortly after his second *carnaval* in February 1938 he became paralysed in the arms and legs after being struck down with acute peripheral neuritis, a form of beri-beri: 'The cause of the disease was all a bit of a mystery. Some people said it was a deficiency of vitamin B. There was a wonderful Brazilian doctor called D'Utra Vaz who had experience of this sort of disease. He said it was often brought on by excessive drinking or childbirth. He prescribed for me a diet of raw vegetables, lots of tomatoes (which I hate), daily injections in the bottom (I had nearly a hundred!) and lots of massage and sunbathing.' Johnston was nursed back to health at the home of the Deighton family, where Dorothy Deighton looked after him 'like a child', until he could walk again. He pored over old copies of *Wisden* to while away the time. In the meantime, his mother Pleasance rushed out to Brazil and accompanied him on a boat back to England when he was well enough. Johnners's Brazilian adventure was over.

\*     \*     \*

The large flowing white lace dresses and headscarves worn by black women in Salvador are offset by beaded necklaces in all the colours of the rainbow. It is a dazzling welcome for our visit to the cosmopolitan port city on the north-east coast. Salvador once served as Brazil's capital, and is one of the oldest cities founded by Europeans in the Americas. We discover that many of the Afro-Brazilian women wearing the eye-catching traditional Baiana de Acarajé dresses are followers of Candomblé – a syncretism of Catholicism and the Yoruba religion, featuring elements of witchcraft, voodoo-type rituals and tribal dances. Black African slaves brought to a number of Brazil's mines and plantations had first docked in Salvador at the same time the city's British merchants started to do business there.

Salvador is separated into an upper and lower town, and from sea level we take the Elevador Lacerda – the first public lift in Brazil – and walk to the Largo do Campo Grande. Overlooked by modern apartments, hotels and the Teatro Castro Alves, it is a well-maintained plaza. The centrepiece is the Monumento ao Caboclo, which commemorates the fierce battles that took place on the site as Bahia fought for its independence from Portugal in the 1820s. Half a century after that bloody conflict, the Bahia Cricket Club began more sedate pursuits on the very same patch of land.

John Wild, professor of literature at the University of Melbourne in Australia, was on HMS *Challenger* when it arrived in 1873. He sketched a match between the ship and Bahia CC at Campo Grande in all its glory. Wild's illustration depicts a black woman, in typical Candomblé dress, resting a basket of fruit on the ground and keenly watching play unfold.

The *Challenger* would circumnavigate the globe, a trip documented by Herbert Swire, who made 'a duck's egg' and 'six or seven' in matches against Bahia CC. Swire and his team-mates were 'whipped pretty soundly' in one game watched by a large crowd. 'The Brazilians were immensely amused whenever a ball was sent spinning into their midst,' Swire added. 'The negroes among them were especially jovial, and their resonant cachinations [*sic*] were heard on all sides.' In 1921, Bahia CC was incorporated in the Bahia Athletic Association, which exists as an exclusive members' club inside an intimidating white glass-fronted building, with surly security guards and gleaming metal turnstiles.

The best cricketer with a Bahian connection was Leonidas de Toledo Marcondes de Montezuma, born in April 1869 to a Brazilian father and British mother in Crowborough, Sussex. Montezuma's Salvador-born grandfather Francisco shunned the priesthood, studied law, was a partisan figure in Bahia's fight for independence where he founded *O Constitucional* newspaper and spoke out against the Portuguese. When Brazil separated from Portugal, Francisco was awarded the Ordem Imperial do Cruzeiro by Dom Pedro I and marked independence by changing the family name from Gomes Brandão to Montezuma in homage to the Aztecs. His grandson L. D. M. de Montezuma would light up scorecards during his eight first-class appearances for Sussex in 1898 and one for W. G. Grace's London County in 1904. He made 80 not out, his sole Championship fifty, against the fine Nottinghamshire attack of Thomas Wass and Dick Attewell at Hove.

The sheer size of the world's fifth-largest country meant Brazilian cricket was not so much a structure as a collection of isolated outposts. Up at Pernambuco, the first mainland stop from Europe, it may even have stretched back to the early 1800s, according to C. T. Nash, owner of the *Anglo-Brazilian Chronicle*. 'Recife in those days had a big British colony, and British men-of-war and sailing vessels, after crossing the Atlantic, frequently called there to take in supplies and fresh water,' he wrote in the 1930s. 'What is more natural than a pitch laid down to give sailors, after a long spell at sea, an opportunity of stretching their legs?'

By 1864 the British were playing at a sugar-cane mill. The Pernambuco Cricket Club followed soon after, initially on the seafront in Santo Amaro das Salinas, close to Recife's beaches, which we find plastered with signs warning against bathing in shark-infested waters. Visiting ships were their main opposition, though staff working for the Central & South American Telegraph Company on the Fernando de Noronha archipelago would scrape an XI together and sail the 200 miles to Pernambuco for a game.

Pernambuco CC played in what the *Brazilian Review* hyperbolically called 'the most luxuriant and best laid out public gardens in the world', before a change to a more suitable venue in 1907. 'The cricket club for many years occupied a field at Santa Anna where the ground, although excellent, was considerably smaller than the new one,' added the *Review*. 'And had the great disadvantage of being open to the public, and the hordes of small nigger boys infesting the field on match days constituted an annoyance of a serious nature.'

Thankfully, there was no evidence of outdated racist attitudes during our visit to the British Country Club in Recife, where the same ground still exists. Of most interest was a team photograph at the bottom of a filing cabinet in the club's cramped offices. Dated 1907, it is of a group of women cricketers and most likely the first match of its kind in Brazil.

There was cricket wherever the British dropped anchor on the Brazilian coastline during this era – from Fortaleza on the north-east tip, to Porto Alegre 2000 miles away down by the Uruguayan border. And the rubber boom would slowly take it inland, with the Pará and Belém cricket clubs founded near the mouth of the Amazon. A tributary of the Amazon, the Rio Xingu, runs through the state of Pará down into Mato Grosso, and it is there where Percy Fawcett, son of ex-Sussex cricketer

Edward Fawcett and a handy player himself, mysteriously disappeared when he went in search of the famed Lost City of Z. Ed Giddins tapped into the spirit of Fawcett and Roy Sheffield by canoeing up the Amazon just weeks after making his Test debut at The Oval in 1999.

We are fleeced paying for hammocks from a market seller at Belém docks, before hopping aboard a weathered passenger ferry, the *Anna Karoline III* (it sank in February 2020), for our journey along the Amazon to Manaus. The boat has special open-air decks with hooks to hang our beds for the next five nights, and is the only option for backpackers on a shoestring budget unable to stretch to a cramped windowless cabin. We leave Belém, covering ourselves in pungent mosquito spray, and head deep into Brazil's interior. Facilities on board the ferry are basic at best, and the romantic notion of sailing down the Amazon fizzles out by the third night. An air-conditioned hotel on our arrival in Manaus becomes a must.

The Manaus Athletic Club sprang up in the early 1900s with a pavilion constructed entirely out of wood from the jungle and a roof of thick leaves. Sixty years later Richard Gordon, a physician who wrote the *Doctor* comic novels, sailed to Manaus as a ship's medic and played a game in the city. On a grassless outfield 'racked like a dropped eggshell', fielding was difficult because players had to watch for snakes. Rain curtailed play early: 'The locals agreed it wouldn't stop for another three months, so we decided to abandon the match as a draw'.

Gordon, with a dash of poetic licence, also described a cricket-mad colleague who would perform a nightly ritual on board the ship. 'Each evening when he came off watch, the engineer would dress in full kit – pads, and all, even a box – to practise shots before an invisible wicket against imaginary bowling on the poop deck,' he wrote in 1972. 'In sparkling, beautifully pressed flannels he would make a diverting sight against the flaming tropical sunset on the Amazon.'

Once the British influence had receded it was Rio and São Paulo that kept cricket going in the years after the Second World War. Boy Cunningham was still around, and struck a six so big it went out of the ground at Niterói, through a window and into a baby's cot. Thankfully the infant was in its mother's arms at the time. Cunningham took to the field with his son Gerry, whose Brazil career would also span four decades, when MCC arrived with a strong side in 1958–9 and thrashed the hosts. 'The local bowling lacked variety. There is no regular supply of young players, and many must travel vast distances to play,' Dennis Silk wrote of a crushing win over Brazil at Niterói. 'One player "Sputnik" Wickham flew down especially from the Amazon to play. The weather was more suited to a Monday morning at Old Trafford than a fairy-tale in the tropics.'

And yet the fast hands of Frank Miroslav Filgas, born to a Czech mother and an Irish father, who had played one first-class match for Ireland, had helped Brazil spring a surprise 2–0 home series win against Argentina in September 1955.

When MCC returned in 1964–5, Brazil had just had a military coup, and cultural resistance in the bars and clubs came in the hypnotic slow dance of the bossa nova of João Gilberto and *tropicália* embodied by Gilberto Gil. Worcestershire's Alan Duff and Surrey's Richard Jefferson took an excursion up Sugar Loaf mountain on the morning of a match to take in spectacular views of Rio. A delay on the cable car back down meant they missed the ferry and turned up at Niterói just 20 minutes before play started, and were cut from the XI by the humourless captain A. C. Smith.

That incident was a drop in the Atlantic Ocean compared to when the cream of England's young cricketers arrived in Rio with the D. H. Robins XI in 1979. Tour managers Peter Parfitt and Henry Blofeld had their hands full trying to keep a group of testosterone-filled young county cricketers in check among the bright lights of Rio. 'I trusted them and they didn't let me down,' Parfitt says solemnly, before his face loosens and he bursts into laughter. 'They were bloody wild! I didn't try to control them.'

Parfitt managed to ensure Robins never got wind of the worst high jinks, when one player streaked through the team hotel and several had their trousers pinched at a party. 'Mr Robins was going to write reports on the boys which would go back to their respective counties, so I tried to keep a lid on it,' Parfitt says. Captain Chris Cowdrey had his wallet stolen after an evening in the company of a Brazilian beauty and had to auction off his kit to pay for the rest of the tour.

Despite their escapades the young county cricketers won easily in Rio and at SPAC, who by this time were playing at the club's present site in Santo Amaro. We discover SPAC's home is not far from the Interlagos race circuit; ex-players tell us the roar of Formula One engines used to make the job of umpires listening for a faint edge somewhat challenging. When the Brazilian Grand Prix moved to Interlagos, Jackie Stewart and Nigel Mansell would drop in at SPAC at the start of the race weekend. Appropriately, Gerry Cunningham had himself helped young Paulista Emerson Fittipaldi get his big break in F1.

Cricket also had a long-standing presence at the Frigorífico Anglo in Barretos, a meat-processing plant some 250 miles inland in Estado de São Paulo. On a breezy day the unmistakeable smell of freshly slaughtered meat would waft under the players' noses. For many years Barretos would host a Camps v. Frigorífico match. After one game, on an isolated farm called Guariroba near the village of Ormiga, the players were desperate for a late-night sing-song, but didn't have any musical instruments for accompaniment. Until they remembered an Italian, who worked with farm machinery, had a battered old piano which a tractor was duly despatched to collect. 'I spent the night on the back of a trailer playing until the early hours,' recalls Marie Young, the wife of one of the players.

The Troubadours included Barretos on their 1989 itinerary. The team flew to São Paulo, drove six hours past endless orange groves – Brazil is the world's biggest producer of orange juice as well as coffee – and played the game on zero sleep. 'I'll never forget the sight of three Hasidic Jews, in full dress, dropping by to watch the match,' tour organiser Barney Miller says. 'Presumably they had come from Israel to inspect the meat factory to see if the cows had been slaughtered in a kosher way, and took in some cricket over lunch.'

Boy Cunningham's other son Murray, a fine cricketer who made a century against Argentina in 1962, later became the plant's manager, and São Paulo and Barretos would subsequently compete for the Cunningham Cup. Barretos's cricketers beefed up São Paulo's side for the interstate matches against Rio, and hosted the fixture at the *frigorífico* ground from time to time. The most bizarre interlude to the annual clash came one year at SPAC when an unmanned ice-cream truck rolled off a nearby road and landed upside down on the outfield. The sweltering players, Gerry and Murray Cunningham among them, flocked to help themselves to free ice cream, only for their father to boom sonorously out from the pavilion: 'Get on with the match!'

One regular spectator at Niterói was the Great Train Robber Ronnie Biggs. He famously fled to Rio in 1970, taking advantage of the lack of an extradition treaty between the UK and Brazil. Even though he was not a member of RC&AA or Paissandu, officially at least, Biggs struck up a friendship with Rio's cricketers. 'Although he was a kind of a celebrity in the UK, that wasn't really the case in Rio,' remembers Neville Thorley, who once dated Plum Warner's granddaughter before moving to Brazil to work with precious gems. 'He was a trained carpenter so ended up as a bit of a handyman for expats.'

Biggs's presence at matches, however, caused periodic awkwardness for cricketing British diplomats who were frightened to death about being reported socialising with a notorious escaped criminal. 'He became part of the furniture here – although I think life was a struggle for him in Brazil,' says Anglo-Brazilian Johnny Hughes. It would have been even more embarrassing had the cricket-loving John Major accepted an invitation for a game at Niterói with Biggs watching on, when the British prime minister was in town for the Earth Summit in 1992. 'I would love to play,' Major wrote in a cryptic reply to Rio's cricketers, 'but unfortunately, the Queen needs me to do my duty.' Finally in 2001, suffering from ill health, Biggs went back to the UK; British ambassador Keith Haskell, a cricketer who had represented Peru on a previous posting in Lima, was instrumental in negotiating his return.

Brazil hold football bragging rights over Argentina with five World Cup wins to two, but you have to go back to 1994 for their cricketers' last victory over Argentina's men. Thorley was skipper when they won by eight wickets at SPAC, but by then cricket at RC&AA was starting to wither away. By the time Princess Diana visited the club in 1997, the year of her death, the interstate match had not been played for two years because Rio were unable to raise a side.

Cricket lived on at SPAC, where Aussie burger chef and national team captain Gregor Caisley tells us he once starred in a Brazilian soap opera that wanted a cricket scene – and belted a straight drive at a startled cameraman. The void left by Rio's demise was filled, to an extent, by the emergence of cricket in Brasília, the country's capital since 1960, when British agronomist John Landers arrived to promote a green cultivation technique known as zero tillage. Landers is a throwback bounder. He sports a fetching cravat, and twice finished runner-up in an Ernest Hemingway lookalike competition in the US. 'I stopped going after the second time. They would never let a Brit win,' he tells us, twiddling his pencil moustache. Landers started the Brasília Cricket Club in 1989 where 'two gin net sessions' were the main attraction as the players honed their skills next to dog kennels, and took on the motto 'from doghouse to victory'. Landers once almost died of hypothermia while on a tour to Chile. He arrived back from a party in the small hours of the morning at the Andean mountain retreat of the Australian consul, where the team were staying. Rather than wake the household, he slept in the doorway and when the maid found him the next morning he had almost frozen to death.

As the years rolled by Landers added a serious dimension. He helped establish the Associação Brasiliense de Cricket, which did much to promote the sport in the federal district. Cricket was offered as an accredited PE course at the University of Brasília, the first serious steps taken to inculcate cricket in young Brazilians through higher education. This led to the formation of the Candangos – a team named after the Brazilians who built Brasília in the 1950s and immortalised in Bruno Giorgi's bronze minimalist sculpture *Os Guerreiros*. Rudyard Hartmann was among the PE students and rose to national-team opening bowler before he switched his focus to captaining Brazil's water-polo team.

Women's cricket, in particular, has blossomed in Brasília. Especially at São Sebastião Cricket Club, who chose a burrowing owl as the club's logo after the birds were spotted watching their training sessions. The space-age modernism of the planned city designed by Oscar Niemeyer provides the otherworldly backdrop when we join a mixed-sex game with Brasília's cricketers one Sunday lunchtime. At fine leg is the Catedral Metropolitana Nossa Senhora Aparecida, a spiky futuristic version of Liverpool's Metropolitan Cathedral. While the bowler delivers from behind the Congresso Nacional, two saucers – one upright, one facing down – are either side of a pair of soaring rectangular blocks. 'This area used to be a popular late-night copulation spot,' Landers whispers to us from square-leg umpire. 'Back in the day, I used to have to bring a pair of rubber gloves to clear up the condoms before play.'

Brazil's economic boom in the 2000s brought more foreigners to the country and cricket back to life in Salvador, Recife and Manaus, and established footholds in areas previously untouched such as Belo Horizonte, on the coast at Macaé and Vitória, near the breathtaking waterfalls at Foz do Iguaçu, and most significantly in the spa town of Poços de Caldas where it has been taken into the hearts of young Brazilians. Players in Curitiba, we discover during a visit to the eco-friendly city, have to overcome more local obstacles than most. Nesting *quero-quero* birds lay their eggs in the grass on the outfield, and if fielders stray too close they can be fearlessly divebombed. On the plus side, the ground is surrounded by a species of pine tree found only in the Paraná region, and the edible pinhão nut comes in handy when tea supplies run low in an increasingly pricey country.

In 2011, the year Brazil's GDP overtook the UK's to become the world's sixth-largest economy, cricket returned to Rio. RC&AA were reticent to turn over the ground at Niterói for a spiritual homecoming since they no longer had any cricket-playing members. So Carioca Cricket Club (CCC) found their home ground – dubbed 'the corridor of sun certainty' in homage to Geoff Boycott and the local climate – at a polo club in the suburb of Itaguaí. CCC imported a cricket matting, listing it on the customs form as a Turkish rug to avoid paying duties, and built a basic pavilion thanks to sponsorship from a beauty-care firm.

We join a CCC training session on a baseball diamond in downtown Rio, and glancing up find a more inspiring backdrop than we would back in England. Next to Rodrigo de Freitas Lagoon, a few blocks from Ipanema beach, the distant figure of Christ the Redeemer watches down over us as we fend off the slow-mediums of a bona fide Carioca, Felipe Lima de Melo. It did not escape the notice of Rio's latest band of cricketers that Christ seemed to be signalling a wide up on Mount Corcovado. Forever self-deprecating, CCC wasted little time in adapting the pose for their club crest, dressing Jesus up as an umpire in white jacket, black trousers and a sunhat.

## 12

# Suriname and French Guiana

## *Polders and Papillon*

C OGGESHALL IS AN incongruous setting for an international cricket scandal. Best known as a retirement spot for East End gangsters, it's a particularly elegant Essex village used as a location in episodes of *Lovejoy*, and about as far removed from Latin America as possible. But there's a history of cricketing controversy at Coggeshall's genteel cricket ground, not least when, reportedly, Billy Godleman smashed up a vacuum cleaner with his bat and Tom Westley kicked in two doors after being on the wrong end of umpiring decisions in a Second XI game for Essex a decade ago.

In 2015, Raj Narain perches up against a tree, taking notes in his A4 jotter. A plump man with a pencil moustache, he is plotting how Suriname can overcome Vanuatu in this World Cricket League Division Six semi-final and earn promotion to the highest level at which the small Dutch-speaking country has ever competed. All the countries in this tournament have fascinating and largely untold stories about their cricket. Narain, a softly spoken man, talks passionately about how cricket came to Suriname. He is chairman of the Surinaamse Cricket Bond, has represented his country in International

Duck Curry Tournaments, and is a good enough draughts player that there is a championship named after him back home.

The ICC's introduction of the WCL global pyramid system provided steps on a ladder for small and relatively insular cricketing communities such as Suriname. With more money and profile at stake, there is a considerable carrot for fielding the strongest eligible team – even if it means issuing passports or visas to players with a tenuous link to your country. Plenty of other higher-ranked countries are at it, finding classy South Africans, Australians and New Zealanders keen to make their mark on the international stage.

The ICC have long been twitchy about staging Associate tournaments in affluent 'Western' countries, after Ugandan players absconded from tournaments in Australia, New Zealand and Canada. Saudi Arabia had themselves not travelled to WCL Division Six in Essex and Hertfordshire, due to problems acquiring visas. The Saudis' absence this time leaves Vanuatu and Suriname with an excellent chance of qualification.

Suriname have at least three good spinners, plus Banerd Bailey, an energetic quick, and Chris Patandin, who took six for 22 in a defeat against Canada in a regional tournament in Indianapolis earlier in 2015. He runs through the Vanuatu batting with five for 18, as they muster just 140. Although Suriname wobble early on, there is no panic on the sidelines as the awaiting batsmen kick back and enjoy a massage from physiotherapists laid on by the ICC. Suriname reach their target with four overs to spare and parade the country's flag in front of the Coggeshall pavilion as they begin to contemplate Division Five. Suriname go on to beat Guernsey in the Division

Six final at the County Ground, Chelmsford, with no suggestion of stage fright on a first-class ground.

It turns out there's a reason for that. Mumblings around Coggeshall suggest there are more than a few Guyanese players in the Suriname side, with experience of good-level club cricket in Guyana, the US and the UK. True, they all seem to be speaking English, though that's not much proof of anything, since – much like the Dutch – Surinamers tend to speak very good English.

Vanuatu and Botswana each raise concerns with the ICC that Suriname are fielding a number of ineligible players. Their claims are given credence by a dramatic press conference called back in Paramaribo by a local politician, publisher and cricket supporter, Radjen Kisoensingh, who says that the squad is made up of three Surinamers and eleven Guyanese, at least five of whom do not live and work in Suriname. 'It is a shame that Suriname was guilty of forgery and fraud,' he said. 'The question is how the selection was made, since there is no competition going on . . . People cannot continue playing cricket in Suriname like this.'

Vanuatu submit a 15-page dossier and 19 pages of supplementary evidence claiming that six of Suriname's players are ineligible to play for the country. Between them the sextet scored two-thirds of their team's runs in Division Six, and took all but two of their wickets. Countries were allowed to field non-citizens, so long as they resided for at least 183 days a year four years before the tournament in question. Vanuatu's evidence – made up of scorecards and timestamps from the players' social media feeds – suggests that this was improbable. Some of the players were playing club cricket and running businesses in New York.

The whistle has been blown on the most blatant eligibility scandal in international cricket for some years, though many in the Associate world may reflect that Suriname's worst crime was getting caught – given how often the residency rules have been flouted by other countries. Suriname forfeit their $25,000 prize and their spot in Division Five, which goes instead to Vanuatu.

The matter reaches Suriname's parliament, and fierce debates ensue between the board and the ministry of sport. Kisoensingh claims it was only a lack of funds that prevented his group from taking the matter to court: 'These figures are still in power. They do nothing. We had some rumours that they were just sitting out the suspension and then going on with the funding from the ICC. We tried to out the board in Nickerie county. But as judicial procedures cost a lot of money, we did not continue this fight. The present board have not organised any tournament in Nickerie.'

When we meet Narain again two years later at Dr E. Snellenpark in Paramaribo, the home of Suriname cricket, he strikes a conciliatory tone. 'What people have to understand is that there's a different culture here around how our season operates,' he says, and stresses how many Guyanese East Indians have come over to settle in the border town of Nickerie during the years of ethnic violence in Guyana. 'It's about using Guyanese players in the right way. I'd like the ICC to come here and audit everything. We are gentlemen.'

*     *     *

Suriname has been a Dutch corner of Latin America ever since 1667, when the Netherlands agreed to relinquish their colony of New Amsterdam, on Manhattan Island, in exchange for the British giving up their claims east of the Courantyne River. For many years Dutch teachers would tell their schoolchildren they had the better deal, since the British had lost New York, while they still had Suriname.

'Man's inhumanity to man just about reached its limits in Surinam,' wrote the historian Charles Boxer of life on the 200 or so Dutch sugar, cotton and coffee plantations. Emancipation came comparatively late, in 1863, and by then thousands of 'Maroons' had escaped the brutality of the *plantages* and taken up arms against their former captors. Their descendants form an influential part of Suriname's cosmopolitan population today. A number of European planters went bankrupt due to the loss of this slave labour, and were saved only by the Anglo-Dutch Treaties of 1870, which provided the Dutch West Indies with thousands of indentured labourers from the Raj – just as many Indians had already sailed to British Guiana and Trinidad.

The British lost Suriname, but cricket still found a way of knitting into the colony's life. Some say it arrived with the first generation of East Indian labourers in what was called Old Bilo, then Nieuw Rotterdam – which was completely destroyed by a flood, before being rebuilt as Nieuw Nickerie in 1879. Others say that by the 1880s, any colonist arriving from the western Netherlands would have known cricket. Or, most likely, it blew east across the Courantyne River with workers from British Guiana. Whatever the reason, the sap of the balata tree had something to do with it.

*Balatableeders* were a common sight in the inland rainforests of Suriname from the 1850s. A *balatableeder* would winch himself up and cut a V-shape into the bark to extract the latex, to be dried in the sun. The rubbery product was used for the soles of shoes and to make golf balls. Locals siphoned off some of it to make their own cricket balls, with the rubbery layer coated around a cacao fruit and tied up with laces. They would use them in a basic game of underarm street cricket in Suriname, called *bat en bal.*

Cricket put down strong roots in Nickerie on the back of the lucrative balata business. Often it was the black players who were most dedicated, because some had heritage in British Guiana or other British Caribbean islands. It helped that descendants of slaves were allowed to move freely, unlike the indentured East Indians tied to their landlord's estate.

There were, inevitably, some clubs of the white elite: Royal Scotts Cricket Club was the first on record, in 1895, and not long afterwards Boonacker CC, founded by Jacob Boonacker, the Nickerie district commissioner. Many other teams were, however, a refreshing combination of Europeans, blacks, Indians, Javanese and Chinese. None of these ethnic groups holds a majority in the country today, and between the wars Suriname cricket might have been more cosmopolitan than in any place on earth.

The game spread on to the polders – the plantation fields surrounded by dykes, then reclaimed for rice and other crops. Rust en Work, a *plantage* that once had 1000 coffee fields, then converted to sugar and employed 1000 East Indians and 1400 Javanese workers, fielding a cricket team under the supervision of a passionate British Guianese manager. On non-match days young boys would flock to the polders for impromptu *bat en bal* games using limes, stones and balata balls.

\* \* \*

Richenel Small has a cage covered by a cloth on the passenger seat when he collects us in his pick-up truck in Nickerie. As well as being the chairman of Cricket Bond Nickerie, Small proudly peels back the cloak and informs us he is a multi-time national champion in one of the most popular 'sports' in Suriname: bird-singing contests.

This may sound like an antiquated throwback pastime, but it's serious business. There are clubs, leagues and trophies, and the best birds can change hands for as much as US$3000. The black piculet and the brown twatwa are renowned as the champion performers.

Head-to-heads between two birds, their cages facing each other, are scored by referees who tally the number of songs they can manage in a set period, typically 15 minutes. A successful bird needs a caring owner to nurture their vocal talents. The secret is getting the birds to sing in short passages, as opposed to the longer melodies they may sing in the wild. 'Most people nowadays use recordings of birds on CDs for training, but there is still a traditional approach,' says Small. 'Truly skilled trainers use whistling to coax their birds into singing.'

Contests typically take place early on Saturday mornings – leaving Small enough time to make it to cricket in the afternoon. Small whistles to himself as he drives us to Nickerie's cricket ground – and we are both too polite to ask if this is an important late training session, or if he is just in a good mood. When we arrive, Small brings the cage out on to the ground with him: 'I had an offer of two hundred dollars for this guy the other day, but I reckon he is worth double that.'

Although unremarkable from the outside, Nickerie's ground has a rustic charm. The walls have been beautifully hand-painted with cricket-themed adverts for local businesses. Even visits by touring teams are granted their own murals – the most eye-catching is three cowboys on horses with raised cricket bats, celebrating the visit a few years back by the Dutch side Zamigos.

Small takes us on a tour of the Westelijke Polders that surround Nickerie. Many of them are still being cultivated, though cricket is rarely played there these days. The names of the countless clubs that once played in the western polders reflect the diverse make-up of Surinamer society: Waterloo, Hamptoncourt, Paradise and Hong Kong mixed it with the likes of Hindekeserie, Hindostan Boys and Jai Hind. Victoria, a club from one of the polders, boasted Ajong Tjon Tjauw Liem, a skilful Chinese-Indonesian wicketkeeper who played many years alongside his brother Asang. Montaj Ali became the first centurion in Nickerie in May 1956, finishing a match on 105 not out.

Hindostani were rocked in 1924 by the death of their chairman, Koengbeharry Oedayrysingh, at just 24. C. R. Singh, born in 1904, took up the baton of organiser-in-chief of cricket in Nickerie for decades, selling tickets for big games from his house, advertised in each day's edition of *Die West*. When India won its independence in 1948, East Indians felt emboldened: Jai Hind came on to the field chanting Hindu songs, wearing Nehru caps and occasionally sharing in prayers with a pundit.

Resourceful East Indian traders struck up close relations with their contemporaries in British Guiana and Trinidad. In the 1950s Singh made friends with West Indies cricketers such as Basil Butcher, Charran Singh and Joe Solomon, and was able to bring back enough equipment, including coconut matting wickets, to keep the game healthy. Lance Gibbs and Rohan Kanhai are among the Guyanese greats to have graced Nickerie's cricket fields.

*　　*　　*

On the far eastern tip of Suriname is the town of Albina, where the River Marowijne provides another natural border, with neighbouring French Guiana. Between the wars Albina's residents founded the Van Hecke CC – appropriately the name translates into English as 'from the fence' – and would take ten-minute boat rides across the water to Saint-Laurent-du-Maroni for matches.

It is a journey we repeat, as there is still no direct road from Suriname into French Guiana. There is a car ferry, but we clamber aboard one of the many long motorboats queuing up to ferry foot passengers. After changing our Surinamer dollars into euros we head into the French Republic – strange sensations in the New World – and towards the Camp de la Transportation.

Van Hecke's opponents were, unusually enough, a team of French officers and guards who worked in the penal camp in Saint-Laurent-du-Maroni, a transit point after the long boat journey from France, where prisoners were processed before being sent on to other camps. As we have arrived on La Fête de la Victoire – VE Day – on 8 May, the camp is closed to tourists during our visit, but we manage to sneak inside to take a look in cell 47, where Henri Charrière scrawled his nickname 'Papillon' on the wall. Charrière was there in 1933, at which time the officers of Saint-Laurent still played cricket for their team, patriotically called Verdun CC.

Our curiosity with Papillon takes us to Kourou, where boats head out to the haunting Îles du Salut. Eighty thousand prisoners died there, and Alfred Dreyfus of the infamous Dreyfus Affair was incarcerated after being sentenced to life imprisonment. Charrière claimed to have escaped from the most famous of the islands – Devil's Island – but unlike Steve McQueen's evocative film portrayal of an escape on the seventh wave on a raft made of coconuts, no records exist that Papillon was ever on the island. It seems Charrière dreamed it up to help sales of his blockbuster autobiographical novel.

Getting around this *département d'outre-mer* is tricky: transport is very much informal. Many French Guianese hitchhike, although drivers usually expect a contribution towards fuel. While in Kourou we drop in on their cricket team, a mix of English and French speakers who play against a club from Cayenne, the capital of French Guiana. Their matches on a football ground in Le Quartier Bonhomme are occasionally interrupted by spectacular but utterly expected explosions in the background: Kourou is home to the rocket launches of the European Space Agency.

*       *       *

West of Nickerie, the Courantyne River forms one of the most porous borders in the world. It's no surprise when some eager owners of wooden boats with outboard motors approach us to say they know of the quiet inlets to get across into Guyana without needing our passports checked. We have no reason to risk any illegal entry, as we are heading in the opposite direction – to Suriname's capital Paramaribo. It is a 150-mile journey, which takes us through coastal towns called Totness and Groningen, which used to raise their own cricket teams.

Paramaribo has classical Dutch wooden colonial architecture cheek-by-jowl with Hindu temples, mosques, synagogues and Anglican churches. In spite of Suriname's relative harmony, at the end of the First World War – in which the Netherlands stayed neutral – Paramaribo went through a period of sectarian strife that played out on the sports field. The government had decided that too many civilians in the stately old town were being struck by flying balls on the lawn – and often these were not balata balls, but hard leather balls imported from British Guiana – in front of the governor-general's palace, and urged the sports clubs to find new grounds.

When, in July 1919, the Katholike Sport Centrale found one, it did not take long for rival clubs to accuse the authorities of siding with the Catholics. Within two years the Suriname Catholic CC had bowed to political pressure and rebadged themselves under the more unifying title of Dutch Guiana CC, with many players drawn from the British firms Bettencourt and Fogarty. The Katholike Sport Centrale morphed into the Nieuwe Generatie Voetbal Bond (NGVB).

The canny minister of agriculture, a German settler called Dr E. Snellen, had his eye on an unkempt field next door to the ministry office. It was too charged an atmosphere to openly lobby for a sports ground, so Snellen applied to use the field to grow rice on behalf of the ministry, and secured funds of 10,000 guilders for it. All the time, he and a band of besotted cricketers were covertly converting the land into a workable cricket pitch.

The NGVB got wind of it and took him to court, but Snellen managed to brush off the challenge. By the time it was too late to stop him he came clean on the purpose of the Cultuurtuinlaan (which roughly translates as the 'culture promenade'), christening it Het Huis Voor de Neutralen ('the House of the Neutrals')

– trumpeted as a place where Surinamers could play sport free
from Catholic dogma.

In 1923 the grand opening of the Cultuurtuinlaan, attended by
the colony's football, cricket, athletics and korfball clubs, injected
new life into sport in Suriname. Snellen was a cricket man first and
foremost, so the maiden visitors to the Cultuurtuinlaan would be
a Guianese cricket team of *balatableeders*.

Back then it took an entire day to sail from Nickerie to the
capital. But Snellen and the other cricket leaders were determined to do all they could to make cricket popular in
Paramaribo, the centre of civic society, and started a regular
competition between the best players from Nickerie and
Paramaribo. This tale of two cities drew so many fans to the
inaugural clash on the Cultuurtuinlaan that signs went up all
over the city, declaring: '*Eer kon geen kip meer bij*' – 'We cannot
cram any more chickens into the coop'. Locals packed on to
the wooden bleachers and the colony's elite took their place in
the posh seats dressed in full white suits.

On a drenched pitch, Paramaribo were sent in and locals
feared for their chances. Gomes and Tjeendre surprised everyone by putting on a century partnership, and as the wicket
dried Nickerie's spinners began cutting through, taking all ten
Paramaribo wickets for 40 runs. Nickerie appeared to be cruis-
ing towards the target in their second innings the following
day, when Wim Anijs was thrown the ball. His seldom-seen
leg-spinners scythed through the Nickerie batting and somehow Paramaribo stole it.

Willem Anijs was one of the most celebrated of Surinamer
cricketers. A black man, he was born in 1899 in Nickerie,
surrounded by football and cricket. His father's career in the
balata trade meant the Anijs family never struggled for money,

but Wim's education was basic until the family moved to Paramaribo and he enlisted in the Nautical School. He had to leave at the age of 15 due to poor eyesight, forcing him into an office job. A bit like Clive Lloyd a few hundred miles to the west in Georgetown, Anijs never let his short-sightedness harm his cricket, and he went on to captain Excelsior and Suriname for many years.

Eventually football grew dominant at the Cultuurtuinlaan, and cricket sought a field with bigger boundaries. In 1954 they moved over the road and christened their new home Dr E. Snellenpark in homage to the great patron of cricket. Although cricket found security at Snellenpark, it was harmed by wider political issues. Work conditions on the sugar plantations got tougher and morale plunged so much that turning out for the *plantage* did not appeal any longer.

In the years leading up to independence in 1975, many Surinamers emigrated to the Netherlands for more money or security, in the fear that life in South America was about to get worse. Walther Braithwaite – holder of Suriname's record batting score, and voted their Cricketer of the Century – played in Topklasse-winning teams at Rood en Wit of Haarlem, west of Amsterdam, during the mid-1960s. Braithwaite was apparently courted by West Indies, but instead became the first Surinamer selected for the Netherlands, and scored 36 opening the batting against Oxford University at The Hague in 1966.

A football cap for Suriname eluded Braithwaite, though he did manage the national team in the 1978 and 1986 World Cup qualification campaigns. He was unable to call on talents such as Frank Rijkaard and Ruud Gullit, as their parents had already emigrated to Amsterdam. Football is pre-eminent in both the Netherlands and Suriname, though there are still cricket teams in Amsterdam and The Hague made up primarily of Dutch Surinamers, and a number of umpires too.

The worst fears of many Surinamers were realised in a coup in 1980. In December 1982, soldiers loyal to the then-dictator, Dési Bourtese, shot 15 people who had been critical of the regime on a boat next to Fort Zeelandia. Sugrim Oemrawsingh, from a Nickerie cricketing family, was among the slain, as was André Kamperveen, a former footballer and sports minister. Bourtese returned to power through democratic means in 2010, despite allegations he was involved in the global drug trade. Europol issued an arrest warrant, but as president he enjoys immunity from arrest in his own country.

And so cricket soldiers on at Snellenpark and Nickerie, even if Suriname have been out of international action since their Essex farrago in 2015. Football – not content with dominating the Cultuurtuinlaan, later renamed the André Kamperveen Stadion – now has swish new training facilities opened by FIFA on the Owru Cul (old field), which not so long ago was used for cricket. Snellenpark does not look like it has had a bean spent on it by the ICC. Narain says he has tried to make cricket more open, relaxing such strictures as the requirement to wear a tie to Snellenpark. He sighs as he considers his burden: 'Paramaribo is known as the city of smiles . . . until you have to pick a cricket team.'

# 13

## The future of cricket in Latin America

### *Salir a los barrios*

PUCK, PUCK, PUCK. Hugo Ambrosio was on the way to his friend's house when the shots flew out from behind a nearby stall. He fell for cover, but one of the bullets caught him in his abdomen. A little girl yards away from him, eight years old, was shot in the chest.

They were both rushed to hospital, the girl in a critical condition. While doctors tended to him, Hugo phoned Luke Humphries, the co-founder of the religious school where he studies, and asked him to pray alongside him. Mercifully, after a nervous few hours, both Hugo and the girl pulled through and made a full recovery. As soon as he could stand again, he was back at cricket training with his friends.

Shootings are a fact of life in Santiago Sacatepéquez, a nondescript, mainly indigenous town just off the highway between Guatemala City and Antigua. Guatemala City is the country's capital, where *Chapins* go for business and not much else; Antigua is the impossibly elegant colonial city of stuccoed houses and cobbled streets decorating every postcard or Instagram post sent from Guatemala.

Having ourselves swiftly moved on from Guatemala City to Antigua, we take a 'chicken bus' – the elongated US school buses decommissioned from use and shipped south to Latin America's poorest countries, where they are creatively daubed in a kaleidoscope of colours and Christian messages – from the bustling market through the invigorating mountain air to Santiago. In this town of 35,000 there are just eight policemen, rotating on shifts of four, each driving around by day or night in the same van. It is not hard for various gangs to outwit them. No one was apprehended for shooting Hugo, and life just carried on as normal.

Luke Humphries first arrived in Guatemala in 2003, still a young teenager, with his father Russell and mother Linda, after the family 'heard the calling from God' to head out to the mission field. They sold their house in Gosport and bunked in friends' spare rooms to save the money to fund a Christian centre where they could make the biggest difference.

That was only seven years after Guatemala had emerged from a brutal 36-year civil war. A quarter of a million either died or remain unaccounted for. Unlike some countries in the region, Guatemala still has a substantial indigenous population, and one consequence of the war was that Mayans, as they are referred to here, converted en masse from Catholicism to Evangelism. So there was no shortage of takers in Santiago when the Humphries family formed El Refugio Centro Cristiano in 2006.

Religious teaching and baptism are the main purpose at El Refugio, though they also offer a step into further education. Already 350 mainly indigenous boys have graduated from the school. Some were former gang members; others deemed to be most in danger of falling into that life.

Free periods presented a challenge to Luke and Russell. Football dominates the schoolyard conversation. But its adversarial atmosphere does not chime too well with the overriding message at El Refugio. 'The thing about football is that people get so worked up about it,' says Luke, himself a big Spurs fan. 'I found it hard to control the boys' anger and disappointment if they lost. And with all the prejudice towards the indigenous people by Ladinos, the Guatemalans of mixed indigenous and European descent, it can get really nasty.'

At first, father and son messed around with a bat and ball to remind themselves of English summers. Soon, though, they began to see what cricket was doing for their congregation. 'When we started cricket, there was visibly more respect between the players,' says Luke. 'The boys weren't under quite so much pressure to win, and a lot of them responded to that. They were just enjoying learning to play an unusual game.'

The boys told Luke the duel between bat and ball felt like a metaphor for something deeper. The way a batsman guards his wicket could be likened to him placing value on his life. A dropped catch, or a narrow escape thanks to a sympathetic umpire, is comparable to a stay of mercy. A bowler has to strive for wickets, rather than resort to the quick fix of a gun or machete.

The best training ground Luke could lay his hands on was a £200-a-month five-a-side football court in San Lucas, a 15-minute moped ride away. So far the Humphries have been allowed to carry on their strange English preoccupation without rubbing up against local interests, and Luke's role in keeping boys off the streets of Santiago lends him a degree of credit with the authorities.

Reminders are everywhere. A tribute to a slain gang leader – '*Adiós Pinky, el barrio te extrañará*' ('Goodbye Pinky, the neighbourhood will miss you') – is scrawled on the wall at one end of the stadium where Luke's team play in Santiago. No municipal worker or local politician would dare scrub off this graffiti. It is a vivid reminder to Geovanny Jolón Yucute every time he stops at the top of his mark to send down a leg-break. He was one of the kids in Santiago most at risk of being recruited as a junior drug pusher.

'Cricket was unlike anything I'd tried before,' says Geovanny. 'I first got interested in spinning the ball when I saw Russell bowling off-spin. I went to an internet café and looked up all the different grips to spin the ball different ways, some YouTube videos of Shane Warne, and I really got into it. There are so many different possibilities in this game. None of my friends understand cricket. They think I'm weird. They only know football.'

At first Geovanny's two younger brothers, Kevin and Marvin, looked on in consternation. Marvin was starting to hang around on street corners with other boys, some of whom now sport the tattoos betraying their gang affiliation. He caught the cricket bug just in time, after seeing Geovanny honing a leggie's flick of the wrist for hours on end. Now both of his brothers have taken up seam bowling – in Kevin's case some handy left-arm inswing – with no hint of a kink in their actions. Luke and Russell were surprised when the teenagers developed orthodox batting techniques, rather than the across-the-line slogging that most first-time cricketers slip into.

They innocently named their outfit the Guatemala Cricket Club, assuming that no one else had gone through all this. It turned out, though, that a few years ago a teacher in Guatemala City, Manuel Farfán, had introduced cricket at his sports college at the suggestion of English friends; and an NGO, Asociación

Manos Amigas – 'Friendship Through Joined Hands' – had run cricket sessions for similarly disadvantaged children. And there were some serious club cricketers in the country: a team of Indian call-centre workers; and keen Guatemalans too, including Stuardo Monroy, who discovered cricket while up at Oxford and runs a centre for autism in the capital.

This was enough to form a spit-and-sawdust league playing on a field at the Antigua International School, in view of the region's three great volcanoes, one of which, Fuego, would regularly blow its top during play. Some of the exclusive private schools in the area asked the Guatemala CC to teach cricket to their pupils: for boys such as the Yucutes to play a role tutoring rich kids would have been a significant social barrier to cross in Guatemala. But the school relocated, so the cricketers are back at the Santiago municipal ground. 'Actually it does the foreigners who play in Guatemala some good to come and see a place like this,' adds Luke.

Guatemala have taken on El Salvador for the Easter Cup, and entered the Volcano Cup between the Central American countries. Luke does his best sensitively to introduce his young congregation into match scenarios, rather than them unceremoniously bat them at number 11, despatch them to fine leg and never throw them the ball. 'By going to El Salvador to play cricket, Geo is experiencing Salvadorian life, British life, Indian life, Zimbabwean life,' says Humphries. 'Getting to know other people opens their minds to an existence outside the *barrio*.' Even four hours by car to Santa Tecla is a step into the unknown for many of the boys, most of whom had never left Santiago. To cover costs, El Salvador have started charging $900 for teams to compete in the Volcano Cup, which is a drain on El Refugio's budget.

All this would be enough to deter lesser men. But Humphries is dreaming big. A fundraising drive – with the ultimate aim to tour England – has allowed Luke to install Guatemala's first proper net complex. If they ever make it to England, they plan to fly via Madrid to avoid zealous US border forces. 'It will give our boys a connection with what cricket means, and what we might achieve in Guatemala. This will be an amazing opportunity for them to play on a proper grass wicket, in a match longer than T20, and to see how a village club works. We hope to visit Lord's so they can see the history of cricket and what it means.' Guatemalan cricket is still waiting for a coffee or banana plantation generous enough to clear some crops for a ground.

Humphries's link to the elite cricketing world is the former South Africa all-rounder J.-P. Duminy, himself a born-again Christian and a member of the Proteas team bible group, who is spreading the word on social media on their behalf. 'Other than that,' adds Luke, 'we will trust God to bring us something.'

\*      \*      \*

At the other end of Latin America's social spectrum, Lautaro Musiani combines studying for an economics degree with playing international cricket for Argentina. He broke into the side as a 15-year-old leg-spinner having honed his smooth action at St Alban's College, one of the traditional bilingual cricket-playing schools in the prim southern suburbs of Buenos Aires. He became so obsessed that he started printing his own cricket magazines and populating his own websites. Musiani has an EU passport through his Spanish ancestry, which has allowed him to play club cricket in England as a domestic player.

While Musiani was at St Alban's the school acquired a red Routemaster bus decommissioned from use in London – a cheap way of ferrying pupils to cricket matches during the Argentine financial crisis of the early 2000s. He rolls his eyes at the memory. 'It stood out like a sore thumb. We would get pelted with stones whenever we drove through a poorer part of town.'

It should have been obvious to everyone in Argentine cricket that unless the sport ventured beyond these clubs and appealed to a wider section of society, it would always be the half-forgotten cousin of rugby and hockey – 'the sport for all the kids who aren't cool', as Dan Sutton, a former head coach of Argentina, put it.

In two centuries of Argentine cricket, Daniel Juarez was one of the first to seriously tackle the issue. He had dabbled with cricket at his and Musiani's club, Lomas AC. When he was appointed auditor for the Archdiocese of Buenos Aires, he had the platform to prove his theory. His new boss, Jorge Mario Bergoglio, the archbishop of Buenos Aires, was already encouraging his pastors to go and work in the *villas miserias* to tackle rampant crime and drug problems – exactly the kind of impoverished shantytowns where Diego Maradona had emerged kicking a football.

Juarez knew a local pastor, Padre José Maria Di Paola – 'Padre Pepe' – whose patch in Barracas included the slum town of Villa 21–24. Many of the inhabitants were poor immigrants from Paraguay. The Argentine military dictatorship of the late 1970s had tried and failed to clean out this 'transit neighbourhood' during the grimly named National Reorganisation Process, and the scars were still evident. Di Paola was run out of Barracas in 2009 after threats to his life from gangs, but not before he gave his backing to Juarez hosting cricket clinics with the poor youngsters of Villa 21. Bergoglio, soon to be Pope Francis, came by and blessed the team and their ground. And so cricket in Buenos Aires came full circle, returning to Barracas, the very *barrio* where James Brittain first gave the game to the city two centuries ago.

'Where we try to be different to other sports is that we really do care about these kids' family, their schooling, their food and what they need in life,' Juarez tells us from his spartan sports hall in an unprepossessing part of town. He found that, unlike much of the gilded youth of upper-middle-class Buenos Aires, a lot of the poorer kids were only too keen to run around and be part of a team. Sergio Arvallo, a spiky-haired player-turned-coach in the project, said: 'For me, cricket is the most complete sport. You have to be alert because anything can happen. It is hard to recruit, because football is a religion. But once a boy starts cricket they don't want to stop.'

Di Paola launched a second team in José León Suárez, and a third in neglected Belén de Escobar 20 miles out of the city, next to a rubbish dump. The projects have been combined together into an NGO, Cricket Sin Fronteras, which uses cricket to improve life skills for struggling 8-to-25 year-olds. With Pope Francis installed in the Vatican, Cricket Sin Fronteras earned the backing of the Pontifical Council for Culture. The cricketers of Sin Fronteras flew to Rome to meet South America's first pope in 2017; his cricket team of priests and seminarians, St Peter's CC, came to Buenos Aires in 2019 on a Light of Faith tour. They took on Los Leónes de Judah, a team of inmates, in the yard of the San Martín prison where they had been carving handmade cricket bats in their carpentry classes. After ten training sessions in four weeks Los Leónes scored a respectable 94 off St Peter's bowling. Their bats are believed to be the first ever handcrafted in Argentina, and the Pope proudly hangs one of the blades in his office.

The danger is that Sin Fronteras becomes an initiative on the periphery of Argentine cricket – a sop to a development programme. Of 1500 boys and girls to pass through it, only a handful have gone on to represent the established Buenos Aires clubs. Arvallo was good enough to be selected for Argentina Under-19s. 'We had to get him a passport,' says Sutton. 'It was his first time on a plane. A few hours later he was booked into a five-star hotel in the Bahamas and didn't speak for two days, so in awe was he. But then you remember that he has to go back to the *villas* and make his life.'

It is hard to keep up the arrangement when some kids in the *barrios* struggle to afford a bus ticket across the city to the club. 'We did our best, hosting matches between Belgrano and Sin Fronteras teams, putting on some food,' says Sutton. 'Ultimately there's still a big gap in Argentina between rich and poor, and not many in the middle. And there's still mistrust. Given that Cristina [Fernández de Kirchner, of the Peronist party] is now back in power, that might get worse.'

\*     \*     \*

Many of the roadblocks in producing Latin American cricketers emerge when an ambitious local attempts to take his or her cricket beyond the softball-and-plastic-bat stage. In Mexico, Argentina, Chile and Peru, the historic multi-sport clubs that are the centre of the game are dominated by football, rugby or hockey. While Chile's poorest cricketers are occasionally able to access the Prince of Wales Country Club, exempt from the pricey membership fees, most clubs of its ilk are haemorrhaging members and in desperate need of cash. They are less inclined to do the old cricketers a favour on the cheap.

Samantha Hickman, Cricket Peru's tireless development officer, says: 'It's hard at Lima Cricket & Football Club – yes, cricket is in the name but it's a private club. To them it's a little sanctuary where they don't have to mix with the peasants. The club are a little hesitant to just let poorer players come in. I gather the relationship used to be better.'

Even in Argentina, crippling import duties mean bulk equipment orders from the UK or the US have had to be sent to one of the 12 Free Trade Zones in nearby Uruguay. 'Cris Nino has a farm in Uruguay, so he used to receive all the kit and cram it into a massive shed,' says Musiani. 'We'd go over in dribs and drabs and bring it back on the *buquebus* ferry.' Cricket Argentina now urge touring sides to pack battered old bats, gloves and pads among their luggage. To raise funds, the ACA started an in-house equipment shop selling off this donated gear for a small price. The economy may be perpetually slumping, but it has proven hard to build a 'cricket aid' narrative around Argentina which, for all its economic problems, can hardly count as a post-conflict hotspot.

Overseas trips remain the lifeblood of Latin American cricket. Hickman encountered this ahead of the 2017 Junior South American Championship. 'A lot of our players had never left the country before, so it was a huge deal for them. One of the boys we selected was Eric Cajahuaman. We knew he was struggling with money, but we couldn't pay for all the kids to go. He was due to be paying his own way until his mum got ill with cancer, and he had to use the money he had saved to pay for her chemotherapy. He had no choice but to support his family.' On this occasion there was a happy ending of sorts: someone in Cricket Peru donated their spare air miles to Cajahuaman so he could make the trip after all.

The following year Colombia hosted the men's and women's South American Championships at the Los Reyes Polo Club in the foothills outside Bogotá. Even though Colombia is not an ICC member, Brazil, Chile and Mexico all made their women's T20 international debuts under long-overdue ICC changes to expand the T20 format and allow all nations to plot their course on cricket's world rankings. Peru should have debuted too, but one of their qualified players had to drop out late on, and it meant their matches lost official ICC status. The organisers managed to bus all the players out of their hostels on the edge of Bogotá each day – one morning the bus crashed and spirits were lifted by an impromptu Spanish sing-song sparked by the Peruvian girls.

Argentina sent a men's A-side of development players, dredging up old accusations about the Texans of South America. Their senior side were about to tour South Africa, and felt playing on a hastily cut grass wicket on a polo field was not the best preparation. The absence altogether of their women, Las Flamingos, was more a symptom of the Argentine recession. Field hockey is the chosen sport of middle-class Argentine females, and most cricket clubs have bumper sections. It is easy to find girls with transferable hand–eye coordination and athleticism; harder to lure them away from a more popular sport with a wider international footprint. And yet Argentina claimed the early bragging rights when women's cricket in the Americas was given a concerted push by the ICC 15 years ago, beating the USA and Bermuda in one of their early tournaments, with teenagers Dirce Yuli and Veronica Vasquez to the fore.

Musiani played much of his junior cricket against members of the pioneering Flamingos. 'You could tell they were talented hockey players – loads of sweeps or quick singles, very disciplined in the field. It's the wider problem in Argentina – they were very good at hitting the ball and very athletic. The girls enjoy it, and loads play at softball level – at *colonias*, these summer camps. But it's quite hard to retain them and get them into the proper sport.'

Sutton arrived in Buenos Aires in late 2012. 'The men's team were sliding down the World Cricket League but were quite stuck in their ways. The women were keener to learn. There are twenty-odd senior hockey teams at Belgrano, so there was an endless clash about whether they would come to hockey or cricket training. Alison Stocks, who was a very high-level hockey player, decided it wasn't for her and committed herself entirely to cricket, so that's a sign of what can be done. With the boys, we had to shock them into it a bit. We surprised them in their last rugby session of the season – we did half-rugby, half-cricket – and got twenty-odd new kids who now play in the league.'

Brazil have nudged ahead of Argentina in women's cricket, winning the last four Women's South American Championships. The absence of one or the other of the South American giants from a regional tournament can have a demoralising effect on women's cricketers across the region. 'It's not only money,' explains Sian Kelly, women's head coach in Argentina. 'It's studies, holiday allocations – it's hard for most people to go away twice in a year. Even though some of our girls come from wealthier families, I think there's an element of shame in asking for money from their family to play sport.'

Brazil, with their cheek-to-cheek grins and samba beats pumping out from their phones on the sidelines, are the new poster boys and girls of the ICC Development Programme. Cricket Brasil boast more than 3000 juniors playing cricket every week, thanks to a wildly successful scheme launched in Poços de Caldas, 200 miles north of São Paulo. An unprecedentedly large gear shipment from the Lord's Taverners – 300 bats and all manner of kit – means there are now a surprising number of children walking around the streets of this spa town wearing powder-blue Surrey one-day shirts. Lucas Jagger, son of Mick and Luciana Gimenez, his Brazilian former lover, has turned out for Brazil's youth teams, but most of the other young Brazilian cricketers have no family connection to the sport. This is a significant boundary to cross in any country; even in England, many women's cricketers traditionally come to the sport through a cricket-loving father or brother.

The *chefe* of Cricket Brasil is Matt Featherstone, once a prolific batsman for Gore Court CC who played a couple of List A matches against the counties for the Kent Cricket Board. He made the move to Brazil in the early 2000s, finding love and settling down. A familiar story, though he has achieved far more at the grassroots than most expats. Fashionably greying, square-jawed, musclebound with a bronze tan – he looks more like a recently retired open-side flanker than a former batsman – his straight-up, can-do personality goes down just as well in the *favelas* as it does in a Dubai boardroom. No one in world cricket seems to have a cross word to say about him.

Brazilian cricket always revolved around the city and state rivalry between Río de Janeiro and São Paulo. Featherstone changed that. Although Cricket for Change and Cricket Brasil have ventured into the *favelas* of the big two cities, it has proved hard to make a cricket programme sustainable. Poços, as his wife's hometown, was an easier target. The contacts Featherstone made there persuaded a private club to open their doors for Cricket Brasil to build a dedicated high performance centre with four artificial nets for young Brazilians to groove their cricket, in addition to a dedicated ground. 'Just to speak to the governor of São Paulo you might be waiting a year to set up a meeting,' says Featherstone. 'It's much easier to access the corridors of power and make more of a splash in a smaller city.' A cabal of young Brazilian coaches are specialising in cricket as part of their degree, so they have an incentive to keep developing the sport.

Dan Sutton suspects Brazil's looming challenge will be finding experienced coaches who can turn enthusiastic youths into teenage batsmen able to crack it at the Associate level. At the start of 2020, Cricket Brasil addressed this by introducing central contracts for 14 women's players and 16 members of staff – 30 Brazilians whose lives have been changed by cricket. Featherstone received an email from a high-ranking ICC official titled 'Thank you for leading the way', as Brazil became the first country in the region to centrally contract its best women.

The most important scorecard in world cricket records not runs and wickets, but participation and performance. The ICC scorecard determines the funding each Associate member receives in the great dividend of global broadcasting revenues. In the current cycle the world's 100 or so Associate members receive $30 million over eight years – just 14 per cent of the overall share. It's a given among all Associate administrators and aficionados that the ICC should divert more money to the developing nations, not that they feel they can always say so on the record.

In light of Brazil's grassroots explosion, Cricket Brasil's annual ICC funding has rocketed from US$10,000 a decade ago to $60,000 in 2019. That was still half the sum received by Argentina, due to their superior track record in tournaments. Although the ICC upgraded all Affiliate members to Associate status in 2017, world cricket remains a three-tier system, where past Affiliates Brazil, Chile, Peru, Panama, Mexico and Costa Rica still lack the voting rights of longstanding Associates Argentina and Suriname. Easing a board's reliance on ICC funding is hard to achieve in a continent where cricket is barely known outside the walls of a club. It was less of a problem in the days when British companies were operating in the countries and filled cricket clubs with their employees. If today's administrators need to make a whole new set of friends, no one in the region seems better at it than Featherstone.

For now, social media is the great tool of free advertising. It has been used astutely by the young locals now involved at the cricket boards, especially the tech-savvy captains of Brazil and Chile, Roberta Moretti Avery and Jeannette Garces García. Video montages of *Las Loicas* (The Meadowlarks) on shuttle-runs, or netting in the back yard of Simon Shalders's hostel in Santiago, flash up on Twitter feeds of cricket fans the world over. When Kevin Pietersen responded to Cricket Peru's montage of their young Peruvian players practising their best switch-hit – KP famously hit Muttiah Muralitharan for six in a Test match with the stroke – it went viral. Women's cricketers across the region combined during the Covid-19 crisis for an inventive montage celebrating the Spice Girls. Moretti – so obsessed that she guested alongside us in a game in Costa Rica when in the country for work – posted daily videos of batting practice in her back yard during the lockdown.

There is clearly something stirring among a swathe of South American women: Garces and other cricketers were among those who took to the streets to protest on International Women's Day 2020. Emotions were particularly high in Chile, where campaigners chanted '*Nunca más sin nosotras*' ('Never again without us women') as the country debated reforms to the Pinochet-era constitution. In Brazil, President Jair Bolsonaro, right-wing admirer of Donald Trump, has come to power pushing a conservative agenda which takes issue with aspects of this social movement.

The ICC some years ago announced their ambition for a 50–50 split between boys and girls in their development programmes. Already in Brazil girls account for more than half of junior players. But, as always with the ICC, there are mixed messages: for the last three Women's T20 World Cups they have made it impossible for any country in the Americas south of the West Indies to enter qualification, on budgetary grounds. In May 2019, ICC Americas finally bowed to pressure and allowed a combined XI from Central and South America to take on the USA and Canada in friendly matches leading up to the qualifier itself. The Americas XI beat Canada and may well have overcome USA were it not for rain. Even then, one of the Peruvian players had her visa application rejected by US immigration, without even a phone call or letter to Cricket Peru or the ICC, after she had stumped up the $250 fee to have it notarised.

The ICC's recent street cricket initiative, Criiio, may not be a means to an end, but an end in itself. Two days before the 2019 World Cup final at Lord's, the Criiio Cup on Trafalgar Square featured teams from eight nations competing against each other in their own forms of street cricket. Some cynics pointed out it was the closest any Associate nation would get to competing in the ICC's ten-team World Cup. The Brazilian team played *taco* – a form of the game dating back to when curious Paulistas first noticed British railwaymen playing cricket next to the São Paulo Railway. As the British were reluctant to let them join in, they carved their own bats, or begged the Brits for their cast-offs. *Taco* is still played with enthusiasm on Brazil's streets and beaches, with thin plywood bats, tennis balls and a twist on traditional cricket rules: a batsman needs to keep their bat on the ground behind the crease at all times, and can be run out by being hit on the body. Prince Harry was unceremoniously stumped when he went in to bat on a diplomatic mission ahead of the Rio Olympics. It is the best starting point for any Brazilian cricketer.

*Taco* is not radically different from the tapeball cricket loved by many immigrants from the subcontinent. A few years ago a group of Indian IT workers were playing every week on Las Ramblas, the Montevideo promenade, in a tapeball competition they grandiloquently labelled the Uruguayan Premier League (UPL). At Christmas 2018 they joined forces with the dormant cricket association in Uruguay to regenerate the second-oldest rivalry in international cricket – a 150th anniversary match against an Argentina XI at Belgrano to mark the inaugural meeting between Buenos Aires CC and Montevideo CC. Uruguay won the South American Championship that year too, and in 2019 fielded a father-and-son pairing, Rob and Alistair Sharp; Alistair, via his mother, is distantly related to the great Dennet Ayling.

Uruguay's cricketing heritage was bought into by Club Atlético Peñarol, the Uruguayan football giants. The club has its roots in the Central Uruguay Railway Cricket Club, their black and orange colours borrowed directly from Robert Stephenson's *Rocket* locomotive built in Newcastle. The manager of the Central Uruguay Railway would double up as chairman of the sports club until violence on the special services laid on for football matches led to a messy split in the club in 1913, and the formation of Peñarol.

More than a century later, Peñarol gave permission for one of the UPL teams to play under their name, paraded their cricketers at a match at their vast stadium Campéon del Siglo, and produced an atmospheric video trailer of a batsman emerging from a British-built railway station. Some fans lauded this heralding of the club's glorious past; others debated how much Peñarol actually owe to a defunct English club which showed scant inclination to involve the average Uruguayan. The new Uruguayan Cricket Association is a more inclusive, multiracial set-up. The next step, introducing the game back into schools and clubs in Uruguay, will be a monumental challenge.

Featherstone has spent a decade as South America's representative in the ICC Americas region, and is in no doubt as to the decision that would change the calculus. 'What will really make a difference – what will make cricket truly go worldwide – is getting cricket into the Olympics. It would entirely transform the money we would get and what we could achieve.' Up to now cricket's superpower, the Board of Control for Cricket in India, have not wanted their schedule clogged up or their cricketers subjected to external doping controls, so have vetoed any Olympic application process.

But cricket cannot just blame India. David Parsons is contrite in old age when we say our goodbyes in Buenos Aires. 'I blame us, the British,' he says. 'I think we felt this game was too sacred, too special, to be ruined by the locals. We clung on to it too tightly.'

Really, after all that has happened in the countries of Latin America, and the fluctuating interest and money from the ICC, the wonder is that this expensive, unwieldy sport is played at all. The great lesson of cricket is that it arrives through waves of migration, then survives if the foundations are built strong enough. The British who brought cricket to this fascinating part of the world did not have much faith in the locals to look after their game. It has taken a while, but the baton is being passed on. '*Este deporte*,' one of the boys in Guatemala whispers to us, out of Luke Humphries's earshot, '*es mágico*.'

# Acknowledgements

A HUGE DEBT OF gratitude is owed to our commissioning editor Andreas Campomar at Constable for his belief and enthusiasm for the concept of this book when we took the idea to him, and Rob Sharp for suggesting he was the man for the job. Andreas's patience and editorial judgement proved invaluable. Also, to the efficient and helpful Claire Chesser at Constable for her diligence to deal with our queries and requests no matter how small. Thanks to our agent Nick Walters at David Luxton Associates, whose knowledge of the nitty gritty enabled us to dedicate ourselves solely to writing.

Having a few sets of eyes on the copy during its genesis was extremely beneficial. Owen Amos kept us on track with his nose for a story and decisive editorial suggestions, while Matthew Brown, Professor of Latin American History at Bristol University, embraced the project and brought a wealth of academic and historical knowledge to the table. We were extremely fortunate to be able to call upon Steven Lynch's extensive cricket knowledge and forensic proofreading skills as we edged closer to deadline. Howard Watson did a superb job of spotting slips that had eluded us.

Our wives, Rachel and Baiba, have suffered more than anyone in putting up with our fretting and moaning (possibly at each other). Rachel's daily love and support during the writing and editing stages allowed Timothy to dedicate himself to the task at hand. Her constructive challenges to our perceptions of Latin America also helped immensely. The sacrifices Baiba made and the love she showed while James spent time overseas researching the book and the missed weekends while he wrote it up will never be forgotten. He is doing his best to repay her now.

To our families we are indebted for the support when both of us quit our jobs and took a leap of faith. Ingo and Doris Abraham have learned to embrace left-field risk-taking wholeheartedly. Ian and Angela Coyne suppressed their scepticism and could not have been more supportive. We know Andrew Abraham secretly relished those trips to the National Maritime Museum on our behalf. Ronald and Maria Waltemeyer were gracious hosts and opened doors to valuable academic resources.

Thanks to Liverpool journalist Simon Hughes for his regular encouragement to Timothy in the bowels of Anfield's press room. Also to Andrew Ingham for buying that 1933 *Wisden Cricketers' Almanack* for James' thirtieth birthday, containing reports on the 1932 South American tour. To Ed Cowan for his kind words about the project early on. At the BBC thanks are due to Sam Sheringham, Paul Fletcher, Justin Goulding, Tim Oscroft, Marc Higginson, Mark Mitchener, Stephan Shemilt and Alison Mitchell. Friends and colleagues, too numerous to mention, at the *Cricketer*, Free Foresters, Wyncote Ramblers, Windsor Wesleyans, XL Club, Crusaders Australia, Carmel & District CC and Flitwick CC are praised for their curiosity, interest and bemusement. To Lawrence Booth and Hugh Chevallier of *Wisden*, whose approach to us to compile the 'Cricket Round the World' section in 2011 gave us the launch-pad to consider this kind of book.

Roger Mann set aside considerable time digging out photos of Latin American cricket in his superb photograph collection, some of which graces the plate section. We were fortunate to access several superb archives and libraries across the Americas and Europe.

Especial thanks go to the Lord's library, run brilliantly (and patiently) by Neil Robinson and Rob Curphey, for allowing us in to look at every sliver of detail on cricket in Latin America. Peter Wynne-Thomas in the glorious Trent Bridge library allowed us to access his exhaustive index of the *Cricketer*. The Biblioteca Max von Buch at the Universidad de San Andrés in Buenos Aires provided superb insights into Argentina, as did the stream of material combed from old Argentine and Uruguayan sports magazines in the impressive archive at the Rosario Athletic Club, diligently maintained by the dependable Mario Milano. The C. C. Morris Library in Philadelphia, overseen by the amiable Joe Lynn, the British Library and National Archives in London should not be taken for granted. The Church Mission Society in Oxford for allowing us in to see the South American Missionary Society archives, and to Lloyds Bank for their considerable archives.

General thanks to Michael Blumberg, Charles Fellows-Smith and Mahendra Mapagunaratne for their love of this subject area and willingness to give expert first-hand advice. Brian Adams for generously allowing us to quote from his diary of the New Zealand Ambassadors tour, and to John 'Mystery' Morrison for speaking so entertainingly about that trip. Ditto

Peter Parfitt on the D. H. Robins XI tour. Roy Morgan was always on hand to check any Associate cricket statistical queries, no matter how obscure.

Sadly, a few of those who assisted us during our time in Latin America passed away before publication. In Asunción, Peter 'Pingu' Logan was a gentleman who could not do enough for us while John Mills in São Paulo was integral to charting Charles Miller's cricketing prowess. John Abell in Guayaquil left no stone unturned while Dean Lindo was forthright, charming and hospitable in Belize City. Anthony Adams Sr and Chris Abbott helped to fill in some of the blanks in Chile and Peru's more recent cricket history.

*　　*　　*

All those mentioned in the book are thanked for being generous with their time, but we must additionally thank the following.

In the Argentina chapter, Thomas Gibson for opening up his family history, David Parsons, the don of Argentine cricket history, Brian O'Gorman for his scrapbooks and hospitality in Sussex, Natalia Westberg and Silvana Lucia Piga at the Biblioteca Max von Buch, Mauricio Runnacles, John Watson, Dafydd Timothy, Ceris Gruffudd, Daniel Juarez, Matías Gibson, Pedro Arrighi, Bernardo Irigoyen, Sam Hatt for picking us for Hurlingham, Nick Ulivi, Dirce Yuli, John Sylvester, Ian Butcher, Malcolm Henderson, Louisa Brown, Mike Ryan, Luigi Ross, Tom Meneer, Sandra Handley, Willie Rumboll, Martin Chandler, David Frith, Patrick Eagar, and Gina Worboys and the Old Bedfordian Club.

In Belize, Souad Lindo and Lan Sluder.

ACKNOWLEDGEMENTS

Simon Hart, Jackie Rae, Alan Shave, David Auty, Chris Wall, Luis Oporto for Bolivia, plus the country's ex-president (although we didn't realise at the time) Carlos Mesa.

For Brazil, Rick Avery, John Milton, Eddie Edmundson, Patrick Reason, David Gilman, Andréa Rezende Porto, Chris Ritchie, Soren Knudsen, Tobias Hanbury, Craig Allison, Patricia Sobral de Miranda, Mark Thompson, Barry Johnston, Glória Kok, Richard Miller, Robert Greenhill, Victor Melo, Derrick Marcus, Matt Barlow, David Sentance, Karen Cunningham, Dave Juson, Abhijit Khan, João Manoel, Kevin Mecone Silva, Luis Felipe Oliveira, Savannah Staubs, Steven Mahoney, Willian Garcia and Ricardo Rosado at the British Society São Paulo.

In Chile, Chris Emmott, Jonny Bensted, Sergio Díaz Valencia, Bernardo Guerrero, Enrique Lago, Ricardo Pereira Viale, Duncan Campbell, Michael Smith, Jimmy Wilkins, Pedro Zegers, David Woods, Manuel Requena Castro, Daniel Davies, Michelle Prain, Salvatore Cirillo and Carol King.

For Colombia, Nick Barsby, David Kay, Enrique Santos Molano, Ronald Williamson, Andrew Wright, Simon Willis, Claribel Carabali and Olly West.

In Costa Rica, Robert Moers and Sam Arthur.

In Ecuador, Matthew Haines, Gina Rivera, Jessica Ruiz, Leghinsh Pallares, Nick Appleyard, Margaret Morris, Gina Rivera, Paulette Ramsay, Ricardo Castellanos, Rocio Torres, Mark Summers and family, Javier Wright, Eduardo Wright, John Tindall, Reetesh Dalmia and Eleodoro Portocarrero Clark.

Clémence Léobal and Rudi Floquet in French Guiana.

Nic Wirtz in Guatemala.

David Evans and Daine Etches in Honduras.

413

For Mexico, Ben Owen, Stephen Lay, Bridget Gouldsworthy, C. Ricardo de Paola Kakneviciute, Brian Gay, Jackie Gay, Roger Kenyon, Stephen Riley, Chris Westphal, Keith Gerrish, Bob Thomas, Jon Wilton, David Renton, Mike Reeve, Forrest Mohler, Tom Seifert, Clyde Louis Young, Clare Stephens, Roger Sherman, Charles Pigott, Jack Palazzo, Gabriela Mota at the Fototeca Nacional in Hidalgo and Sergio Iglesias Rodriguez.

In Nicaragua, Mickey Peart and Andy Mathieson.

In Panama, thanks to Ross Alford, Paola Martinez Zanardo, Aisa Sarfaraz Alibhai, Ron Headley, Dean Headley and Gordon Smith.

In Paraguay, Grizzie Logan, Anne Bradley, Andrew Nickson, Tony Cantor, Victor Isaacs, Ralph Hannah, Ben Stubbs, Juan Rickman, Chris Monnox and Fabrizzia Aquino.

In Peru, Richard Brown for sharing the family history and memories of his father, plus Miles Buesst, Jan Perrins, Chris Morgan, Alex James, Chris Hodgson, Tony Sandford, Noel Conway, Matthew Spry, Viv Ash, George Glynn, Hans Reijer de Wit and Matthew Andrews.

For Suriname, Rene Schoonheim, Raj Sewnarine, Radjen Kisoensingh and Alan Butcher.

In Uruguay, Malcolm Henderson, Peter Stanham, Alvaro Cuenca, Rene Borretto and Eduardo Irigoyen García.

Thanks in Venezuela to Gustavo Ocando, Robert Jones, Yasir Patel, Javier González, Randy Trahan, Miguel Tinkler Salas and Patricia de Gomez.

Anyone we have accidentally left out, please accept our profound apologies.

# Bibliography

## Books

Aguirre Achá, José, *De los Andes al Amazonas* (Velarde, Aldazosa y Company, 1902).

Alexander, Caroline, *Endurance: Shackleton's Legendary Antarctic Expedition* (Alfred Knopf, 1998).

Arellano, Jorge Eduardo, *El Beisbol en Nicaragua* (Academia Nicaragüense de la Lengua, 2009).

Ashley-Cooper, F. S., *Cricket Highways and Byways* (George Allen & Unwin, 1927).

Attwood, Shaun, *Pablo Escobar's Story* (Gadfly Press, 2018).

Avila Martel, Alamiro de, *Cochrane y la independencia del Pacífico* (Editorial Universitaria, 1976).

Ayling, Eric, *The Ayling Family in Argentina – 1900–1980* (unknown).

Bagot, A. G., *Travel and sport in India and Central America* (Mittal, 1984).

Baronov, David, *The Abolition of Slavery in Brazil* (Greenwood Publishing, 2000).

Beaty, Jonathan and S. C. Gwynne, *The Outlaw Bank: A Wild Ride into the Secret Heart of BCCI* (Beard Books, 2004).

Beckles, Sir Hilary, *The Development of West Indies Cricket: Vol 2, The Age of Nationalism* (University of the West Indies Press, 1998).

Beezley, William H., *Judas at the Jockey Club and Other Episodes of Porfirian Mexico* (University of Nebraska Press, 2018).

Bethell, Leslie, *Brazil: Essays on History and Politics* (University of London, 2018).

Blakemore, Harold, *From the Pacific to La Paz: the Antofagasta (Chili) and Bolivia Railway Company, 1888–1988* (Lester Crook, 1990).

Blofeld, Henry, *A Thirst for Life: With the Accent on Cricket* (Hodder, 2001)

Bowen, Rowland, *Cricket: A History of Its Growth and Development around the World* (Eyre & Spottiswoode, 1970).

Bradley, Leo, *Glimpses of Our History* (Bliss Institute, 1962).

Bridger, Gordon, *Britain and the Making of Argentina* (WIT Press, 2012).

Bridger, Kenneth E., *North and South: A History of the Annual Cricket Classic in Argentina* (Privately printed, 1974).

Brown, Freddie, *Cricket Musketeer* (N. Kaye, 1954).

Bullock, W. H., *Across Mexico in 1864–65* (Macmillan, 1866).

Burrowes, S. I. and J. A. Carnegie, *George Headley* (Nelson, 1971).

Burton, Richard F., *Explorations of the Highlands of the Brazil* (Tinsley Brothers, 1869).

Buzzetti, José L. and Eduardo Gutierrez Cortinas, *Historia del Deportee en el Uruguay* (Talleres Gráficos, 1965).

Calvert, Peter, *Mexican Revolution 1910–1914: The Diplomacy of the Anglo-American Conflict* (Cambridge University Press, 1968).

Campomar, Andreas, *¡Golazo! A History of Football in South America* (Quercus, 2014).

Cardus, Neville, *Autobiography* (Collins, 1947).

Caro, Montserrat, *Valparaíso – Capital Cultural* (Cultura Puzzle, 2010).

Chalmers, Ian, *A Chalmers Miscellany* (MPG Biddles, 2008).

Chapman, Peter, *Jungle Capitalists* (Canongate, 2009).

Charrière, Henri, *Papillon* (HarperCollins, 2012).

Chester, Frank, *How's That!* (Hutchinson, 1956).

Chomsky, Aviva, *West Indian Workers and the United Fruit Company in Costa Rica, 1870–1940* (Louisiana State University Press, 1996).

Clark, Kim, *The Redemptive Work: Railway and Nation in Ecuador, 1895–1930* (Rowman & Littlefield, 1998).

Coldham, James P., *Lord Hawke* (I. B. Tauris, 2003).

Connelly, Charlie (ed.), *Elk Stopped Play; and Other Unlikely Tales from Wisden's Cricket Round the World* (Bloomsbury, 2014).

Conniff, Michael L., *Black Labor on a White Canal: Panama 1904–1981* (University of Pittsburgh Press, 1981).

Corfield, Richard, *The Silent Landscape: The Scientific Voyage of HMS Challenger* (Henry Joseph Press, 2003).

Cushman, Gregory T., *Guano and the Opening of the Pacific World* (Cambridge University Press, 2013).

Díaz Valencia, Sergio, *La industria del salitre contada por el yodo, 1811–2004* (Unknown, 2005).

Dooley, Elizabeth, *Streams in the Wasteland: A Portrait of the British in Patagonia* (Imprenta Rasmussen, 1993).

Eakin, Marshall C., *British Enterprise in Brazil: The St John del Rey Mining Company and the Morro Velho Gold Mine 1830–1960* (Duke University Press, 2013).

Edmundson, William, *A History of the British Presence in Chile* (Palgrave Macmillan, 2009).

—, *The Nitrate King: A Biography of John Thomas North* (Palgrave Macmillan, 2011).

Fariña, José, *William Paats: Padre del fútbol Paraguayo* (El Lector, 2014).

Feldwick, W., Oliver T. Breakspear, L. T. Delaney (eds), *Twentieth Century Impressions of Argentina: Its History, People, Commerce, Industries and Resources* (Lloyd's Greater Britain, 1911).

Ferguson, Ian, *Cricket's Far Horizons* (Rex Thompson, 1996).

Forstall Comber, Biddy, *Crepúsculo en un balcón: Ingleses y la pampa salitrera* (Editorial Universitaria de Chile, 2019).

Foss, Clive, *Juan and Eva Peron* (The History Press, 2006).

Frankson, A. S., *Caribbean Identity: Memoirs of the Colonial Service* (I. B. Tauris, 2008).

Frith, David, *Silence of the Heart: Cricket Suicides* (Mainstream Digital, 2011).

Galsworthy Estavillo, Bridget et al., *Cornwall & Hidalgo: An Enduring Connection* (San Ángel Ediciones, 2013).

Garavini, Giuliano, *The Rise and Fall of OPEC in the Twentieth Century* (Oxford University Press, 2019).

García Márquez, Gabriel, *The General in His Labyrinth* (Alfred Knopf, 1990).

Garner, Paul, *British Lions and Mexican Eagles* (Stanford University Press, 2011).

Gillespie, Major Alexander, *Gleanings and Remarks: Collected During My Many Months of Residence at Buenos Aires* (B. Dewhirst, 1818).

Gmelch, George A. (ed.), *Baseball without Borders* (University of Nebraska Press, 2006).

Godden, Charles H., *Trespassers Forgiven: Memoirs of International Service in an Age of Independence* (Radcliffe Press, 2009).

González, Daniel, *The Kings of Money Laundering: The Rise and Fall of BCCI – an Extraordinary Story* (9 Signos Grupo Editorial, 2019).

Grace, W. G., *The History of a Hundred Centuries* (L. Upcott Gill, 1895).

Graham-Yooll, Andrew, *The Forgotten Colony: A History of the English-speaking People in Argentina* (LOLA, 1999).

—, *Goodbye Buenos Aires* (Eland, 2011).

—, *A State of Fear: Memories of Argentina's Nightmare* (Eland, 2009).

Greene, Graham, *The Honorary Consul* (The Bodley Head, 1973).

Haigh, Gideon (ed.), *Peter the Lord's Cat; and Other Unexpected Obituaries from Wisden* (Bloomsbury, 2006).

Hart Dyke, Tom and Paul Winder, *The Cloud Garden* (Corgi Books, 2011).

Hawke, Lord, *Recollections and Reminiscences* (Williams & Norgate, 1924).

Heald, Tim, *Brian Johnston: The Authorised Biography* (Methuen, 1996).

Henderson, Captain George, *An Account of the British Settlement of Honduras* (R. Baldwin, 1811).

Hesketh-Prichard, H., *Through the Heart of Patagonia* (T. Nelson, 1902).

Heywood, Benjamin, *Memoir of Captain Prescot William Stephens* (J. Nisbet, 1886).

Hill, Stephen and Barry Phillips, *Somerset Cricketers 1919–39* (Halsgrove, 2017).

Hinchcliff, Thomas Woodbine, *South American Sketches* (Longman, Green, Longman, Roberts & Green, 1863).

Holder, Arthur L., *British and North American Sports and Pastimes in the Argentine Republic* (Privately printed, 1923).

Hollett, Dave, *More Precious than Gold: The Story of the Peruvian Guano Trade* (Associated University Presses, 2008).

Howat, Gerald, *Plum Warner* (HarperCollins, 1987).

Howe, Martin, *Rockley Wilson: Remarkable Cricketer, Singular Man* (Association of Cricket Statisticians and Historians, 2008).

Hyde, Evan X., *Sports, Sin and Subversion* (Ramos, 2008).

Ingleby-MacKenzie, Colin, *Many a Slip* (Oldbourne, 1962).

Iorio, Patricia and Vitor Iorio, *Paissandu Atlético Clube* (PAC, 2001).

—, *Rio Cricket e Associação Atlética* (Arte Ensaio, 2008).

Ishmael, Odeen, *The Guyana Story: From Earliest Times to Independence* (Xlibris Corporation, 2013).

Jacobs, Michael, *Ghost Train Through the Andes* (John Murray, 2007).

James, C. L. R., *Beyond a Boundary* (Hutchinson, 1963).

—, *A Majestic Innings: Writings on Cricket* (Aurum, 2006).

Johnston, Brian, *A Further Slice of Johnners* (Virgin, 2011).

—, *Letters Home, 1926–45*, ed. Barry Johnston (Orion, 1998).

Jones, Tom, *Patagonian Panorama* (Outspoken Press, 1961).

Kepner, Charles D., *Social Aspects of the Banana Industry* (AMS PR Inc., 1936).

Kipling, Rudyard, *Brazilian Sketches* (P. E. Waters, 1989).

—, *Just So Stories* (Macmillan, 1902).

Knightley, Phillip, *The Vestey Affair* (The Book Service, 1981).

Lacey, Josh, *God is Brazilian: Roger Miller – The Man Who Brought Football to Brazil* (Tempus, 2005).

Laffaye, Horace A., *The Evolution of Polo* (McFarland, 2009).

—, *Polo in Argentina: A History* (McFarland, 2014).

Lambert, Peter and Andrew Nickson, *Paraguay Reader: History, Culture, Politics* (Duke University Press, 2013).

Lawrence, Bridgette, *Masterclass: The Biography of George Headley* (Polar, 1995).

Léobal, Clémence, *Saint-Laurent du-Maroni, une porte sur le fleuve* (Ibis Rouge Éditions, 2014).

Lewis, Tony, *Playing Days: An Autobiography* (Hutchinson, 1985).

Lindo, Dean R., *Cricket, Lovely Cricket* (Unknown, 2013).

McCann, Thomas P., *An American Company: The Tragedy of United Fruit* (Crown, 1976).

McCrery, Nigel, *Final Wicket: Test and first-class cricketers killed in the Great War* (Pen & Sword Military, 2015).

McGough, James, *The Book of Hundreds; Being a List of Centuries Made in Argentine Cricket* (The British Printery, 1921).

—, *Chronicles of Cricket in Argentina* (The British Printery, date unknown).

—, *The Year Book of Argentine Cricket* (Souvenir Publishing Co., various years).

McKellar, Margaret, *Life on a Mexican Ranche* (Lehigh University Press, 1994).

McLynn, Frank, *Villa And Zapata: A Biography of the Mexican Revolution* (Pimlico, 2001).

McNamara, Patrick J., *Sons of the Sierra: Juárez, Díaz, and the People of Ixtlán, Oaxaca, 1855–1920* (University of North Carolina Press, 2007).

Manley, Michael, *A History of West Indies Cricket* (André Deutsch, 1995).

Marshall, Oliver (ed.), *English-speaking Communities in Latin America* (Palgrave Macmillan, 2000).

Mazur, Robert, *The Infiltrator* (Back Bay Books, 2016).

Metzgen, Monrad, *Blazing Trails on Bicycles and Motor Cars in British Honduras* (BRC Printing, 2002).

—, *The Handbook of British Honduras* (1925).

Mill, Hugh Robert, *The Life of Sir Ernest Shackleton* (W. Heinemann, 1923).

Miller, Douglas, *M. J. K. Smith: No Ordinary Man* (Association of Cricket Statisticians & Historians, 2013).

Miller, John, *Memoirs of General (William) Miller* (Longman, Rees, Orme, Brown and Green, 1829).

Mills, John, *Charles William Miller, 1894/1994 – Memoriam S.P.A.C.* (Price Waterhouse, 1996).

Morales, Franklin, *100 Años de Fútbol: los albores del fútbol Uruguayo* (Vertice, 1969).

Morgan, Roy, *The Encyclopedia of World Cricket* (Sportsbooks, 2007).

—, *Real International Cricket: A History in One Hundred Scorecards* (Pitch, 2016).

Naipaul, V. S., *The Middle Passage: Impressions of Five Colonial Societies* (Picador, 2012).

Neruda, Pablo, *Canto General* (University of California Press, 1950).

Ogilvie, Campbell P., *Argentina from a British Point of View* (Wertheimer, Lea & Co., 1910).

O'Hagan, Andrew and Julian Assange, *Julian Assange: The Unauthorised Autobiography* (Canongate, 2011).

Paige, Jeffrey M., *Coffee and Power: Revolution and the Rise of Democracy in Central America* (Harvard University Press, 1997).

Palmer, Paula, *What Happen: A Folk History of Costa Rica's Talamanca Coast* (Zona Tropical, 2005).

Paraíso, Rostand, *Esses ingleses* (Bagaço, 1997).

Parker, Matthew, *Hell's Gorge: The Battle to build the Panama Canal* (Cornerstone, 2011).

Perez, Danae, *Language Competition and Shift in New Australia, Paraguay* (Springer Nature, 2019).

Portocarrero Clark, Eleodoro, *Jamaica en Ecuador* (Imprenta Mariscal, 2007).

Porto Filho, Ubaldo, *História da Associação Atlética da Bahia* (Associação Atlética da Bahia, 2012).

Rabling, William, *Captured by Brigands* (Camborne, 1897).

Raffo, Víctor, *Historia del Club Social Ingles de Lomas de Zamora* (Lomas English Social Club, 2000).

—, *El Origen Británico del Deporte Argentino* (Prendergast, 2004).

Redfield, Peter, *Space in the Tropics: From Convicts to Rockets in French Guiana* (University of California Press, 2000).

Renshaw, Andrew (ed.), *Wisden on the Great War* (John Wisden & Co, 2014).

Rice, Jonathan, *Curiosities of Cricket* (Pavilion, 1993).

Rijks, Miranda, *The Eccentric Entrepreneur: Sir Julien Cahn* (The History Press, 2011).

Rock, David, *The British in Argentina: Commerce, Settlers and Power 1800–2000* (Palgrave Macmillan, 2018).

Rueda, Tomás, *Vargas Escritos* (Antares, 1963).

Russell, William Howard, *A Visit to Chile and the Nitrate Fields* (Virtue & Co., 1890).

Rutter, Owen, *If Crab No Walk: A Traveller in the West Indies* (Hutchinson, 1933).

Sarti, Ricardo, *Temas Sobre el Callao* (Unknown, 2011).

Schwartz, Sharron P., *The Cornish in Latin America: 'Cousin Jack' and the New World* (Cornubian Press, 2016).

Sheffield, Roy, *Bolivian Spy?* (Marchand, 1935).

Sierra e Iglesias, Dr J. P., *The Life and Work of the Leach Brothers* (Provincia de Jujuy, 1998).

Smith, Michael, *MI6: The Real James Bonds 1909–39* (Dialogue, 2011).

—, *Shackleton: By Endurance We Conquer* (Oneworld, 2015).

Souter, Gavin, *A Peculiar People: The Australians in Paraguay* (Sydney University Press, 1981).

Stewart, Iain, *Don Heriberto: Knight of the Argentine* (Melrose, 2008).

Stubbs, Ben, *Ticket to Paradise* (HarperCollins, 2012).

Stutgard, Ricky W., *De eerste Surinaamse sportencyclopedie 1893–1988* (Alberga, 1990).

Swan, Michael, *British Honduras* (Phoenix, 1957).

Swanton, E. W., *Gubby Allen: Man of Cricket* (Hutchinson, 1985).

Swanton, E. W. (ed.), *Barclays World of Cricket* (Guild, 1986).

Swire, Herbert, *The Voyage of the Challenger: A Personal Narrative of the Circumnavigation of the Globe in the Years 1872–76* (Golden Cockerel Press, 1938).

Synge, Allen and Leo Cooper, *Tales from Far Pavilions* (Ward & Lock, 1984).

Tambiah, Stanley J., *Edmund Leach: An Anthropological Life* (Cambridge University Press, 2002).

Tarran, Bruce, *George Hillyard: The Man Who Moved Wimbledon* (Matador, 2013).

Thomas, Donald, *Cochrane: Britannia's Own Sea Wolf* (Cassell, 2012).

Thompson, Harry S., *Penguins Stopped Play* (John Murray, 2007).

Tinker Salas, Miguel, *The Enduring Legacy: Oil, Culture, and Society in Venezuela* (Duke University Press, 2009).

Tritton, Pieter, *El Infierno* (Ebury Press, 2017).

Vasconcellos, Ricardo, *Historias del Fútbol Guayaquileño* (Asociación de Fútbol del Guayas, 2012).

Vigne, Godfrey, *Travels in Mexico, South America, Etc.* (W. H. Allen & Company, 1863).

Warner, Pelham, *Long Innings: The Autobiography* (Harrap, 1951).

Watson, Francis, 'White Gold of Chile' (unpublished).

White, Noel, *Atlas: George Headley* (Institute of Jamaica, 1974).

Whitehead, Anne, *Paradise Mislaid: In Search of the Australian Tribe of Paraguay* (University of Queensland Press, 1997).

Whymper, Edward, *Travels Amongst the Great Andes of the Equator* (Thomas Nelson, 1911).

—, *Whymper's London Diary, 1855–1859* (London Record Society, 2008).

Williams, J. W., *La Tranca* (Privately printed, 1881).

*Wisden Cricketers' Almanack* (various editions).

Woods, David J., *The Bombardment of Paradise* (WTA Publishing, 2011).

Wright, Winthrop R., *British-Owned Railways in Argentina: Their Effect on the Growth of Economic Nationalism, 1854–1948* (University of Texas Press, 1974).

Young, Rusty, *Marching Powder* (Pan Macmillan, 2003).

Young, Sidney A. (ed.), *Isthmian Echoes: A Selection of the Literary Endeavours of the West Indian Colony of the Republic of Panama* (Benedetti, 1928).

## Magazines, periodicals and handbooks

*Anenas 85 Anos: Resena Historica del Tucuman Lawn Tennis Club*

*The Anglo-South: the staff journal of the Anglo-South American Bank*

Argentine Cricket Association handbook

*Banister Court School Magazine*

*Bell's Life in London, and Sporting Chronicle*

*Bogotá Ilustrado*

Bogota Sports Club handbooks

British Chamber of Commerce magazine

British Council Minutes – Paraguay

Buenos Aires Cricket Club handbook

*Caras y Caretas*

*Caribbean Way: Ministero de Cultura de Costa Rica*

Central Uruguay Railway Cricket Club handbooks

*Cien años del Club Británico de Río Gallegos 1911–2011*

*Cricket: a weekly record of the game/ World of Cricket*
*Cricketer/Wisden Cricketer*
*The Economist*
*Estatutos Calama Football and Cricket Club* (1907)
*Estatutos Club de Sport Tarapaca*
'The First Britons in Valparaíso', lecture by Benjamín Vicuña Mackenna
*Georgian School Magazine*
Clement Gibson's scrapbooks
*El Gladiador*
*Goddard Association of Europe Newsletter* (no. 49, 1999)
*El Gráfico*
The Grange School handbooks
Graham Hammond diaries aboard HMS *Spartiate*
*Helsinki Cricketer*
*The History of the Hurlingham Club of Argentina*
Richard Latham's scrapbook
*Lima Cricket & Football Club – 60th anniversary handbook* (1945)
Lomas Athletic Club handbooks
*Mundo Argentino*
C. T. Nash, 'Brazil tour of the Argentine, 1953'
*Peru Ilustrado*
*Prince of Wales Country Club Chile – 70 Años*
*Quarterly Review* (1824)
*Reforma Athletic Club – Club Centenario 117 años*
Rio Cricket & Athletic Association handbooks, fixture cards and newsletters
Rosario Athletic Club centenary handbook
*Rotarian*
Rules and regulations of the Mexican Union Cricket Club (1838)
Rules of the Taltal Cricket Club (1885)
St Peter's School handbooks
Santos Athletic Club minute books
*South American Missionary Magazine*
*Spectator*
'Stranger's Club History: silver jubilee' (2008)
*Time Magazine*
*Token: home magazine of the Bank of London and South America*

*Valparaiso Sporting Club 1882–1957*
Valparaiso Cricket Club annual reports
*Wileman's Review*


# Newspapers

Argentina: *Anglo-American Review, British Packet and Argentine News, Buenos Aires Herald, Bulletin, Critica, La Nación, La Prensa, River Plate Sport & Pastime, River Plate Times, Standard.*

Belize: *Amandala, Belize Billboard, Belize Independent, Belize Times, Central American Telegraph, Colonial Guardian, Observer, Times of Central America.*

Bolivia: *El Diario, El Imparcial, La Razon.*

Brazil: *Anglo-Brazilian Chronicle, Anglo-Brazilian Times, Brazilian Review, Correio Paulistano, O Cruzeiro, Diario de Pernambuco, Dolha do Amazonas, O Estado, O Imparcial, Jornal do Comercio, Jornal do Recife, Latin American Daily Post, A Provincia do Para, A Provinica de Sao Paulo, Rio News, Rio Times, Times of Brazil.*

Chile: *Chilean Times, El Lota, Magellan Times, El Mercurio, El Mercurio de Antofagasta, Punta Arenas Mail, South Pacific Mail.*

Costa Rica: *Limon Searchlight, Limon Times, La Nación, Tico Times.*

Ecuador: *El Comercio, Los Andes*

French Guiana: *La Dépêche Coloniale, Journal Officiel de la Guyane Française.*

Jamaica: *Daily Gleaner.*

Mexico: *Mexican Herald, Mexican Post, Mexican Sportsman, El Mundo Ilustrado, Two Republics.*

Nicaragua: *Bluefields Messenger, Bluefields Sentinel, Recorder.*

Panama: *Daily Echo, Estrella de Panama, La Nacion, Panama American, Panama Canal Review, Panama Star and Herald, Panama Tribune, Silver People Chronicle.*

Paraguay: *Cosme Monthly Notes.*

Peru: *El Comercio, Peruvian Times, West Coast Leader.*

Suriname: *Koloniaal Nieuws, Times of Suriname, Die West.*

UK: *Aberdeen Press and Journal, Bruce Castle Chronicle, Brucian, Cornishman, Cornish Post, Daily Mail, Daily Mirror, Daily News,*

*Daily Record, Daily Sketch, Daily Telegraph, Edinburgh Evening News, Evening Standard, Guardian, Hampshire Telegraph and Sussex Chronicle, News of the World, Ousel, Royal Cornish Gazette, Scotsman, Southampton Times, Southern Daily Echo, Star, The Times, West Briton, Western Daily Press.*

Uruguay: *Montevideo Times, Times of Montevideo.*

USA: *Chicago Tribune, Los Angeles Herald, Los Angeles Times, New York Herald, New York Times, St Louis Post-Dispatch, Spirit of the Times, Topeka.*

Venezuela: *El Cojo Ilustrado, Guyana Times, Maracaibo Herald, Maracaibo Times, Mediapart, La Opinión Nacional, Tropical Sun, Venezuelan Herald.*


## Other articles

Andrade de Melo, Victor, 'Os Britânicos e os clubes de cricket na são paulo do século xix anos 1870–1890', *Revist de História*, no. 178 (July 2019).

—, 'O esporte nos arrabaldes do Rio de Janeiro: o cricket em Bangu 1904–1912', *Movimento*, vol. 24, no. 3 (2018).

—, 'Para inglês ver? Os clubes de cricket E a sociabilidade britânica em Recife 1865–1906', *Revista Territórios e Fronteiras*, vol. 10, no. 1 (2017).

—, 'A sociabilidade britânica no Rio de Janeiro do século XIX: os clubes de Cricket', *Almanack*, no. 16 (2017).

Baptiste, Fitzroy André, 'Trinidad and Tobago as the hinge of a primary and secondary diaspora between Africa, the Caribbean and South America, especially Venezuela circa 1797 to 1914', paper, University of the West Indies (2002).

Childs, Matt D., 'Master-Slave Rituals of Power at a Gold Mine in Nineteenth Century Brazil', *History Workshop Journal*, vol. 53, no. 1 (2002).

Costeloe, Michael P., 'To Bowl a Mexican Maiden Over: cricket in Mexico, 1827–1900', *Bulletin of Latin America Research*, vol. 26, no. 1 (2007).

Greenhill, Robert and Carlos Gabriel Guimarães, 'Trading in an

Emerging Market: E. Johnston & Co and the Brazilian Coffee Trade 1840–1880', *Revista de Historia Económica* (July 2019).

Guerrero Jiménez, Bernardo, 'Pero alguien trajo el fútbol: historia del fútbol Tarapaqueño', *Revista de Ciencias Sociales*, no. 15 (2005).

Healy, Claire, 'Daniel Florence O'Leary', *Irish Migration Studies in Latin America*, vol. 4, no. 2 (2006).

Johnson, Melissa A., 'The Making of Race and Place in British Honduras', *Environmental History*, no. 8 (2013).

Putnam, Lara, 'The Panama Cannonball: Transnational Ties, Migrants and Sport', *Journal of Sport History*, vol. 41, no. 3 (2014).

White, Craig, 'Golden Age of Mexican Cricket', *Playing Pasts* (8 November 2018), https://www.playingpasts.co.uk/articles/team-sports/golden-age-of-mexican-cricket-part-1/.

—, 'The Thin Red Line: The British Community in Porfirian Pachuca and Real del Monte', Canning House (2020), https://www.canninghouse.org/canning-insights/the-thin-red-line.

Willasey-Wilsey, Tim, 'A Hundred Years of Costa Rican cricket, 1890–1990: an untold chapter of Caribbean history', Costa Rica Cricket Federation (1992), http://www.costaricacricket.org/history.html.

—, 'Jamaica, Headley and the heyday of Costa Rican Cricket', *Cricket World* (29 January 2013).

## Websites

BBC, Brink Adventures, CricketArchive, Cricket Europe, Emerging Cricket, ESPNCricinfo, ICC.

# Index

The abbreviations AC or CC after a name indicate Athletic Club or Cricket Club

429